The Lion Christian Meditation Collection

THE LION

CHRISTIAN
MEDITATION
COLLECTION

compiled by
Hannah Ward
and
Jennifer Wild

A LION BOOK

This collection copyright © 1998
Hannah Ward and Jennifer Wild

Published by
Lion Publishing plc
Sandy Lane West, Oxford, England
ISBN 0 7459 3836 1 (hardback)
ISBN 0 7459 3989 9 (paperback)

First hardback edition 1998
10 9 8 7 6 5 4 3 2 1 0
First paperback edition 1998 (special edition only)
10 9 8 7 6 5 4 3 2 1 0

A catalogue record for this book is available
from the British Library

Typeset in 11.5/13 Berkeley Oldstyle
Printed and bound in Spain

CONTENTS

PREFACE

In making this collection, our natural instinct was to turn first to passages that have meant a lot to us in the past and to build round that material. In the end, we have found ourselves reading a great many books or parts of books which we never dreamt of reading – and we feel all the richer for it! We hope very much that you will have something of the same experience. You may not find all *your* favourite passages here, but we hope that you will find some old friends as well as many new ones. Obviously, this is a book to be used reflectively, indeed, meditatively, as a source of companionship and inspiration, not read through in large chunks at a sitting.

The ten sections are intended as a help to occasional browsing, and certainly not as watertight compartments. We have begun with God's creation and ended with an ancient outpouring of gladness at God's work among us – and in between are reflections on the many ways that human beings have encountered life's pleasures, hardships, challenges and tasks, baffling experiences of God's absence and fiery awareness of God's presence. Sometimes the emphasis is on the individual in his or her apparent solitude, sometimes the writer's preoccupation is with all that connects human beings with each other as well as with God.

Our sources are all Christian, but from a wide range over time and space. Some writings from earlier Christian centuries need more effort to appreciate, and no doubt some of the contemporary extracts in this collection will seem far removed from each other in cultural or religious attitudes. There are contributions from women and men, and from Christians in poorer as well as richer parts of the globe. We have followed the present move towards making the language about men and women more inclusive, where slight alterations were possible without intruding on the author's thought; but, as will be seen, we have retained the original words in many instances where change seemed impracticable or inappropriate to the writer concerned. Sometimes we have added a Bible reference where this makes the passage easier to follow.

Within the ten sections each piece has been given a title to indicate something of its mood or tone. The indexes are intended to help the reader to track down the contributions of particular authors, and also to provide a way of finding passages on themes that are of interest at any given time.

In making our selection we have tried not to overlook the fact that meditation is not an activity that removes the need for serious thought. Some of the passages in this collection offer an invitation to think hard, partly to tease out their meaning, partly because their subject matter calls for careful thought. But we do not forget that, in meditating, thought as well as feeling is able to lead towards prayer.

We hope that this collection will provide opportunities for getting to know something of the deepest experiences of many different kinds of writers, and so serve to enlarge our hearts and minds and draw us closer to God. By seeing how our own experiences connect with those of others, we may discover afresh the awareness of God's gracious presence in our world.

PART 1

The Gift of Life

Creation

Creation pizzazz
1.1

Of all known forms of life, only about ten per cent are still living today. All other forms – fantastic plants, ordinary plants, living animals with unimaginably various wings, tails, teeth, brains – are utterly and forever gone. That is a great many forms that have been created. Multiplying ten times the number of living forms today yields a profusion that is quite beyond what I consider thinkable. Why so many forms? Why not just that one hydrogen atom? The creator goes off on one wild, specific tangent after another, or millions simultaneously, with an exuberance that would seem to be unwarranted, and with an abandoned energy sprung from an unfathomable font. What is going on here? The point of the dragonfly's terrible lip, the giant water bug, birdsong or the beautiful dazzle and flash of sunlighted minnows, is not that it all fits together like clockwork – for it doesn't, particularly, not even inside the goldfish bowl – but that it all flows so freely wild, like the creek, that it all surges in such a free, fringed tangle. Freedom is the world's water and weather, the world's nourishment freely given, its soul and sap: and the creator loves pizzazz.

Annie Dillard, *Pilgrim at Tinker Creek* (Picador/Macmillan 1976), pp. 125–26.

A sense of beauty
1.2

In ancient times the love of the beauty of the world had a very important place in men's thoughts and surrounded the whole of life with marvellous poetry. This was the case in every nation in China, in India, and in Greece…

Today one might think that the white races had almost lost all feelings for the beauty of the world, and that they had taken upon them the task of making it disappear from all the continents where they have penetrated with their armies, their trade and their religion. As Christ said to the Pharisees: 'Woe to you for ye have taken away the key of knowledge; ye entered not in yourselves and they that were entering in ye hindered' (Luke 11:52).

And yet at the present time, in the countries of the white races, the beauty of the world is almost the only way by which we can allow God to penetrate us, for we are still further removed from the other two. Real love and respect for religious practices are rare even among those who are most assiduous in observing them, and are practically never to be found in others. Most people do not even conceive them to be possible. As regards the supernatural purpose of affliction, compassion and gratitude are not only rare but have become almost unintelligible for almost everyone today. The very idea of them has almost disappeared; the very meaning of the words has been debased. On the other hand a sense of beauty, although mutilated, distorted and soiled, remains rooted in the heart of man as a powerful incentive. It is present in all the preoccupations of secular life. If it were made true and pure it would sweep all secular life in a body to the feet of God, it would make the total incarnation of the faith possible. Moreover, speaking generally, the beauty of the world is the commonest, easiest and most natural way of approach.

Simone Weil, *Waiting on God*, tr. Emma Craufurd (Collins 1974), p. 115.

Life in awareness
1.3

With regard to the world around one, there should be a conscious willed period of attentiveness each day. It is the will that has to be used to raise the consciousness from the depths of the self to the world outside. It is important to notice positively the objects in one's environment, the things in the familiar street, the flowers and trees in the garden and park, and above all the people one passes to and from one's work. Each is complete in itself, but it needs our recognition, just as we need the recognition of others to be fully human. If we do not trouble to recognize others because of inner preoccupation, no one will trouble to recognize us. It is important not only to recognize and acknowledge the uniqueness of each object and each person but also to flow out to them in silent gratitude for being what they are. All life in awareness is a blessing, and we show this by blessing those around us. This does not require a formula or an articulated statement; it is essentially an inner gratitude.

This awareness of the meaningfulness of the surroundings and our gratitude that it should be so is the precursor of the prayer of thanksgiving and praise.

Martin Israel, *An Approach to Spirituality* (The Mysticism Committee of the Churches Fellowship for Psychical and Spiritual Studies 1971), p. 28.

Gifts through the senses
1.4

I will thank him for the pleasures given me through my senses, for the glory of the thunder, for the mystery of music, the singing of birds and the laughter of children. I will thank him for the pleasures of seeing, for the delights through colour, for the awe of the sunset, the beauty of flowers, the smile of friendship and the look of love; for the changing beauty of the clouds, for the wild roses in the hedges, for the form and beauty of birds, for the leaves on the trees in spring and autumn, for the witness of the leafless trees through the winter, teaching us that death is sleep and not destruction, for the sweetness of flowers and the scent of hay. Truly, oh Lord, the earth is full of thy riches! And yet, how much more I will thank and praise God for the strength of my body enabling me to work, for the refreshment of sleep, for my daily bread, for the days of painless health, for the gift of my mind and the gift of my conscience, for his loving guidance of my mind ever since it first began to think, and of my heart ever since it first began to love.

Edward King, Sermons and Addresses (Longmans, Green and Co. 1911), p. 37.

Human potential
1.5

Achieving wholeness and holiness requires traversing the difficult terrain of real life with all its challenges and crises. Even at the end of a lifetime of effort, we still need to be completed by the finishing touch of the divine artist. God will then bring to completion in us the eternal design of people destined to love wholeheartedly. While awaiting that unifying touch of divine grace, we pilgrims are called to follow the way of Jesus. And the Lord who walks with us assures us that we will always be blessed. The blessings sent our way may not always be enjoyable, but they will always nudge us forward in our efforts to love as God intended.

A rabbi was once asked, 'What is a blessing?' He prefaced his answer with a riddle involving the creation account in chapter one of Genesis. The riddle went this way: After finishing his work on each of the first five days, the Bible states, 'God saw that it was good.' But God is not reported to have commented on the goodness of what he created on the sixth day when the human person was fashioned. 'What conclusion can you draw from that?' asked the rabbi. Someone volunteered, 'We can conclude that the human person is not good.' 'Possibly,' the rabbi nodded, 'but that's not a likely explanation.' He then went on to explain that the Hebrew word translated as 'good' in Genesis is the word *tov*, which is better translated as 'complete'. That is why, the rabbi contended, God did not declare the human person to be *tov*. Human beings are created incomplete. It is our life's vocation to collaborate with our creator in fulfilling the Christ-potential in each of us.

Wilkie Au, *By Way of the Heart: Toward a Holistic Christian Spirituality*
(Geoffrey Chapman 1990), pp. 202–203.

You are unique
1.6

Think of yourself for a moment. *There is no one on this earth who is like you.* This may be just as well, but it is true. You may have an identical twin who was removed at birth for all you know, but there is not, and cannot ever have been, nor will there ever be, a person who is exactly like you. Even if someone has exactly the same genes and chromosomes, the environment in which he (or she) grew up will have been different and so he will have become a different person. It is not possible for someone else to have the same loves and hates and lusts and fears and anxieties and hopes and desires as you yourself have. You are unique, you are yourself and there never has been, or can be, someone who is just like you, or who fills your place in the world. And if religion is, as it claims to be, a personal relationship with God, your relationship with God will be something unique to yourself and him. You can listen to preachers preaching, you can read about religion – and probably ought to do so because we can learn from each other's experience – but in the last resort your religion and your prayer is something of your own self. Finally, at the end of your life, you will stand before the judgment seat by yourself. You are responsible for yourself. Many people have contributed towards your goodness and your badness. Many of them may well be blamed and have some responsibility for what is in you, but in the last resort, you are *you* and no one can take your place.

Gonville ffrench-Beytagh, *Encountering Light* (Fontana 1975), p. 17.

My garden gives me joy
1.7

For many years I had a dream: I wanted to plant *my* garden. Not a garden but *my* garden. I say *my* garden because it had to be able to evoke the stories and images I love. Many gardens are delights to the senses but they are dumb. They say nothing. They lack the power to evoke. I walk through their alleys and my inner garden continues to sleep. Yes, there is an inner vegetal world inside our bodies…

I dreamed about planting *my* garden because I couldn't. The plot where my house was built was too small. But one day I managed to buy the vacant plot by the side of my house, and my dream came true.

For those whom I have not told my dreams, my plants are only plants: vegetal entities which offer a bit of pleasure to the body. For me, however, they are magical: they have the power to conjure up the past. The lilac was given by my father. Every time I smell its odour I see my father's face and hear his voice. The myrtle takes me back to the public garden of my home town. The emperor's jasmine grew in the backyard of my grandfather's huge colonial house, filled with mysteries, where I played as a boy. I walk by my plants. There are invisible presences in their midst. The past becomes present. My garden is a text. Each plant is a poetic metonymy. Many other plants give me pleasure. But my garden gives me joy.

Rubem A. Alves, *The Poet, The Warrior, The Prophet*
(SCM Press/Trinity Press International 1990), p. 46.

Soul and body

1.8

Is it the soul, as such, that constitutes the human being? No. That is only the soul. Is it the body, then, that is called human? No. That is only the body. Consequently, since these two components, separately, do not constitute a human being, it must be the unity formed by the conjunction of both that alone deserves the name. It is the whole person, certainly, whom God has called to life and to resurrection, not merely a part. It is the human being, whole and entire, who is called, that is to say, the soul, but also the body. If that is so, how can it be conceded that one should be saved without the other when together they form an indissoluble union? Once the possibility of the flesh knowing a new birth has been admitted, what an unfair discrimination it would be for the soul to be saved without the body.

Justin Martyr, Fragment 8 in Olivier Clément, *The Roots of Christian Mysticism*,
tr. Theodore Berkeley and Jeremy Hummerstone
(New City 1993).

Drinking in creation
1.9

Today, I had a delightful walk. At first the ascent was rather dull – along an almost invisible path winding amidst chalk embankments through a forest of low, sparse pines. However, there were incidents to compensate for this: a hare sprang from almost under my feet; I wandered across barberry-bushes and sweet-briar, shedding its blossoms. I walked slowly, reading as I went, the matins service and the hours, sitting down to rest from time to time. I mounted the hill for about two hours and then reached the pass: immediately the whole landscape was transformed. To the left, a small village scattered round a church; to the right, lovely meadows; and, directly beyond the pass, an endless view opening on the mountains, streaked and spotted with snow. Around me and quite near to me – torn, craggy rocks. Below – green slopes of forest; and above all, an extraordinary, snow-saturated atmosphere and absolute silence. Only from below came the sound of the brook, and a hidden spring was babbling somewhere under a rock. I sat for a long time, enjoying the stillness, the mountains, the fragrance. At my side some immortelles were blooming, such as I have never seen before, blue with a heart of deep violet. In the valley below there were no flowers at all, but here on the hillside they were as abundant as if they had sprung, not from the earth, but from the air and sun. And I thought: this is why mountains are so beautiful; through them, as through a friendship with some wise human being, one drinks in freshness, clarity, calm – the qualities born of high altitudes.

Alexander Elchaninov, *The Diary of a Russian Priest* (Faber & Faber 1967), pp. 152–53.

This amazing structure
1.10

When we contemplate the physical creation, we see an unimaginable complex, organized on many planes one above another; atomic, molecular, cellular; vegetable, animal, social. And the marvel of it is that at every level the constituent elements run themselves, and, by their mutual interaction, run the world. God not only makes the world, he makes it make itself; or rather, he causes its innumerable constituents to make it. And this in spite of the fact that the constituents are not for the most part intelligent. They cannot enter into the creative purposes they serve. They cannot see beyond the tip of their noses, they have, indeed, no noses not to see beyond, nor any eyes with which to fail in the attempt. All they can do is blind away at being themselves, and fulfil the repetitive pattern of their existence. When you contemplate this amazing structure, do you wonder that it should be full of flaws, breaks, accidents, collisions and disasters? Will you not be more inclined to wonder why chaos does not triumph; how higher forms of organization should ever arise, or, having arisen, maintain and perpetuate themselves?...

Though a thousand species have perished with the mammoth and the dodo, and though all species, perhaps, must perish at the last, it is a sort of miracle that the species there are should have established themselves. And how have they established themselves? Science studies the pattern, but theology assigns the cause: that imperceptible persuasion exercised by creative will on the chaos of natural sources, setting a bias on the positive and achieving the creatures.

Austin Farrer, *Saving Belief* (Hodder & Stoughton 1967), p. 51.

Water
1.11

Is oxygen-and-hydrogen the divine idea of water? Or has God put the two together only that man might separate and find them out? He allows his child to pull his toys to pieces: but were they made that he might pull them to pieces? He were a child not to be envied for whom his inglorious father would make toys to such an end! A school examiner might see therein the best use of a toy, but not a father! Find for us what in the constitution of the two gases makes them fit and capable to be thus honoured in forming the lovely thing, and you will give us a revelation about more than water, namely about the God who made oxygen and hydrogen. There is no water in oxygen, no water in hydrogen; it comes bubbling fresh from the imagination of the loving God, rushing from under the great white throne of the glacier. The very thought of it makes one gasp with an elemental joy no metaphysician can analyze. The water itself, that dances and sings, and slakes the wonderful thirst... – this lovely thing itself, whose very wetness is a delight to every inch of the human body in its embrace – this live thing which, if I might, I would have running through my room, yea, babbling along my table – this water is its own self, its own truth, and is therein a truth of God. Let him who would know the truth of the maker, become sorely athirst, and drink of the brook by the way – then lift up his heart – not at that moment to the maker of oxygen and hydrogen, but to the inventor and mediator of thirst and water, that man might foresee a little of what his soul may find in God.

George Macdonald, 'The Mirrors of the Lord' in C.S. Lewis,
George Macdonald: An Anthology (Geoffrey Bles 1946), p. 81.

Books without words

1.12

The easiest place to begin is with nature. It is not difficult to see that the created order has something to teach us. Isaiah tells that 'the mountains and the hills before you shall break forth into singing, and all the trees of the field shall clap their hands' (Isaiah 55:12). The handiwork of the Creator can speak to us and teach us if we will listen. Martin Buber told the story of the rabbi who went to a pond every day at dawn to learn 'the song with which the frogs praise God'.

We begin the study of nature by paying attention. We *see* flowers or birds. We observe them carefully and prayerfully. André Gide described the time when during a classroom lecture he observed a moth being reborn from its chrysalis. He was filled with wonder, awe, joy at this metamorphosis, the resurrection. Enthusiastically he showed it to his professor who replied with a note of disapproval, 'What! Didn't you know that a chrysalis is the envelope of a butterfly? Every butterfly you see has come out of a chrysalis. It's perfectly natural.' Disillusioned, Gide wrote,

> Yes, indeed, I knew my *natural* history as well, perhaps better than he… But because it was natural, could he not see that it was marvellous? Poor creature! From that day, I took a dislike to him and a loathing to his lessons.

Who wouldn't! Gide's professor had only amassed information, he had not studied. And so the first step in the study of nature is reverent observation.

Richard Foster, *Celebration of Discipline* (Hodder & Stoughton 1980), p. 63.

All is silence

1.13

When we did find a road, the ruts were so deep and wedged the cart wheel until the axles writhed with pain that found an echo in our bones. We struggled out and walked. Our feet sunk into sand or trod on hard sun-burned mud that cut our shoes. Hour after hour we went on, and at sunset we camped for the night. There was no village by the wayside, but wherever there was a clump of trees there was a group of mud huts, and there was always a well – these are the villages of India. The people plough the land and sow their crops, and then wait for harvest. The damp mists rise when the sun goes down, and out in the country all is silence. Wide spaces, lofty mountains, freedom to go where you will, and a people always ready with patience to listen to good news. Could anything be more attractive to a missionary?

The silent awe of the dawn when the sun rises over the highest mountains in the world, seen from the plains of India, brings something into the soul that nothing else can. Alone with God, in space ineffable and untellable, the soul is stilled. Those mountains are the messengers to remind us that though they seem secure and unmovable, they may be removed. But there is something more than they, it is the word of God.

Who are we that such a treasure should be entrusted to us?

Mary Warburton Booth, *'They That Sow'* (Pickering & Inglis n.d.), pp. 22–23.

Nature's wisdom
1.14

A willow-wren had built in a bank in my fields. This bird a friend and myself had observed as she sat in her nest; but were particularly careful not to disturb her, though we saw she eyed us with some degree of jealousy. Some days after as we passed that way we were desirous of remarking how this brood went on; but no nest could be found, till I happened to take up a large bundle of green moss, as it were, carelessly thrown over the nest, in order to dodge the eye of any impertinent intruder.

The flycatcher… builds every year in the vines that grow on the walls of my house. A pair of these little birds had one year… placed their nest on a naked bough, perhaps in a shady time, not being aware of the inconvenience that followed. But a hot, sunny season coming on before the brood had half fledged, the reflection of the wall became insupportable, and must inevitably have destroyed the tender young, had not affection… prompted the parent-birds to hover over the nest all the hotter hours while, with wings expanded, and mouths gaping for breath, they screened off the heat from their suffering offspring.

Gilbert White, *Natural History and Antiquities of Selborne* (1789).

Image of God
1.15

Know to what extent the creator has honoured you above all the rest of creation. The sky is not an image of God, nor is the moon, nor the sun, nor the beauty of the stars, nor anything of what can be seen in creation. You alone have been made the image of the reality that transcends all understanding, the likeness of imperishable beauty, the imprint of true divinity, the recipient of beatitude, the seal of the true light. When you turn to him you become that which he is himself… There is nothing so great among beings that it can be compared with your greatness. God is able to measure the whole heaven with his span. The earth and the sea are enclosed in the hollow of his hand. And although he is so great and holds all creation in the palm of his hand, you are able to hold him, he dwells in you and moves within you without constraint, for he has said, 'I will live and move among them' (2 Corinthians 6:16).

Gregory of Nyssa, *Second Homily on the Song of Songs*,
tr. Theodore Berkeley and Jeremy Hummerstone.

This spring of nature
1.16

What astonishing variety of artifices, what innumerable millions of exquisite works, is the God of nature engaged in every moment! How gloriously are his all-pervading wisdom and power employed in this useful season of the year, this spring of nature! What infinite myriads of vegetable beings is he forming this very moment in their roots and branches, in their leaves and blossoms, their seeds and fruits!… What endless armies of animals is the hand of God moulding and figuring this very moment throughout his dominions! What immense flight of little birds are now fermenting in the egg, heaving and growing toward shape and life! What vast flocks of four-footed creatures, what droves of large cattle, are now framed in their early embryos, imprisoned in the dark cells of nature!… What unknown myriads of insects in their various cradles and nesting places are now working toward vitality and motion! And thousands of them with their painted wings just beginning to unfurl, expand themselves into fluttering and daylight.

An exquisite world of wonders is complicated even in the body of every little insect – an ant, a gnat, a mite – that is scarce visible to the naked eye. Admirable engines! which a whole academy of philosophers could never contrive – which the nation of poets has neither art nor colours to describe – nor has a world of mechanics skill enough to frame the plainest or coarsest of them. Their nerves, their muscles and the minute atoms which compose the fluids fit to run in the little channels of their veins, escape the notice of the most sagacious mathematician, with all his aid of glasses. The active powers and curiosity of human nature are limited in their pursuit and must be content to lie down in ignorance.

It is a sublime and constant triumph over all the intellectual powers of man which the great God maintains every moment in these inimitable works of nature – in these impenetrable recesses and mysteries of divine art.

Isaac Watts, 'Meditation on the First of May', *Reliques Juveniles*.

Beyond the horizon
1.17

Standing on the shore and looking at the sea you can think of the horizon as a meeting of the sky and sea in one of two ways. Either it is simply a line running right and left, and denoting the limit of your vision, or it is something beyond which other horizons lie which in their turn reveal other seas and lands and civilizations. The latter view has no part of fantasy. What your perspective tells you is provable fact. You may not be able to see beyond the line of the horizon, but your knowledge of the physical nature of the universe is adequate assurance of the facts and forms – that they do exist. If you wish to inspect them for yourself you may do so by travelling to them, but you do not need assurance of their existence. The line of the horizon is an arbitrary demarcation, a purely contingent affair, unlike the edge of a table or the drop of a shutter.

The acceptance of the world of the spirit can become a normal way of looking at life – matter-of-fact as looking at television, but with a new dimension added. Our knowledge of the spiritual nature of the universe should tell us that our physical horizon is not the only one, that the concreteness of things is not the entire reality, and that it is the added dimension of the spiritual which gives to the created order its total reality.

Hubert van Zeller, *The Current of Spirituality* (Templegate Publishers 1970), pp. 64–65.

God's gifts our delight
1.18

Let this be our principle: that the use of God's gifts is not wrongly directed when it is referred to that end to which the author himself created and destined them for us, since he created them for our good, not for our ruin. Accordingly, no one will hold to a straighter path than he who diligently looks to this end. Now if we ponder to what end God created food, we shall find that he meant not only to provide for necessity but also for delight and good cheer. Thus the purpose of clothing, apart from necessity, was comeliness and decency. In grasses, trees, and fruits, apart from their various uses, there is beauty of appearance and pleasantness of odour [cf. Genesis 2:9]. For if this were not true, the prophet would not have reckoned them among the benefits of God, 'that wine gladdens the heart of man, that oil makes his face shine' [Psalm 104:15]. Scriptures would not have reminded us repeatedly, in commending his kindness, that he gave all such things to men. And the natural qualities themselves of things demonstrate sufficiently to what end and extent we may enjoy them. Has the Lord clothed the flowers with the great beauty that greets our eyes, the sweetness of smell that is wafted upon our nostrils, and yet will it be unlawful for our eyes to be affected by that beauty, or our sense of smell by the sweetness of that odour? What? Did he not so distinguish colours as to make some more lovely than others? What? Did he not endow gold and silver, ivory and marble, with a loveliness that renders them more precious than other metals or stones? Did he not, in short, render many things attractive to us, apart from their necessary use?

John Calvin, Institutes III, 10, tr. Ford Battles in *Calvin: Institutes of the Christian Religion*, ed. John T. McNeill (The Westminster Press 1960).

The gift of beauty
1.19

The beauty of the world, as many have felt, is the strongest evidence we have of the goodness and benevolence of the creator. Not, of course, that the world was made beautiful for our sakes. It is beautiful because its author is beautiful, and we should remember that when the old writers spoke of God as the author of nature, they used the word in much the same sense as if we said that a man was the author of his own photograph. But we are allowed to see and enjoy beauty, although the gift cannot be proved to promote our own survival. It looks like a free gift of God. Beauty is a general quality of nature, and not only of organic nature; crystals are very beautiful; the perceiving mind must also be beautiful and healthy. The vile or vulgar mind not only cannot discern beauty; it is a great destroyer of beauty everywhere.

The love of beauty is super-personal and disinterested, like all spiritual values; it promotes common enjoyment and social sympathy. Unquestionably it is one of the three ultimate values, ranking with goodness and truth.

W.R. Inge, *Outspoken Essays* (Longmans, Green & Co. 1922), Second Series, p. 30.

The edge of chaos
1.20

There should be a rational response to everything, we thought; it should be possible to make a better world.

It hasn't worked. Management and control are breaking down everywhere. The new world order looks very likely to end in disorder. We can't make things happen the way we want them to at home, at work or in government, certainly not in the world as a whole. There are, it is now clear, limits to management. We thought that capitalism was the answer, but some of the hungry and homeless are not so sure.

Scientists call this sort of time the edge of chaos, the time of turbulence and creativity out of which a new order may jell. The first living cell emerged, some four million years ago, from a primordial soup of simple molecules and amino acids. Nobody knows why or how. Ever since then the universe has had an inexorable tendency to run down, to degenerate into disorder and decay. Yet it has also managed to produce from that disorder an incredible array of living creatures, plants and bacteria, as well as stars and planets. New life is forever springing from the decay and disorder of the old.

At the Santa Fe Institute, where a group of scientists are studying these phenomena, they call it 'complexity theory'. They believe that their ideas have as much relevance to oil prices, race relations and the stock market as they do to particle physics. In his book about their work, *Complexity*, Mitchell Waldrop describes the edge of chaos as the one place where a complex system can be spontaneous, adaptive and alive. It is also uncomfortable if you are in the middle of it, as so many of our social institutions are right now.

Charles Handy, *The Empty Raincoat* (Arrow Books 1995), p. 16.

And it was good
1.21

Sometimes at dusk we see the loveliness of a doe and her fawn walking across the field, but they have stayed away from the garden, chewing instead the bark of tender new trees.

Broccoli, Brussels sprouts, carrots, don't mind the cold. We'll be picking them long after the ground is rimed with frost. We have discovered a new vegetable this summer, spaghetti squash, which we scrape out with a fork, after cooking, in long, spaghetti-like strands. Leeks are a delight, creamed, or in soup, and spinach salad. We glory in the goodness of creation every day. All that weed-pulling was worth it, though weeds have their own beauty, and, like mosquitoes and flies, are an inevitable part of the summer.

At night now the sky is clear, with no heat haze. One night we eat supper out on the little terrace which we have made with flagstones and lots of honest sweat. We linger at the picnic table through sunset and star rise, and suddenly someone says, 'How light it is on the northern horizon!' We blow out the lamps and there is the staggering beauty of the northern lights. There is something primal about those lights pulsing, in pale green and rose, upwards from the horizon. They give me the same surge of joy as the unpolluted horizon near the Strait of Magellan, showing the curve of the home planet; the same lifting of the heart as the exuberance of the dolphins sporting about the ship after we had crossed the equator.

I sit at the table as we all watch the awesome display of beauty, and there again is the promise of the rainbow covenant of Easter, radiant, affirming.

And it is good.

Madeleine L'Engle, *And It was Good: Reflections on Beginnings*
(Harold Shaw Publishers 1983), pp. 210–11.

The music of the universe
1.22

There are things that we must see in a relation of use to ourselves, if we are to live at all. For instance, food is to us rightly and naturally that which we eat; and, if we grow cabbages, we are necessarily in a relation of use to them. But there are other things that we cannot understand at all if we see them only in the relation of use. For instance, music. If I listen to a symphony by Beethoven, expecting it to give me some information of use to myself, information that will help me to increase my income or cure my indigestion, I shall not hear the music at all, and it will be to me a mere chaos of sounds. The music does not exist to give me useful information... True, to perceive it will profit me; I shall have the delight of experiencing beauty. But the paradox of the process is this, that I shall not experience the beauty if I try to experience it with an eye to my own profit. For in that case I shall have certain expectations and make certain demands of my own upon it, not perhaps that it shall increase my income or cure my indigestion, but that it shall give me just the kind of pleasure I expect of it. If I am to experience the music as it is, I must forget about myself and all my demands and expectations, and allow myself to fall in love with it, if I can; I must allow that relation, which is the music, to happen to me.

Now, according to Christ, the universe, in its nature, is not like cabbages that we grow for our own kitchens; it is like music. Its reality consists in a relation that is not a relation of use to us at all; and we must get ourselves and our own wants and demands and expectations out of the way if we are to be aware of that reality. But, further, to be aware of that reality of the music of the universe is the highest good, the highest happiness. Then we ourselves become part of the music; we are by hearing the music constrained to make ourselves part of it; for it is a real music, irresistible in its beauty, and we cannot but dance to it when we hear it. He himself heard it and danced to it; and the beauty of his dance, of his life, of his whole state of being, has for two thousand years allured the world, even while the world would not understand the meaning of it.

Arthur Clutton-Brock, *What is the Kingdom of Heaven?* (1919).

My knowledge was divine
1.23

Certainly Adam in paradise had not more sweet and curious apprehensions of the world, than I when I was a child. All appeared new, and strange at first, inexpressibly rare and delightful and beautiful. I was a little stranger, which at my entrance into the world was saluted and surrounded with innumerable joys. My knowledge was divine. I knew by intuition those things which since my apostasy, I collected again by the highest reason. My very ignorance was advantageous. I seemed as one brought into the estate of innocence. All things were spotless and pure and glorious: yea, and infinitely mine, and joyful and precious. I knew not that there were any sins, or complaints or laws. I dreamed not of poverties, contentions or vices. All tears and quarrels were hidden from mine eyes. Everything was at rest, free and immortal. I knew nothing of sickness or death or rents or exaction, either for tribute or bread. In the absence of these I was entertained like an angel with the works of God in their splendour and glory. I saw all in the peace of Eden; heaven and earth did sing my creator's praises, and could not make more melody to Adam, than to me. All time was eternity, and a perpetual Sabbath. Is it not strange, that an infant should be heir of the whole world, and see those mysteries which the books of the learned never unfold?

The corn was orient and immortal wheat, which never should be reaped, nor was ever sown. I thought it had stood from everlasting to everlasting. The dust and stones of the street were as precious as gold: the gates were at first the end of the world. The green trees when I saw them first through one of the gates transported and ravished me, their sweetness and unusual beauty made my heart to leap, and almost mad with ecstasy, they were such strange and wonderful things. The men! O what venerable and reverend creatures did the aged seem! Immortal cherubims! And young men glittering and sparkling angels, and maids strange seraphic pieces of life and beauty! Boys and girls tumbling in the street, and playing, were moving jewels. I knew not that they were born or should die; but all things abided eternally as they were in their proper places. Eternity was manifest in the light of the day, and something infinite behind everything appeared: which talked with my expectation and moved my desire. The city seemed to stand in Eden, or to be built in heaven. The streets were mine, the temple was mine, the people were mine, their clothes and gold and silver were mine, as much as their sparkling eyes, fair skins and ruddy faces. The skies were mine, and so were the sun and moon and stars, and all the world was mine; and I the only spectator and enjoyer of it. I knew no churlish proprieties, nor bounds, nor divisions: but all proprieties [i.e. properties] were mine: all treasures and the possessors of them. So that with much ado I was corrupted, and made to learn the dirty devices of this world.

Thomas Traherne, *Centuries* (Faith Press/Clarendon Press 1960), Third Century, pp. 2–3.

The surprises of paradox
1.24

We need a new way of thinking about our problems and our futures. If the contradictions and surprises of paradox are going to be part of those futures, we should not be dismayed. The acceptance of paradox as a feature of our life is the first step towards living with it and managing it.

I used to think that paradoxes were the visible signs of an imperfect world, a world which would, one day, be better understood by us and better organized. There had to be one right proven way to bring up children, I thought. There should be no reason for some to starve while others gorge. Freedom need not mean licence, violence or even war. Riches for some should not necessarily imply poverty for others. We lacked only the knowledge and the will to resolve the paradoxes…

I no longer believe in a Theory of Everything, or in the possibility of perfection. Paradox I now see to be inevitable, endemic and perpetual. The more turbulent the times, the more complex the world, the more the paradoxes. The Theory of Complexity has been added to the Theory of Chaos. The turbulence, the theory goes, is a necessary prelude to creativity and some new order. We can therefore, and should, reduce the starkness of some of the contradictions, minimize the inconsistencies, understand the puzzles in the paradoxes, but we cannot make them disappear, nor solve them completely, nor escape from them, until that new order becomes established. Paradoxes are like the weather, something to be lived with, not solved, the worst aspects mitigated, the best enjoyed and used as clues to the way forward. Paradox has to be *accepted*, coped with and made sense of, in life, in work, in community and among the nations.

Charles Handy, The Empty Raincoat (Arrow Books 1995), pp. 17–18.

Work as worship
1.25

How can we best show our respect, or in other words, worship, to the giver of all good? Reasoning by analogy I would say, by increasing our endeavours to make the best use of the gifts God has bestowed on us whether bodily or mental. We all have a gift either small or great; it matters not how small, be earnest in trying to make the best of it... Get all the available knowledge in the direction your gift leads and go ahead... learn your business thoroughly from every source, it does not matter where, people, books or nature, but don't be content to do a thing because 'it has been done so for the last generation or two and will do for you'; it won't do for you, be sure of that. 'The Lord requires his own with usury,' and the usury can be best attained by improving your gift and making your land produce more than your predecessor by the skill you bring to bear on it.

By doing this you have three causes of satisfaction: you are doing the will of God by improving your talents, you have increased the yield of your land, and you have also the satisfaction of being a direct encourager (by example, which is better than precept), of others in the same path, and lastly, all the time you have been working, you have been worshipping God by doing his will. This will be found to be the case throughout all the gifts of God; if the gift be small make it of use by constant practice of it; if it be large, then, my friend, a greater responsibility rests upon you, 'the greater the gift, the greater the burden'. An earnest worker is one of God's true nobility; he is trying to do all he knows, and by respecting the gift, he respects the giver.

There is as much worship in good workmanship done in the right spirit, as in any other act; the spirit of the thing done and not the act itself is the key to tell whether anything done be worship or not, but God, the master workman, who has made the minutest insect with as much care as the mammoth elephant, sets us the example of good works. Imitation is the sincerest praise.

C.B. Bostwick, 'The Shaker Manifesto' XI, 2, pp. 29–30, in The Shakers: Two Centuries of Spiritual Reflection, ed. R.E. Whitson (Paulist Press 1983), pp. 284–85.

Relationship

Members one of another
1.26

All mankind is of one author, and in one volume; when one man dies, one chapter is not torn out of the book, but translated into a better language; and every chapter must be so translated;… God's hand is in every translation, and his hand shall bind up all our scattered leaves again, for that library where every book shall lie open to one another. As therefore that bell that rings to a sermon, calls not upon the preacher only, but upon the congregation to come; so this bell calls us all… Who casts not up his eye to the sun when it rises? But who takes off his eye from a comet when that breaks out? Who bends not his ear to any bell, which upon any occasion rings? But who can remove it from that bell, which is passing a piece of himself out of this world? No man is an island, entire of itself; every man is a piece of the continent, a part of the main; if a clod be washed away by the sea, Europe is the less, as well as if a promontory were, as well as if a manor of thy friends or of thine own were; any man's death diminishes me, because I am involved in mankind; and therefore never send to know for whom the bell tolls; it tolls for thee.

John Donne, *Devotions upon Emergent Occasions*, XVII (1624).

Persons in relation
1.27

For our lives to be fully human, we have to be persons-in-relation – persons who relate 'rightly' to God, to our neighbour, to ourselves and to the cosmos. And we cannot relate rightly to God unless we relate rightly to our neighbour. For human relationships to be life-giving, there is need to recognize the other's human worth and dignity; there is need for mutual respect and reciprocity.

Mary Magdalene as woman symbolizes this life-in-relation. Her relationship to Jesus was a life-giving relationship. In the social setting of her time, women were 'non-persons' who 'belonged' to some male individual, with no rights of their own. And yet Jesus showed respect for Mary's personhood by calling her by name (John 20:16) and gave recognition of her personal dignity as a woman, thus dignifying womanhood as well. There is something significant in the fact that Jesus appreciated Mary's worth for who she was as a person, and not because she was 'wife of', or 'mother of', or 'daughter of' a superior male. She carried her own identity: she was Mary of Magdala... Jesus not only recognized Mary's value as a person but called forth her potential as a woman, and confirmed her trustworthiness and capability, above his other disciples, to be his first witness to life.

Virginia Fabella, 'Symbols in John's Resurrection Scene: Reflections on the Garden and Mary Magdalene' in *Women of Courage: Asian Women Reading the Bible*, ed. Lee Oo Chung et al. (Asian Women's Resource Centre for Culture and Theology 1992), pp. 188–89.

No passing feeling
1.28

Friendship is an unpretentious relation, for 'friend' is not a designation of office, nor an exalted title, nor a function one must perform from time to time, nor a role one is supposed to play in society. Friendship is a personal relation, 'someone who likes you', someone you like...

Friendship also combines respect with affection... One does not have to submit to a friend. One neither looks up to nor down at a friend. One can look a friend in the face. In friendship one experiences oneself, just as one is, readily accepted and respected in one's own freedom. When one person likes another, then one respects the other in his or her individuality, and delights in his or her singularities as well.

Friendship is no passing feeling of affection. It combines affection with faithfulness. You can depend upon a friend. As a friend you become someone upon whom others can depend. A friend remains a friend even in misfortune, even in guilt. For between friends there rules no prejudice that defines one, and no ideal image after which one must strive. Nor is friendship an alliance for mutual advantage, as is the case with so-called business friends. Between friends there rules only the promise to walk with each other and to be there for each other, in other words, a faithfulness that has to do not with acting and possessing, but with the individual person and with being.

Friendship is then a deep human relation that arises out of freedom, consists in mutual freedom, and preserves this freedom.

Jürgen Moltmann, *The Open Church* (SCM Press 1978), p. 51.

Having a friend
1.29

In order to be capable of friendship, somehow I need to *have* a friend. The friend I need is one who confirms me, confronts me and celebrates me. When others confirm me, I feel firm on my own ground. I know that as they stand before me they are really *for* me. They will not pull out the rug from under my feet, nor invade the sacredness of my own being. They affirm my own needed space and my own unique style.

Nevertheless, my friend also confronts me, challenging me to acknowledge the ways in which I am being destructive toward myself or others. Confrontation is not just condemnation. My friend does not just condemn me for having a vice, but urges me to resist it. My friend does not simply point to a life-denying tendency within me, but also calls upon me to draw upon the life-affirming resources that are within and around me.

If friendship involves confirmation and confrontation, it also involves celebration. These three, but the greatest of these is celebration. When I look on another as a close friend, I celebrate that other's very existence. My friend's unique way of expressing life evokes feelings of thanksgiving in me. My friend's breakthroughs toward fuller and more creative life evoke rejoicing in me. Just as my friend's times of discouragement and despair can draw me out of my own preoccupation and elicit my reaching out in care, so also my friend's 'highs' can draw me into celebration. In a good liturgical word, friends not only celebrate each other, they also 'concelebrate' life around them.

If these are the dynamics of human friendship, they may also be a clue to friendship with God.

James Nelson, *The Intimate Connection* (SPCK 1992), p. 65.

The nature of friendship
1.30

Maintaining spiritual distance is a more personal matter than I realized yesterday. It is essential to the understanding and living of true friendship. Jonas and I are trying to deal with our friendship. In the beginning we touched upon it only indirectly, but in the past few days we have been able to explore our relationship more directly. It is hard for me to speak of my feelings of being rejected or imposed upon, of my desire for affirmation as well as my need for space, of insecurity and mistrust, of fear and love. But as I entered into these feelings, I also discovered the real problem – expecting from a friend what only Christ can give.

I feel so easily rejected. When a friend does not come, a letter is not written, or an invitation not extended, I begin to feel unwanted and disliked. I gravitate toward dark feelings of low self-esteem and become depressed. Once depressed, I tend to interpret even innocent gestures as proofs of my self-chosen darkness, from which it is harder and harder to return. Looking carefully at this vicious circle of self-rejection and speaking about it directly with Jonas is a good way to start moving in the opposite direction.

Two things happened when Jonas and I spoke. First, he forced me to move out of the centre! He too has a life, he too has his struggles, he too has unfulfilled needs and imperfections. As I tried to understand his life, I felt a deep compassion and a desire to comfort and console him. I no longer felt so strongly the need to judge him for not paying enough attention to me. It is so easy to convince yourself that you are the one who needs all the attention. But once you can see the other concretely in his or her life situation, you can step back a bit from yourself and understand that, in a true friendship, two people make a dance.

Henri J.M. Nouwen, *The Road to Daybreak* (Darton, Longman & Todd 1989), pp. 64–65.

Jesus the friend
1.31

When, in the field of human relationships, the parent–child relation comes to an end, when the master–servant connection is abolished and when the privileges based on sexual position are removed, then what is truly human emerges and remains; and that is friendship. The new man, the true man, the free man is the friend. Existence *for* others within the regulation and functioning of the social order is necessary. But it is only legitimated as long as the necessity continues to exist. On the other hand existence *with* others, in unexacting friendliness, is free from necessity and compulsion. It preserves freedom because it unites receptivity with permanence. Friendship is the reasonable passion for truly human fellowship; it is a mutual affection cemented by loyalty. The more people begin to live with one another as friends, the more privileges and claims to domination become superfluous. The more people trust one another the less they need to control one another. The positive meaning of a classless society free of domination, without repression and without privileges, lies in friendship. Without the power of friendship and without the goal of a friendly world there is no human hope for the class struggles and struggles for dominance.

... The inner reason for Jesus' friendship with 'tax collectors and sinners' was to be found in the joy of the messianic feast which he celebrated with them. It was not sympathy, it was overflowing joy in the kingdom of God, a joy that sought to share and to welcome, that drew him to people who were outcasts in the eyes of the law. The dawn of the kingdom is celebrated in the messianic feast, often described as a marriage feast. The regard which Jesus showed for the unregarded and despised when he ate and drank with them was determined by the law of grace. Jesus laid claim to this law by forgiving sins and by living in fellowship with tax collectors and sinners.

Jürgen Moltmann, *The Church in the Power of the Spirit*
(SCM Press 1977), pp. 116–17.

Glimpses of eternity
1.32

Ecstasy is an experience of temporary boundary dissolution – of perception and living. Ecstasy is a moment in which some otherwise distant reality is glimpsed as here and now and at one with itself. This is a peak experience. Whether in the context of contemplation or sexuality it is something that it is dangerous and damaging to grasp for its own sake. It is, after all, possible to become addicted to altered states of consciousness. But peak experiences do have their place in human life and are *not* to be viewed with suspicion. In contemplative mysticism such experiences point to a transformation of the whole of life towards the source of all being and meaning that is God. The same, I would suggest, can be true of the ecstasy of intimacy or sexual union. In other words, the 'glimpses' of eternity provided by sexual or contemplative ecstasy serve to deepen our personalities and our perceptions of reality.

We need to maintain a certain delicacy here. A true human intimacy is a mirror of God's relationship with us. This involves holding in proper balance an appropriate dissolution of personal boundaries and a continued respect for personal space. It is an unfortunate fact, of which we are being made increasingly aware these days, that the sexual crossing of boundaries has often been violent and abusive. At the heart of most cases of sexual abuse, including rape, lies the desire to gain power over another human being.

True human desire, like God's desire for us, is respectfully tuned both to the self and to the partner. Each person may be lost in the other but individual boundaries are not abused. Each person freely allows them to be crossed in a way that enhances each partner rather than destroys his or her identity. In the end the commandment in the gospel of John is to learn how to love in a truly human way that is, at the same time, a God-shaped way: 'This is my commandment, that you love one another as I have loved you.'

Philip Sheldrake, 'Befriending our Desires' in *The Way*,
vol. 35, no. 2 (April 1995), pp. 99–100.

Openness to each other
1.33

Prayer is best understood on the analogy of a shared human relationship. The right context in which to understand prayer is the context of presence rather than power, after the pattern of a personal relationship rather than a market transaction.

Since this is the case, prayer must be something far richer and far deeper than a matter merely of making requests. Prayer is more than asking God to give us this or that.

Asking need not and should not vanish away into thin air. Asking is the expression of desire, and the sharing of desire has its proper place even in the most sensitive and loving of human relationships. But it can no longer become the be-all and end-all of prayer. If there is no more to a human relationship than what each can get from the other, then the relationship is barely personal at all. Persons are being used, not appreciated and enjoyed.

Once, however, human beings are respected for what they are in themselves and regarded as ends rather than means, then the relationships which are formed between persons acquire a value of their own, and as they develop they find expression in a rich variety of communication and communion.

At the centre of such a relationship is an openness to each other. This makes possible and sustains a process of sharing, of giving and receiving. Persons share because they care, and in the process their whole selves are involved, together with all the varied resources of feeling, imagination and thought.

Peter Baelz, *Does God Answer Prayer?* (Darton, Longman & Todd 1982), p. 7.

Connection in the Spirit
1.34

As we breathe in the power of the Holy Spirit, so we are transformed personally. As we undergo personal transformation, so the power of the Holy Spirit radiates from us to all those around us – and at a distance in the prayer of intercession. Now at last we can effect a deep, caring relationship with other people, both individually and collectively. We do not need to strive to know people by displaying our gifts and social eligibility. Instead, we can remain completely still and at peace within, while a stream of love so pours down from us that we are in the most intimate fellowship even with complete strangers. True personal knowledge is a state of union with the other; indeed, unitive knowledge is the apogee of all understanding. In this knowledge the two, while retaining their unique identities, are now functionally one, and there follows an unembarrassed sharing of inner problems, tensions and fears. There is also an unlimited flow of spiritual strength from the one to the other, and with this there comes an undisturbed trust and a warmth of love that far exceeds any superficial affection that we may experience on a purely social level.

When we know this degree of spiritual intimacy with another person, we are inevitably in close fellowship with many other people also, for with the breaking down of our own barriers, we are fully available to the world while remaining rooted in our own unique nature. In this state of open friendship it would be impossible to betray anyone, let alone give false evidence against them. On the contrary, as the barriers of the personality drop from us, so we can rejoice in the splendid uniqueness of each fellow being while participating with delight in that special gift. Thus we acknowledge and support the individual nature of each person we encounter in a day's work. It is indeed a social duty to uphold our fellow creatures, supporting their legitimate endeavours and protecting them against injury and injustice. But what starts as a law of social action becomes a passionate response from the soul as we live in the depths of our fellow human beings.

Martin Israel, *The Discipline of Love: The Ten Commandments for Today*
(SPCK 1985), pp. 80–81.

How to be free
1.35

Detachment frees us from the control of others. No longer can we be manipulated by people who hold our livelihoods in their hands. Things do not entice our imaginations, people do not dominate our destinies.

The Desert Fathers renounced speech in order to learn compassion. A charming story is told of Abbot Macarius, who said to the brethren in the church at Scete, 'Brethren, flee.' Perplexed, one of the brothers asked, 'How can we fly further than this, seeing we are here in the desert?' Macarius placed his finger to his mouth and said, 'Flee from this.' When Arsenius, the Roman educator who gave up his status and wealth for the solitude of the desert, prayed, 'Lord, lead me into the way of salvation,' he heard a voice saying, 'Be silent.'

Silence frees us from the need to control others. One reason we can hardly bear to remain silent is that it makes us feel so helpless. We are accustomed to relying upon words to manage and control others. A frantic stream of words flows from us in an attempt to straighten others out. We want so desperately for them to agree with us, to see things our way. We evaluate people, judge people, condemn people. We devour people with our words. Silence is one of the deepest disciplines of the Spirit simply because it puts the stopper on that.

When we become quiet enough to let go of people, we learn compassion for them. We can be with people in their hurt and need. We can speak a word out of our inner silence that will set them free. Anthony knew that the true test of spirituality was in the freedom to live among people compassionately: 'With our neighbour there is life and death: for if we do good to our brother, we shall do good to God: but if we scandalize our brother, we sin against Christ.'

Richard Foster, *Freedom of Simplicity* (Harper & Row/Triangle 1981), pp. 57–58.

The extent of love
1.36

You are as prone to love, as the sun is to shine; it being the most delightful and natural employment of the soul of man: without which you are dark and miserable. Consider therefore the extent of love, its vigour and excellency. For certainly he that delights not in love makes vain the universe, and is of necessity to himself the greatest burden. The whole world ministers to you as the theatre of your love. It sustains you and all objects that you may continue to love them. Without which it were better for you to have no being. Life without objects is sensible emptiness, and that is a greater misery than death nor nothing. Objects without love are the delusion of life. The objects of love are its greatest treasures: and without love it is impossible they should be treasures… To love all persons in all ages, all angels, all worlds, is divine and heavenly. To love all cities and all kingdoms, all kings and all peasants, and every person in all worlds with a natural intimate familiar love, as if him alone, is blessed. This makes a man effectually blessed in all worlds, a delightful lord of all things, a glorious friend to all persons, a concerned person in all transactions, and ever present with all affairs. So that he must ever be filled with company, ever in the midst of all nations, every joyful, and ever blessed. The greatness of this man's love no man can measure; it is stable like the sun, it endureth for ever as the moon, it is a faithful witness in heaven. It is stronger and more great than all private affections.

It representeth every person in the light of eternity, and loveth him with the love of all worlds, with a love conformable to God's, guided to the same ends, and founded upon the same causes. Which however lofty and divine it is, is ready to humble itself into the dust to serve the person beloved. And by how much the more sublime and glorious it is, is so much the more sweet and truly delightful, majesty and pleasure concurring together. Now you may see what it is to be a son of God more clearly. Love in all its glory is the friend of the most High. It was begotten of him, and is to sit in his throne, and to reign in communion with him. It is to please him and to be pleased by him, in all his works, ways and operations. It is ordained to hold an eternal correspondence with him in the highest heavens. It is here in its infancy, there in its manhood and perfect stature.

Thomas Traherne, *Centuries* (The Faith Press 1969), p. 86.

A life of love
1.37

Every human being is unique. If follows that every human being has some unique gift to give to his family; to his parents and brothers and sisters in the ordinary narrow sense, first of all, and thence to his country and to the world. The small world of the human home is built up of the gifts of each member of it; the larger world without is built up in the same way of the various gifts, economic, political, cultural, religious, of its individual citizens. If we are Christians we dismiss once and for all the idea that our business in the world is to serve ourselves and nobody else, to become holy ourselves and pay no attention to anyone else… Live your life in the unity of the home first of all: train yourself to think in terms of what will make the home a better and a happier place; and then in your building up of the home think of the needs and wellbeing of your immediate neighbours, and thence of your country and of the whole world; and so you will necessarily live a life of love, and fulfil that much at least – and it is a great deal – of the law of God.

Gerald Vann, *The Divine Pity* (William Collins 1956), p. 56.

We are sexual beings
1.38

One of the Desert Fathers, Abbot John, reported triumphantly to his confessor that, after a long struggle, he had finally overcome all passion in himself. His confessor wasn't pleased at all. 'Go back,' he told him, 'and pray to be tempted again.' Like the wise old man he was he knew that passion, whether of anger or sexual desire, was part of normal human experience; woe to the man who is 'too good' for that sort of thing, since, by pride or repression, he has abdicated his humanity.

... In fact it is not easy to live, as a human being must, with being a sexual creature. It is all right for the animals for whom sexual longing is a seasonal frenzy to be satisfied as suddenly, and often as violently, as it occurs. It is much harder for us for whom sex seems to touch upon so many other things – our loyalties to others, our wish for stable family life, our need for social acceptance on the one hand, and our need to grow as individuals, our need for ecstasy, even our longing to find God on the other. Sex lies at the very quick of our lives – in our deepest hope to love and be loved, to heal and to be healed.

It is the tremendous hope that all of us invest in sex which makes me feel we should be more compassionate to one another's sexual longings than to anything else. (In practice, however, because of fear and envy, we are just the opposite.) We are muddled and foolish, and we make terrible mistakes. Sexual desire then slides easily towards lust, the condition in which love becomes swallowed in hunger.

Yet for all our capacity to get it wrong, we do so desperately want to get it right, knowing even in our lost moments that, if we *can* get sexual love and desire together in the same place at the same time, then we have achieved one of the greatest delights of being human, a truly religious moment.

... It is a miracle of salvation that creativity springs not from our strength and virtue but from our weakness, emptiness and shame. So that lust, if accepted simply, almost humorously, without excuses or justifications, is turned from our crucifixion to our resurrection. 'One of the elders said it is not because evil thoughts come to us we are condemned but only because we make use of the evil thoughts. It can happen that from these thoughts we suffer shipwreck, but it can also happen that because of them we may be crowned.'

Monica Furlong, *Christian Uncertainties* (Hodder & Stoughton 1975), pp. 41–43.

Guilt, real and false
1.39

A conversation with a friend helped open my eyes. Connie is about ten years older than I am, and her mother died a year ago, and Connie is filled with guilt.

Now I happen to know that Connie was more than just a dutiful daughter; she kept her mother at home until a hospital was inevitable; she visited her daily thereafter; the difficult old woman was treated with love and kindness; and I told Connie that if anybody had little cause for guilt, it was she. But the guilt was obviously there, and a sore weight. So I said that we all, all of us without exception, have cause for guilt about our parents, and that I had far more cause than she. Then I heard myself saying, 'I don't think real guilt is ever much of a problem for us. It's false guilt that causes the trouble.' Connie gave me a funny, surprised look, and said, 'I think you're right.'

And a load of guilt fell from my own shoulders.

I certainly have legitimate cause for both real and false guilt with my mother. But when I try to be the perfect daughter, to be in control of the situation, I become impaled on false guilt and become overtired and irritable.

It is only by accepting real guilt that I am able to feel free of guilt as I sit on the stone bridge and cool my feet in the dappled shade and admire the pop eyes of the frog; and it comes to me that if I am not free to accept guilt when I do wrong, then I am not free at all. If all my mistakes are excused, if there's an alibi, a rationalization for every blunder, then I am not free at all.

Madeleine L'Engle, *The Summer of the Great-Grandmother*
(Harper & Row 1974), p. 50.

Marriage
1.40

Marriage, says the Christian, is for life; and the wedding is a declaration that it is so. It is a fearsome declaration to make, and without the grace of God, arrogant and absurd...

This is why the wedding is an act of worship, and not merely a formal indication in a register office: because the Christian, saying these terrible things, dare not just nod them off before a clerk; but must come and put his vows into the hand of God, trusting that God will hold [the couple] where he wants them held. To turn a wedding into worship is to recognize that marriage is bigger than we are; that it is not just a pleasant arrangement we have made for our own convenience, but a vocation into which we have been drawn by nature and by God.

The truth is that very few marriages remain all the time, day and night, summer and winter, pleasant or convenient. We have to give things up for each other: sometimes hobbies and pastimes, habits of spending, friends. Some glib talkers about marriage say that we do not need to 'give up': we must enrich each other's lives, not rob them. But this is unreal... If we mean business about marriage, we shall throw a good deal overboard in painful but decisive abandon; we shall bring along with us whatever is shareable, and a few things that are not; and we shall discover new things that we never did alone, but which we can start together and use as the basis for 'mutual society, help and comfort, in prosperity and adversity'... Then Christians know they are committed, that they are in it for good or ill; and in a curious way the situation is lightened by the knowledge.

Harold Loukes, *Christians and Sex: A Quaker Comment*
(1962), pp. 26–27.

Family idols
1.41

We might define the family as 'a dynamic, interdependent psychological unit made up of individuals, and the interactions between them, a nucleus of whom form a household over time and are maybe related by either blood or law. Whilst a family will evolve and change through the course of its life-cycle, its members will retain crucial, emotional significance for one another, of both a positive and negative kind...'

We need to stop 'sacralizing' one kind of family structure – the nuclear unit of a first marriage plus children. Not only does this marginalize the majority of people, who do not belong to such a structure, but it has the effect of encouraging a kind of idolatry which stands in the way of challenging individuals to 'leave their father's house' and attend to the claims of the Kingdom. The family is a natural human institution not a Christian invention, and the claims of family naturally and obviously absorb people's attention and concern to an enormous extent, whether they define themselves as an 'insider' or an 'outsider' to a family group. The effect of the Church's 'sacralization' of the family (and of this one form of family structure) is to accentuate these natural tendencies so that Christians, far from being freer to be at the disposal of Kingdom claims often seem more encumbered than everyone else by their perception of the prior claims of family life. Jesus sat very lightly indeed to the family. His few comments about it are mainly disparaging and he showed no inclination to found one himself. There is therefore little support from the gospels for the kind of idolatrous position given by the church to the family as an institution.

Sue Walrond-Skinner, 'Creative Forms of Family Life: Can the Church let it Happen?'
in *Mirror to the Church,* ed. Monica Furlong (SPCK 1988), p. 73.

The space between us
1.42

In the deepest intimacy, it seems to me, there is no merging; but there is indwelling, to such an extent that people can live in one another and be part of one another even when separated by thousands of miles. What makes the difference between merging and indwelling is, I believe, personal love and commitment and trust. Two people can enter into deeply altered states of consciousness either through drugs or hypnosis, or even by the practice of non-attachment, and they can float into one another's psyche with a terrifying loss of identity. But where there is no love and trust, what human value can this possibly have? And where love and trust are lacking, how terrible can be this 'forced' intimacy! Furthermore, love and trust must grow; and ordinarily this takes time. I cannot believe that we can blandly walk into the core of another's being by altering our consciousness with drugs or hypnosis or other techniques. Nor can we do so by staring for hours at another's face, unless our love and trust correspond to the length of our gaze. It must be awful to be stared at for hours by someone who does not love you; and it must be awful to stare for hours at someone we do not love. All this is so different from the ecstatic love affair in which the beloved is 'the mountains, the solitary wooded valleys, strange islands... silent music'. Without the mystical dimension of love and trust, meditation runs the risk of inhumanity and mechanical manipulation.

William Johnston, *Silent Music: The Science of Meditation*
(Fontana 1974), p. 147.

An intuition of beauty
1.43

A better starting point in thinking about romantic love would be to stay with the classical understanding: to see it as an intuition of beauty, a moment of revelation both about God and about creation. As an emotion it should be seen as an awakening – a summons to other emotions and other commitments. As a revelation of God it should lead to worship. As a revelation about creation it should lead to an appropriate engagement with the created order – possibly art, poetry or political endeavour; possibly, but not necessarily, to relationship with the person whose beauty has been seen. It may be appropriate for such a moment to lead to marriage, to friendship, or to some affectionate sexual relationship. The discernment of what outcome is appropriate cannot lie with the experience of romantic love itself; it must be discovered within creation and within responsible and affectionate society. For a gay man who finds himself 'falling for' another man, a society that interprets his insight as intrinsically perverse can offer him little guidance on how wisely to 'order his affections'.

Michael Vasey, *Strangers and Friends: A New Exploration of Homosexuality and the Bible* (Hodder & Stoughton 1995), p. 236.

Partner for life
1.44

As quite a young girl I made up my mind. He must be a sincere Christian; not a nominal one or a mere church member, but truly converted to God. I resolved that he should be a man of sense. I knew that I could never respect a fool, or one much weaker mentally than myself.

The third essential consisted of oneness of views and tastes, and any ideas of lordship or ownership being lost in love. There can be no doubt that Jesus Christ intended, by making love the law of marriage, to restore woman to the position God intended her to occupy. Of course there must be mutual yielding whenever there is proper love, because it is a pleasure and a joy to yield our own wills to those for whom we have real affection, whenever it can be done with an approving conscience.

Neither party should attempt to force an alliance where there exists a physical repugnance. Natural instinct in this respect is usually too strong for reason, and asserts itself in after life in such a way so as to make both supremely miserable.

Another resolution that I made was that I would never marry a man who was not a total abstainer, and this from conviction, and not merely to gratify me.

Besides these things, which I looked upon as being absolutely essential, I had, like most people, certain preferences. The first was that the object of my choice should be a minister, for I felt I could be most useful to God as a minister's wife. Then I very much desired that he should be dark and tall, and had a special liking for the name, 'William'. Singularly enough, in adhering to my essentials, my fancies were also gratified.

Catherine Booth, 'On Choosing a Husband' in *The Training of Children and Courtship and Marriage* (Salvationist Publishing and Supplies 1953).

Vulnerable to God
1.45

More than anything else, the example of Jesus' life teaches us [i.e. men] that all our activity needs to be rooted in contemplative communing with God. Initially, the Spirit leads Jesus into the desert to discern the meaning of the revelation of his identity, given at baptism. There Jesus opens himself to understand that revelation in all its implications. He becomes vulnerable to God and to all the temptations we experience that try to distort our sense of ourselves. Yet, out of that struggle emerges a man whose life flows directly from the appropriation of his identity in relation to God. That sense of self and mission must be refined over and over in the rhythm of involvement with others and contemplative withdrawal.

Without the willingness to open ourselves to such moments of solitude, we men will never be able to sort through the images which clamour for our attention, promising true masculinity. Only by shifting our attention away from what others tell us we should be, can we discern who we truly are. The revelation of our true identity comes when we are willing to risk openness to God's Spirit speaking to our own. It is a precarious enterprise for, like Abraham, we will be called to forsake the nest of patriarchy to embark on a strange, new journey. We need community to cultivate the new ways of being that we discover in prayer. In community, we discover what it means to be open and vulnerable to God through the practice of being open and vulnerable to one another. In community we receive support from one another to sustain the commitment to return anew to prayer and to continue the rhythm of revelation and appropriation. Finally, it is in community that we can establish relationships of mutual mentorship with one another, modelling for one another the courageous fidelity to the task of discovering our true selves in partnership with God.

Robert A. Repicky, 'Discovering Ourselves as Men before God' in *The Way*, vol. 35, no. 2 (April 1995), pp. 119–20.

The Path of Life

The precious gift
1.46

Life is our most precious gift from God, and we are called to make it most truly human. Neither a subhuman life, nor one that is simply passive, is a fully human life. The Hebrew conception of life is always one of action, movement and enjoyment. The evangelist John speaks of eternal life as the true life. But to John, eternal life is not the future resurrected life of believers; it is a life that we already presently enjoy in our earthly existence. Eternal life begins now when we live out Jesus' words of enduring life: 'Love one another.' Our life is one, so there is no division between physical life and spiritual life, between our life of food and drink and our life of relationship to God and neighbour.

The resurrection of Jesus announces that true life is available to, and the right of, all human beings; it is not something reserved for a few, or something that we await to happen on the 'last day': it is something we already live now. It is not compensation for the miseries of life, but a continuation of an earthly existence lived out according to God's will and purpose for humanity.

Virginia Fabella, 'Symbols in John's Resurrection Scene: Reflections on the Garden and Mary Magdalene' in *Women of Courage: Asian Women Reading the Bible*, ed. Lee Oo Chung et al. (Asian Women's Resource Centre for Culture and Theology 1992), pp. 189–90.

God in everything
1.47

Expectant people are watchful, always looking for him they expect, always ready to find him in whatever comes along; however strange it may be, they always think he might be in it. This is what awareness of the Lord is to be like and it requires diligence that taxes a man's senses and powers to the utmost, if he is to achieve it and to take God evenly in all things – if he is to find God as much in one thing as in another.

In this regard, one kind of work does indeed differ from another but if one takes the same attitude toward each of his various occupations, then they will be all alike to him. Thus being on the right track and God meaning this to him, he will shine, as clear in worldly things as heavenly...

To be right, a person must do one of two things: either he must learn to have God in his work and hold fast to him there, or he must give up his work altogether. Since, however, man cannot live without activities that are both human and various, we must learn to keep God in everything we do, and whatever the job or place, keep on with him, letting nothing stand in our way. Therefore, when the beginner has to do with other people, let him first commit himself strongly to God and establish God firmly in his own heart, uniting his senses and thought, his will and powers with God, so that nothing else can enter his mind.

> Meister Eckhart, *The Treatises*, ch. 7, in *Meister Eckhart: A Modern Translation*,
> tr. Raymond B. Blakney (Harper Torchbooks 1941), pp. 10–11.

The meaning of life

1.48

Together with the whole people of God, with people from all over the world, you are invited to live a life exceeding all your hopes. On your own, how could you ever experience the radiance of God's presence?

God is too dazzling to be looked upon. He is a God who blinds our sight. It is Christ who channels this consuming fire, and allows God to shine through without dazzling us.

Christ is present, close to each one of us, whether we know him or not. He is so bound up with us that he lives within us, even when we are unaware of him. He is there in secret, a fire burning in his heart, a light in the darkness.

But Christ is also someone other than yourself. He is alive; he stands beyond, ahead of you.

Here is his secret: he loved you first.

That is the meaning of your life: to be loved for ever, loved to all eternity, so that you, in turn, will dare to live your life. Without love, what is the point of living?

From now on, in prayer or in struggle, only one thing is disastrous, the loss of love. Without love, what is the good of believing, or even of giving your body to the flames?

Do you see? Contemplation and struggle arise from the very same source, Christ who is love.

If you pray, it is out of love. If you struggle to restore dignity to the exploited, that too is for love.

Will you agree to set out on this road? At the risk of losing your life for love, will you live Christ for others?

Roger Schutz (Brother Roger of Taizé), *Parable of Community:*
Basic Texts of Taizé (Mowbray 1980), pp. 49–50.

God in our own history
1.49

There is a definite and proper end or issue for every person's existence: an end which, to the heart of God, is the good intended for him or for which he was intended; that which he is privileged to become, ought to become; that which God will assist him to become and which he cannot miss, save by his own fault. Every human soul has a complete and perfect plan, cherished for it in the heart of God – a divine biography marked out, which it enters into life to live.

This life, rightly unfolded, will be a complete and beautiful whole, an experience let on by God and unfolded by his secret nurture, as the trees and the flowers, by the secret nurture of the world. It is a drama cast in the mould of a perfect art, with no part wanting; a divine study for the person themselves and for others; a study that shall forever unfold in wondrous beauty the love and faithfulness of God, great in its conception, great in the divine skill by which it is shaped; above all, great in the momentous and glorious issues it prepares… We live in the divine thought. We fill a place in the great everlasting plan of God's intelligence. We never sink below his care, never drop out of his counsel.

… Your life is a school, exactly adapted to your lesson, and that to the best, last end of your existence. No room for a discouraged or depressed feeling, therefore, is left you. Enough that you exist for a purpose high enough to give meaning to life and to support a genuine inspiration… The tallest saints of God will often be those who walk in the deepest obscurity, and are even despised and quite overlooked by others. Let it be enough that God is in your history and that the plan of your biography is his.

Horace Bushnell, 'Every Man's Life a Plan of God',
Sermons for the New Life (New York 1872),
pp. 120–22.

A strong storyline
1.50

Those who are finding life very difficult at present, who having once left their familiar ways can't find their feet at all and heartily wish they might return to the way of life that was second nature to them – these may receive some comfort from the fact that what they are going through is an essential part of the process of unlearning the past, which constitutes their initiation into the future…

When we relearn what has been unlearned, it is as if we are retranslating the past into a language which can be used for the future, as a source of meaning in life. Real changes in the way we understand and experience life only happen when the new has somehow been accommodated within the framework of the old, built into the fabric of a personal story as a change in the action: a new direction, but the same plot. Only a strong storyline can sustain real changes in the plot. Most of us have put in a good deal of hard work since we were children wearing our personal narratives, which constitute the foundation of our self-image. It is this tough fabric of interwoven ideas and experiences that bears the weight of changes that take place in our lives. If the change is an important one, particularly if it is unexpected, we may feel that our narrative strength is simply unequal to the task; we simply cannot cope with the necessity to take it in. Perhaps every really new event in our lives has this effect on us; if it doesn't, then it isn't really new or really an event. The plot shifts, but the story continues, even though, for us, the world has stopped.

Roger Grainger, *Change to Life* (Darton, Longman & Todd 1993), pp. 51–52.

True worship
1.51

The real worship, the only thing that God really cares for, is a Christ-like life. To live all the time in the consciousness of the love and nearness of God, to merge all our desires and purposes in his will, to walk humbly before him and justly and lovingly with everyone, this is the real Christian worship. Without that no prayer, no song, no 'divine service' on Sunday is more than discordant noise in the ears of God. That is what Paul means when he tells us to offer our bodies, our own selves, as a living sacrifice and says that will be our 'reasonable service' [Romans 12:1], that is, our rational form of worship. He was well acquainted with many irrational forms of worship. When James says that a pure and undefiled 'religion' consists in helping the helpless and keeping ourselves unspotted from the world [James 1:27], the word 'religion' means liturgy or ceremonial. A loving and pure life is the true liturgy of Christian worship.

The life of Jesus was as full of religion as a nightingale is full of song or a rose full of fragrance, but the bent of his life was away from the inherited forms of worship, and he can scarcely be said to have taught new forms. He taught a prayer when his disciples asked for it, but that prayer was meant to teach utter simplicity. In our common worship we shall come closest to the spirit of true Christianity if every act is full of joy in God and his fellowship, love for one another, hatred for all evil, and an honest desire to live a right life in the sight of Christ. Our worship should eliminate as far as possible all selfish greed, all superstition, and all untrue and unworthy ideas about God. It should clear our conception of the right life by instructing our moral nature; it should give our will strong, steady, lasting impulses toward righteous action; and it should breed and foster habits of reverence and the faculty of adoration.

Walter Rauschenbusch, 'Why I am a Baptist' in *The Colegate–Rochester Divinity School Bulletin*, vol. XI, no. 2 (1938), pp. 104–105.

Liberating men
1.52

Many of us men are confused, but it's not part of the male role to admit it. We will water the garden, clean the car, storm out to the pub, escape into golf, fight back our tears, show we can go it alone, and, above all, busy ourselves in our work.

We know in our hearts that we have to change, but we try to avoid it. At forty we may be faced with the fundamental question, 'What's our life for?' – and duck away from it. If we cannot find this ability to change, we shall probably make life miserable for our wife and children, for the people we work with, and mostly for ourselves. It is as though we believe that mid-life crises, like religion, are best left to women. We can find ways of side-stepping the question. We will perhaps do anything except the one thing which we ought to do; that is, get through the painful experience of inner change and find the renewed and growing self...

Men do considerable violence to themselves by refusing to allow their gentler side to emerge. Pretending to be what we are not, refusing to admit our feelings, even to ourselves, disables us. It can lead to the loss of our own real self, behind the role we believe the male should play. Of course, staying vulnerable is more costly – but not in the long run, because the sustained hypocrisy and pretence lead to a disfigured personality.

Jim Thompson, *Stepney Calling: Thoughts for Our Day* (Mowbray 1991), pp. 82–83.

Homely food
1.53

'Well, Sadie,' said an American mother to her little girl, who was devouring everything within reach, 'I reckon you won't long have the use of that breakfast.' There are intemperate devotional meals to which the same risk is attached. It is left to us to feed our souls wisely and carefully – not too many spiritual sweets, not too much effervescent emotion. We are to be content with the food we find suits us – strengthens us, makes us grow – not make wild efforts to get the food we like best. Nor are we to be fastidious in our rejection of everything we do not think 'essential', until we reach what we choose to regard as a 'purely spiritual' type of prayer. Our ghostly insides are much like our natural insides; they need a certain amount of what doctors call 'roughage', and seldom thrive on too refined a diet.

The homely mixed food, the routine meals, of institutional religion, keep our digestions in good order. Particularly at times when we are drawn to fervour, or our spiritual sensibility seems to transcend the average level, we need the wholesome corrective of the common religious diet, the average practice, with its rough and ready adaptation to ordinary needs and limitations, to remind us that we are not pure spirits yet. In that excellent parable, *The History of Sir John Sparrow*, a logical insistence on the reduction of his food to its essential constituents at last left the hero face to face with a saucer of canary seed. He had proved that it contained all the human body needed; but somehow the position was not a satisfactory one. Therefore temperance will restrain us from simplifying or ethercalizing our religious diet over-much. We are mixed feeders, and must do as our fellows. Fastidious choices, special paths, look rather ridiculous in the 'perpetual bright clearness of eternity'.

Evelyn Underhill, *The House of the Soul* (Methuen [1929] 1947), pp. 97–98.

The road to resurrection
1.54

We cannot bear to put ourselves in the same class as the afflicted. Yet this is also the road to resurrection, to fuller, richer life. For it is our hatred of what is buried within us, our fear of it and guilt about it, which keeps it excluded from our awareness. And it is precisely this exclusion which maintains it as an enemy felt to be working against us. When received into awareness, it loses its power to hurt or destroy, and, in time, contributes positively to the well-being and depth of the personality. I may, for instance, have the habit of quarrelling with my friends and tend therefore to lose their friendship. It is easy for me to explain this fact as due either to something wrong in them or to my own circumstances, such as the necessity to overwork. I am too frightened to receive into awareness the buried child within me, who is terrified of losing his own identity by parental domination or possessiveness. It is this buried child who is losing me my friends, for he converts them into the dominating possessive parents with whom I have to quarrel in order to preserve my individuality. It is painfully terrifying to acknowledge this child and to receive him into awareness, for it looks as though, once acknowledged thus, he will make havoc of me altogether. He will make me fall out completely with everybody and everything so that I shall no longer be able to live. But this in fact does not happen. Received into awareness, the child disappears. But he leaves behind something of enormous value – that instinct to be myself and to give expression to what I am, from which flow all the highest achievements of human life, whatsoever things are lovely, whatsoever things are good [Philippians 4:8], of which the greatest is the capacity to give myself away in love. It is thus that I pass through involvement with an alienated self, the cross and the passion, to the glory of the resurrection.

H.A. Williams, 'Theology and Self-awareness' in *Soundings*, ed. A.R. Vidler
(Cambridge University Press 1963), pp. 74–75.

Living is dancing
1.55

There is no universal recipe for living. Living has to do with a choice of contexts. It is up to us to choose the relevant points of reference – the horizons – the directions – or, if you will, the stimuli which are going to make up the world to which we are responsible. Living is like dancing. As you dance you move your body according to a rhythm and a harmony which fill the space. The complexity of our human predicament is due to the fact that a number of conflicting rhythms and harmonies are being played at the same time. You cannot dance them all; if you try, you become schizophrenic and your body is split (or immobilized) by contradictory dynamics. Personality demands integration. As Kierkegaard once said that purity of heart is to will one thing only, so we might say that purity of heart is to dance to one rhythm only.

You may dance the tune played by the present reality. Your style of life will be realistic and pragmatic. Or you may choose to move your body under the spell of a mysterious tune and rhythm which come from a world we do not see, the world of our hopes and aspirations. *Hope is hearing the melody of the future. Faith is to dance it.* You risk your life, and you take your risk to its ultimate conclusion, even the cross, because you detect a strange odour of death mixed with the fascinating music of Mephisto, lord of the 'present evil world'. The rhythms of the future, on the other hand, contain promises of freedom, love and life. It is worth the risk – even if we lose!

Rubem A. Alves, *Tomorrow's Child: Imagination, Creativity, and the Rebirth of Culture* (SCM Press 1972), pp. 194–96.

To prepare for eternity
1.56

Time is precious, but we do not comprehend all its value. We shall know it only when it will no longer be of any advantage to us. Our friends make demands upon it, as if there were nothing, and we bestow it in the same way. Often it is a burden to us. We know not what to do with it. A day will come, when a simple quarter of an hour may appear of more worth to us than the riches of the whole world. God, who is so free and liberal in his bounty to us in everything else, teaches us, by the wise economy of his providence, how careful we should be of the use of time; for he gives us but one instant, and withdraws that as he gives us a second, while he retains the third in his own hands, leaving us in entire uncertainty whether it will ever be ours.

Time is given us to prepare for eternity, and eternity will not be too long for our regrets at the loss of time, if we have misspent it. Our lives as well as our hearts belong to God; he has given them both for his service. We cannot always be doing something that belongs to our condition. To be silent, to suffer, to pray when we cannot ask, is acceptable to God. A disappointment, a contradiction, a harsh word received and endured as in his presence, is worth more than a long prayer; and we do not lose time if we bear its loss with gentleness and patience, provided the loss was inevitable, and was not caused by our own fault.

Thus let us spend our days, redeeming the time, by quitting vain amusements, useless correspondence, those weak outpourings of the heart that are only modifications of self-love, and conversations that dissipate the mind, and lead to no good. Thus we shall find time to serve God; and there is none well employed that is not devoted to him.

François de la M. Fénelon, in *Selections from the Writings of Fénelon*, tr. 'Mrs Follen' (Edward T. Whitfield 1850), p. 246.

Death the connecting link

1.57

If we would become wise we must learn that we have here no abiding city (Hebrews 13:14).

To have life in focus we must have death in our field of vision. Within this vision we see life as preparation for death and death as preparation for life.

If we are to meet our own death with hope it must be a hope built not on theory or on belief alone but on experience. We must know from experience that *death is an event in life*, an essential part of any life which is lived as a perpetually expanding and self-transcending mystery.

Only the experience of the continuous death of the ego can lead us into this hope, into an ever-deepening contact with the power of life itself.

Only our death to self-centredness can really persuade us of death as the connecting link in the chain of perpetual expansion, and as the way to fullness of life.

John Main OSB, in *The Joy of Being*, ed. Clare Hallward
(Darton, Longman & Todd 1989), p. 19.

Refusing the task

1.58

There are so few people who become what they have it in them to be. It may be through lethargy and laziness, it may be through timidity and cowardice, it may be through lack of discipline and self-indulgence, it may be through the involvement in second bests and byways. The world is full of people who have never realized the possibilities which are in them. We need not think of the task which God has in store for us in terms of some great act or achievement of which everyone will know. It may be to fit a child for life; it may be at some crucial moment to speak that word and exert that influence which will stop someone ruining life; it may be to do some quite small job superlatively well; it may be something which will touch the lives of many by our hands, our voices or our minds. The fact remains that God is preparing us by all the experiences of life for *something*; and the fact remains that there are so many who refuse the task when it comes, and who never realize that they are refusing it.

William Barclay, *The Gospel of John*, vol. 1
(Saint Andrew Press 1965), p. 40.

Necessary losses
1.59

Our birth is a death. We leave the only world we know, the strange, dark, watery, secure world of our mother's womb and we pass into a baffling, noisy, colourful world beyond it. Given the choice, we would not leave the womb and would probably not believe in the existence of the fabled world that lay beyond it. We come to life only by letting go. So it will be at the end. Given the choice none of us would leave this world. It is only faith that can grasp the existence of the world beyond, that defies our imagination and eludes our words. We shall come to that world only by dying. From the outset to the end of our lives, we are having to learn to let go, to accept loss. Nor should we gloss over the reality of that loss by interpreting every loss as pure gain. There is something lost in leaving places that have brought us happiness because, however effective we may be in creating happiness in new places, what we have known in one cannot be repeated in another. We can never transplant the past into the present. There is the great gain of having children and there are the losses we experience as they grow up. All too quickly they pass from the openness of childhood to the turbulent years of youth. The day they leave home to share a flat with friends, or move to another city to work, or go to university, it is like death. A part of our life is irrevocably ended. There are, of course, as every parent of grown children knows, great compensations. They are of a different order and we can push them into the pattern of the past only by violating and distorting our relationship with our children.

Michael Walker, 'Human and Spiritual Development' in
Spirituality and Human Wholeness (BCC 1986), pp. 72–73.

Moving day
1.60

It's moving day again. As a boy the world I knew was the world of city apartments. Life was carried on high up in a building, so that one could not run out of doors on to a lawn or into a yard; it was bound by elevators and stairways and people one never spoke to. Apart-ment, being apart, and so close together; not communicating, yet hearing sounds through the walls.

Did we move more because we lived in apartments? Moving day meant up and down in elevators, the moving man taking everything down. The walls bare, the funny-looking empty rooms, the rugs up and the pictures down, I suddenly realized this was my home, *my home*. It was time to go, but I hadn't even left a mark on my home – not a mark.

Yet what mark could I have left there but my breath on the walls, my footsteps on the floors, my life in the rooms? And had I not been given something to take away with me and puzzle over, this easygoing informal community amid anonymity? There were possibilities for sharing with others that I had let slip because I felt both attracted and threatened.

It's moving day again: an opportunity for new people, new choices.

Malcolm Boyd, *Malcolm Boyd's Book of Days*
(Heinemann/SCM Press 1968), p. 7.

A farewell party
1.61

At first sight it looked like any other luncheon party. The day was warm enough for it to be held outdoors and dozens of friends of the host couple were eating and drinking, talking and laughing. What was not so obvious was that they had gathered to help say farewell to a house and a garden in which their hosts had lived for nearly thirty years, raised their children, consolidated their careers, worked through the highs and lows of their marriage. The impending move was both timely and desirable and there was much to be said in its favour. Leaving the old house, however, was a wrench which they both felt. Some sort of recognition seemed desirable, both in celebration of what had been and in acknowledgment of what would not be in the same way again. The couple had decided that the appropriate rite was a garden party with friends old and new who had shared something of the significance of their living in that house and playing in that garden.

This couple recognized their need of help in making an important transition. They found a rite which worked for them and in which significant others could share without embarrassment. And they found that their participation in the rite really did make it easier for them to cope with a major change in their lives which, though positive in many ways, nevertheless involved genuine grief at what was lost in the process. These impending losses were not unimportant. They included a loss of neighbours who had become friends, a loss of familiar patterns of living, a loss of things and of spaces which could evoke powerful memories, a loss of identity in the local community and many other losses which they could not identify so clearly.

Graeme M. Griffin, 'Deaths in Life', *The Way*, vol. 33, no. 4
(October 1993), p. 304.

After divorce
1.62

I walked in mud for years after the end of my marriage, enjoying little, barely alive, somewhat like Samuel Johnson who wrote of his bereavement:

> I have ever since seemed to myself broken off from mankind, a kind of solitary wanderer in the wild of life, without any direction, or fixed point of view: a gloomy gazer on the world to which I have little relation.

Those years of heaviness were also, I think, years of silent growth. I have said *ad nauseam* that during much of my life I have felt lonely, but I had never had actually to live alone in a house. At first I was anxious and fearful, locking doors and leaving lights on all night. I also felt unreal. Johnson also commented that marriage may have many trials but celibacy has no pleasures. Celibacy was the least unbearable part of it. Far worse was the endless experience of having to carry myself the whole time, to learn to be complete within myself, to laugh or weep alone, think of what to shop for, make time to buy it, bring it home, cook it and then dine alone. I made a point of keeping up appearances even to myself because I instinctively knew how easy it would be to slip into self-neglect. So I would polish the table and the silver, starch the linen, lay the table properly, open the wine and enjoy the meal. I would light the fire every evening and cocoon myself in the little heavily beamed sitting-room. To friends I appeared to have become rather a donnish figure, alone with books, music, fire, pipe and wine. They did not know that I was simply trying to survive and hold on to some self-respect. The silent growth came through my being forced to face myself and the reality about myself. In the evenings the silence is total, and if there is nothing that appeals on Radio 3 I sink into the silence. After a time the fearfulness passed, but I would warn anyone who has not been bereaved that grief and fear feel very much the same.

Anthony Faulkner, *To Travel Hopefully* (Darton, Longman & Todd 1994), pp. 53–54.

The silence of old age
1.63

I feel closed in. I have reached the age where people hem me in on all sides. I am not free anymore. I cannot take an airplane and go to Europe if I want to. In many things I cannot dispose of myself. Everything in me seems to be tied up. I walk with small steps. I used to be able to walk out into the woods and see many kinds of landscapes. I roamed up and down mountains and valleys. I was free. But now I feel all bound up. 'When you grow old you will stretch out your hands, and somebody else will put a belt around you and take you where you would not go' (John 21:18). Now I have only one landscape: the heart of God.

But how stupid of me to talk like this, one who has stood at the edge of the silver sands and jumped into the infinity of God's silence. I'm letting the old smother the new. I am losing myself in the past, and God looks at me going over my life. I guess it never occurs to us that tomorrow, or the day after, our steps will falter, that we will be too weak to do this or that. And yet, I think this unfreedom of old age is also an entry into the silence of God.

God offers us many silences – the silence of babyhood, the silence of childhood, the silence of youth and maturity, and finally the silence of old age. My own heart must learn to accept this lack of freedom. People undoubtedly say about me, 'Oh well, she is old now. She can't do this and she can't do that.' This is good. It is good because then I enter a new depth of silence, the very essence and depth of poverty for which I have so longed. I am now exceedingly free.

Catherine de Hueck Doherty, *Molchanie: The Silence of God*
(Collins Fount 1982), pp. 81–82.

The silence is strange

1.64

There are long hours in the day now in which I find myself alone, and see no one… Or it may be that in the company of others amid the liveliness of general conversation, deafness leaves me alone in an awkward silence. I feel the constraint of being against my will a non-conductor of geniality, and wish that I could disappear unobserved. Then, perhaps, I shall find that I am deprived of the opportunity of contributing to the general cheerfulness in order to discover another function given to me instead, and I may learn to forget myself and the constraint of my position, and reverence the presence of God in my companions and in myself. Thus I might without observation prove in my silence a link for them with the eternal truth and the infinite love. If deafness separates me from my brethren, it is only an outward separation, and for the moment, and gives occasion for a closer fellowship in Christ through prayer.

Or, again, I remember that when I have been alone in times past, nature has been wont sometimes to speak to me, and fill me with happiness too great for words. But now as eyesight begins to fail me, the sun, the moon and the stars, grow dim for me… Through this dimness the voices of nature no longer reach me. The sun rises and sets, and the bright stars come out, but they say nothing to me now. I remember 'the hour of splendour in the grass, of glory in the flower', but I no longer hear the canticle of the creatures. The daughters of music are brought low, and I am left to myself in silence. And now in the stillness I become aware of one who lures me into the wilderness in order that he himself may speak to my heart. The silence is strange: I must rouse myself and stand to hear what the Lord will say to me. As I awake to listen in stillness and serenity of soul, all my past life,

The noisy years, seem moments in the being
Of the eternal Silence.

The silence that enfolds me in this solitude is the eternal love, and I no longer want his messengers, the creatures, to speak to me of him, for God has come to speak to me, and his message is himself.

George Congreve, *Treasures of Hope for the Evening of Life*
(Longmans & Co. 1920), pp. 189–90.

The mystery
1.65

Barry, the youngest person I have attempted to minister to, was a young man suffering from Kaposi's sarcoma, a form of cancer involving not only the skin but also the internal organs of the body. At fifteen, Barry 'came out' to his parents as being homosexual and at twenty-one (when I met him) had been sharing his life with another man in a monogamous relationship for three years. Trevor (his partner) was about twenty-four. It was obvious that they were devoted to each other and each family felt that it had gained another son. Both men were quite popular and genuinely loved by their parents. Barry was hardly ever without a visitor. As he became increasingly weaker and more aware of his dying, he became more and more consoling to Trevor – 'my mate' – and their respective parents. Whether Barry or Trevor ever went to church is debatable. However, both believed in what they called 'the mystery'.

About two days before he died, Barry asked me, and the others round his bed, to 'think of me going on a voyage and that my bags are packed for the greatest trip ever. My passport has been approved and I am simply waiting for the plane to take off into the mystery.' He added that when he got to his destination, he would wait for us. Barry had clearly gone through all the stages of letting go and he was now, simply, waiting for the journey to begin.

I was not with Barry when he died. However, my last picture was of him surrounded by those he dearly loved and who dearly loved him. His mother was holding his left hand, his partner was holding his right hand, and his father was embracing them all. This, for me, was a real live symbol of 'Our Father' who embraces and enfolds us all within the love of understanding acceptance.

Bill Kirkpatrick, *AIDS: Sharing the Pain: Pastoral Guidelines*
(Darton, Longman & Todd 1988), p. 33.

Two ways of growing old
1.66

Old age is the most precious time of life, the one nearest eternity. There are two ways of growing old. There are old people who are anxious and bitter, living in the past and illusion, who criticize everything that goes on around them. Young people are repulsed by them; they are shut away in their sadness and loneliness, shrivelled up in themselves. But there are also old people with a child's heart, who have used their freedom from function and responsibility to find a new youth. They have the wonder of a child, but the wisdom of maturity as well. They have integrated their years of activity and so can live without being attached to power. Their freedom of heart and their acceptance of their limitations and weakness makes them people whose radiance illuminates the whole community. They are gentle and merciful, symbols of compassion and forgiveness. They become a community's hidden treasures, sources of unity and life. They are true contemplatives at the heart of community.

Jean Vanier, *Community and Growth* (Darton, Longman & Todd 1991), p. 140.

Reflections in old age
1.67

I recognize, of course, that this statement of belief is partly governed by the circumstances that I am old, and in at most a decade or so will be dead. In earlier years I should doubtless have expressed things differently. Now the prospect of death overshadows all others. I am like a man on a sea voyage nearing his destination. When I embarked I worried about having a cabin with a porthole, whether I should be asked to sit at the captain's table, who were the more attractive and important passengers. All such considerations become pointless when I shall so soon be disembarking.

As I do not believe that earthly life can bring any lasting satisfaction, the prospect of death holds no terrors. Those saints who pronounced themselves in love with death displayed, I consider, the best of sense; not a Freudian death-wish. The world that I shall soon be leaving seems more than ever beautiful; especially its remoter parts, grass and trees and sea and rivers and little streams and sloping hills, where the image of eternity is more clearly stamped than among streets and houses. Those I love I can love even more, since I have nothing to ask of them but their love; the passion to accumulate possessions, or to be noticed and important, is too evidently absurd to be any longer entertained.

A sense of how extraordinarily happy I have been, and of enormous gratitude to my creator, overwhelms me often. I believe with a passionate, unshakable conviction that in all circumstances and at all times life is a blessed gift; that the spirit which animates it is one of love, not hate or indifference, of light, not darkness, of creativity, not destruction, of order, not chaos; that, since all life and all that is known about it, now and henceforth, have been benevolently, not malevolently or indifferently conceived. If it is for nothing, then for nothingness I offer thanks; if another mode of existence, with this old worn-out husk of a body left behind, like a butterfly extricating itself from its chrysalis, and this floundering muddled mind, now at best seeing through a glass darkly, given a longer range and a new precision, then for that likewise I offer thanks.

Malcolm Muggeridge, Jesus Rediscovered (Collins 1982), p. 57.

Waiting
A Meditation on Luke 2:22–35
1.68

Did Simeon feel impatience? We can imagine him divided, torn between two feelings. The longer the messiah delays, the longer he will live. Love of life invites him to hope for delay. But the longing to see the messiah impels him to want the time to be shorter, even though that means living less long. Impatience for the event or the enjoyment of a long evening. But by now Simeon does not live to enjoy what remains of life. Life has already given him everything it was going to give. He only goes on living in order to keep his appointment.

Simeon lives with the mature serenity of his years and the joy given him by the Holy Spirit in whom he trusts. The scriptures speak in general of the coming of the messiah: the Spirit has read him the classic texts giving them a personal application. In his intimacy with the Spirit Simeon also represents the best of Israel. What is said in Amos 3:7 goes for him: the Lord God does nothing without revealing his plan to his servants the prophets.

We too go on living, we have passed sixty-six. Perhaps because we live in an age when the average life span has considerably lengthened (in our countries). Perhaps because an operation delayed or removed the danger of death. Perhaps because of our genes or a robust constitution: seventy years is the span of our life, eighty if our strength holds (Psalm 90). The reasons are not important. Does this stage of our life have no other meaning? Is it just living to go on living? The messiah has already come centuries ago, it is not for us to wait for him. Hope has been succeeded by memory, which is also a sign of our old age. On the other hand, if we refer to the second coming or *parousia,* this meeting will come in its own time. We must not hasten it or impatiently expect it. It is enough simply to watch out for it.

Luis Alonso Schökel, *In the Autumn of Life* (St Paul Publications 1991), pp. 124–25.

Death in Donegal
1.69

I remember very vividly my hitch-hike travels through the dark, melancholy hills of Northern Ireland. I wrote stories about the storytellers of Donegal in the Dutch newspapers and, while Kerry and Killarney left hardly any memories in my mind, Donegal I will never forget.

There was something sombre but also profound and even holy about Donegal. The people were like the land. I still see vividly the simple funeral of a Donegal farmer. The priest and a few men carried the humble coffin to the cemetery. After the coffin was put in the grave, the men filled the grave with sand and covered it again with the patches of grass which had been laid aside. Two men stamped with their boots on the sod so that it was hardly possible to know that this was a grave. Then one of the men took two pieces of wood, bound them together in the form of a cross and stuck it in the ground. Everyone made a quick sign of the cross and left silently. No words, no solemnity, no decoration. Nothing of that. But it never has been made so clear to me that someone was dead, not asleep but dead, not passed away but dead, not laid to rest but dead, plain dead. When I saw those two men stamping on the ground in which they had buried their friend, I knew that for these farmers of Donegal there were no funeral-home games to play. But their realism became a transcendent realism by the simple unadorned wooden cross saying that where death is affirmed, hope finds its root. 'Unless a grain of wheat falls on the ground and dies, it remains only a single grain; but if it dies, it yields a rich harvest' (John 12:24).

Henri J.M. Nouwen, *Genesee Diary* (Doubleday 1976), pp. 77–78.

PART 2

A Broken World

The reality of evil
2.1

We do not have to travel far to explore the reality of evil, because it can and should be studied in the battlefield of our own mind. If we find it there, we can be sure that in the affairs of society, in the great affairs of the nations, it will be rampant. I am convinced that some of the bad things I have done and imagined are not just the result of being hard-done-by. The hurts which I have received have seemed to make me more ready to hurt others, but it is difficult to escape the idea that some of my worst thoughts and actions arrive in my mind under their own power. The conversation in my mind suggests that there is a voice or an impulse which offers me the bad alternative. I can then have all sorts of arguments with another alternative voice or set of impulses which try to prevent me. Is this just the 'computerized' response based on my past experience? Am I programmed to respond in this way by the 'parent' in me, or by the hurt I have suffered in the past? It is puzzling, if that is the case, that I can analyze and explain it to myself, point out all the possible damage it will do, yet at the same time do it. The sources of evil in myself could be in part the result of stored resentment and anger, and in part the replay of the strongest and most passionate experiences on my own tape, in part the fearful reaction to the threatened loss of love. Yet those descriptions do not seem to me to describe adequately the independence of the evil within me. I am led to believe that the impulse, the energy and the will behind the evil I have done are not just a facet of my past experience, but rather a reality against which I have to struggle...

Nothing could be more dangerous than to underestimate the reality of evil – except possibly to credit it with too much power. Whether this tendency to do wrong comes from within myself or within the human race, its reality is vivid and challenges us to fight the good fight. We have the drama of the struggle. If the darkness and shadow are not part of the portrait, the human being is drawn in pale pastel and bears little resemblance to the sharply defined conflict of our experience. The battle within us is not just an unravelling of the self and the maturity of the 'adult' who is there in waiting, because when the adult emerges he or she will still have the battle against evil. The more maturity, the deeper the perceptions, the higher the virtue – the stronger will be the sensitivity to evil and the ensuing battle.

Jim Thompson, *Stepney Calling: Thoughts for Our Day*
(Mowbray 1991), pp. 33–35.

Structural injustice
2.2

Christians frequently restrict the scope of ethics to a narrow class of 'personal' sins. A few years ago in a study of over 1,500 ministers, researchers discovered that the theologically conservative pastors speak out on sins such as drug abuse and sexual misconduct. But they fail to preach about the sins of institutionalized racism, unjust economic structures and militaristic institutions which destroy people just as do alcohol and drugs.

There is an important difference between consciously willed, individual acts (like lying to a friend or committing an act of adultery) and participation in evil social structures. Slavery is an example of the latter. So is the Victorian factory system where ten-year-old children worked twelve to sixteen hours a day. Both slavery and child labour were legal. But they destroyed people by the millions. They were institutionalized or structural evils. The Bible condemns both.

Ronald J. Sider, *Rich Christians in an Age of Hunger* (Hodder & Stoughton 1978), p. 120.

Having my own way
2.3

The liberty of the God who would have his creature free, is in contest with the slavery of the creature who would cut his own stem from his root that he might call it his own and love it; who rejoices in his own consciousness, instead of the life of that consciousness; who poises himself on the tottering wall of his own being, instead of the rock on which that being is built. Such a one regards his own dominion over himself – the rule of the greater by the less, inasmuch as the conscious self is less than the self – as a freedom infinitely larger than the range of the universe of God's being. If he says, 'At least I have it my own way!' I answer, you do not know what is your way and what is not. You know nothing of whence your impulses, your desires, your tendencies, your likings come. They may spring now from some chance, as of nerves diseased; now from some roar of a wandering bodiless devil; now from some infant hate in your heart; now from the greed or lawlessness of some ancestor you would be ashamed of if you knew him; or, it may be, now from some far-piercing chord of a heavenly orchestra: the moment it comes up into your consciousness, you call it your own way, and glory in it.

George Macdonald, 'Freedom' (Third series), in C.S. Lewis, *George Macdonald: An Anthology* (Geoffrey Bles 1946), p. 85.

Contemporary idolatries
2.4

The worship of idols takes many forms, some direct and unmistakable, some far more deceptive and subtle. In our own times we witness people, relationships, institutions, ideologies, movements and nations caught in the grip of contemporary idolatries. The contemporary idolatries that have captured our worship and servitude are familiar realities; money, possessions, power, race, class, sex, nation, status, success, work, violence, religion, ideology, causes and so on. The militant power of the contemporary idolatries has captured the corporations and institutions of commerce, the state and the branches of government, the private and public bureaucracies, the various professions, the schools and universities, media and entertainments, and the churches. The presence of these idols or gods is felt in our economic and political systems, our social and cultural patterns, crucially affecting the way we relate to one another. Idols perpetuate themselves by erecting self-justifying ideologies and informational systems with the ability to turn falsehood into seeming truth by the distortion of language itself.

Biblically understood, idolatry originates in the human decision to seek life and salvation apart from the source of life in God. Idols are 'imposters of God', as William Stringfellow has described them. They may be things, ideas, persons or institutions exalted and worshipped as gods. Rather than these finite realities serving people, people come to serve and worship them as objects of ultimate concern that are allowed to substitute for God. Idolatry denies the place of God as the giver of life and the author of salvation, dehumanizes people by making them pay homage to objects not deserving of worship, and denigrates the proper vocation of things meant to be servants of human life, not rulers over it.

Jim Wallis, *Agenda for Biblical People* (Triangle 1986), pp. 38–39.

Deadening
2.5

I think sin is anything which leads to a greater deadening of one's mind, one's personality, one's feelings. God is ultimately interested in my being totally alive: everything that comes from him is life-giving. I think that my belief in the devil – call him what you like – sees him as the personification of the inbuilt false promise that goes with a great many experiences – they hold out false hopes of greater vitality. We think: if I do that, I'll get a kick out of it. Well, each time you get less and less of a kick, and it ends up making you deader instead of more alive. Whatever we do that creates deadness is a sin. And in terms of society, if I organize some institution the end result of which is the greater deadening of the human community, then that is a gigantic sin.

John V. Taylor, in Gerald Priestland, *Priestland's Progress*
(BBC 1982), p. 70.

A cosy world?
2.6

That calm, beautiful face [of William Cowper], it moves me strangely as I look upon it. We read his poems and letters, and we can picture the daily life at Olney. The evening is drawing on. The curtains are drawn. The urn is brought in, grace is said, and either Lady Hesketh or Mrs Unwin pours out 'the cup that cheers but not inebriates'; the poet reads some good book; the day closes with family prayers, and they all retire to rest. The very model of a Christian home of the eighteenth century. But if they had looked out of their windows, it would have been upon an England of brutal sports, of bestial drinking, of the darkened lives of children, in which the common people were untaught and had no chance. There is no sign of a social conscience in the writings of Cowper. It was Shelley, the atheist, not the evangelical poet, who pleaded passionately for the rights of man. We have little understood the temper of the new age and of the days that are before us if we have not seen that a vast change is coming upon our world, that nothing will be taken for granted and nothing respected in our social, economic and religious institutions that conflicts with human rights and brotherhood. We cannot return as a nation... to the old system of sweated labour, rookeries, insanitary surroundings and the darkening of child life by excessive labour. We want to see a better world, a brighter world, a world in which there shall not be the old glaring inequalities. In the heart of every right-thinking person there is something that responds to this note of hope. Such a cause will not lack recruits. The sacrifice and agony of the world will not have been in vain if, thereby, it casts aside evils and wrongs and there is the emergence of a worthier future.

J.H. Shakespeare, *The Churches at the Crossroads*
(Williams & Morgate 1918), pp. 8–9.

The truth about us
2.7

Let us see what the wisdom of God will do.

'Expect neither truth,' she says, 'nor consolation from men. I am she who formed you, and who alone can teach you what you are. But you are now no longer in the state in which I formed you. I created man holy, innocent, perfect. I filled him with light and intelligence. I communicated to him my glory and my wonders. The eye of man saw then the majesty of God. He was not then in the darkness which blinds him, nor subject to mortality and the woes which afflict him. But he has not been able to sustain so great glory without falling into pride. He wanted to make himself his own centre, and independent of my help. He withdrew himself from my rule; and, on his making himself equal to me by the desire of finding his happiness in himself, I abandoned him to himself. And setting in revolt the creatures that were subject to him, I made them his enemies so that man is now become like the brutes, and so estranged from me that there scarce remains to him a dim vision of his author. So far has all his knowledge been extinguished or disturbed! The senses, independent of reason, and often the masters of reason, have led him into pursuit of pleasure. All creatures either torment or tempt him, and domineer over him, either subduing him by their strength, or fascinating him by their charms, a tyranny more awful and more imperious.

'Such is the state in which men now are. There remains to them some feeble instinct of the happiness of their former state, and they are plunged in the evils of their blindness and their lust, which have become their second nature.

'From this principle which I disclose to you, you can recognize the cause of those contradictions which have astonished all men, and have divided them into parties holding so different views. Observe, now, all the feelings of greatness and glory which the experience of so many woes cannot stifle, and you see if the cause of them must not be in another nature.'

Blaise Pascal, *Pensées*, tr. W.F. Trotter (Random House 1941), p. 137.

Unable to love
2.8

In guilt the other is experienced not as a presence but as pressure. Under this pressure I feel a powerlessness to love. The felt powerlessness to love is the very nerve of guilt. Because my root inclination is to enter into relationships, I tend to interpret the unlovableness of someone as something I am producing by strangling this inclination. This makes me feel guilty. Although there is only a limited sense in which it is true to say that the unlovableness of another is my fault, it is something I can never be happy about. This unhappiness is a feeling of guilt.

When something is going badly wrong with an intimate relationship, we experience this 'ugliness of the other' in an intense way. Suddenly the beloved can appear hateful. This is due to the sudden failure of my normal love-current, which leaves the beloved before me in all his or her closeness and involvement in my life, while I am powerless to respond. Guilt is acute when the intimate other becomes alien. In all guilt, the other appears alien. Guilt is when the other changes from partner to alien. Because partnership is natural and congenial to me, is the way my life wants to flow, this 'alienation' of the partner is experienced by me as a contradiction with myself. This self-contradiction, this inner friction of the spirit, is the experience of guilt.

Sebastian Moore, *The Fire and the Rose are One*
(Darton, Longman & Todd 1980), p. 64.

Alienation
2.9

Mammoth productive facilities with computer minds, cities that engulf the landscape and pierce the clouds, planes that almost outrace time – these are awesome, but they cannot be spiritually inspiring. Nothing in our glittering technology can raise us to new heights, because material growth has been made an end in itself, and, in the absence of moral purpose, we ourself become smaller as our works become bigger. Gargantuan industry and government, woven into an intricate, computerized mechanism, leave the person outside. The sense of participation is lost, the feeling that ordinary individuals influence important decisions vanishes, and we become separated and diminished.

When an individual is no longer a true participant, when they no longer feel a sense of responsibility to their society, the content of democracy is emptied. When culture is degraded and vulgarity enthroned, when the social system does not build security but induces peril, inexorably the individual is impelled to pull away from a soulless society. This process produces alienation – perhaps the most pervasive and insidious development in contemporary society.

Martin Luther King, in *The Words of Martin Luther King*,
sel. Coretta Scott King (Collins 1986), p. 19.

A full humanity?
2.10

What does it mean to be fully human? This is the question Asian women ask when they encounter overwhelming suffering and injustice in their lives. Asian women ask hard questions about the meaning of humanity and God because they are hurt. They want to find meaning in their seemingly meaningless suffering in order to survive as human beings with dignity and integrity. From birth to death Asian women have to fight against 'death-wishes' from male-dominated society. In fact, this curse against Asian women begins even before their biological conception. Asian parents pray to the gods and goddesses asking for the conception of a son. Once conception has occurred, they hope for a son throughout the pregnancy. Upon the birth of a daughter, many Asian parents are greatly disappointed. Some Korean women are named Sup-sup-ie, which means regrettable or disappointing. Others are called Keun-nae-mi, which means terminating (the birth of the next daughter). Many Asian women arrive in this men-worshipping, women-despising world only to receive 'curse-full' names. Some are destroyed in their mother's womb after amniocentesis or right after birth by the hands of family members who wanted a son. Female children generally are more poorly fed, less educated and overworked when compared with male children. Even after they grow up, women's lives only get worse under oppressive public and domestic structures based on classism, racism, sexism, castism and cultural imperialism. Their bodies are controlled and their labours are exploited.

Asian women's self-understanding grows out of this brutal reality…

In their brokenness and longing for a full humanity, Asian women have met and come to know God.

Chung Hyun Kyung, *Struggle to Be the Sun Again* (SCM Press 1991), pp. 38, 39.

Invitation to connect
2.11

How do we understand our own individuality?… What overwhelms us too often is compassion-fatigue, inertia, the inability of the prevailing ethic to change anything. Neither reasoned analysis nor response to catastrophes based on the generosity of a few individuals appears to be able to shift the grip of unjust systems on a global scale or prevent the suffering they bring about. Any 'drive to connect' takes place amid the brokenheartedness of oppressed communities and crucified peoples. It is a brokenheartedness caused partially by a *structured separateness*. If this sounds an exaggerated claim, think of the way we organize our world, our institutions and our relationships, following in part from the way we understand the human person. To what degree are all of these structured by the notion of separation and, on the level of subjectivity, by separative individualism and its far-reaching consequences? 'The individual deserves what he gets and gets what he deserves' is still a very popular slogan.

This is why the political and social transformation must first be on the level of our philosophical consciousness and symbolic order. Invitations to connect, reconnect, or build relationships around the notion of mutuality will make no difference until the all-pervasiveness of the notion of separation – even within theology itself – is recognized, together with the difficulties of moving away from this to restructure on the basis of connection: *to discover 'the connected self' in a connected world*.

Mary Grey, *The Wisdom of Fools: Seeking Revelation for Today* (SPCK 1993), p. 67.

A painful reality
2.12

Opposed to any notion of mutual sharing is the concept of alienation. This is more than a fashionable word with Marxist and psychiatric overtones; it corresponds to a painful reality by which everyone is to some extent afflicted. To be exploited or merely used, to be compelled to perform inhuman, mechanical, unrewarding tasks yielding no intrinsic satisfaction, to be denied an adequate wage for one's work, to have no choice of livelihood except one that involves continual frustration – these are forms of alienation as it is commonly understood. They are symptoms of a deeper malaise: the lack of fellow-feeling of human beings with one another and a cleavage within the individual...

Religion may be regarded in practical terms as an attempt to deal with the problem of alienation. Its aim is to bring about a situation in which people are not strangers to one another – to actualize that one touch of nature which makes the whole world kin – or at odds with themselves. The second part of the problem is the more fundamental: remove the inner conflict within individuals and reciprocal good fellowship is likely to follow. Disharmony within the self, however, can only be put to rest in the light of genuine self-knowledge – and this in its turn, or rather simultaneously, calls for a realization of the supreme self, which we call God.

Aelred Graham, *Contemplative Christianity* (The Catholic Book Club 1975
[by arr. with A.R. Mowbray]), pp. 69–70.

Desires indulged
2.13

Desires indulged grow faster and farther than gratifications extend. Ungratified desire is misery. Expectations eagerly indulged and terminated by disappointment are often exquisite misery. But how frequently are expectations raised only to be disappointed, and desires let loose only to terminate in distress! The child pines for a toy; the moment he possesses it, he throws it by and cries for another. When they are piled up in heaps around him, he looks at them without pleasure and leaves them without regret. He knew not that all the good which they could yield lay in expectation, nor that his wishes for more would increase faster than toys could be multiplied, and is unhappy at last for the same reason as at first: his wishes are ungratified. Still indulging them, and still believing that the gratification of them will furnish the enjoyment for which he pines, he goes on, only to be unhappy.

Men are merely taller children. Honour, wealth, and splendour are the toys for which grown children pine; but which, however accumulated, leave them still disappointed and unhappy. God never designed that intelligent beings should be satisfied with these enjoyments. By his wisdom and goodness they were formed to derive their happiness and virtue from him alone.

Moderated desires constitute a character fitted to acquire all the good which this world can yield. He who is prepared, in whatever situation he is, therewith to be content, has learned effectually the science of being happy, and possesses the alchemic stone which will change every metal into gold. Such a man will smile upon a stool, while Alexander the Great sits weeping on the throne of the world.

Timothy Dwight, Sermon (c. 1799), in *The World's Great Sermons*,
comp. Grenville Kleiser, vol. 3 (Funk and Wagnalls 1908).

One in the eye?
2.14

There is anger in the eye of another. In your eye, however, there is a beam [Matthew 7:3–5]. If you hate someone, how can you see what has to be removed from the other's eye? There is a beam in your own eye. How does this happen? The reason is that you neglect the splinter which lodged there. With that splinter you go to bed and you rise. You have cultivated it yourself, you have watered it with false suspicions, and you have fed it by giving credence to the words of flatterers and of people who came speaking ill of your friend. You have not been diligent enough to pull the splinter out, and you have made a beam of it... I say to you: you shall not hate. But you are quite unconcerned about it and you answer me: 'Hate, what is that? And what harm is there in a person hating his enemy?'... Whoever hates is a murderer (1 John 3:15). Now you can surely not say: 'What difference does it make to me if I am a murderer!'... You have, so to speak, done no more than to hate someone. But, in doing this, you have first killed yourself and then another.

Augustine of Hippo, Sermon 49.7.7, in *The Rule of St Augustine*, intro. and comm. by Tarcisius J. van Bavel, tr. Raymond Canning (Darton, Longman & Todd 1984), p. 95.

Flowers of resurrection
2.15

Latin American Christians of our century have added to the fourteen traditional stations of the cross, which came from Spain, a fifteenth, which they call the resurrection. In Canto Grande the many cardboard crosses are taken back down from the wooden cross and replaced by white carnations as signs of the resurrection. The cross of hunger is replaced by the flower of sharing which takes place in the *comedores populares*, the kitchens for the poor, where mothers come together to prepare in common economical and nutritious meals for their children. The cross of injustice is replaced by the justice that the people demand on their protest marches, so that the officials will finally meet their obligations towards the families by providing water, light, health care, and schools. The cross of disease becomes the flower of health, for which voluntary health workers speak up by carrying out education and organizing campaigns for hygiene. The cross of poverty becomes the flower of water, reflected in the water project: all residents of the communities have agreed to communal work Sunday after Sunday to construct a drinking water tank for Motupe and Montenegro.

The cross of death is replaced by the flower of life. In this symbolic action the cross of dark wood appears whiter and whiter, covered by the flowers of resurrection. Then the people also kiss this new cross.

Dorothee Soelle, *Celebrating Resistance: The Way of the Cross in Latin America*, tr. Joyce Irwin (Mowbray 1993), p. 5.

Creative leisure
2.16

Sloth or accidie, to give it its ancient name, is the last of the seven capital sins. It refers to something more than mere physical self-indulgence; it is lethargy of the spirit, a weariness of life, a boredom in which nothing seems worthwhile. Frank Lake has shown the close resemblance between the symptoms of *accidie* as outlined by the old ascetic writers and those which the modern psychotherapist associates with depression. Doctors now recognize that depression can be a disease which requires medical treatment. But there is a normal depression which often succeeds a burst of activity in which much nervous energy has been expended, or some big disappointment or painful bereavement. It is as though a black dog lurks within some people waiting its opportunity to leap out and occupy the centre of the mental stage. The old writers recognized that underneath *accidie* there lived the demon of bottled-up rage. When a person who has for long restrained their anger under severe provocation of a sudden completely loses their temper they often experience a wild lifting of their spirits. It is often the inability to express anger openly that is the prime cause of depression. If sloth is often linked with bottled-up anger, it can also be allied with pride. So long as I maintain a masterly inactivity I can cling to my picture of myself as a person of great talents.

If I were to act, this picture might be shattered; therefore better do nothing. By inactivity I can keep up my sense of superiority to all the people who run around trying to make themselves important. Many evils have been tolerated because those who could have put an end to them were too lazy to act. All the same, sloth is not wholly evil, or rather, it is the corruption of an attitude potentially good. The world is not something merely to be exploited and used; it is something to be appreciated and delighted in; to those whose ears are open it can speak of the creator who made it. It is good sometimes just to stand and stare. There is a creative leisure out of which is born the vision which makes action fruitful. Perhaps this creative, contemplative leisure is what the world above all needs today.

Christopher Bryant SSJE, *The Heart in Pilgrimage*
(Darton, Longman & Todd 1980), p. 41.

This silly disposition
2.17

A vain man is a nauseous creature: he is so full of himself, that he has no room for anything else, be it ever so good or deserving. It is I, at every turn, that does this, or can do that. And as he abounds in his comparisons, so he is sure to give himself the better of everybody else; according to the proverb, 'All his geese are swans.' They are certainly to be pitied that can be so much mistaken at home. And yet I have sometimes thought that such people are, in a sort, happy, that nothing can put out of countenance with themselves, though they neither have, nor merit, other people's. But at the same time, one would wonder they should not feel the blows they give themselves, or get from others, from this intolerable and ridiculous temper; nor show any concern at that which makes others blush for, as well as at, them viz. their unreasonable assurance. To be a man's own fool is bad enough; but the vain man is everybody's. This silly disposition comes of a mixture of ignorance, confidence and pride: and as there is more or less of the last, so it is more or less offensive, or entertaining. And yet, perhaps, the worst part of this vanity is its unteachableness. Tell it anything, and it has known it long ago; and outruns information and instruction, or else proudly puffs at it. Whereas the greatest understandings doubt most, are readiest to learn and least pleased with themselves; this, with nobody else. For though they stand on higher ground, and so see further than their neighbours, they are yet humbled by their prospect, since it shows them something so much higher above their reach.

And truly then it is that sense shines with the greatest beauty when it is fed in humility.

William Penn, *Fruits of Solitude* (A.W. Bennett 1863), p. 91.

Pride: the deadliest of sins
2.18

Jealousy is probably the most important factor leading us to give false evidence against a neighbour. What we ourselves have failed to achieve we begrudge in the life of someone more favoured than we are. That we may in fact be less worthy than the other person is too intolerable to consider, and instead we conjure up fantasies of intrigue and subversion to explain how others always fare better than we do. That underhand manipulations do sometimes allow us less worthy contenders to win the accolade of public esteem is well known. That secret cabals may play a part in misdirecting justice is no idle thought, but in the end those who work subversively earn their reward of exposure and humiliation. People attaining spiritual mastery do not patronize these circles. The false accusations levelled at Christ were an amalgam of jealousy and fear. His opponents could not bear his effortless spiritual superiority and they were afraid that he would expose their weakness to the crowds. In fact, had they trusted Jesus, he would have supported their frailty and given them strength to face the darkness within them. But pride prevented them from either opening themselves to him or permitting his healing love to suffuse their distorted personalities with new life. Pride is certainly the deadliest of the sins because it will neither yield itself nor receive love from anyone else. Therefore it leads to absolute stagnation, until its proverbial departure before the inevitable fall: only a major calamity can force it to be relinquished, and then at last the power of love can penetrate the bereft personality. Rancour, jealousy and the fear of being exposed in one's naked impotence all feed pride, which in turn will plot to put an end to anyone who may threaten its tenuous security.

Martin Israel, *The Discipline of Love: The Ten Commandments for Today*
(SPCK 1985), pp. 84–85.

Hypocrisy
2.19

Although we cannot abide the double dealing and contrariness that we find in others, we would find that we are as bad as the worst if we only had a good look at ourselves. If we could face up to the truth, we would have to admit that we do not seek after what is true, or what is reasonable. Instead, our choices are made by caprice, or we do not choose at all, but simply allow ourselves to be led by others, and only afterwards look for reasons to justify what we have done.

We try to persuade ourselves that we are practising moderation, when in fact we are being indolent. When we fear to give offence, we pride ourselves on our restraint. We think we are being brave when we are proud and presumptuous; prudent and circumspect when in fact we are only pandering to others. We make no effort to strive after real virtue, but merely pretend to ourselves that we are good, and try to appear so to others... The hypocrisy involved in keeping up appearances is a very laborious business. None the less, that is our aim, and provided we can amuse ourselves with one or two superficial little practices of virtue, and tell ourselves how well we are doing, then we are satisfied.

... When shall I begin to be honest with myself, and cease to put on false appearances for the benefit of others, and even in order to fool myself? When shall I be content to be nothing, in my own eyes, and in the sight of others, instead of bolstering up my own self-respect and posturing as someone of importance? When shall I find that God is sufficient for me?

J.B. Bossuet, *Letters of Spiritual Direction*, tr. G. Webb and A. Walker
(A.R. Mowbray 1958), pp. 38–39.

A 'hidden' sin
2.20

Envy: this is the sin which affects those who hate to see others better, or more handsome, or abler, or more successful than themselves. This shows itself in jealousy. It is a very subtle fault and one to which religious people are often prone. Envious people are often snobbish, jealous and possessive. At bottom they do not respect other people. They do not like thanking anyone for a gift or a service. Envy leads to tale-bearing, spiteful gossip and detraction. This means 'running a person down', sometimes to the extent of taking away a person's reputation with a word or a look, or by means of a 'whispering campaign'. In spite of these obvious signs, envy is often a 'hidden' sin, which may be disguised under fair words and pleasant manners. Thus envy begins out of sight, deep down in the heart, but it is finally expressed by the tongue. The words of St James on these sins of the tongue are not too strong. 'The tongue is a fire... it infects the whole body... it is a pest that is never allayed, all deadly poison.'

Olive Wyon, *On The Way*
(SCM Press 1958), p. 50.

Unfair!
2.21

Envy is the child of pride. The envious are less able than the proud to repress their sense of inadequacy by building up a self-image of superiority to others. The realization that others are or seem to be more fortunate, abler, richer, happier than they is painful to the envious and makes them feel dejected. The failure or misfortune of others gives them a secret pleasure. On the other hand the success or good luck of others depresses them.

Envy is sometimes unwittingly encouraged by parents and others who urge children to aim at achievement which is beyond the reach of their limited ability and talent. The competitive structure of modern society is apt to breed envy in the less able or the handicapped. Some people go through life haunted by the feeling that people, circumstances or life itself have not been fair to them.

Christopher Bryant SSJE, *The Heart in Pilgrimage*
(Darton, Longman & Todd 1980), p. 38.

'Gather up the fragments'
2.22

There is a great waste of power in our failure to appreciate our opportunities. 'If I only had the gifts that this man has I would do the large and beautiful things that he does. But I never have the chance of doing such things. Nothing ever comes to my hand but opportunities for little commonplace things.' Now, the truth is that nothing is commonplace. The giving of a cup of cold water is one of the smallest kindnesses anyone can show to another, yet Jesus said that God takes notice of this act amid all the events of the whole world, any busy day, and rewards it. It may not be cabled half round the world and announced with great headlines in the newspapers, but it is noticed in heaven. We do not begin to understand what great waste we are allowing when we fail to put the true value on little opportunities of serving others. Somehow we get the feeling that any cross-bearing worthwhile must be a costly sacrifice, something that puts nails through our hands, something that hurts till we bleed...

When the great miracle of the loaves had been wrought [John 6:1–14], Jesus sent his disciples to gather up the broken pieces, 'that nothing be lost'. The Master is continually giving us the same command. Every hour's talk we have with a friend leaves fragments that we ought to gather up and keep to feed our heart's hunger or the hunger of others' hearts, as we go on. When we hear good words spoken or read a good book, we should gather up the fragments of knowledge, the suggestions of helpful thoughts, the broken pieces, and fix them in our hearts for use in our lives. We allow large values of the good things we hear or read to turn to waste continually because we are poor listeners or do not try to keep what we hear. We let the broken pieces be lost and thereby are great losers. If only we would gather up and keep all the good things that come to us through conversations and through reading, we would soon have great treasures of knowledge and wisdom.

James Russell Miller, *The Book of Comfort.*

Cynicism
2.23

The cynic in society becomes the pessimist in religion. The large embrace of sympathy which fails him as interpreter of human life, will no less be wanting when he reads the meaning of the universe. The harmony of the great whole escapes him in his hunt for little discords here and there. He is blind to the august balance of nature, in his preoccupation with some creaking show of defect. He misses the comprehensive march of advancing purpose, because, while he himself is in it, he has found some halting member that seems to lag behind. He picks holes in the universal order; he winds through its tracks as a detective, and makes scandals of all that is not to his mind. He trusts nothing that he cannot see; and he sees chiefly the exceptional, the dubious, the harsh. The glory of the midnight heavens affects him not, for thinking of a shattered planet or the uninhabitable moon. He makes more of the flood which sweeps the crop away, than of the perpetual river that feeds it year by year. For him the purple bloom upon the hills, peering through the young green woods, does but dress up a stony desert with deceitful beauty; and in the new birth of summer, he cannot yield himself to the exuberance of glad existence for wonder why insects tease and nettles sting. Nothing is so fair, nothing imposing, as to beguile him into faith and hope… In selfish minds the same temper takes a meaner turn, and resorts to the pettiest reasons for the most desolate thoughts: 'If God were good, why should I be born with a club-foot? If the world were justly governed, how could my merits be so long overlooked?'

James Martineau, *Hours of Thoughts on Sacred Things*, vol. 1
(Longmans, Green, Reader & Dyer, 1880), p. 97.

Different kinds of noise

2.24

Could we pause to ask ourselves what spirituality has to do with noise? At first glance nothing at all, for the general tendency of those in search of spirituality is to flee the world and strive to find oneself and the absolute in silence, in prayer and in quietude. I, too, love silence because above all it permits me to recall better so many memories and yearnings, it helps me to reflect deeply on challenging problems at hand, it helps me to rest and also because my formation has made me love silence and be at ease with it. But the question lies beyond this level. Here, when I speak of noise, I refer to those deafening noises that are the product of our consumer society, and sold to or imposed on people at large, more specially on the poor. This noise paralyzes all thought, keeps on beating ceaselessly at the eardrums, alienates the person and rends one's heart apart, away from one's self. This is the noise that is being boomed out from all kinds of factories, by loud and noisy music. It is these and other such intoxicating noises that do great harm to people. Yes, sonorous pollutions among so many other pollutions! Visual, corporal, material, environmental…

Then there is this noise, particularly of ideas that come to cloud our minds, us pastoral workers. I speak analogically of this noise, yet it is intense and always present. We produce plenty of ideas on every possible thing. It is said that a well-informed person is worth two. So, we keep on selling and buying ideas and opinions to such an extent that in the end we become intoxicated and never arrive at being the well-informed persons we wanted to be. And more than that, we have lost ourselves in this haze of floating ideas. We are supplied with information of all sorts, sometimes true, sometimes false, at other times more or less true, so that ultimately we do not know for sure which is true. Each tries to make the other believe that one version is the truth. Little bits of truths that rip the body and mind apart, that lead to the disintegration of that desire for unity among us. Who can save us from this noise of senseless sounds and ideas? How can we withstand all this noise which creates such emptiness and dissatisfaction with us: could we really speak of spirituality in the midst of such noise?

> Ivone Gebara, 'A Cry for Life from Latin America' in *Spirituality of the Third World*,
> ed. K.C. Abraham and Bernadette Mbuy-Beya (Orbis Books 1994), pp. 111–12.

Suffering humanity
2.25

Holding oneself together theologically in Holy Week takes a bit of doing. We are plunged ever deeper into the passion, gazing upon the sacred head ill used, the disfigured features of the man of sorrows, caught up in the horror of unsolicited violence, man's appalling inhumanity. And even if we have no time or heart to contemplate the sacred mysteries, they are splashed unrelentingly every day on our television screens. Christ dies in Bosnia, in Belfast, in Warrington. He is a Muslim woman raped and bleeding, a schoolboy blown to pieces by bombs and a toddler tied to a railway track. Father forgive them, for they know not what they do.

These are the mysteries we should be pondering each Good Friday, not trying vainly to imagine how Jesus looked as he climbed the hill to Golgotha. We know well enough what he looked like: like any desperate Kurd or Slav, stumbling barefoot over mountain paths, eyes blinded by tears, shoulders bowed with fatigue. He looked like the youngster I ignored yesterday in the street, a bedraggled booted teenager, sitting hopelessly on the pavement clutching a mongrel puppy, her face contorted with emptiness and pain. We know what he looked like; what we need to learn is how to comfort him suffering here and now. Jesus Christ, son of the living God, have mercy on us, have mercy on them. Show us what we should do. Give us diviners of living water lest we die of thirst.

But he *has* given us diviners of the water of life, and we do not recognize them. We ignore today's prophets because they are unshaven pop stars like Bob Geldof, scruffy missionaries from Latin America, or Indian-skirted social workers talking of child abuse and the death of the inner city. It is so much easier to believe that some are born wicked than that most have wickedness thrust upon them.

Sheila Cassidy, *Light from the Dark Valley: Reflections on Suffering and the Care of the Dying* (Darton, Longman & Todd 1994), pp. 63–64.

Love creating life
2.26

Fundamentally the cross represents the astonishing reality that God's power is not controlling. Fundamentally the cross shows God's power standing silently by while violence does its worst, while rage is unleashed in the world in paroxysms of attempts to control the religious, ethical and social structures of life. Fundamentally the cross shows God not in armed combat with the forces of evil, as so much Christian imagery would have it, but rather it shows God quietly, deeply, almost imperceptibly changing the terms of the conflict. The cross shows us that armed conflict with the forces of evil is precisely *not* the way to image God's power, a power that is not simple acquiescence but rather the generative power of life in *all* situations. God resets the terms of violent conflict, and the terms are loving.

Just as the cross is not a violent symbol, so also it is not a passive one. It does not show us a God who stands by and lets violence win. It shows us a God who will not let violence win because God does not engage that particular contest. Rather, in the midst of the worst that violence can do, love creates life.

Sally B. Purvis, *The Power of the Cross* (Abingdon Press 1993), p. 88.

A fallen world
2.27

For in our age all are separated into self-contained units, everyone crawls into his own hole, everyone separates himself from his neighbour, hides himself away and hides away everything he possesses, and ends up by keeping himself at a distance from people and keeping other people at a distance from him. He accumulates riches by himself and thinks how strong he is now and how secure, and does not realize, madman that he is, that the more he accumulates the more deeply does he sink into self-destroying impotence. For he is used to relying on himself alone and has separated himself as a self-contained unit from the whole. He has trained this mind not to believe in the help of other people, in men and mankind, and is in constant fear of losing his money and the rights he has won for himself. Everywhere today the mind of man has ceased, ironically, to understand that true security of the individual does not lie in isolated personal efforts but in general human solidarity. But an end will almost certainly come to this dreadful isolation of man, and everyone will realize all at once how unnaturally they have separated themselves from one another. Such will be the spirit of the time, and everyone will be surprised at having remained so long in darkness and not having seen the light. And then the sign of the Son of man will appear in the heavens... But till then we must still keep the banner flying and, even if he has to do it alone, a man has to set an example at least once and draw his soul out of its isolation and work for some great act of human intercourse based on brotherly love, even if he is to be regarded as a saintly fool for his pains. He has to do so that the great idea may not die.

Fyodor Dostoevsky, *The Brothers Karamazov*, tr. David Magarshack
(Penguin 1963), p. 357.

Community of the guilty
2.28

At the end of it all we need to recognize that it is an inevitable part of our moral being as humans that we are sinners, sharing every one of us in a quality of guiltiness. Perhaps we can only help people to cope with guilt if, first of all, we can agree on that. We may then go on to make some sense of the diversities of guilt, and, of course, accept that some guilts are much more publicly serious or more morally destructive than others, but it is from within a community of the guilty that we have to approach guilt, not as people who stand outside or think that it is even possible to stand outside. There is no us and them. We must come, all of us, as publicans not as pharisees [Luke 18:10]. If we do so we may need to proclaim rather different standards of guiltiness from those presented by the law, by society or even by the church. Outside prison, as much as within it, there is a full range of guilt. Perhaps that is true even within the ranks of the clergy. In our ministry it may be no less important to point to the guiltiness of those outside prison as to help cope with the guiltiness of some of those within, and the one could be a key to the other. Yet, if guilt is pervasive and largely immeasurable, it can never be the end of the story. Maybe it is only when someone recognizes that he or she personally participates in a community of guilt that the gospel analysis of sin, a divine Saviour and the offer of forgiveness none of us can merit, begins to make some sense. We may then be empowered to help others discover another community far beyond guilt, a community of the genuinely humane, of hope, of forgiveness, of love. Theologically, the universality of guilt is but the backdrop to the universality of forgiveness. Perhaps in practice it is when we recognize convincingly the reality of the first that we can become credible guides to the reality of the second.

Adrian Hastings, *The Shaping of Prophecy* (Geoffrey Chapman 1995), pp. 173–74.

PART 3

The Search for God

God our home
3.1

All this beauty that haunts us comes by revelation to those who are able to hear it. It is all around us, pressing in upon us, if only we could hear, if only we could learn to listen. And news of that other country we are born trying to remember comes the same way. We are homesick for something that lies beyond the universe yet strangely affects the movement of the sea. Our sense of regret points to a primordial homesickness – a sorrow that afflicts us precisely because we turn ourselves away from God who is the country we long for, the land of lost content. Most of us are mildly aware of this, but we are more than half afraid of the consequences of really finding God – 'Lest, having him, we must have naught beside', in the words of Francis Thompson. The saints have a raging sense of their need for God. He is the country of their soul, and tidings from that far country break in upon them. That is the meaning of Christ, who brought tidings, news of that country. He brought the very air of it into our land of exile. And there have been other moments of revelation, brief glimpses beyond the curtain. The world rolls back, and we are left forlorn, but sustained by the memory of it and the sense we have that history, including our own private history, is the story of a return.

Richard Holloway, *Paradoxes of Christian Faith and Life* (Mowbray 1984), p. 25.

One whom I can trust
3.2

Have you never cried in your hearts with longing, almost with impatience, 'Surely, surely, there is an ideal holy one somewhere – or else, how could have arisen in my mind the conception, however faint, of an ideal holiness? But where? Oh where? Not in the world around strewn with unholiness. Not in myself, unholy too, without and within. Is there a holy one, whom I may contemplate with utter delight? And if so, where is he? Oh that I might behold, if but for a moment, his perfect beauty, even though, as in the fable of Semele of old, "the lightning of his glance were death".'... And then, oh, then – has there not come that for which our spirit was athirst – the very breath of pure air, the very gleam of pure light, the very strain of pure music for it is the very music of the spheres – in those words, 'Holy, holy, holy, Lord God Almighty, which was, and is, and is to come'? Yes, whatever else is unholy, there is a holy one – spotless and undefiled, serene and self-contained. Whatever else I cannot trust, there is one whom I can trust utterly.

Whatever else I am dissatisfied with, there is one whom I can contemplate with utter satisfaction and bathe my stained soul in that eternal fount of purity. And who is he? Who, save the cause and maker and ruler of all things past, present and to come?

Charles Kingsley, Daily Thoughts (Macmillan & Co. 1884), p. 73.

Living is longing
3.3

Life is a search for this 'something', a search for something or someone to give meaning to our lives, to answer the question, who am I, why am I here, what is the purpose of my life?

I believe that this great need we all feel is caused by a longing which cannot be satisfied by the usual goals we set ourselves in this journey of life. Even when they have been achieved they so often fall short of our hopes and expectations. The longed-for objective is not something which can be possessed, it cannot be held or kept, can only be fleetingly glimpsed as it comes and goes.

It can only be hinted at, referred to obliquely; indescribable in words, it can only be felt, and all we know of it is that it is what we are looking for. The promise of it is there in our love for another person. In the glory of a sunrise or sunset, the silver path of the moon on the sea, the sad haunting cry of seabirds, the touching protective courage of a wild thing for its young or its mate. In the mountains and the streams, in the flowers and the forests, in the sufferings and sorrows of mankind as well as in the joys and the laughter.

This longing is all bound up with memories too, it carries its light like a will-o'-the-wisp through the scents and sounds and sights which suddenly bring back to us the magical moments when we were very young and in love with life. But it is also there, playing its part in the despair and the sorrowing and the regrets and the remorse. Sadly it seems that this yearning can become misdirected into channels which lead to drugs or drink or other excesses for excitement to assuage the longing when it has not been recognized for what it is.

There are countless ways in which the longing can be expressed, by poets and painters, musicians and dancers, and by so many of those whose talent is for living and loving in awe and worship.

Perhaps the whole of life is concerned with this yearning. Nothing can be left out, but it carries us on into death and beyond when we dare to hope that we shall come face to face with the source of all our longing.

Elizabeth Bassett, The Bridge is Love (Darton, Longman & Todd 1981), p. 31.

What am I looking for?
3.4

It would be well if every now and again in life, we were to ask ourselves: 'What am I looking for? What am I trying to extract from life? What's my aim and goal? If I am honest, what, in the depth of my heart, am I really trying to get out of life?' There are some who are searching for *security*. They would like a position which is safe, money enough to meet the needs of life and to put some past for the time when work is done, a material security which will take away the essential worry about material things. It is not a wrong aim, but it is a low aim, and an inadequate thing to which to direct all life; for, in the last analysis, there is no safe security in the uncertainty of the chances and the changes of this life. There are some who are searching for what they would call a *career*, for power, for prominence, for prestige, for a place to fit the talents and the abilities they believe themselves to have, for an opportunity to do the work they believe themselves capable of doing. Again it is not a bad aim. If it be directed by motives of personal ambition it can be a bad aim; if it be directed by motives of the service of our fellow human beings it can be a high aim. But it is not enough, for its horizon is limited by time and by the world. There are some who are searching for some kind of *peace*, for something to enable them to live at peace with themselves, and at peace with God, and at peace with one another. That is the search for God; that is the aim that only Jesus Christ can meet and supply.

William Barclay, *The Gospel of John*, vol. 1 (Saint Andrew Press 1974), p. 70.

Where are you?
3.5

Come then, Lord my God, teach my heart where and how to seek you, where and how to find you. Lord, if you are not present here, where, since you are absent, shall I look for you? On the other hand, if you are everywhere why then, since you are present, do I not see you? But surely you dwell in 'light inaccessible' [1 Timothy 6:16]. And where is this inaccessible light, or how can I approach the inaccessible light? Or who shall lead me and take me into it that I may see you in it? Again, by what signs, under what aspect, shall I seek you? Never have I seen you, Lord my God, I do not know your face. What shall he do, most high Lord, what shall this exile do, far away from you as he is? What shall your servant do, tormented by love of you and yet cast off 'far from your face'? He yearns to see you and your countenance is too far away from him. He desires to come close to you, and your dwelling place is inaccessible; he longs to find you and does not know where you are; he is eager to seek you out and he does not know your countenance. Lord, you are my God and my Lord, and never have I seen you. You have created me and recreated me and you have given me all the good things I possess, and still I do not know you. In fine, I was made in order to see you, and I have not yet accomplished what I was made for.

… Let me discern your light whether it be from afar or from the depths. Teach me to seek you, and reveal yourself to me as I seek, because I can neither seek you if you do not teach me how, nor find you unless you reveal yourself. Let me seek you in desiring you; let me desire you in seeking you; let me find you in loving you; let me love you in finding you.

I acknowledge, Lord, and I give thanks that you have created your image in me, so that I may remember you, think of you, love you. But this image is so effaced and worn away by vice, so darkened by the smoke of sin, that it cannot do what it was made to do unless you renew it and reform it. I do not try, Lord, to attain your lofty heights, because my understanding is in no way equal to it. But I do desire to understand your truth a little, that truth that my heart believes and loves. For I do not seek to understand so that I may believe; but I believe so that I may understand. For I believe this also, that 'unless I believe, I shall not understand' [cf.. John 8:43].

Anselm of Canterbury, *Proslogion*, ch. I, tr. M.J. Charlesworth
(Clarendon Press 1965).

Aspects of reality
3.6

God reveals himself also in art of all kinds – written, visual, audible. For art, when true to itself, attempts to bring into the sharpest possible focus some aspect or other of reality, how it threatens and ennobles, destroys and creates, its tragedies and triumphs, thus waking us up from our comforting dreams and consoling illusions – or maybe from our nightmares.

… There is the story of Charles Gore, encountered one evening 'in the corridor of the Queen's Hall after the orchestra had played a Brandenburg concerto'. His almost unconscious comment on the music showed where it had led his thoughts: 'If *that* is true, everything must be all right.'

Wherever reality of any kind is revealed, there God must be. For it is only in his light that we can see light, which means also that it is only in his light [Psalm 36:9], that we can perceive darkness.

H.A. Williams and C.R. Mitchell, *The Joy of God* (Mitchell Beazley 1980), p. 65.

True living
3.7

No man or woman begins to live a full life until they realize they live in the presence of something greater, outside and beyond themselves. Self-consciousness truly means that you are standing over against that other than yourself and you cannot be living in truth. Wonder is at the base of true living, and wonder leads to worship and after that the great other than self; it is yet kin to you, you are one with it. When you begin to live more completely and realize the kinship between you and nature, that out of nature you came and are part and parcel with it, this brings nearer faith which is self-conscious life (opposed to birds, trees, etc.), reaching out to perfection.

G.A. Studdert Kennedy, *The New Man in Christ* (Hodder & Stoughton 1932), p. 132.

A spirituality for everyone
3.8

We have, I think, much too readily talked of God's plan for the world, too easily presumed to set it out for a programme to be carried out. But God whose concern for the freedom in which love is born is absolute, is not a divine puppeteer. Human history must exhibit that freedom, the choice set out so clearly by the Deuteronomic writer: 'I have set before you life and death, blessing and cursing, therefore choose life, that both thou and thy seed may live, that thou mayest love the Lord thy God' (Deuteronomy 30:18). Human history must likewise afford that distillation of spiritual experience which gives an increasing reality to the choices that have to be made. It is one of the chief functions of historical inquiry to dethrone the idols that otherwise obstruct this freedom, to dispel the fantasies that the fearful are inclined to give way to. It applies furthermore to theology which if it be not liberating from all idolatries including those of its own construction, is not honest to God who loves his creatures.

It seems to me then that the spirituality we seek is not that of either laity or religious, but that of the one holy people of God, a thing in which we have not hitherto made much way. It will be concerned to replace those sometime exclusive walls that have divided people into denominational groups and churches over against the non-churched, by something more like a sensitive skin which registers contact and communication of pain and delight. We have made a start towards this. There is a great deal of pain to be faced ahead, and it may well be that Christians have not yet, in their spirituality, learned to exercise that great solvent of rigidities, God's gift of laughter.

Alan Ecclestone, 'Some Intimations of Spirituality' in
Spirituality and Human Wholeness (BCC 1986), pp. 23–24.

Whom do you seek?
A Meditation on John 20:11–18
3.9

Jesus said to her: 'Woman, why are you weeping? Whom do you seek?' He asked the reason for her sorrow to increase her desire, so that when he asked whom she was seeking she might feel a more vehement love for him.

She thought that it was the gardener... Perhaps this woman was not as mistaken as she appeared to be when she believed that Jesus was a gardener. Was he not spiritually a gardener for her, when he planted the fruitful seeds of virtue in her heart by the force of his love? But why did she say to the one she saw and believed to be the gardener, when she had not yet told him whom she was seeking, *'Sir, if you have taken him away'*? She had not yet said who it was who made her weep from desire, or mentioned him of whom she spoke. But the force of love customarily brings it about that a heart believes everyone else is aware of the one of whom it is always thinking. It is understandable that the woman did not say whom she was seeking, and yet said, *'If you have taken him away'.* She did not believe that the one for whom she herself so constantly wept in her desire was unknown to the other.

Jesus said to her: 'Mary'. After he had called her by the common name of 'woman', he called her by her own name, as if to say, 'Recognize him who recognizes you'... And so because Mary was called by name, she acknowledged her creator, and called him at once *'rabboni'*, that is, *'teacher'*. He was both the one she was outwardly seeking and the one who was teaching her inwardly to seek him.

Gregory the Great, Homily 25 [Migne], tr. David Hurst, in *Gregory the Great:
Forty Gospel Homilies* (Cistercian Publications 1990), pp. 192–93.

Affirming life
3.10

The religious need is the need for experienced meaning, the yearning for a truth that has been promised and that is becoming increasingly visible.

Religion is the attempt to regard nothing in this world as alien, hostile to human beings, a matter of fate, without meaning. Religion is the attempt to change everything that is experienced and encountered in all of life and to integrate it totally into a humane world. Everything should be interpreted in such a way that it becomes something 'for us'. Everything that is rigid should become flexible; everything that is chance, necessary; everything that appears to be meaningless should be regarded and believed to be true and good. Religion is the attempt to tolerate no nihilism and to live an unending and unrefutable affirmation of life.

As a variation of Freud's statement 'Where It was, I shall become' one could say, 'Where there was strangeness and chance and nothing, there shall be home, identity, and "God".' The word 'God' then, no longer means a super-power dwelling in some world other than this, a world that intervenes in ours from without. Nor does 'God' mean another realm, a heaven, another time after death, another kind of immortal, all-powerful being that stands over against us as a person. To be sure, we need the word 'God' in order to express what we mean by the as yet unrealized totality of our world and the truth of our life which is yet to appear. In this sense it can be said that everyone has already decided over and over whether they believe in God or nothing, in the meaning of life or in total meaninglessness, by the way they live.

Dorothee Soelle, *The Inward Road and the Way Back*, tr. David L. Scheidt
(Darton, Longman & Todd 1979), pp. 132–33.

Real dialogue
3.11

Dialogue was not a mere talking about religion; that is very often pure babble, vanity, self-glorification. Nor was dialogue the 'comparative religion' of experts. The comparison of religions is interesting only so long as one has not understood what religion is really all about. One can only compare what lies on the surface – *maya*. The real dialogue takes place in an ultimate, personal depth; it does not have to be a talking about religion. But something does distinguish real dialogue: the challenge. Dialogue challenges both partners, takes them out of the security of their own prisons their philosophy and theology have built for them, confronts them with reality, with truth: a truth that cannot be left to gather dust in libraries, a truth that demands all. Truth was there in so many a true dialogue; never before had he felt so small, so helpless, so inadequate. All of a sudden the shallowness of all religious routine was laid bare, the compromise with the world, that which is essentially un-Christian in so many things that bear Christ's name. Suddenly he became aware of the fact that he, too, had to be 'converted', that he could not confront his neighbour as one who demands, but that they both jointly would have to ask God for his grace. If dialogue is taken seriously, Christianity must be deeply sincere and upright – different from what it is now. He understood that the lack of 'conversion' of the nations was not due to their obstinacy but to the lack of conversion among those who had sent themselves... Dialogue in depth shatters the self-confidence of those who regard themselves as guardians of the whole and only truth. Truth has to be searched for in order to be had; the kingdom of God is arriving, and only those who are on their way will reach it.

Klaus Klostermaier, *Hindu and Christian in Vrindaban* (SCM Press 1969), pp. 102–103.

The great fight for life
3.12

The spirituality of resistance is one which, in spite of the aggression surrounding the communities [in El Salvador], goes on maintaining the hope that reality will change. It is the hope based on the conviction that this change can only come from below. This spirituality is moving some men and women to commit themselves to the search for the integral development of their communities, but as a development which starts from solidarity with the most defenceless sectors of the communities. This approach seeks to maintain a critical conscience, in the face of the convenience of letting oneself be dragged along by the current of the 'individual well-being', or the passivity of 'we can't do anything'. We call this the spirituality of resistance because from it gospel values are kept alive, leading people to commit themselves to life, especially the life of the poorest. And it is a spirituality of resistance, too, because it sets itself against the reigning priorities which are now the market, competition, production, capital. These are priorities with no regard for the environment, or the growing impoverishment of the great majority, or the values of solidarity, of mercy – in other words, where life in all its multiple manifestations counts for nothing.

From this spirituality the actual situation can be read as part of the road which has to be trodden in this great fight for life. From this spirituality can be discovered the God who hides himself, who is in the resistance, accompanying people in the fight which, as it was before, is unequal but, also as it was before, where God's presence is what gives strength to go on fighting from weakness. God is discovered as the one who continues to invite us to make an option, and to opt for *life* in spite of *death*.

Carmen Manuela Del Cid, 'In El Salvador: Discovering a God Who Hides Himself' in *The Way*, vol. 36, no. 1 (January 1996), p. 34.

Going to church
3.13

We must not be too solemn about it but, on the whole, going to church – coming together as Christians – is not something which more than a small number can possibly be expected to do; and I, for one, do not blame them. Going to church, taking part in church affairs generally, on the whole is not exposure to an exploration into a mysterious and attractive, awe-inspiring and ever-deepening reality. On the whole going to church and being attached to various church affairs forms a series of operations which protect us from the realities around us. The whole process tends to make people less human and less realistic. I once saw a poster up outside a place I was driving through which said 'Come to church'. I had a great sense that I ought to get out and put up another poster which said: 'This is the *last* thing you should do.' Which, I still think, is right. People have to know quite a lot about God before they can stand up to going to church.

So much churchgoing is just religious practices and not godly living and godly exploring. Something seems to have gone very wrong. I believe, as so often in the history of the church and of the various communities which go to make up the church, that just as God is bringing pressures upon us about one world, so he is bringing pressures to bear on us which could and should reawaken us to the immense God possibilities which are around in the world and in people and in the church. I would not be a bishop if I were not absolutely clear that even the church cannot keep a good God down. This is a fundamental axiom, as far as I am concerned. We ought to be reawakened to the powerful resources and insights which are available in and through the biblical records and in and through the various Christian traditions – if only we will not shut them up in the practices of religion.

David E. Jenkins, *God, Jesus and Life in the Spirit*
(SCM Press 1988), pp. 23–24.

Call to conversion
3.14

Is there someone among you who desires to be satisfied and would like this desire to be fulfilled? Then let him begin to be hungry for righteousness, and he cannot fail to be satisfied. Let him yearn for those loaves which abound in his father's house, and he will immediately find he is disgusted with the husks of swine [see Luke 15:11ff]. Let him endeavour, however little, to experience the taste of righteousness that he may desire it more and thus merit more; as it has been written: 'He who eats me will hunger for more, and he who drinks me will thirst for more' [Sirach 24:21]. This desire is more akin to the spirit, and because it is natural to it, the heart is more eagerly preoccupied with this and manfully shoves out all other desires. In this way a strong man fully armed is overcome by one stronger than he; in this way one nail is driven out by another. 'Blessed are they who hunger and thirst for righteousness' [Matthew 5:6]. Then, 'for they will be satisfied'. Not yet by that one thing by which we are never sated, the one thing by which we live, but by everything else, all those things for which we previously longed insatiably, so that thereafter the will ceases delivering up the body to obey its former passions, and delivers it over to reason, urging it to serve righteousness for holiness' sake with no less zeal than it formerly showed in serving evil for iniquity's.

Bernard of Clairvaux, *Sermons on Conversion*, tr. Marie-Bernard Said
(Cistercian Publications 1981), pp. 61–63.

The world God's body
3.15

The world is our meeting place with God, and this means that God's immanence will be 'universal' and God's transcendence will be 'worldly'.

To say that God's presence to us, God's immanence, is universal means that it is not limited to special times and places, or to particular people or institutions, although special times and places, as well as particular people or institutions, may have paradigmatic importance. If the world, the cosmos, is our point of contact with God, *the* place where we join God to work on a project of mutual importance – the well-being of the body for which we have been given special responsibility – then it is here that we find God, become aware of God. This means we look at the world, all parts and aspects of it, differently: it is the body of God, and hence we revere it, find it special and precious, not as God but as the way God has chosen to be visible, available, to us. In addition, then, to special, paradigmatic individuals and to the church as the fellowship of friends, both of which are illuminating places where God is immanent, there is also the world that belongs to God in so intimate and special a way that we call it God's body. It is not, then, mere earth or dead matter; it is 'consecrated', formally dedicated to a divine purpose. We do not know in all ways or even in many ways what this purpose is, but the world is not *ours* to manipulate for *our* purposes. If we see it as God's body, the way God is present to us, we will indeed know we tread on sacred ground. God's immanence, then, being universal, undergirds a sensibility that is open to the world, both to other people and to other forms of life, as the way one meets

God. In this picture we do not meet God *vis-à-vis* [face to face], but we meet God only and always as mediated, as embodied.

Sallie McFague, *Models of God: Theology for an Ecological, Nuclear Age*
(Fortress Press 1987), p. 185.

Greater than our hearts
3.16

If religion is to be meaningful in modern society, it has to develop a sense of the gratuitous, the non-assimilable. In her book *The Need for Roots*, Simone Weil attacks a form of education in which everything can be absorbed, assimilated, reduced and rendered banal; such an education, she says, runs the risk of snuffing out the spark of energy in humankind. On the contrary, a true education is one that places the human being before the irreducible, that which cannot be harnessed but which sheds light on all things, that which is gratuitous, that which is beautiful. Religion does just that: it leads us into the presence of a gratuitous, illuminating, both hidden and revealed reality – a reality that is to be contemplated, not assimilated. It is here that the religious factor acts as a powerful anthropological and social lever. It presents us not with a useful and consumable God, but with a gratuitous God who, as a result, is a source of salvation. It reaffirms the purpose of existence as being one of celebration, as being a festival.

Olivier Clément, 'Witnessing in a Secularized Society' in *Your Will Be Done:
Orthodoxy in Mission* (Katerini/Geneva, Tertios/WCC 1989), p. 123.

Freedom above all
3.17

The mystery of the world abides in freedom: God desired freedom and freedom gave rise to tragedy in the world. Freedom is at the beginning and at the end. I might say that all my life I was engaged in hammering out a philosophy of freedom. I was moved by the basic conviction that God is truly present and operative only in freedom.

Freedom alone should be recognized as possessing a sacred quality, whilst all the other things to which a sacred character has been assigned since history began ought to be made null and void.

I found strength to renounce many things in life, but I have never renounced anything in the name of duty or out of obedience to precepts and prohibitions: I renounced for the sake of freedom, and, maybe, also out of compassion. Nothing could ever tie me down, and this, no doubt, has to some extent weakened my efficiency and diminished my possibilities of self-realization. I always knew, however, that freedom gives birth to suffering, while the refusal to be free diminishes suffering. Freedom is not easy, as its enemies and slanderers allege: freedom is hard; it is a heavy burden…

All things in human life should be born of freedom and pass through freedom and be rejected whenever they betray freedom. The true meaning and origin of the fallen condition of humanity is to be seen in the primordial rejection of freedom.

Nicolas Berdyaev, *Dream and Reality*, tr. Katherine Lampert
(Geoffrey Bles 1950), p. 46.

Catching a frog
3.18

When we draw water from a well, it can happen that we inadvertently also bring up a frog. When we acquire virtues we can sometimes find ourselves involved with the vices which are imperceptibly interwoven with them. What I mean is this. Gluttony can be caught up with hospitality; lust with love; cunning with discernment; malice with prudence; duplicity, procrastination, slovenliness, stubbornness, wilfulness and disobedience with meekness; refusal to learn with silence; conceit with joy; laziness with hope; hasty condemnation with love again; despondency and indolence with tranquillity; sarcasm with chastity; familiarity with lowliness. And behind all the virtues follows vainglory as a salve, or rather a poison, for everything.

John Climacus, *The Ladder of Divine Ascent*, Step 26, tr. Colm Luibhead and Norman
Russell (slightly adapted) (Paulist Press 1992), p. 237.

Way of love
3.19

Once I asked Blessed François how one may best become perfect. 'You must love God with your whole heart,' he answered, 'and your neighbour as yourself.'
'I did not ask in what perfection consists,' I replied, 'but how to attain it?'
'Charity', he repeated, 'is both the means and the end, the one and the only

way by which we can attain that perfection which in truth is charity itself... And just as the soul is the life of the body, so charity is the life of the soul.'

'I am aware of that,' I said, 'but I want to know *how* one is to love God with one's whole heart and one's neighbour as oneself?'

Again he answered the same: 'We must love God with our whole heart and our neighbour as ourselves.'

'I am still just where I was,' I rejoined. 'Tell me how I may acquire such love.'

'The best way, the shortest and easiest way of loving God with one's whole heart – is simply to love him wholly and heartily!'

This is the only answer he would give.

Finally, however, François said: 'There are many others who would also like me to tell them of techniques and methods and secret ways of attaining perfection. Yet I can only tell them that the sole secret is a hearty love of God and the only method of acquiring that love is by loving. You learn to speak by speaking, to study by studying, to run by running, to work by working. All those who wish to learn in any other way only deceive themselves. If you really want to love God, go on and love him more and more. Never look back. Move forward constantly. Begin as a humble apprentice and the very power of love will draw you on to become a master in the art. Those who have made most progress will constantly press ahead, never for a moment thinking that they have reached the goal. For charity should continue to increase in us until we draw our last breath.'

Jean Pierre Camus, The Spirit of St François de Sales, ed. and tr. C.F. Kelley
(Harper & Brothers 1952), p. 1.

The crucified hands
3.20

On the side wall of Newman College Chapel in Melbourne there is a bronze sculpture of Jesus on the cross. I used to look at it every day, since it was located on our short path to the grocery store. The nails brutally pierced the palms of the hands of Jesus. The weight of his body was painfully focused on these nails. He is in agony. He is gasping. He is neither like the Japanese Buddha with webbed hands, attractive and merciful, nor like Lenin with his confident ideological fist. Jesus looks defenceless. He is beaten. He is defeated. 'He was crucified in weakness...' (2 Corinthians 13:4). His hands are neither open nor closed. Perhaps he wanted either to open them all the way or to close them all the way. I don't know. 'My father, if it be possible, let this cup pass from me; nevertheless, not as I will, but as thou wilt' (Matthew 26:39) – this is what we hear. Did the nails actually pierce through the palms of his hands? I don't know. I am speaking the language of symbolism. I 'saw' that his hands are neither open or closed. If his hands are closed tight, theology can become ideology. I am not suggesting that ideology is something inherently evil. There are good ideologies and bad ideologies. And none of us is free from ideologies. What concerns me here at this moment is that there is a distinction between theology and ideology. Theology is 'neither open nor closed'. 'And blessed is he who takes no offence at me' (Matthew 11:6). If his hands were open – very much open with symbolic webs – then theology can get rid of its quality of being a 'stumbling block'.

As I pondered the bronze figure of the crucified Jesus, I began to see gradually that the saving truth which the gospel speaks is spoken through hands which are neither open nor closed, the crucified hands...

The crucified hands are the hands of ultimate love and respect for our history. They are the hands of divine invitation. The mind that contemplates the crucified hands, neither open nor closed, is the crucified mind. The crucified mind is perceptive about the varieties of forms of hands and their relationship to the crucified hands.

Kosuke Koyama, *No Handle on the Cross: An Asian Meditation on the Crucified Mind* (SCM Press 1976), pp. 25–26.

The language of faith
3.21

To look for a sort of 'rock-bottom' solidity in language, and for certain words that are unchangeable and adequate to mediate God to us is, I think, to mistake the nature of language. Worse, it is also to mistake the nature of faith.

It is tempting to assume that words, rather like counters, 'stand for' or define a reality that lies behind them; that they can be formulated so as to do this in a timeless way. In a church context it is easy to suppose, for instance, that the creeds represent just such an eternally valid definition of faith. However, a little reflection reveals that the creeds were formulated in the context of fierce controversy about what it meant to be Christian. The rolling phrases of the Nicene Creed about the second person of the Trinity were not devised as a piece of dispassionate definition, but were affirmations set against other prevalent views of Christ's nature. The language of faith is forged in an atmosphere of human and historical polemic; and therefore certain words and emphases will emerge not because they are 'true' in a realm quite separate from immediate issues, but because in the context of conflict they desperately need to be said. This does not mean that the creeds are *not* true, or that religious language has failed to express faith; it is simply to recognize something about language which is necessarily the case. Indeed, it may be more helpful to think about words, not as inherently defining or naming reality, but as *doing* or affecting things within society as it is lived.

Janet Morley, 'Liturgy and Danger' in *Mirror to the Church*,
ed. Monica Furlong (SPCK 1988), p. 26.

God around and within
3.22

'God is not far from each one of us, for in him we live and move and have our being' [Acts 17:28]. If ultimately only God satisfy our infinite longing, only he fill the hole in the heart, it might look as if we had to set out on a desperate search for him. And because the words of earth can only indirectly and obliquely indicate the realities of heaven, there is a sense in which we do indeed have to search for God, to seek if we are to find, to knock if it is to be opened to us. But it is an odd sort of searching, for it ends with the discovery that God is and has been with us all the time, that he is not far off, but nearer to us than the air we breathe, and that, like the air, his presence with us is not something we have earned, but is a free gift to all. Because we can speak of God only obliquely, in our talk about him we shall get tied up in all sorts of inconsistent spatial metaphors. That doesn't matter. What godly men try to tell us makes sense in spite of the apparent contradictions.

We discover God as our environment. In the homely image of the psalmist, he is about our path and about our bed and familiar with all our ways. It is in him, to quote Paul again, that we live and move and have our being. But if God is around us he is also within us. And if he is within us it is not as an alien, not as another, but as our truest selves. A human individual with a powerful personality may be said to invade us as an alien, destroying our autonomy and forcing us into his own mould so that we lose our own identity and become mere copies of his...

But unlike another human being, God is our creator, and by dwelling within us he makes us our true selves and establishes our personal identify. He negates himself in us in order to find himself in us. That is to say, he limits himself so that, instead of overwhelming us, he gradually and gently calls forth into being the tender, vulnerable fragility of our true selfhood, the fragility which when made perfect is his presence, it is himself which he discovers in us. 'God begins to live in me,' says Thomas Merton, 'not only as my creator but as my other and true self' – other and true because I spend much of my time fabricating a false self instead of allowing God to create me.

H.A. Williams and C.R. Mitchell, *The Joy of God* (Mitchell Beazley 1979), p. 20.

Thirst of the Spirit
3.23

All our spirits are born of God's Spirit; the likeness of God's own nature is planted in every one of us; and therefore our spirits can never be at rest till they reach the heavenly fountain from which they came. Unhappily we do not understand our own selves: we feel the thirst within us, but we are long before we learn what alone will quench it.

The thirst of the spirit is chiefly of two kinds, the desire of light and the desire of love. No one surely is without the desire of light. We all are constantly meeting with things which provoke us to ask within ourselves, what is this? how is this? why is this? If we are not curious about such things as books might tell us, we still are troubled with much greater questions. We cannot help seeing what is going on around us among our friends and neighbours, and then we ask how it is that this or that event happens to them. We are still more troubled by thoughts about ourselves and our present and future life. We wonder how a world so full of evil and sorrow can be the work of a good God. This is a longing for light. It is partly satisfied every time that a word spoken by anyone else, or a verse from the Bible, or any other cause gives us a hint which throws light upon what was dark before. And the more we know, the more we desire to know, and then we soon find that there is no teaching like God's own: and all his words and works seem to give forth ever fresh light so long as we remember that they do indeed proceed from him. At last we find that nothing less can satisfy us than God himself to shew us all truth, and we fall on our knees before him, and pray him to scatter all our darkness, and fill us wholly with his own light.

The desire of love is a still deeper thirst of the spirit. There is to us a delight in the presence and affection of those who are dear to us, which we would not exchange for anything that a person could give us, whether it be child, or father, or mother, or husband, or wife, or brother, or sister that we love. They partly satisfy the thirst of our hearts, as God meant that they should. But they are not always the same to us; sometimes, it may be, fretful, sometimes cold: and then, it may be, they die from among us, and our eyes can behold them no more. The more tenderly we love them, the more we shall feel that they cannot exhaust our love, that there is something within us which longs after one who cannot change like poor weak mortals, whose love is as deep and constant as the everlasting heavens, from whose presence death itself cannot cut us off. Our love is therefore never fulfilled till it lays hold upon God himself, and renews itself from that never-failing source.

F.J.A. Hort, *Village Sermons* (Macmillan & Co. 1905), p. 198.

The door of the heart
3.24

The gospel tells us that the kingdom of God is within us first of all. If we cannot find the kingdom of God within us, if we cannot meet God within, in the very depth of ourselves, our chances of meeting him outside ourselves are very remote. When Gagarin came back from space and made his remarkable statement that he never saw God in heaven, one of our priests in Moscow remarked, 'If you have not seen him on earth, you will never see him in heaven.' This is also true of what I am speaking about. If we cannot find a contact with God under our own skin, as it were, in this very small world which I am, then the chances are very slight that even if I meet him face to face, I will recognize him. St John Chrysostom said, 'Find the door of your heart, you will discover it is the door of the kingdom of God.' So it is inward that we must turn, and not outward – but inward in a very special way. I am not saying that we must become introspective. I don't mean that we must go inward in the way one does in psychoanalysis or psychology. It is not a journey into my *own* inwardness, it is a journey *through* my own self, in order to emerge from the deepest level of self into the place where he is, the point at which God and I meet.

Anthony Bloom, *School for Prayer*
(Darton, Longman & Todd 1970), p. 19.

Conscience
3.25

Conscience is that depth of human nature at which it comes in touch with God, where it receives God's message and hears his voice... Conscience is the remembrance, in our sinful life, of God and of life divine. When, in the most sinful and criminal people, conscience awakes, this means that they remember about God, and how it is to live a godly life, although they may not express it in these words. Conscience is the organ of reception of religious revelation of truth, of good, of integral truth. It is not a separate side of human nature or a special function, it is the wholeness of our spiritual nature, its very heart... Conscience is also the source of original primary judgments about the world, and about life. More than this, conscience judges God, or about God, because it is an organ of the perception of God. Conscience may judge about God only because it is an organ of the perception of God. God acts on our conscience, awakens our conscience, awakens our memories of a higher world. Conscience is the remembrance of what we are, to what world we belong to by the idea of our creation, by whom we were created, how and why we were created. Conscience is a spiritual, supernatural element in us, and it is not at all of social origin. What is of social origin is rather an obstruction or deformation of conscience. Conscience is that depth of human nature when it has not fallen completely away from God, where it has maintained contact with the divine world.

Nicolas Berdyaev, *Christian Existentialism*, selected and tr. Donald A. Lowrie
(George Allen & Unwin 1965), p. 88.

Led by truth
3.26

Do you see that only truth leads and brings one to this mountain? Truth leads; truth is that which guides. I gladly follow truth; I do not hold suspect such a guide. Truth knows to lead; truth does not know how to mislead. But what is truth? 'I am', he says, 'the Way, the Truth, and the Life' (John 14:6). Therefore let one who wishes to ascend the mountain follow truth. Follow Christ, whoever you are who wish to ascend this mountain. We have learned from the teaching of the evangelist: 'Then Jesus took his disciples, viz., Peter, James and John, and led them into a high mountain apart' (Matthew 17:1). Thus the disciples of Jesus are led above and apart, that they may take possession of this high mountain. It is a steep way unknown to many, which leads to the summit of this mountain. I think only those run without error, only those arrive without impediment, who follow Christ, who are led by truth. Whoever hastens to high things, you go in security if truth goes before you. Without it you labour in vain. As truth does not wish to deceive, so it is not able to be deceived. If you do not wish to err, follow Christ.

Richard of St Victor, *The Twelve Patriarchs*, chapter LXXVII, tr. Grover A. Zinn,
(Paulist Press 1979), p. 135.

My own truth
3.27

What I really lack is to be clear in my mind *what I am to do*, not what I am to know, except in so far as a certain understanding must precede every action. The thing is to understand myself, to see what God really wishes *me* to do; the thing is to find a truth which is true *for me*, to find *the idea for which I can live and die*. What would be the use of discovering so-called objective truth, of working through all the systems of philosophy and of being able, if required, to review them all and show up the inconsistencies within each system; what good would it do me to be able to develop a theory of the state and combine all the details into a single whole, and so construct a world in which I did not live, but only held up to the view of others; what good would it do me to be able to explain the meaning of Christianity if it had *no* deeper significance *for me and for my life*; what good would it do me if truth stood before me, cold and naked, not caring whether I recognized her or not, and producing in me a shudder of fear rather than a trusting devotion? I certainly do not deny that I still recognize an *imperative of understanding... but it must be taken up into my life*, and *that is* what I now recognize as the most important thing. That is what my soul longs after, as the African desert thirsts for water. That is what I lack, and that is why I am left standing like a man who has rented a house and gathered all the furniture and household things together, but has not yet found the beloved with whom to share the joys and sorrows of his life.

Søren Kierkegaard, *The Journals of Kierkegaard 1834–1854*, ed. and tr. Alexander Dru (Fontana 1958), p. 44, from Gilleleie, 1 August 1835.

PART 4

Meditations on God

Visions and Revelations

A Christian dream

4.1

Ruminating one evening on this chequered scene of mortal life, its pains and pleasures, hopes and cares; and endeavouring to reduce my thoughts into some kind of order, it produced the following reverie.

I fancied myself beginning a difficult and hazardous journey, I knew not at first from whence I came nor whither I was going… I had only a little dubious light, like the first faint glimmerings of approaching morn; but as daylight by degrees came on I could discover something of the prospect before me, and found myself at the foot of a very high mountain; the side-extended scene on the right and the left as far as my eye could reach presented an endless variety of objects…

I saw before me a variety of paths, some were smooth and verdant, and winding seemed to promise an easy ascent to the top of the mountain which I wished to reach, others appeared difficult and dangerous. I should have been at a loss to know the right path, had not my conductors (who at my first setting out led me and were still near) put into my hands a book, in which I found a map of the country through which I was travelling; a description of the place to which I was going, and plain instructions concerning the road I was to take: this book, of so much importance to my safety and comfort, I was informed was written by the direction of a person of consummate skill and undoubted veracity, and who had also promised such powerful protection and assistance to those travellers who might sincerely desire it, as should preserve them through every danger and enable them to surmount every difficulty.

Desiring to follow the directions of this book, and imploring the protection and assistance of its great author, I chose a narrow path, which I was assured led to life, another name for the land of happiness.

Anne Steele ('Theodora'), *Miscellaneous Pieces in Verse and Prose*,
vol. III (Bristol 1780).

The things that make for peace
4.2

Jesus Christ reveals the last things to his followers, for he can scan the horizon of history from beginning to end. He sees the twilight of the day, the twilight of life and the twilight of the world. And in the all-consuming desire of his love he says, 'Would that even today you knew the things that make for peace!' We, however, do not hear him. We are too wrapped up in our daily work, our life's work and the world's work.

At the beginning of the war I stood in the bell tower of St Katharine's Church in Danzig with the church organist. He sat down at the keyboard of the carillon to play a hymn on the hour. His mighty proclamation of the gospel rang out over the whole town. The bells beat upon my ears and the sound of their message so filled me that no other sound could intervene. Far below, though, I could see men going on about their business. They were building an air-raid shelter. The excavator clattered, pneumatic drills hammered away and traffic surged along. No one looked up to listen to the music that was pounding in my ears and filling me to the brim. What sounded all around us up above remained inaudible down there below amidst the noise of people's daily work.

Have we heard the sound that comes from above? We certainly cannot stop our machines. Nor should we try. But we can pay attention to the sound that filters through our earthly noise. For the air is full of promises, and we would lose everything if we failed to hear them.

Helmut Thielicke, 'What Are We to Make of the Biblical Exposition of the End
of All Things?', *How Modern Should Theology Be?*, tr. H.G. Anderson
(Collins Fontana 1970), pp. 80–81.

Cause to be merry
4.3

Then this creature asked our Lord Jesus how she should best love him. And our Lord said, 'Be mindful of your wickedness and reflect on my goodness.' She said again, 'I am the most unworthy creature that you ever showed favour to on earth.' 'Ah daughter,' said our Lord, 'do not be afraid. I take into account not what a person has been, but what they will be.'

'Daughter, you are as sure of the love of God, as God is God. Your soul is more sure of the love of God than of your own body, for your soul will part from your body, but God will never part from your soul, for they are joined together for ever. And so, daughter, you have as good cause to be merry as any lady in this world, and if you knew, daughter, how much you please me when you willingly allow me to speak in you, you would never do otherwise, for this is a holy life and the time is very well spent. Daughter, this life of yours pleases me more than if you wore a hair-shirt and fasted on bread and water, for if you said a thousand *Pater nosters* every day, you would not please me as well as you do when you remain silent and allow me to speak in your soul.'

Margery Kempe, *The Book of Margery Kempe* (1436).

Oneness in the Eucharist
4.4

On a certain Pentecost Sunday I had a vision at dawn. Matins were being sung in the church, and I was present. My heart and my veins and all my limbs trembled and quivered with eager desire and, as often occurred with me, such madness and fear beset my mind that it seemed to me I did not content my beloved, and that my beloved did not fulfil my desire, so that dying I must go mad, and going mad I must die. On that day my mind was beset so fearfully and so painfully by desirous love that all my separate limbs threatened to break, and all my separate veins were in travail. The longing in which I then was cannot be expressed by any language or any person I know; and everything I could say about it would be unheard of to all those who never apprehended love as something to work for with desire, and whom Love had never acknowledged as hers. I can say this about it: I desired to have full fruition of my beloved, and to understand and taste him to the full. I desired that his humanity should to the fullest extent be one in fruition with my humanity, and that mine then should hold its stand and be strong enough to enter into perfection until I content him, who is perfection itself, by purity and unity, and in all things to content him fully in every virtue. To that end I wished he might content me interiorly with his Godhead, in one spirit, and that for me he should be all that he is, without withholding anything from me. For above all the gifts that I ever longed for, I chose this gift: that I should give satisfaction in all great sufferings. For that is the most perfect satisfaction: to grow up in order to be God with God. For this demands suffering, pain and misery, and living in great new grief of soul: but to let everything come and go without grief, and in this way to experience nothing else but sweet love, embraces and kisses. In this sense I desired that God give himself to me, so that I might content him.

Hadewijch, in *Hadewijch: The Complete Works*, Vision 7,
tr. Mother Columba Hart OSB (Paulist Press 1981), pp. 280–81.

Encountering Jesus
4.5

All my feelings seemed to rise and flow out; and the utterance of my heart was, 'I want to pour my whole soul out to God.' The rising of my soul was so great that I rushed into the back room of the front office, to pray. There was no fire and no light in the room; nevertheless it appeared to me as if it were perfectly light. As I went in and shut the door after me, it seemed as if I met the Lord Jesus face to face. It did not occur to me then, nor did it for some time afterwards, that it was wholly a mental state. On the contrary, it seemed to me that I saw him as I would see any other man. He said nothing, but looked at me in such a manner as to break me right down at his feet. I have always since regarded this as a most remarkable state of mind; for it seemed to me a reality that he stood before me, and I fell down at his feet and poured out my soul to him. I wept aloud like a child, and made such confessions as I could with my choked utterance. It seemed to me that I bathed his feet with my tears; and yet I had no distinct impression that I touched him, that I recollect. I must have continued in this state for a good while; but my mind was too absorbed with the interview to recollect anything that I said. But I know, as soon as my mind became calm enough to break off from the interview, I returned to the front office, and found that the fire that I had made of large wood was nearly burned out. But as I turned and was about to take a seat by the fire, I received a mighty baptism of the Holy Spirit.

Charles Grandison Finney, *The Memoirs of Rev. Charles G. Finney* (1876).

Moment of conversion
4.6

As I was walking in a dark thick grove, unspeakable glory seemed to open to the view and apprehension of my soul. I do not mean any external brightness, for I saw no such thing; nor do I intend any imagination of a body of light, somewhere away in the third heavens, or anything of that nature. But it was a new inward apprehension or view I had of God, such as I never had before, nor anything which had the least resemblance of it. I stood still, and wondered, and admired. I knew that I never before had seen anything comparable to it for excellency and beauty. It was widely different from all the conceptions that ever I had of God or things divine.

I had no particular apprehension of any one person in the Trinity, either the Father, the Son, or the Holy Spirit, but it appeared to be divine glory that I then beheld. My soul 'rejoiced with joy unspeakable' to see such a God, such a glorious divine being, and I was inwardly pleased and satisfied that he would be *God over all*, forever and ever. My soul was so captivated and delighted with the excellency, loveliness, greatness and other perfections of God, that I was even swallowed in him, at least to the degree that I had no thought, as I remember at first, about my own salvation, and scarce reflected there was such a creature as myself.

... I continued in this state of inward joy and peace, yet astonishment, till near dark, without any sensible abatement, and then began to think and examine what I had seen; and felt sweetly composed in my mind all the evening following. I felt myself in a new world, and everything about me appeared with a different aspect from what it was wont to do.

At this time the way of salvation opened to me with such infinite wisdom, suitableness, and excellency, that I wondered I should ever think of any other way of salvation, and was amazed that I had not dropped my contrivances, and complied with this lovely, blessed, and excellent way before.

David Brainerd, *The Diary and Journal of David Brainerd* (London 1902).

In broad daylight
4.7

Then very suddenly I was shown what to do... I looked through advertisements of vacant posts for nursing sisters in the *Nursing Mirror*. There was one asking for sisters to go to work in India where (at the time) there was only one trained nurse for thousands of people. The longing returned to do medical missionary work. I knew again that evening it was the only thing I really wanted to do with my life.

The next morning I prepared to go to Chester on the bus and as I looked out from the window of my room I had what I can only describe as a 'Spiritual Experience'. In a split moment of time, suddenly away in the distant sky, there was a dark outline of India as on a map. Then instantaneously two strong arms came, embraced me and carried me strongly and swiftly to that India. Then with the sound of a click I was back into my shoes. In a fraction of a second I had been shown what to do. I was dazed. This was broad daylight. I had no idea that such things ever happened. I went for the bus and to Chester for the day as I often did on my off duty days. The one thing that stood out clearly was that I was directed to go to India. The experience was so humbling. I could scarcely think of what had happened without a feeling of emotion. Then I thought, when I tell my family what would their reaction be, but I wasn't ready to tell them yet and the spiritual experience was so personal and so very wonderful to me that I did not, or could not, speak of it.

Two days later I was again standing at my window thinking, 'Well I am to go to India. I must make no mistake, I must go with the church.' As I made this decision I was, as it were, filled to overflowing with a power that I had never before experienced. I had heard of the Holy Spirit and now I was myself experiencing it. I was filled with tremendous joy, difficult to describe. Such joy was coupled with deep humility. From then onwards I was able to tell people that I was applying to go to India as a medical missionary.

> May Bounds and Gladwys M. Evans, *Medical Mission to Mizoram*
> (Handbridge 1986), p. 8.

The riches of God
4.8

Once I was in the cell where I had enclosed myself for the Great Lent. I was enjoying and meditating on a certain saying in the gospel, a saying which I found of great value and extremely delightful. I had by my side a book, a missal, and I thirsted to see that saying again in writing. With great difficulty I contained myself and resisted opening this book in my hands, for I feared I might do so out of pride or out of too great a thirst and love. I became drowsy and fell asleep still in the throes of this desire. Immediately, I was led into a vision, and I was told that the understanding of the epistle is something so delightful that if one grasped it properly one would completely forget everything belonging to this world. And he who was leading me asked me: 'Do you want to have this experience?' As I agreed and ardently desired it, he immediately led me into this experience. From it I understood how sweet it is to experience the riches of God and I immediately and completely forgot the world. He who was leading me added that the understanding of the gospel is even more delightful, so much more so that if one understood it one would not only forget the world but even oneself, totally. He led me still further and enabled me to directly experience this. Immediately I understood what it is to experience the riches of God and derived such delight from it that I not only forgot the world but even myself. This state was so delightful and holy that I begged the one who was leading me not to let me ever leave it. He replied that what I was asking was still not possible; and he immediately led me back to myself. I opened my eyes and felt an immense joy from what I had seen, but also great sorrow at having lost it. Recalling this experience still gives me great pleasure. From then on, I was filled with such certitude, such light, and such ardent love of God that I went on to affirm, with the utmost certainty, that nothing of these delights of God is being preached. Preachers cannot preach it; they do not understand what they preach. He who was leading me into this vision told me so.

Angela of Foligno, *The Book of the Blessed Angela of Foligno (Memorial)*, ch. I, in *Angela of Foligno: Complete Works*, tr. Paul Lachance OFM (Paulist Press 1993), pp. 130–31.

The wise counsellor
A Meditation on 1 Kings 19:11–13
4.9

Persons come to the minister of God in seasons of despondency; they pervert with marvellous ingenuity all the consolation which is given them: turning wholesome food into poison. Then we begin to perceive the wisdom of God's simple homely treatment of Elijah, and discover that there are spiritual cases which are cases for the physician rather than the divine.

God calmed his stormy mind by the healing influences of nature. He commanded the hurricane to sweep the sky, and the earthquake to shake the ground. He lighted up the heavens till they were one mass of fire. All this expressed and reflected Elijah's feelings. The mode in which nature soothes us is by finding meeter and nobler utterance for our feelings than we can find in words – by expressing and exalting them. In expression there is relief. Elijah's spirit rose with the spirit of the storm. Stern wild defiance – strange joy – all by turns were imaged there. Observe, '*God* was not in the wind', nor in the fire, nor in the earthquake. It was Elijah's stormy self reflected in the moods of the tempest, and giving them their character.

Then came a calmer hour. Elijah rose in reverence – felt tenderer sensations in his bosom. He opened his heart to gentler influences, till at last out of the manifold voices of nature there seemed to speak, not the stormy passions of the man, but the 'still small voice' of the harmony and the peace of God.

Frederick W. Robertson, *Sermons on Bible Subjects* (J.M. Dent/E.P. Dutton 1906).

The light of hope
4.10

The world has in fact begun to crack. The moment of truth for humanity seems to have arrived. We seem destined for destruction at our own hands. But behold, miracle of miracles, out of the cracks a light shines. The venomous snake has not crushed the light. The light burns. It gives warmth. It gives hope. And as the dreamer timidly advances toward the light, he discovers that there are many, many others who are also moving toward it from different directions – from behind iron curtains, from across human barriers, from behind the walls of our own frightened souls. Yes, we all need that light, for that light is the only hope – we, the poor and the rich, the oppressed and the oppressors, the theists and the atheists, Christians, Muslims, Jews, Buddhists and Hindus. We all must get to that light, for it is the light of love and life, the light of hope and future. The movement of persons toward that light must have constituted a formidable power, for the snake, the demon, begins to loosen its grip on the globe. Its power is broken. Its threat is removed.

And so God moves on. God moves from the Tower of Babel to Pentecost, from Israel to Babylon. God moves in Europe, in Africa, in the Americas, in Asia. As God moves, God suffers with the people, sheds tears with them, hopes with them, and creates the communion of love here and there... Until the time when the communion of love is firmly established in the world of strife and conflict, of pain and suffering, God moves on in compassion. We have no alternative but to move on with God toward that vision of a community of compassion and communion of love.

Choan-Seng Song, *The Compassionate God: An Exercise in the Theology of Transposition* (SCM Press 1982), p. 260.

God's Greatness and Goodness

Loving God
4.11

I said in the beginning: the reason for our loving God *is* God. I spoke the truth, for he is both prime mover of our love and final end. He is himself our human love's occasion; he also gives the power to love, and brings desire to its consummation. He is himself the lovable in his essential being, and gives himself to be the object of our love. He wills our love for him to issue in our bliss, not to be void and vain. His love both opens up the way for ours and is our love's reward. How kindly does he lead us in love's way, how generously he returns the love we give, how sweet he is to those who wait for him! He is rich unto all that call upon him, for he can give them nothing better than himself. He gave himself to be our righteousness, and keeps himself to be our great reward. He sets himself to the refreshment of our souls, and spends himself to free the prisoners. Thou art good, Lord, to the soul that seeks thee, What, then, art thou to the soul that finds? The marvel is, no one can seek thee who has not found already. Thou willest us to find that we may seek, to seek that we may find. We can both seek and find thee, but we can never be before with thee. For though we say 'Early shall my prayer come before thee', a chilly, loveless thing that prayer would be, were it not warmed by thine own breath and born of thine own Spirit.

Bernard of Clairvaux, *On the Love of God*, tr. A Religious of CSMV
(A.R. Mowbray [1950] 1961), p. 38.

Life's greatest response
4.12

Adoration is the first and greatest of life's responses to its spiritual environment; the first and most fundamental of spirit's movements towards

Spirit, the seed from which all other prayer must spring. It is among the most powerful of the educative forces which purify the understanding, form and develop the spiritual life. As we can never know the secret of great art or music until we have learned to look and listen with a self-oblivious reverence, acknowledging a beauty that is beyond our grasp – so the claim and loveliness remain unrealized till we have learned to look, to listen, to adore. Then only do we go beyond ourselves and our small vision, pour ourselves out to that which we know not, and so escape from our own pettiness and limitations into the universal life.

Evelyn Underhill, *The Golden Sequence* (Methuen & Co. 1932), p. 162.

In love I find you
4.13

Only in love can I find you, my God. In love, the gates of my soul spring open, allowing me to breathe a new air of freedom and forget my own petty self. In love, my whole being streams forth out of the rigid confines of narrowness and anxious self-assertion, which make me a prisoner of my own poverty and emptiness. In love, all the powers of my soul flow out toward you, wanting never more to return but to lose themselves completely in you, since by your love you are the inmost centre of my heart, closer to me than I am to myself.

But when I love you, when I manage to break out of the narrow circle of self and leave behind the restless agony of unanswered questions, when my blinded eyes no longer look merely from afar and from the outside upon your unapproachable brightness, and much more when you yourself, O incomprehensible one, have become through love the inmost centre of my life, then I can bury myself entirely in you, O mysterious God, and with myself all my questions...

When I abandon myself in love, then you are my very life, and your incomprehensibility is swallowed up in love's unity. When I am allowed to love you, the grasp of your very mystery becomes a positive source of bliss. Then the farther your infinity is removed from my nothingness, the greater is the challenge to my love. The more complete the dependence of my fragile existence upon your unsearchable counsels, the more unconditional must be the surrender of my whole being to you, beloved God. The more annihilating the incomprehensibility of your ways and judgments, the greater must be the holy defiance of my love. And my love is all the greater and more blessed, the less my poor spirit understands of you.

111

God of my life, incomprehensible, be my life. God of my faith, who leads me into your darkness – God of my love, who turns your darkness into the sweet light of my life, be now the God of my hope, so that you will one day be the God of my life, the life of eternal love.

Karl Rahner, 'God of My Life' in *Encounters with Silence*,
tr. James M. Demske SJ (Newman 1966).

Preaching the gospel
4.14

I said to the officers of the church, 'There is a man coming from England and he wants to preach. I am going to be absent on Thursday and Friday. If you will let him preach on those days, I will be back on Saturday and take him off your hands.' They did not care about him preaching, being a stranger; but at my request they let him preach.

On my return on Saturday I was anxious to hear how the people liked him, and I asked my wife how that young Englishman got along. She said, 'They liked him very much. He preaches a little different from what you do. He tells people God loves them. I think you will like him.' I said he was wrong. I thought I could not like a man who preached contrary to what I was preaching. I went down Saturday night to hear him, but I had made up my mind not to like him. He took his text, and I saw everybody had brought their Bibles with them. 'Now', he says, 'if you will turn to the third chapter of John and the sixteenth verse, you will find my text.'

He preached a wonderful sermon from that text, 'For God so loved the world that he gave his only begotten Son, that whosoever believes in him should not perish, but have everlasting life.' My wife had told me he had preached the two previous sermons from that text, and I noticed there was a smile over the house when he took the same text. Instead of preaching that God was behind them with a double-edged sword to hew them down, he told them God wanted every sinner to be saved, and he loved them. I could not keep back the tears. I didn't know God thought so much of me. He went from Genesis to Revelation, and preached that in all ages God loved the sinner.

... I have never forgotten those nights. I have preached a different gospel since, and I have had more power with God and man from that time.

Dwight L. Moody, 'God is Love', *The Gospel Awakening*
(Chicago 1879).

The power that embraces the universe
4.15

Given that the Good transcends everything, as indeed it does, its nature, unconfined by form, is the creator of all form. In it is non-being really an excess of being. It is not *a* life, but is, rather, superabundant Life. It is not a mind, but is superabundant Wisdom. Whatever partakes of the Good partakes of what pre-eminently gives form to the formless. And one might even say that non-being itself longs for the Good which is above all being. Repelling being, it struggles to find rest in the Good which transcends all being, in the sense of a denial of all things.

In my concern for other matters I forgot to say that the Good is the cause even for the sources and the frontiers of the heavens, which neither shrink nor expand, and it brought into being the silent (if one must put it this way) and circular movements of the vast heavens…

And what of the sun's rays? Light comes from the Good, and light is an image of this archetypal Good. Thus the Good is also praised by the name 'Light', just as an archetype is revealed in its image. The goodness of the transcendent God reaches from the highest and most perfect forms of being to the very lowest. And yet it remains above and beyond them all, superior to the highest and yet stretching out to the lowliest. It gives light to everything capable of receiving it, it creates them, keeps them alive, preserves and perfects them. Everything looks to it for measure, eternity, number, order It is the power which embraces the universe. It is the cause of the universe and its end.

Dionysius the Areopagite, in *Pseudo-Dionysius: The Complete Works*
tr. C. Luibheid (Paulist Press 1987), pp. 73–74.

Who created all these?
4.16

We read in Isaiah 40:26, 27:

Lift your eyes and look to the heavens: who created all these? He who brings out the starry host one by one, and calls them each by name. Because of his great power and mighty strength, not one of them is missing. Why do you say, O Jacob, and complain, O Israel, 'My way is hidden from the Lord; my cause is disregarded by my God'?

The prophet places himself in the great cosmic movements in heaven and on earth, all in the same glory of God. And within these mighty outlines lie the little things too, even those concerning the smallest midge, the sparrows and the flowers. The same great power encompasses them all.

There is a great power always present; the sun runs its course; the earth, the stars, everything makes its mighty circuit. This mighty circuit must come into human hearts too, so that good will come just as surely as the sun and the rain.

The earth is so beautiful, the earth is so lovely and full of joy, every little midge rejoices, every tree rejoices. All things are arranged delightfully and beautifully by God so that we too can live and move among them in joy and graciousness. We are peculiar people, though; we would rather have melancholy, just as folk songs are mostly melancholic. We often think that our human misery is the only thing that should occupy God. But alongside our weak nature God's power is always present in creation. He is always the life-bringing, wonderful God who touches us also so that we have hope for our own life. Just as God goes up with a merry noise, you should arise too, O man, and let yourself be found strong in the God who has become your Father.

Christoph Friedrich Blumhardt, *Action in Waiting* (Plough Publishing House,
Hutterian Society of Brothers 1979), p. 250.

Trinity
4.17

The Fathers of the church saw an analogy of the image of God in three persons in the original nuclear family: Adam, Eve and Seth. In spite of all the problems and limitations of this analogy it allows some insights which may give us a better understanding of human relations. The human family as image of God, shows us that God is the mystery of love – and a fruitful love – and that God's trinitarian being is not closed in on itself but is fulfilled by surrendering itself and giving itself freely out of the richness of its immanent being. Moreover, if the woman, man, and child are images of God on earth, then eternal paternity, maternity, and infancy are revealed to us in the Triune God. Femininity and infancy, then, have an assured place in the divine mystery.

María Clara Bingemer, 'Reflections on the Trinity' in *Through Her Eyes:
Women's Theology from Latin America*, ed. Elsa Tamez
(Orbis Books 1989), p. 79.

Sin and grace
4.18

Grace strikes us when we are in great pain and restlessness. It strikes us when we walk through the dark valley of a meaningless and empty life. It strikes us when we feel that our separation is deeper than usual, because we have violated another life, a life which we loved, or from which we were estranged. It strikes us when our disgust for our own being, our indifference, our weakness, our hostility, and our lack of direction and composure have become intolerable to us. It strikes us when, year after year, the longed-for perfection of life does not appear, when the old compulsions reign within us as they have for decades, when despair destroys all joy and courage. Sometimes at that moment a wave of light breaks into our darkness, and it is as though a voice were saying:

> You are accepted. *You are accepted*, accepted by that which is greater than you, and the name of which you do not know. Do not ask for the name now; perhaps you will find it later. Do not try to do anything now; perhaps later you will do much. Do not seek for anything; do not perform anything; do not intend anything. *Simply accept the fact that you are accepted!*

If that happens to us, we experience grace. After such an experience we may not be better than before, and we may not believe more than before. But everything is transformed. In that moment, grace conquers sin, and reconciliation bridges the gulf of estrangement. And nothing is demanded of this experience, no religious or moral or intellectual proposition, nothing but *acceptance*.

And in the light of this grace we perceive the power of grace in our relation to ourselves. We experience moments in which we accept ourselves, because we feel that we have been accepted by that which is greater than we. If only more such moments were given to us! For it is such moments that make us love our life, that make us accept ourselves, not in our goodness and self-complacency, but in our certainty of the eternal meaning of our life. We cannot force ourselves to accept ourselves. We cannot compel anyone to accept themselves. But sometimes it happens that we receive the power to say 'yes' to ourselves, that peace enters into us and makes us whole, that self-hate and self-contempt disappear, and that our self is reunited with itself. Then we can say that grace has come upon us.

'Sin' and 'grace' are strange words; but they are not strange things. We find them whenever we look into ourselves with searching eyes and longing hearts. They determine our life. They abound within us and in all of life. May grace more abound within us!

Paul Tillich, *The Shaking of the Foundations* (SCM Press 1957), pp. 161–63.

Judgment is God's
4.19

I claim… that the only 'just' appraisal, the only 'judgment' which can take all the facts into account, is God's. And only he can make a 'final' judgment. His appraisal will be accurate, while at the same time it will be merciful. In stating it in this way, I am trying to indicate what seems to me the insight in the traditional view that God is just, not in the human sense of meting out, distributively or retributively, the proper rewards or punishments according to some prior set of laws or regulations, but in the divine sense… of complete understanding. Further, I am trying to indicate, by the word 'mercy', that God's appraisal is more than accurate, in terms of complete understanding; it is also characterized by God's *chesed*, his 'loving-kindness', his never-failing mercy, which always makes the best out of every situation and finds the best in every person. In saying this about 'the best', I do not intend the idea that this is read into the situation or the person. On the contrary, I suggest that precisely because God does know all desires, the secrets of human hearts and the depths of each situation, he also knows there the 'initial aim' which in the first instance he gave, the entire condition of things which was there present, the possibilities which were offered, the efforts that were made, the failures that were experienced, and *everything else*. Knowing that, God's appraisal is 'charitable' appraisal in the true sense of that word – that is, it is *really* loving and thus can both see the best that is there and be prepared to use that best in the augmenting of good in the creative advance which is the cosmic process.

Norman Pittenger, *'The Last Things' in a Process Perspective*
(Epworth Press 1970), pp. 53–54.

God and the church
4.20

It simply is not true that there is anywhere a church which is guaranteed to get it right under God. As there are no knock-down miracles which prove to everybody that God is around, so there is no church with knock-down authority which can settle decisively and definitely for ever what God is like and what God wants. To claim this, or to behave as if this were so, is to present an impossible and unworthy picture of God. For if it were the case that there exists a church which is bound to be right when it speaks for God, speaks of God, or acts for God, then we should all be bound to be atheists. For the records of all churches contain acts of inhumanity, declarations of stupidity and indications of triumphalism, arrogance and insensitivity which are a disgrace to God – or, indeed, to ordinary humanity. It is surely quite clear that it is practically and morally impossible to believe in an ecclesiastical God or a God of the church. God must be far more than, and at times very distanced from, the church or all churches. We worship God, not the church in any shape or form. That was one of the most fundamental reassertions of Protestantism and of the Reformation, and it has to be reasserted again and again. This sort of Protestantism is an essential part of catholic and apostolic faith and practice. Within, under and through this worship of God we thankfully accept that there is a church of God, which he calls, judges, changes and sustains and, above all, mercifully and graciously uses. There is a church of God but there is no God of the church. He is the God of the whole earth and mystery of all things. We belong to him, but he does not belong to us. He identifies himself with us and saves us, but he is sovereign, free, glorious and mysterious.

David E. Jenkins, *God, Miracle and the Church of England*
(SCM Press 1987), p. 7.

God as mother
4.21

If we are God's children it might be helpful to imagine ourselves sometimes as in her womb. There could not be a closer image of warmth, security and protection. There we have all our needs provided for in perfect measure, as the baby receives oxygen and nourishment without deficiency or excess through the umbilical cord. In God's womb we can stretch and turn in every direction, just as the baby, suspended in water, is as happy upside down as the right way up, and in the early months can exercise its limbs freely. Wherever God our mother takes us we will be safe and provided for; whether in cold or heat, storm or drought, we will be protected. Wherever we journey to we will still be at home, for the presence of our mother's body is closer to us than our geographical location. God is closer to us than the ground we stand on. Even though we have never seen our mother, perhaps are quite unaware of her, or even deny her existence, she is in perfect and constant intimacy with us, and when we are born into the light of her presence we will recognize that she has been with us all along.

Margaret Hebblethwaite, *Motherhood and God*
(Geoffrey Chapman 1984), p. 21.

God our mother
4.22

It should be known, then, that God nurtures and caresses the soul, after it has been resolutely converted to his service, like a loving mother who warms her child with the heat of her bosom, nurses it with good milk and tender food, and carries and caresses it in her arms. But as the child grows older, the mother withholds her caresses and hides her tender love; she rubs bitter aloes on her sweet breast and sets the child down from her arms, letting it walk on its own feet so that it may put aside the habits of childhood and grow accustomed to greater and more important things. The grace of God acts just as a loving mother by re-engendering in the soul new enthusiasm and fervour in the service of God. With no effort on the soul's part, this grace causes it to taste sweet and delectable milk and to experience intense satisfaction in the performance of spiritual exercises, because God is handing the breast of his tender love to the soul, just as if it were a delicate child.

John of the Cross, *The Dark Night* 1.2, tr. K. Kavanaugh and O. Rodriguez in
The Collected Works of St John of the Cross (ICS Publications 1979), p. 298.

God draws us to his love
4.23

Comparison of the love little children have for their mothers should not be rejected because of its pure, innocent character. Consider, then, a beautiful little child to whom the seated mother offers her breast. It throws itself forcibly into her arms and gathers up and entwines all its little body on that beloved bosom and breast. See how its mother in turn takes it in, clasps it, fastens it so to speak to her bosom, joins her mouth to its mouth and kisses it. Watch again how that little babe is allured by its mother's caresses, and how on its part it co-operates in this union of its mother and itself. As much as it possibly can, it fastens and presses itself to its mother's breast and face. It seems as if it wants to bury and hide itself completely in the beloved bosom from which it came. At such a moment there is a perfect union; it is but a single union, yet it proceeds from both mother and child, although in such wise that it depends entirely on the mother. She drew the child to herself. She first clasped it in her arms and pressed it to her bosom. The child's strength was never sufficient to clasp and hold itself so close to its mother. Yet on its own part the poor little one does as much as it can and joins itself with all its strength to its mother's bosom. It not only consents to the sweet union its mother makes but with all its heart contributes its own feeble efforts. I call them feeble efforts because they are so weak that they resemble attempts at union rather than actual union.

Thus, too, our Lord shows the most loving breast of his divine love to a devout soul, draws it wholly to himself, gathers it in and, as it were, enfolds all its powers within the bosom of his more than motherly comfort.

Francis de Sales, *Treatise on the Love of God*, vol. II, tr. John K. Ryan (Tan Books 1975).

'Trinity, whom I adore'
4.24

O my God, Trinity, whom I adore, help me to forget myself entirely that I may be established in you as still and as peaceful as if my soul were already in eternity. May nothing trouble my peace or make me leave you, O my unchanging one, but may each minute carry me further into the depths of your mystery. Give peace to my soul; make it your heaven, your beloved dwelling and your resting place. May I never leave you there alone but be wholly present, my faith wholly vigilant, wholly adoring and wholly surrendered to your creative action.

O my beloved Christ, crucified by love, I wish to be a bride for your heart; I wish to cover you with glory; I wish to love you... even unto death! But I feel my weakness, and I ask you to 'clothe me with yourself', to identify my soul with all the movements of your soul, to overwhelm me, to possess me, to substitute yourself for me that my life may be but a radiance of your life. Come into me as adorer, as restorer, as saviour. O eternal Word, Word of my God, I want to spend my life in listening to you, to become wholly teachable that I may learn all from you. Then, through all nights, all voids, all helplessness, I want to gaze on you always and remain in your great light. O my beloved star, so fascinate me that I may not withdraw from your radiance.

O consuming fire, Spirit of love, 'come upon me', and create in my soul a kind of incarnation of the Word: that I may be another humanity for him in which he can renew his whole mystery. And you, O Father, bend lovingly over your poor little creature; 'cover her with your shadow', seeing in her only the 'beloved in whom you are well pleased'.

O my three, my all, my beatitude, infinite solitude, immensity in which I lose myself, I surrender to you as your prey. Bury yourself in me that I may bury myself in you until I depart to contemplate in your light the abyss of your greatness.

Elizabeth of the Trinity: Complete Works, vol. 1, tr. Sister Aletheia Kane OCD
(Institute of Carmelite Studies 1984), pp. 183–84.

Recognition
4.25

He knows what we want before we ask it. Then why ask? Why, because there may be blessings which only are effectively blessings to those who are in the right condition of mind; just as there is wholesome food which is actually wholesome only to those who are healthy in body. If you give the best beef to somebody in typhoid fever, you do him great harm. The worst of the diseases of the soul is forgetfulness of God; and if everything that we need came to us while we forgot God, we should only be confirmed in our forgetfulness of him, in our sense of independence of him… Over and over again, it will happen that, whether or not God can give the blessing which, in his love, he desires to give, will depend on whether or not we recognize the source from which it comes. The way to recognize that he is the source of the blessings, and that we need them, is to ask.

William Temple, *Christian Faith and Life* (SCM Press 1931), p. 111.

Singing to the Lord
4.26

Sing to him a new canticle. Have done with the old: you now know the new canticle. The new man, the New Testament, the new canticle. The new canticle does not belong to the old man; none but the new man can learn it, the man who, having once belonged to the Old, is born again by grace and henceforth belongs to the New Testament, which is the kingdom of heaven. Our whole longing yearns after it, singing the new canticle. Let our life, not our tongue, chant this new song. *Sing to him a new canticle. Sing well unto him.* Each one will ask how to sing to God. Sing to him but do not sing out of tune. He does not like his ears wounded. Sing well, brother. Suppose some fine musician is among your audience and you are told: 'Sing, to please him'; you feel terrified to sing, being untrained in the art of music, for you may grate upon the artist, because the expert will censure the flaws which pass unnoticed by the unqualified. Well then, who can offer to sing well before a God who is such a judge of the singer, such a critic of every part, such a keen listener? When will you bring the art of singing to such a pitch as not to jar in the slightest upon such perfect hearing? Lo and behold, he sets the tune for you himself, so to say; do not look for words, as if you could put into words the things that please God. Sing *in jubilation*: singing well to God means, in fact, just this: singing in jubilation. What does singing in jubilation signify? It is to realize that words cannot communicate the song of the heart. Just so singers in the harvest, or the vineyard, or at some other arduous toil express their rapture to begin with in songs set to words; then as if bursting with a joy so full that they cannot give vent to it in set syllables, they drop actual words and break into the free melody of pure jubilation. The *jubilus* is a melody which conveys that the heart is in travail over something it cannot bring forth in words. And to whom does that jubilation rightly ascend, if not to God the ineffable? Truly is he ineffable whom you cannot tell forth in speech; and if you cannot tell him forth in speech, yet ought not to remain silent, what else can you do but jubilate? In this way the heart rejoices without words and the boundless expanse of rapture is not circumscribed by syllables. *Sing well unto him in jubilation.*

Augustine of Hippo, 'Second discourse on Psalm 32', 8 [V.3], *St Augustine on the Psalms: Psalms 30–37*, tr. and ed. Scholastica Hegbin and Felicitas Corrigan (Newman Press/Longmans, Green and Co 1961), pp. 111–12.

The greatest thing
4.27

Love is the greatest thing that God can give us; for himself is love: and it is the greatest thing we can give to God; for it will also give ourselves, and carry with it all that is ours. The apostle calls it the bond of perfection: it is the old, and it is the new, and it is the great commandment, and it is all the commandments; for it is the fulfilling of the law. It does the work of all other graces without any instrument but its own immediate virtue. For, as the love to sin makes a person sin against all their own reason, and all the discourses of wisdom, and all the advices of their friends, and without temptation, and without opportunity, so does the love of God; it makes a person chaste without the laborious arts of fasting and exterior disciplines, temperate in the midst of feasts, and is active enough to choose it without any intermedial appetites, and reaches at glory through the very heart of grace, without any other arms but those of love. It is a grace that loves God for himself, and our neighbours for God. The consideration of God's goodness and bounty, the experience of those profitable and excellent emanations from him, may be, and most commonly are, the first motive of our love; but when we are once entered, and have tasted the goodness of God, we love the spring for its own excellency, passing from passion to reason, from thanking to adoring, from sense to spirit, from considering ourselves to an union with God: and this is the image and little representation of heaven; it is beatitude in picture, or rather the infancy and beginnings of glory.

Jeremy Taylor, 'Of Charity, or the Love of God', *Holy Living*, ch. 4, section 3 (1650).

God's Love Revealed in Christ

Christmas
4.28

Comfort is here; help has come down from heaven. 'The kindness and humanity of God our Saviour hath appeared.'

The kindness was always there, for the Lord's mercy is from everlasting; but it was hidden till the humanity appeared. Before that, it was promised, but it was not felt; and many for that reason disbelieved in it. But lo, peace is no longer promised now, but sent; it is no longer prophesied, it is presented to us. God the Father has sent to earth a sackful of his mercy, as it were; a sack that in the passion must be rent, so that the price of our redemption may pour out of it. Only a little sack it is, but it is full. To us a child is given indeed, but in him dwells the fullness of the Godhead. For when the fullness of the time was come, the fullness of the Godhead came also. He came in flesh, to show himself to people living in the flesh; and his humanity appeared that we might know his kindness. For how could he commend his kindness to me better than by taking my flesh – my flesh, not such as Adam had before he fell? What could so mightily declare his mercy as this assumption of our misery? And the smaller he made himself, so much the kinder did he show himself; the smaller, too, that he is made for me, so much the dearer is he.

Bernard of Clairvaux, in *In Epiphania Domini*, I, tr. A Religious of CSMV, in
St Bernard on the Christian Year (A.R. Mowbray 1954), pp. 37–38.

Where Christ was born
4.29

A North American priest visited a displaced persons' refuge in San Salvador in 1981 and wrote the following reflection.

This year I celebrated Christmas mass with more than 200 displaced people living in the basement of a church in San Salvador.

These people cannot leave the church. Many have been here for a year and a half. During this time they have not seen the sunlight or taken a breath of fresh air. They have organized themselves into groups to cook, clean, take care of the children and stand watch. Nine children have been born here and the community is now expecting four more.

Over the table that served us as our altar the people hung a large newspaper photograph of Archbishop Romero. Even in death Romero continues to be present to the people. 'Monsignor visited our village,' they told me. 'He was one of us. His memory is our most treasured possession.'

Next to the photograph of Archbishop Romero was a faded image of the Sacred Heart of Jesus. Both images served as silent acolytes during our Eucharistic celebration. People offered petitions and thanks and prayed for their dead. They prayed for their children and relatives, and for the nuns who share their lives with them. They also thanked God for many things, especially for life.

It was evident from their prayers that they find encouragement and hope in their belief that Jesus loves them. They believe in Jesus the liberator and saviour.

As I shared the Christmas celebration with these displaced people, it was easy to imagine Jesus being born in a church basement like this one, amidst the smell of *tamales* and the strumming of two old guitars. Here, Jesus would have been at home.

> *El Salvador: A Spring Whose Waters Never Run Dry*, ed. Scott Wright, Minor Sinclair,
> Margaret Lyle and David Scott (Ecumenical Program on Central America and the
> Caribbean (EPICA) 1990), p. 50.

What do I owe him?

4.30

See, Christian soul, here is the strength of your salvation, here is the cause of your freedom, here is the price of your redemption. You were a bond-slave and by this man you are free. By him you are brought back from exile, lost, you are restored, dead, you are raised. Chew this, bite it, suck it, let your heart swallow it, when your mouth receives the body and blood of your redeemer. Make it in this life your daily bread, your food, your way-bread, for through this and not otherwise than through this will you remain in Christ and Christ in you, and your joy will be full...

Now... think of what you owe your Saviour. Consider what he was to you, what he did for you, and think that for what he did for you he is the more worthy to be loved. Look into your need and his goodness, and see what thanks you should render him, and how much love you owe him. You were in darkness, on uncertain ground, descending into the chaos of hell that is beyond redemption... Remember and tremble; think and be afraid.

Consider, O my soul, and hear, all that is within me, how much my whole being owes to him! Lord, because you have made me, I owe you the whole of my love; because you have redeemed me, I owe you the whole of myself; because you have promised so much, I owe you all my being.

Anselm of Canterbury, 'Meditation on Human Redemption', tr. Benedicta Ward in
The Prayers and Meditations of St Anselm (Penguin 1973), pp. 234–36.

'See how I loved thee!'
4.31

Then with a glad cheer our Lord looked unto his side and beheld, rejoicing. With his sweet looking he led forth the understanding of his creature by the same wound into his side within. And then he showed a fair, delectable place, and large enough for all mankind that shall be saved to rest in peace and in love. And therewith he brought to mind his dearworthy blood and precious water which he let pour all out for love. And with the sweet beholding he showed his blessed heart even cloven in two.

And with this sweet enjoying, he showed unto mine understanding, in part, the blessed Godhead, stirring then the poor soul to understand, as it may be said, that is, to think on, the endless love that was without beginning, and is, and shall be ever. And with this our good Lord said full blissfully: Lo, how that I loved thee, as if he had said: My darling, behold and see thy Lord, thy God that is thy maker and thine endless joy, see what satisfying and bliss I have in thy salvation; and for my love rejoice with me.

And also, for more understanding, this blessed word was said: Lo, how I loved thee! Behold and see that I loved thee so much ere I died for thee that I would die for thee; and now I have died for thee and suffered willingly that which I may. And now is all my bitter pain and all my hard travail turned to endless joy and bliss to me and to thee. How should it now be that thou shouldst pray that pleaseth me but that I should full gladly grant it thee? For my pleasing is thy holiness and thine endless joy and bliss with me.

This is the understanding, simply as I can say it, of this blessed word: Lo, how I loved thee. This shewed our good Lord for to make us glad and merry.

Julian of Norwich, *Revelations of Divine Love* (tenth revelation),
ed. Grace Warrack (Methuen n.d.), p. 51.

Breakthrough
4.32

The incarnation is a happening both unique and ordinary. It is so complete and absolute of its kind that it has no parallels, no precedents, no successors, but the flesh-taking of God as Jesus is a unique example of the kind of ordinary event I want to call 'breakthrough'. An impulse – of need, of love, of will-to-power – manages to overcome some obstacle and pass through to a new and desired sphere of experience. This can be a small personal event, such as the achievement of a shared understanding. It can be a physical event, such as the breaking of a dam, when the 'need' of the water to find a way forward breaks the barriers and crashes through to the valley below. It can be a mystical experience or a scientific discovery. It can be a chicken breaking its shell or the signing of a peace treaty.

Even this random collection of examples shows that 'breakthrough' is a category of events which makes nonsense of the division of reality as such – physical, psychological and spiritual reality; and even to use those words introduces a misleading separation, yet a necessary one, since we cannot talk about the oneness of experience unless we can also talk about the fact that we experience reality in ways that can only be described by developing such distinctions. But it shows us that we also need a language about reality which will make it easier not to be handicapped by the separation of these categories. And in attempting to realize the meaning of the Flesh-taking it is essential to transcend those categories if we are to realize it as the manifestation not just of God but of the nature of reality, at its peak. Incarnation is breakthrough, and it involves every level of reality from the most basic particles to the ultimate Being of God.

Rosemary Haughton, *The Passionate God* (Darton, Longman & Todd 1982), p. 18.

Jesus the book of life
4.33

What do I think I am doing, my dear daughter, writing you these little letters of mine to give comfort to your heart, when you can derive much better and more enjoyable comfort from taking and reading that book of life, that scroll of the perfect law which converts our souls, which you have daily before your mind's eye? That law which is perfect, because it takes away all imperfections, is charity, and you find it written with strange beauty when you gaze at Jesus your Saviour stretched out like a sheet of parchment on the cross, inscribed with wounds, illustrated in his own loving blood. Where else, I ask you, my dearest, is there a comparable book of love to read from? You know better than

I do, that no letter could inspire love more passionately. So fix your mind's attention there. Hide in the clefts of this rock, hide yourself away from the clamour of those who speak wickedness. Turn this book over, open it, read it; you will find in it what the prophet found: lamentations, song and woe. Lamentations, because of the pains which he endured; a song of gladness, which he won for you by his pains; and the woe of unending death, from which he redeemed you by his death. In his lamentations, learn to have patience in yourself, learn love in his song of joy, because surely he has the first claim on your love, seeing that he wanted you to be a sharer in such great joys. And when you realize that you have been rescued from that woe, what else should result but thanksgiving and the sound of praise?

Jordan of Saxony OP, Letter 14 to Sister Diana (1229), *Early Dominicans: Selected Writings*, ed. Simon Tugwell OP (Paulist Press 1982), p. 405.

Descent and ascent
4.34

God descends to re-ascend. He comes down from the heights of absolute being into time and space, down into humanity, down further still – if embryologists are right – to recapitulate in the womb ancient and prehuman phases of life. Down into the very roots and sea-bed of the nature he created. But he goes down to come up again and then brings the whole ruined world up with him...

One may think of a diver, first reducing himself to nakedness, then glancing in mid-air, then gone with a splash, vanished, rushing down into green, warm water, into bleak and cold water, down into increasing pressure, into the depth of ooze and slime and old decay. Then up again, back into colour and light. His lungs almost bursting till suddenly he breaks surface, holding in his hand the dripping, precious thing he went to recover. He and it are both coloured now, but they have come back into the light. Down below, where it lay colourless in the dark, he lost his colour, too.

C.S. Lewis, *Miracles* (Geoffrey Bles 1947), p. 135.

Nature's picture of God
4.35

I know it is hard to see in nature what God is; its many voices seem to contradict one another. Its tenderness and cruelty, its order and its chaos, its beauty and its ugliness, make discords in its song and mar the music of its message to the soul of man. There is much truth in the charge that nature is red in tooth and claw. It is hard to see God in a cobra or a shark...

That is the picture of God that nature gives when you look square in her face and refuse to blind yourself either to her failure or her success. God was forced to limit himself when he undertook the task of material creation. He had to bind himself with chains and pierce himself with nails, and take upon himself the travail pangs of creation. The universe was made as it was because it is the only way it could be made, and this way lays upon God the burden of many failures and of eternal strain – the sorrow of God the Father which Christ revealed...

When in nature one sees God suffering and striving as a creative Father Spirit, and when one sees how much that his sorrow has produced is quite perfect, like this red dawn and that white bird upon the wing, the rose that blooms at the cottage door, and the glory of sweet spring days, and the eyes of my dog, and the neck of my horse, and a million other perfect things – and when one sees all this as the fruit not only of God's power, but also of God's pain, then the love of nature's God begins to grow up in one's soul. One remembers the great words, 'He that has seen me has seen the Father', and there comes a burst of light, and one sees nature in Christ and Christ in nature. One sees in Christ the revelation of suffering, striving, tortured, but triumphant love that nature itself would lead us to expect... I have no fear of nature's horror chambers; they are just God's cross, and I know that the cross is followed by an empty tomb and victory.

G.A. Studdert Kennedy, *The Hardest Part* (G.H. Dovan 1918).

No joke
4.36

It is true that Jesus said greatly comforting things to women. He called a girl of twelve 'little darling', according to our new commentators, when he took her small hand and drew her back from death. He speaks to and of mothers and widows. He made no jokes about a mother-in-law, but raised one from her fever, and she ministered in the way that the mothers-in-law I know minister, even when dwelling in 'other people's houses'. I am not sure that the most beautiful story in the whole testament is not that of the old woman, bowed these eighteen years in spirit and body, with no beauty surely on her face, and probably neither rich nor clever; yet one who had come to the place where she could meet with God. He had to 'call' her, for she would not think that a young man of three-and-thirty could seek out herself. But she was in need; and that was sufficient for the good shepherd.

The courtesy of Christ to women goes far deeper than race or appearance; and with that he has raised the nature of his fellow men. Indeed, when I have heard good men tell an audience of women that they ought to be 'grateful' to Jesus, for he has 'raised the status of woman', I shrink, surprised by their blindness. It is just a century since slavery was abolished in the British empire. Would we wish for our own sakes to go back to it, even if we could? Do we not pray to be delivered from the burden of knowing that some of our labour here is still semi-slavery? When we freed slaves, we ourselves were freed just as much as they.

Dorothy Hosie, 'Christ and Women' in *Women in the Pulpit*,
ed. D.P. Thompson (James Clark n.d.).

'I, if I am lifted up...'
A Meditation on John 17
4.37

The relation between Christ and his followers is always, in this gospel [of John], grounded in the archetypal relation in which he stands to the Father. If therefore the washing of the feet, with the intimate converse of Christ with his friends which flows out of it, in some sort represents dramatically the union of human beings with the eternal Son, we still need something which will represent the archetypal union of the Son with the Father; and this is supplied in the only way in which such union can be truthfully represented in human terms. The prayer in some sort *is* the ascent of the Son to the Father. Let us recall its key phrases:

Father, glorify your son...
Glorify me in your own presence...
I am coming to you...
I consecrate myself...
You, Father, are in me and I in you...

and finally the emphatic and pregnant

I have known you.

In such words we apprehend the spiritual and ethical reality of that going or lifting up of the Son of man which is hereafter to be enacted in historical actuality on the cross. This is what is ultimately meant by the words, 'I am going to the Father... that where I am you may be also.' Christ's 'journeying' to the Father is neither a physical movement in space, such as a bodily ascension to heaven, nor is it the physical act of dying. It is that spiritual ascent to God which is the inward reality of all true prayer. And this ascent in prayer carries with it all those who are included in the intercession which is, again, inseparable from all true prayer. In thus praying, Christ both accomplishes the self-oblation of which his death is the historical expression, and 'draws' all people after him into the sphere of eternal life which is union with God: first, the faithful group of his personal disciples, and then all who are to believe in him to the end of time.

C.H. Dodd, *The Interpretation of the Fourth Gospel*
(Cambridge University Press 1960), pp. 419–20.

Words are power
4.38

In Hebrew the term *dabar* means both 'word' and 'deed'. Thus to say something is to do something. 'I love you.' 'I hate you.' 'I forgive you.' 'I am afraid.' Who knows what such words do, but whatever it is, it can never be undone. Something that lay hidden in the heart is irrevocably released through speech into me, is given substance and tossed like a stone into the pool of history, where the concentric rings lap out endlessly.

Words are power, essentially the power of creation. By my words I elicit a word from you. Through our conversation we create one another...

God never seems to weary of trying to get himself across. Word after word he tries in search of the right word. When the creation itself doesn't seem to say it right – sun moon, stars, all of it – he tries flesh and blood... Jesus as the *mot juste* of God.

Frederick Buechner, *Wishful Thinking* (Collins 1973), pp. 96–97.

The crucified is God's chosen
4.39

What I have said so far suggests a provisional definition of the primary stage in preaching the resurrection as an invitation to *recognize one's victim as one's hope*. The crucified is God's chosen: it is with the victim, the condemned, that God identifies, and it is in the company of the victim, so to speak, that God is to be found, and nowhere else. And this is not simply to say, in the fashionable phrase, that God makes his own the cause of the poor and despised. We are not talking of 'the' poor and despised, 'the' victim in the abstract. The preaching of the resurrection, as we have seen, is not addressed to an abstract audience: the victim involved is the victim of the hearers. We are, insistently and relentlessly, in Jerusalem, confronted therefore with a victim who is *our* victim. When we make victims, when we embark on condemnation, exclusion, violence, the diminution or oppression of anyone, when we set ourselves up as judges, we are exposed to judgment (as Jesus himself asserts in Matthew 7:1–2), and we turn away from salvation. To hear the good news of salvation, to be converted, is to turn back to the condemned and rejected, acknowledging that there is hope nowhere else.

Rowan Williams, *Resurrection* (Darton, Longman & Todd 1982), pp. 11–12.

Seeing and hearing
4.40

Jesus challenged us to look at the ordinary things of earthly reality and to discern their depth-dimensions which point to God's reality.

In the Bible the relationship between hearing and seeing, between the word and the image, is a complex one. No one can see God and live. Yet at times this elusive God yields to the human desire to see the divine. There are theophanies, manifestations of God's presence and glory. When Moses insisted on knowing God's design and seeing God's face, he had to be content with the assurance that God knew him. Only from a protected cleft in the rock could he see God's back (Exodus 33:1–23). While there is no direct seeing of God, some visible signs of God's presence are given. The second of the ten commandments (Exodus 20:4ff) is not a prohibition of art and artifacts, as Jews and Christians have often thought. Exodus 35:30ff and the many artistic designs and objects in the temple of Jerusalem show that what is prohibited is idolatry, not art.

In the New Testament the same complex relation between seeing and hearing appears. When Thomas wanted to see the risen Lord, he was told: 'Blessed are those who have not seen and yet have come to believe' (John 20:29). 'Faith comes from what is heard, and what is heard comes through the word of Christ' (Romans 10:17). These and similar texts give hearing precedence over seeing. Yet in Jesus the distorted image of God has been restored and can be seen by those who have eyes of faith. 'We have seen his glory', testifies John (John 1:14; cf. 1 John 1:1); and Paul defends his apostleship with the exclamation: 'Have I not seen Jesus our Lord?' (1 Corinthians 9:1). Jesus himself affirmed: 'Whoever has seen me has seen the Father' (John 14:9). Nevertheless, such seeing of God in the earthly Jesus is only for those who can recognize God's glory in the humiliation of Jesus on the cross. Once, three disciples saw the glory of Jesus on the mountain of transfiguration, but even on that occasion the accent was put more on hearing than on seeing: 'Listen to him!' the divine voice commanded (Mark 9:7). Seeing is always only an anticipation of what is to come. When there is a new heaven and a new earth, then God's servants will 'see his face' (Revelation 22:4).

Hans-Rudi Weber, *The Book That Reads Me: A Handbook for Bible Study Enablers* (WCC 1995), pp. 37–38.

The good news
4.41

Evangelion (that we call the gospel) is a Greek word; and signifieth good, merry, glad and joyful tidings, that maketh a man's heart glad, and maketh him sing, dance and leap for joy: as when David had killed Goliath the giant, came glad tidings unto the Jews, that their fearful and cruel enemy was slain, and they delivered out of all danger: for gladness whereof, they sung, danced, and were joyful. In like manner is the Evangelion of God (which we call gospel, and the New Testament joyful tidings; and as some say, a good hearing) published by the apostles throughout all the world, of Christ the right David; how that he hath fought with sin, with death and the devil, and overcome them: whereby all men that were in bondage to sin, wounded with death, overcome of the devil, are, without their own merits or deservings, loosed, justified, restored to life and saved, brought to liberty and reconciled unto the favour of God, and set at one with him again: which tidings as many as believe laud, praise and thank God, are glad, sing and dance for joy.

This Evangelion or gospel (that is to say, such joyful tidings) is called the New Testament; because that as a man, when he shall die, appointeth his goods to be dealt and distributed after his death among them which he nameth to be his heirs; even so Christ before his death commanded and appointed that such Evangelion, gospel, or tidings should be declared throughout all the world, and therewith to give unto all that repent, and believe, all his goods: that is to say, his life, wherewith he swallowed and devoured up death; his righteousness, wherewith he banished sin; his salvation, wherewith he overcame eternal damnation. Now can the wretched man (that knoweth himself to be wrapped in sin, and in danger to death and hell) hear no more joyous a thing, than such glad and comfortable tidings of

Christ; so that he cannot but be glad, and laugh from the low bottom of his heart, if he believe that the tidings are true.

William Tyndale, 'A Pathway into the Holy Scripture' (c. 1525) in *The Work of William Tyndale*, ed. G.E. Duffield (Sutton Courtenay Press 1964), pp. 4–5.

Only the sick need a doctor
4.42

There is nothing that might be called otherworldly about the ministry of Jesus. He scandalized the religious leaders of his day, the prim and proper ones, because he consorted with the social and religious pariahs of his day. The religious establishment saw him as a young upstart who had no religious training, who had not sat at the feet of any renowned rabbi. What was more, he came to turn upside down everything they knew. He came sowing all kinds of confusion. He had dared to have dinner with Zaccheus, a tax collector, a collaborator with the Roman oppressor, and had had the temerity to call him the son of Abraham. He had invited another tax collector, Levi, to become one of his special followers. He had gone to dinner in his house, and there, quite horribly, incredibly, he had sat at the table with all the riff-raff of the town, those whom every respectable person would not be seen dead with, let alone supping with them – those prostitutes, those sinners, those drug addicts, the so-called scum of society. Moreover, when the establishment men, the Pharisees and the Sadducees, those who knew everything about God and religion, when they challenged him, he was not in the least embarrassed. No, he said: 'Only the sick need a doctor, not those who are well.' He said he had come to find those who were lost. He even said, quite unbelievably, that these prostitutes, these sinners, would precede the religious teachers and leaders into heaven. Jesus revolutionized religion by showing that God was really a disreputable God, a God on the side of the social pariahs. He showed God as one who accepted us sinners unconditionally.

Desmond Tutu, *Crying in the Wilderness*, ed. John Webster (Mowbray 1990), pp. 3–4.

Christ died for me
4.43

How seriously do I believe that Christ died for me? For *me*. How has the consciousness of this revelation formed my life?

Is the thought always before me as a guiding principle? Clearly it should be if I regard myself as a Christian. Of course, I claim to believe this, but if I really do, can it be said that the way I lead my daily life reflects this awareness? That Christ died for me gives me tremendous worth.

I am, as it is, infinitely valuable; I have been redeemed by an infinite sacrifice. Do I see myself as someone of consequence? I should, since, for me, God sent the only begotten Son. Well, if I am, in such a sense, the centre of a universe, am I acting in a fit manner? We might be aware that petty behaviour is *not* what is called for. Rather, action befitting one for whom Christ died. For example, should a person who so received the attentions from God the creator be a gossip? Or a chronic complainer? Am I particularly quick and eager to blame others when the chance arises? Do I really believe in the dignity of my own life? Goethe wrote that good manners have their basis in heaven. Are my manners reflective of this? There is a tremendous responsibility put on me as one who has 'benefited' from the crucifixion. How have I accepted this? By cheating a little in business deals? By admiring athletes who break the rules and don't get caught? By encouraging others to hedge on certain regulations? Do I use language befitting one for whom Christ died? Am I anxious to make snap judgments about other persons? Do I, in fact, reflect enough on what it means that Jesus made me the great gift of himself? That has got to be a humbling thought when realized. Yet it is possible that most who call themselves followers of Christ fail to fully deal with this concept. If we did, most of us would change our lives radically. What does it really mean in my life? Christ died for *me*?

Harry James Cargas, *Encountering Myself* (SPCK 1978), p. 6.

Being childlike
4.44

Behold the Word made flesh, the all-powerful promise of the Father – a helpless babe capable of making only childish cries! And I pride myself on being wise; satisfied that I have a superior mind, I doubt that the world's opinion of my capacities is sufficiently high! No, all that must change. I will be numbered among those happy children who lose all to win all: they no longer care for anything in the world for themselves, and they are indifferent when others scorn them or refuse to rely on their judgment.

Let the world take pride in greatness; let even those with high ideals and zealous in good works increase daily in discretion and decorum and other noteworthy virtues; as for me, my happiness will be in decreasing: silently self will diminish and disappear in lowliness as I quietly accept whatever disapproval and disdain God wills for me – the shame of Jesus crucified united with the helplessness of Jesus the little child.

We would rather die distressfully with him than be bound in swaddling clothes with him in the manger. We dread lowliness more than death, for death can be nobly and bravely endured; but to be treated like a child, to be deprived of self-respect, to return to childlike behaviour and yet to be keenly aware of the ridicule resulting from this action means unbearable anguish for those souls whose courage and sagacity would compensate for every other loss. Human wisdom, reason, courage, these the soul dying to self reluctantly relinquishes; all else has scarcely any hold on us or hardly belongs to us and slips lightly from our fingers; but our own wisdom is so flattering and forms such an intimate part of the soul that to take it away is to flay us alive.

François Fénelon, 'Christmas', *Affective Thoughts*, tr. Elizabeth C. Fenn in
Fénelon: Meditations and Devotions (Morehouse-Gorham Co. 1952/A.R. Mowbray 1954),
pp. 31–32.

Your highest mystery
4.45

My God, make me worthy of knowing your highest mystery – brought about by your most ardent and ineffable charity, with the clarity dispensed by the Trinity – that is, the most high mystery of your most holy incarnation which you accomplished for our sake. The incarnation was the beginning of our salvation and it does two things for us: first, it fills us with love; second, it makes us certain of our salvation.

O incomprehensible charity! There is indeed no greater charity than the one by which my God became flesh in order that he might make me God. O heartfelt love poured out for me! When you assumed human form, you gave of yourself in order to make me. You did not let go of anything in yourself in any way that would lessen you or your divinity, but the abyss of your conception makes me pour out these deep, heartfelt words: O incomprehensible one, made comprehensible! O uncreated one, made creature! O inconceivable one, made conceivable! O impalpable one, become palpable!

O Lord, make me worthy of seeing the depth of the charity which you communicated to us in your most holy incarnation. O happy fault, which merited that we discover the most hidden depths of the divine charity until then hidden from us. Oh, in truth, I cannot imagine anything greater to contemplate! O most high, make me able to understand this most high and ineffable charity.

Angela of Foligno, *The Book of the Blessed Angela of Foligno (Instructions)*,
Instruction XXXV in *Angela of Foligno: Complete Works*, tr. Paul Lachance OFM
(Paulist Press 1993), pp. 308–309.

Make Christ at home
4.46

An African woman perceives and accepts Christ as a woman and as an African. The commitment that flows from this faith is commitment to full womanhood (humanity), to the survival of human communities, to the 'birthing', nurturing, and maintenance of life, and to loving relations and life that is motivated by love.

Having accepted Christ as refugee and guest of Africa, the woman seeks to make Christ at home and to order life in such a way as to enable the whole household to feel at home with Christ. The woman sees the whole space of Africa as a realm to be ordered, as a place where Christ has truly 'tabernacled'. Fears are not swept under the beds and mats but are brought out to be dealt with by the presence of the Christ. Christ becomes truly friend and companion, liberating women from assumptions of patriarchal societies, and honouring, accepting, and sanctifying the single life as well as the married life, parenthood as well as the absence of progeny. The Christ of the women of Africa upholds not only motherhood, but all who, like Jesus of Nazareth, perform 'mothering' roles of bringing out the best in all around them. This is the Christ, high priest, advocate, and just judge in whose kingdom we pray to be.

Elizabeth Amoah and Mercy Amba Oduyoye, 'The Christ for African Women' in
With Passion and Compassion: Third World Women Doing Theology, ed. Virginia Fabella
and Mercy Amba Oduyoye (Orbis Books 1988), pp. 44–45.

The name of Jesus
4.47

If you wish to be on good terms with God and have his grace direct your life and come to the joy of love, then fix this name 'Jesus' so firmly in your heart that it never leaves your thought. And when you speak to him using your customary name 'Jesu', in your ear it will be joy, in your mouth honey, and in your heart melody, because it will seem joy to you to hear that name being pronounced, sweetness to speak it, cheer and singing to think it. If you think of the name 'Jesu' continually and cling to it devotedly, then it will cleanse you from sin and set your heart aflame; it will enlighten your soul, remove turbulence, and eliminate lethargy; it will give the wound of love and fill the soul to overflowing with love; it will chase off the devil and eliminate terror, open heaven, and create a mystic. Have 'Jesu' in your mind, because it expels all wickedness and delusion from his lover... Great will be the love and joy you feel if you are willing to act in accordance with this instruction. There is no need for you to be very eager for a lot of books. Hold on to love in heart and deed, and you've got everything which we can talk or write about. For the fulfilment of the law is love: on that, everything depends.

> Richard Rolle, in *Richard Rolle – The English Writings*, tr. Rosamund Allen
> (Paulist Press 1988), p. 173.

The going-forth of Jesus
A meditation on Luke 9:28–36
4.48

Jesus is praying, and the light shines on his face. We do not know that it is a prayer of agony and conflict like the prayer in Gethsemane, but we know that it is a prayer near to the radiance of God and the prayer of one who has chosen the way of death. Luke tells us that the two witnesses were conversing about the exodus which Jesus would accomplish in Jerusalem: not the death alone, but the passing through death to glory, the whole going forth of Jesus as well as the leading forth of the new people of God in the freedom of the new covenant. Luke tells us that after the resurrection Jesus spoke of the witness of Moses and of all the prophets to his suffering and glory.

It was not a glory which the disciples at the time could fathom. No doubt they would have welcomed a glory on the mountain far away from the conflicts which had happened and the conflicts which were going to happen as Jesus set his face towards Jerusalem. Yet when Jesus went up the mountain to be transfigured he did not leave these conflicts behind, but rather carried them up the mountain so that they were transfigured with him. It was the transfiguration of the whole Christ, from his first obedience in childhood right through to the final obedience of Gethsemane and Calvary.

The disciples could not grasp this at the time, but the writings of the apostolic age were to show that the link between the suffering and the glory came to be understood as belonging to the heart of the Christian message.

Michael Ramsey, *Be Still and Know* (Collins Fount/Faith Press 1982), pp. 64–65.

The power of the cross
4.49

O the marvellous power of the cross, the glory in the passion! No tongue can fully describe it. Here we see the judgment seat of the Lord, here sentence is passed upon the world, and here the sovereignty of the Crucified is revealed. You drew all things to yourself, Lord, when you stretched out your hands all the day long to a people that denied and opposed you, until at last the whole world was brought to proclaim your majesty. You drew all things to yourself, Lord, when all the elements combined to pronounce judgment in execration of that crime; when the lights of heaven were darkened and the day was turned into night; when the land was shaken by unwonted earthquakes, and all creation refused to serve those wicked people. Yes, Lord, you drew all things to yourself; the veil of the temple was torn in two and the Holy of Holies taken away from those unworthy high priests. Figures gave way to reality, prophecy to manifestation, law to gospel. You drew all things to yourself in order that the worship of the whole human race could be celebrated everywhere in a sacramental form which would openly fulfil what had been enacted by means of veiled symbols in that single Jewish temple.., Through your cross the faithful are given strength instead of weakness, glory instead of shame, life instead of death.

Leo the Great, from Sermon 8 on the Passion, in *A Word in Season* II,
ed. Friends of Henry Ashworth (Exordium Books 1982), pp. 201–202.

The meaning of the cross
4.50

We in fact have to agree that, before it became the cross of God, the cross was the nadir of human powerlessness and hopelessness. It was an irreversible end to everything standing for hope and the future. The cross stood for inhumanity, brutality, hell and death. It was the last defiance of satanic power against humanity. The cross was anti-human, anti-Christ and anti-God. In the cross was concentrated the cosmic power of negation. But by rendering God powerless, the cross itself became transformed. For on the cross what was exposed was not the powerlessness of God but the powerlessness of the power of negation. What was revealed was the power of the powerlessness of God. The demonic power of negation proved on the cross to be essentially powerless. The power of hate was consumed in its own hate and the power of death was dissolved in its own death. Thus the demonic power of negation was a self-destructive power. That is why it was powerless. In contrast, the powerlessness of God came from his inability to hate, to destroy and to kill. That is why he was the most powerful God. He was the God who loves, who lets live and who gives hope. The cross was therefore the victory of the powerlessness of God over the power of hate, destruction and death. It was the triumph of love over hate, heaven over hell and life over death. The world was saved by this powerlessness of God.

Choan-Seng Song, *Third-Eye Theology: Theology in Formation in Asian Settings*
(Orbis Books 1979/Lutterworth 1980), pp. 167–68.

Being Christs to one another
4.51

Therefore, if we recognize the great and precious things which are given us, as Paul says [Romans 5:5], our hearts will be filled by the Holy Spirit with the love which makes us free, joyful, almighty workers and conquerors over all tribulations, servants of our neighbours, and yet lords of all. For those who do not recognize the gifts bestowed upon them through Christ, however, Christ has been born in vain; they go their way with their works and shall never come to taste or feel those things. Just as our neighbour is in need and lacks that in which we abound, so we were in need before God and lacked his mercy. Hence, as our heavenly Father has in Christ freely come to our aid, we also ought freely to help our neighbour through our body and its works, and each one should become as it were a Christ to the other that we may be Christs to one another and Christ may be the same in all, that is, that we may be truly Christians.

Who then can comprehend the riches and the glory of the Christian life? It can do all things and has all things and lacks nothing. It is lord over sin, death, and hell, and yet at the same time it serves, ministers to, and benefits all. But alas in our day this life is unknown throughout the world; it is neither preached about nor sought after; we are altogether ignorant of our own name and do not know why we are Christians or bear the name of Christians. Surely we are named after Christ, not because he is absent from us, but because he dwells in us, that is, because we believe in him and are Christs one to another and do to our neighbours as Christ does to us.

Martin Luther, *Treatise on Christian Liberty*, tr. John Dillenberger in *Martin Luther: Selections from His Writings* (Doubleday 1961), p. 76.

Jesus on the cross
4.52

There are we entertained with the wonder of all ages. There we enter into the heart of the universe. There we behold the admiration of angels. There we find the price and elixir of our joys. As on every side of the earth all heavy things tend to the centre; so all nations ought on every side to flow in unto it. It is not by going with the feet, but by journeys of the soul, that we travel thither. By withdrawing our thoughts from wandering in the streets of this world, to the contemplation and serious meditation of his bloody sufferings. *Where the carcase is, thither will the eagles be gathered together.* Our eyes must be towards it, our hearts set upon it, our affections drawn, and our thoughts and minds united to it. When I am lifted up, saith the Son of man, I will draw all men unto me, as fishes are drawn out of the water, as Jeremie was drawn out of the dungeon, as St Peter's sheet was drawn up into heaven; so shall we be drawn by that sight from ignorance and sin, and earthly vanities, idle sports, companions, feasts and pleasures, to the joyful contemplation of that eternal object. But by what cords? The cords of a man, and the cords of love.

... The cross is the abyss of wonders, the centre of desires, the school of virtues, the house of wisdom, the throne of love, the theatre of joys, and the place of sorrows; it is the root of happiness, and the gate of heaven.

Of all things in heaven and earth it is the most peculiar. It is the most exalted of all objects. It is an ensign lifted up for all nations, to it shall the gentiles seek. His rest shall be glorious: the dispersed of Judah shall be gathered together to it, from the four corners of the earth. If love be the weight of the soul, and its object the centre, all eyes and hearts may convert and turn unto this object: cleave unto this centre, and by it enter into rest. There we may see God's goodness, wisdom and power: yea his mercy and anger displayed. There we may see man's sin and infinite value, his hope and fear, his misery and happiness. There we might see the Rock of Ages, and the joys of heaven. There we may see a man loving all the world, and a God dying for mankind.

Thomas Traherne, *Centuries*, The First Century, nos. 56–59
(Faith Press 1960), pp. 28–29.

A vision more wonderful
4.53

The power of Christ is able to control fiercer storms than those of the wind and the sea. It is able to still the torrents of evil of the whole world in the stillness of his own heart. It is the power which enables him to command the floods of all the sorrow in the world and hold them within his peace. It is the power which can not only give life back to the dead, but can change death itself to life. It is the power of divine love.

So, for a moment, a vision more wonderful than that of Tabor is granted to the woman whose compassion drove her to discover Christ in a suffering man. Then Christ passes on, on the way of sorrows, leaving her with the veil in her hands and on it the imprint of that face of suffering that hid the beauty of God.

In Christ burying his face in that woman's veil on the Via Crucis, we are looking at the many children of today whom war has twisted and tortured out of the pattern of childhood, who are already seared and vitiated by fear, persecution, homelessness and hunger.

We see grown-up people who have been maimed or disfigured, those whom chronic illness or infirmity has embittered. We see, too, those most tragic ones among old people, those who are not loved, and are not wanted by their own, those in whom the ugliness, not the beauty of old age is visible. We see the tragic ones who are cut off from all but the very few, the Veronicas of the world, by mental illness. We see, too, many who are dying, who with Christ are coming to the end of their Via Crucis, yet sometimes without realizing that Christ is suffering for and in them.

Caryll Houselander, *The Stations of the Cross* (Sheed & Ward 1955), pp. 62–63.

Fellow-feeling
4.54

The sympathy of Jesus was fellow-feeling for all that is human. He did not condole with Zaccheus upon his trials, he did not talk to him 'about his soul', he did not preach to him about his sins, he did not force his way into his house to lecture him; he simply said, 'I will abide at thy house': thereby identifying himself with a publican: thereby acknowledging a publican for a brother. Zaccheus a publican? Zaccheus a sinner? Yes: but Zaccheus is a man. His heart throbs at cutting words. He has a sense of human honour. He feels the burning shame of the world's disgrace. Lost? Yes: but the Son of man, with the blood of the human race in his veins, is a brother to the lost.

... Remark the power of this sympathy on Zaccheus' character. Salvation that day came to Zaccheus' house. What brought it? What touched him? Of course, 'the gospel'. Yes; but what is the gospel? Speculations or revelations concerning the Divine Nature? The scheme of the atonement? or of the incarnation? or baptismal regeneration? Nay, but the personal sympathy of the Divinest Man. The personal love of God, manifested in the face of Jesus Christ. The floodgates of his soul were opened, and the whole force that was in the man flowed forth. Whichever way you take that expression, 'Behold, Lord, the half of my goods I give to the poor': if it referred to the future, then, touched by unexpected sympathy, finding himself no longer an outcast, he made that resolve in gratefulness. If to the past, then, still touched by sympathy, he who had never tried to vindicate himself before the world, was softened to tell out the tale of his secret munificence. This is what I have been doing all the time they slandered me, and none but God knew it.

F.W. Robertson, 'Triumph over Hindrances' (sermon 1850).

A person came...
4.55

For a person came, and lived and loved, and did and taught, and died and rose again, and lives on by his power and his spirit for ever within us and amongst us, so unspeakably rich and yet so simple, so sublime and yet so homely, so divinely above us precisely in being so divinely near – that his character and teaching require, for an ever fuller yet never complete understanding, the varying study, and different experiments and applications, embodiments and unrollings of all the races and civilizations, of all the individual and corporate, the simultaneous and successive experiences of the human race to the end of time. If there is nothing shifting or fitful or simply changing about him, there are everywhere energy and expansion, thought and emotion, effort and experience, joy and sorrow, loneliness and conflict, interior trial and triumph, exterior defeat and supplantation: particular affections, particular humiliations, homely labour, a homely heroism, greatness throughout in littleness. And in him, for the first and last time, we find an insight so unique, a personality so strong and supreme, as to teach us, once for all, the true attitude towards suffering... With him, and alone with him and those who still learn and live from and by him, there is the union of the clearest, keenest sense of all the mysterious depth and breadth and length and height of human sadness, suffering, and sin, *and*, in spite of this and through this and at the end of this, a note of conquest and of triumphant joy.

Friedrich von Hugel, *The Mystical Element of Religion*
(J.M. Dent/James Clarke [1908] 1961), pp. 26–27.

God's Faithfulness

A word of comfort
4.56

Then Moses said to God, 'If I come to the people of Israel and say to them, "The God of your fathers has sent me to you," and they ask me, "What is his name?" what shall I say to them?' (Exodus 3:13).

... And now – we wait in breathless suspense – what is God going to answer to this most urgent of all human questions in the field of religion? 'I will be that which I will be.' The form of expression in Hebrew makes it plain that this mysterious phrase is intended to paraphrase and to explain the hidden name of God, JHVH. But is this really an explanation? Is it not rather an evasion than an answer? Yes, this is the first impression that is bound to be left upon our minds – God is withdrawing himself from the importunity of human beings. He does not allow anyone to lay claim to him, as we would so gladly do; he preserves his own freedom and the mystery of his being. But we have gone only half way towards expounding this utterance, if we see in it no more than God's refusal to answer our questions. The Hebrew word which we translated above 'I will be' signifies rather 'to be present', or even 'to take place'. Its reference, therefore, is rather to being in act, in activity, than to being at rest; and therefore we can say with certainty that the reference here is not to God 'as he is in himself', but to God 'as he turns himself towards us'. This is, then, a word spoken by a God who condescends to us, who makes us aware of his willingness to help us. We might almost go so far as to translate it, 'I will manifest myself to be that which I will manifest myself to be.'

If God sends to those living in misery the message that he will show himself active according to his own free decision, from the first moment the affirmation is a word of comfort, an assurance that God is 'the One who is always there'; perhaps it is not too much to say that it is an assurance of the faithfulness of God.

Gerhard von Rad, *Moses* (Lutterworth 1960), pp. 19–21.

Sin, judgment and mercy
4.57

To find God all we need to do is to return to ourselves; we shall find God in what he does to us. God's throne is an impenetrable darkness, or, if you prefer to say so, a brightness utterly blinding, out of which proceed lightnings, and thunderings and voices. The points of the lightning are thrown just so far as to touch us, the arrowheads of the voices bury themselves in our hearts.

When we read the ancient prophets, Hosea for example, we are not invited to the centre of the mystery, to spy at God; we are placed at the circumference and our breasts are bared to the arrows that fly out of the throne: arrows of judgment, arrows of love. The God behind the darkness, whose thoughts I cannot see, kills and he makes alive. Whether he shoots from the same bow the shafts of ice and the shafts of fire, I do not know, but I know that both are as sharp as death and both are pushed home by omnipotence, and that I must not turn away, but take both in my heart. To expose sin to holiness is to suffer annihilation. According to the good pasture I gave them, says Hosea's God of his rebellious sheep, they gorged themselves and their heart was uplifted; and so they have forgotten me. Therefore am I a lion unto them, as a leopard I watch their way, I meet them as a bear bereaved of her whelps and I rend the caul of their heart [Hosea 12:7]. But equally, to the first sign of penitence mercy is unconfined. 'I heal their backsliding, I love them freely; mine anger is turned from them; I am as the dew to Israel, he shall flourish as the lily' [Hosea 14:5]. These are the things God does to sin and to repentance; both are immeasurably strong, for both are God; and yet we know that of two immeasurable things, judgment and mercy, mercy prevails.

Austin Farrer, *Words for Life*, ed. Charles Conti and Leslie Houlden
(SPCK 1993), pp. 35–36.

God stays true
4.58

A sailor in World War I once wrote home, 'If you should hear that I have fallen in battle, do not cry. Remember that even the ocean in which my body sinks is only a pool in my Saviour's hand.'… We don't know what destiny is reaching out for us in the remaining years of this decade, but one thing we do know: that hand reaches out for us, too. That is the message of this story. And how can it be said more relevantly or more precisely than by means of sinking Peter [cf. Matthew 14:13] – Peter who is none other than I, with my fever chart of a great 'little faith', with my anxiety and my curiosity, with my experience that God is always greater than my heart and that he stays true to me when I am false to him? And then after all the storms are over, and the sea is smooth once again; when calm weather returns, and I once more come to myself; then may things turn out as they did with the disciple, who could only fall to his knees and stammer. 'Truly you are the Son of God.'

Maybe I have other words, not nearly so rich, to state who Jesus is for me. Maybe I only come up with, 'I don't know who you are, Jesus of Nazareth, but you are different from all the rest of us. I will dare to hold to you. Then I will have secure footing when all around me gives way.' That is not put as fully or as richly as it is stated in the liturgy and the catechism. Yet Jesus Christ would hear it, and for him it would be enough.

Helmut Thielicke, 'How Crises in Faith Arise', *How to Believe Again*,
tr. H.G. Anderson (Collins 1973), pp. 75–76.

God's constancy
4.59

The resurrection does not cancel or merely redress the truth that shines from the cross; it confirms it. This is the eternal nature of divine power and victory, in so far as our human minds are capable of grasping it.

This God does not promise that we shall be protected from the accidents and ills of this life, but that those who open themselves to him will be empowered with the human resources of endurance, insight and selflessness that can turn misfortune to good account. The well-known words of Philippians 4:13 in the older versions, 'I can do all things through Christ who strengthens me,' are in fact a misleading rendering. The truer sense, which is also more appropriate in the context, is, 'I have strength to cope with anything.'

That in which we put our trust is essentially the constancy and reliability of God; and this is, in fact, all the more solidly established through this understanding of his nature and his purpose. His faithfulness consists in his unbreakable commitment to his people and, as the scriptures also indicate, to his whole creation. He will never turn back from the love which binds him to the world and which remains his way with the world to the end of time. It is a way that embraces the 'changes and chances', in all their arbitrary freedom, within the 'eternal changelessness' of a love that bears, believes, hopes, endures all things. By its very nature that love is at once the source of the grace we need in this life, and our hope of glory in the life to come.

The Doctrine Commission of the Church of England, *We Believe in God*
(Church House Publishing 1987).

Don't be afraid
4.60

Don't be afraid of anything. Do not ever be afraid. And don't worry. So long as you remain sincerely penitent, God will forgive you everything. There's no sin, and there can be no sin in the whole world which God will not forgive to those who are truly repentant. Why, no one can commit so great a sin as to exhaust the infinite love of God. Or can there be a sin that would exceed the love of God? Only you must never forget to think continually of repentance, but dismiss your fear altogether. Believe that God loves you in a way you cannot even conceive of. He loves you in spite of your sin and in your sin. And there's more joy in heaven over one sinner that repents than over ten righteous men. This was said a long time ago. So go and do not be afraid. Do not be upset by people and do not be angry if you're wronged... if you are sorry for what you did, then you must love. And if you love, you are of God... Everything can be atoned for, everything can be saved by love. If I, a sinner like you, have been moved by your story and am sorry for you, how much more will God be. Love is such a priceless treasure that you can redeem everything in the world by it, and expiate not only your own but other people's sins. Go and do not be afraid.

Fyodor Dostoevsky, *The Brothers Karamazov*, vol. 1, tr. David Magarshack
(Penguin Books 1963), p. 56.

Disreputable God
4.61

What a tremendous relief it should be, and has been to many, to discover that we don't need to prove ourselves to God. We don't have to do anything at all, to be acceptable to him. That is what Jesus came to say, and for that he got killed. He came to say, 'Hey, you don't have to earn God's love. It is not a matter for human achievement. You exist because God loves you already. You are a child of divine love.' The Pharisees, the religious leaders of the day – the bishops and presidents and moderators – they couldn't buy that. Jesus tried to tell them all sorts of stories to prove this point, like the one about the labourers in the vineyard [Matthew 20:1ff], who were hired in batches at different times of the day. With all but the very last lot the owner of the vineyard came to an agreement about the wages. The last lot worked for no time at all and yet they were paid a full day's wage – God's love and compassion are given freely and without measure, they are not earned. They are totally unmerited and gracious. The religious leaders thought that Jesus was proclaiming a thoroughly disreputable God with very low standards – any Tom, Dick and Harry, Mary and Jane would soon be jostling with the prim and proper ones. Stupendously that was true; no, just part of the truth. Jesus was saying that the unlikely ones, those despised ones, the sinners, the prostitutes, the tax collectors, would in fact precede the prim and proper ones into the kingdom of God.

God is like the good shepherd who goes out looking for the lost sheep [cf. Luke 15:4]. We are misled by the religious pictures which depict Jesus as the good shepherd carrying a cuddly white lamb on his shoulder. A lamb will hardly stray from its mother. It is the troublesome, obstreperous sheep which is likely to go astray, going through the fence, having its wool torn and probably ending up in a ditch of dirty water. It is this dirty, smelly, riotous creature which the good shepherd goes after, leaving the good, well-behaved ninety-nine sheep in the wilderness, and when he finds it, why, he carries it on his shoulder and calls his friends to celebrate with him.

Desmond Tutu, Hope and Suffering (Collins Fount 1984), pp. 137–39.

Overflowing love
4.62

In Tamil we have a polite word, which tells someone who asks for something that we have nothing to give; we have run short of it – Poochiam.

One day I felt like saying Poochiam about love; I had run short of it. I was in the Forest, and I had just read a letter that was hard to answer lovingly. I was sitting by The Pool at the time, and presently began to watch the water flow down through the deep channel worn in the smooth rocks above it. There was always inflow, so there was always outflow. Never for one minute did the water cease to flow in, and never for one moment did it cease to flow out; and I knew, of course, that the water that flowed out was the water that flowed in. The hollow that we called The Pool had no water of its own, and yet all the year round there was an overflow.

God hath not given you the spirit of fear… but of love.

If love flows in, love will flow out. Let love flow in. That was the word of The Pool. There is no need for any of us to run short of love. We need never say Poochiam.

Amy Carmichael, Edges of His Ways:
Selections for Daily Theological Reading (SPCK 1955).

PART 5

Approaches to Prayer

Drawing Closer to God

Christmas memories

5.1

Paradoxically enough, it is often in the secular thoughts that preoccupy us at Christmas that the holy element comes close to us. This is simply because wherever we are open in our humanity the mystery of God is present among us...

Every one of us carries with us something that is very carefully protected from the strains and stresses of everyday life. In these times of silence that occur especially at Christmas, we recall moments during which we experienced life very intensely, times of suffering, great happiness, tender love, shy friendship or unfulfilled longing. A human face, a habitual gesture made by a long-lost friend, a colour, the shape of a countryside well known in the past – these we remember, sometimes with astonishing clarity. We like to keep such memories with us, dwell on them lovingly. We feel at home in them, because what is most precious to us is made present in them. At such times we realize that our lives contain certain unique elements, experiences of special grace and power, and that even insights that we had forgotten long ago can come to light and appear totally convincing again. In those moments of recollection, too, we see with great clarity that convictions and attitudes which can barely survive the hard experiences of daily life are of the greatest value and importance.

... We are not simply at the mercy of the hopeless and often bad experiences that we have in the everyday world. These do not ultimately determine what we are and what we may become. New and unexpected things can always rise up out of our lives because there is, despite all the anxiety and unhappiness that surrounds us, a hidden source of salvation in the world that can begin to flow at any time. Something that is bright and pure and not simply superstitious or wildly enthusiastic is proclaimed in this Christmas mood. It is that, despite all the evidence that exists in the world as we know it, there is a way from darkness into light: there is a light shining in the darkness of the night.

Ladislas Boros, 'Feast of Silence', *Meditations*, tr. David Smith
(Search Press 1973), pp. 27–29.

Journey of surprises
5.2

Our notion of God is mediated to us through parents, teachers and clergy. We do not come to know God directly. If our experience of parents and teachers has been of dominating people who show little affection or respect for us as persons, but value us only in so far as we conform to their expectations, then this experience is bound to affect our notion of God and will influence the way we relate to him...

Although I may know in my mind that God is not like that, I may still experience a strong disinclination to approach him, without knowing why, and find a thousand reasons for not praying – I am too busy, I prefer to find him through my work, etc. We have to pray constantly to be rid of false notions of God, and we have to beg him to teach us who he is, for no one else can. 'God is known by God alone', as one of the early writers of the church said. What we are praying for is not merely an intellectual knowledge, but a felt knowledge which affects our whole being and therefore affects the way we see ourselves, other people and the world around us. This felt knowledge of God changes the patterns of our thinking and therefore of acting, breaks open the cocoon of our minds and hearts and liberates us from the constrictions which our upbringing and present environment are imposing on us.

To become aware that we have a distorted notion of God is to have made progress on our journey towards him. As the journey continues, we shall discover other distortions of which we were not aware. Such discoveries can be very painful at first, but it is like the pain we feel when our limbs are at last free after being constricted; it is the pain of freedom. The journey to God is a journey of discovery and it is full of surprises.

Gerard Hughes, *God of Surprises* (Darton, Longman & Todd 1985), pp. 35–36.

The hidden God
5.3

You do very well, oh soul, to seek him ever as one hidden, for you exalt God immensely and approach very near him when you consider him higher and deeper than anything you can reach. Hence, pay no attention, neither partially nor entirely, to anything which your faculties can grasp. I mean that you should never desire satisfaction in what you understand about God, but in what you do not understand about him. Never stop with loving and delighting in your understanding and experience of God, but love and delight in what is neither understandable nor perceptible of him. Such is the way, as we said, of seeking him in faith. However surely it may seem that you find, experience and understand God, you must, because he is inaccessible and concealed, always regard him as hidden, and serve him who is hidden in a secret way. Do not be like the many foolish ones who, in their lowly understanding of God, think that when they do not understand, taste, or experience him, he is far away and utterly concealed. The contrary belief would be truer. The less distinct is their understanding of him, the closer they approach him, since in the words of the prophet David, 'He made darkness his hiding place' (Psalm 18:11). Thus in drawing near him, you will experience darkness because of the weakness of your eye.

John of the Cross, Commentary on *The Spiritual Canticle*, Stanza 1.12, tr. Kieran Kavanaugh OCD and Otilio Rodriguez OCD in *The Collected Works of St John of the Cross* (Institute of Carmelite Studies 1979), pp. 400–401.

Learning to listen
5.4

It is helpful if we are comfortable while we prepare to listen to the Lord. If our bodies are too tense, or we are too cold, or too hot, or our back aches because the chair is uncomfortable, our minds will keep coming back to our physical discomforts, instead of relaxing and thinking of the Lord. It can be a great blessing, as well, to sit quietly in his presence, not thinking about anything in particular, not wanting anything from him, but just to enjoy his company. That was the testimony of an older lady who told how she would often wake up in the middle of the night and spend an hour or so with God, just enjoying being with him. I felt that my own increasing awareness of the Lord was rather small and insignificant beside her powerful testimony!

Some people find that God speaks to them while they are on the move. Another friend shared that she heard the Lord many times while taking her dog for a walk. For myself, it was while I was hoovering that he put into my mind the idea of writing down these thoughts! And from scripture we have the story of the two disciples walking on the Emmaus road, who said afterwards: 'Did not our hearts burn within us while he talked to us on the road?' (Luke 24:32). God is not limited by any conditions that we lay down; so we need to widen our thinking and expect him to speak to us at any time, in any place. However, this is far more likely to happen when we have already spent time cultivating the two-way relationship in our quiet time.

Jean Holl, *Alone with God: Making the Most of Your Quiet Time*
(Triangle 1986), pp. 103–104.

Why pray if God knows best?
5.5

But, someone will say, does God not know, even without being reminded, both in what respect we are troubled and what is expedient for us, so that it may seem in a sense superfluous that he should be stirred up by our prayers – as if he were drowsily blinking or even sleeping until he is aroused by our voice? But they who thus reason do not observe to what end the Lord instructed his people to pray, for he ordained it not so much for his own sake as for ours. Now he wills – as is right – that his due be rendered to him, in the recognition that everything men desire and account conducive to their own profit comes from him, and in the attestation of this by prayers. But the profit of this sacrifice also, by which he is worshipped, returns to us. Accordingly, the holy fathers, the more confidently they extolled God's benefits among themselves and others, were the more keenly aroused to pray. It will be enough for us to note the single example of Elijah, who, sure of God's purpose, after he has deliberately promised rain to King Ahab, still anxiously prays with his head between his knees, and sends his servants seven times to look [1 Kings 18:42], not because he would discredit his prophecy, but because he knew it was his duty, lest his faith be sleepy or sluggish, to lay his desires before God.

John Calvin, *Institutes of the Christian Religion*, III, 20.

The door to meditation
5.6

Since I learned how to enter the forest of meditation, I have received sweet dewlike drops from that forest. I have found that the door to meditation is open everywhere and at any time, at midnight, or at noonday, at dawn or at dusk. Everywhere, on the street, on the trolley, on the train, in the waiting room, or in the prison cell, I am given a resting place of meditation, wherein I can meditate to my heart's content on the almighty God who abides in my heart.

It is said that Francis of Assisi meditated and prayed, looking up at the sun in broad daylight. Plato has told how Socrates suddenly would pause and stand erect to meditate for a few minutes while walking with his disciples... Jesus withdrew into the wilderness and meditated forty days and forty nights. Sometimes he was lost in meditation and prayer all night long in the mountains of Galilee. Those who draw water from the wellspring of meditation know that God dwells close to their hearts. For those who wish to discover the quietude of old amid the hustle and bustle of today's machine civilization, there is no way save to rediscover this ancient realm of meditation. Since the loss of my eyesight I have been as delighted as if I had found a new wellspring by having arrived at this sacred precinct.

Toyohiko Kagawa, *Meditations*, tr. Jiro Takenaka (Harper & Brothers 1950), p. 1.

Difficult listening

5.7

The most difficult and decisive part of prayer is acquiring this ability to listen. Listening is no passive affair, a space when we happen not to be doing or speaking. Inactivity and superficial silence do not necessarily mean that we are in a position to listen. Listening is a conscious, willed action, requiring alertness and vigilance, by which our whole attention is focused and controlled. Listening is in this sense a difficult thing. And it is decisive because it is the beginning of our entry into a personal and unique relationship with God, in which we hear the call of our own special responsibilities for which God has intended us. Listening is the aspect of silence in which we receive the commission of God.

Mother Mary Clare SLG, *Encountering the Depths*
(Darton, Longman & Todd 1981), p. 33.

Remembrance of God

5.8

Seek and ye shall find. But what is one to seek? A conscious and living communion with the Lord. This is given by the grace of God, but it is also essential that we ourselves should work, that we ourselves should come to meet him. How? By always remembering God, who is near the heart and even present within it. To succeed in all this remembrance it is advisable to accustom oneself to the continual repetition of the Jesus Prayer, 'Lord Jesus Christ, Son of God, have mercy upon me,' holding in mind the thought of God's nearness, his presence in the heart. But it must also be understood that in itself the Jesus Prayer is only an outer oral prayer; inner prayer is to stand before the Lord, continually crying out to him without words.

By this means remembrance of God will be established in the mind, and the countenance of God will be in your soul like the sun. If you put something cold in the sun it begins to grow warm, and in the same way your soul will be warmed by the remembrance of God, who is the spiritual sun. What follows on from this will presently appear.

Your first task is to acquire the habit of repeating the Jesus Prayer unceasingly. So begin and continually repeat and repeat, but all the time keep before you the thought of our Lord. And herein lies everything.

> Theophan the Recluse, in *The Art of Prayer, An Orthodox Anthology*,
> comp. Igumen Chariton of Valamo, tr. E. Kadloubovsky and E.M. Palmer,
> ed. Timothy Ware (Faber & Faber 1973), p. 121.

See and be seen
5.9

Prayer is to look to the omnipresent God and to allow oneself to be seen by him. What is now easier and more simple than to turn our eyes upward and to see the light that surrounds us on all sides? God is far more present to us than the light. In him we live, we move, and we are. He penetrates us, he fills us, he is nearer to us than we are to ourselves. To believe this in simplicity and to think of this simply as well as one can, that is prayer. How can it be difficult to allow oneself to be looked after by so kind a physician who knows better what is troubling us than we ourselves know? We have no need to bring this or that, to present ourselves in this way or in that way or to look too much or to experience much if we wish to pray, but we need only simply and briefly to say how we are and how we wish to be. Indeed, it is not even necessary that we say this, but we need only allow the ever-present good God to see. We are not to let him see only the surface, but at every point we are to remain by him and before him so that he can see us correctly and heal us. We must not say anything to him or allow him to see anything other than what is in us. What will be is what he wills. If you find yourself disturbed, dark, with no spiritual experiences, simply tell God and let him see your suffering; then you have prayed properly. Is there a natural laziness or diffidence at hand? Take heart but a little and turn again with humility to God. If one can remain awake standing better than kneeling, let one fight sleep in such a way; if one can do so better by looking in a book, this is not forbidden. In short, one must help oneself at a particular time as well as one can, so long as one does not disturb one's chief goal by doing so, namely, prayer, but, rather, always turn oneself again to this task. Deny your own will and desires and you will pray properly and easily. For the Lord will work prayer in your soul through his grace.

Gerhard Tersteegen, in *The Pietists: Selected Writing*, ed. Peter Erb (Paulist Press 1983).

The soul's castle
5.10

Now let us return to our beautiful and delightful castle and see how we can enter it. I seem rather to be talking nonsense; for, if this castle is the soul, there can clearly be no question of our entering it. For we ourselves are the castle: and it would be absurd to tell someone to enter a room when he was in it already! But you must understand that there are many ways of 'being' in a place. Many souls remain in the outer court of the castle, which is the place occupied by the guards; they are not interested in entering it, and have no idea what there is in that wonderful place, or who dwells in it, or even how many rooms it has. You will have read certain books on prayer which advise the soul to enter within itself: and that is exactly what this means.

A short time ago I was told by a very learned man that souls without prayer are like people whose bodies or limbs are paralyzed: they possess feet and hands but they cannot control them. In the same way, there are souls so infirm and so accustomed to busying themselves with outside affairs that nothing can be done for them, and it seems as though they are incapable of entering within themselves at all. So accustomed have they grown to living all the time with the reptiles and other creatures to be found in the outer court of the castle that they have almost become like them; and although by nature they are so richly endowed as to have the power of holding converse with none other than God himself, there is nothing that can be done for them. Unless they strive to realize their miserable condition and to remedy it, they will be turned into pillars of salt for not looking within themselves, just as Lot's wife was because she looked back.

Teresa of Avila, *Interior Castle*, ch. 1, tr. E. Allison Peers, in
Complete Works of St Teresa, vol. 2 (Sheed & Ward 1972), p. 203.

Christ the true king
5.11

A much greater love for and confidence in this Lord began to develop in me when I saw him as one with whom I could converse so continually. I saw that he was man, even though he was God; that he wasn't surprised by human weaknesses; that he understands our miserable make-up, subject to many falls on account of the first sin which he came to repair. I can speak with him as with a friend, even though he is lord. I know that he isn't like those we have as lords here on earth, all of whose lordship consists in artificial displays: they have to have designated times for speaking and designated persons to whom they speak. If some poor little creature has any business matter to take up, what roundabout ways they must go through and what trials and favours it costs them in order to get to speak to this lord! Oh, and if it is with the king! Then, people who are poor or those who don't belong to the nobility can't even get near; but they must ask those who are the court minions. And most assuredly these latter are not persons who have trampled the world underfoot, for those who have speak the truth since they know no fear, nor are they obligated to anyone. Such people are not for the palace, for there you mustn't speak out but be silent about what appears to be wrong; you mustn't even dare think about it if you don't want to fall into disfavour.

O king of glory and lord of all kings! How true that your kingdom is not armed with trifles, since it has no end! How true that there is no need for intermediaries with you! Upon beholding your person one sees immediately that you alone, on account of the majesty you reveal, merit to be called Lord. There's no need for people in waiting or for guards in order that one know that you are King.

> Teresa of Avila, *The Book of Her Life*, ch. 37, tr. Kieran Kavanaugh OCD and
> Otilio Rodriguez OCD, in *The Autobiography of St Teresa of Avila*
> (Book-of-the-Month Club 1995), pp. 325–26.

Healing silence
5.12

It seems to me that nothing but silence can heal the wounds made by disputations in the region of the unseen. No external help, at any rate, has ever in my own experience proved so penetratingly efficacious as the habit of joining in a public worship based upon silence. Its primary attraction for me was in the fact that it pledged me to nothing, and left me altogether undisturbed to seek for help in my own way. But before long I began to be aware that the united and prolonged silences had a far more direct and powerful effect than this. They soon began to exercise a strangely subduing and softening effect upon my mind. There used, after a while, to come upon me a deep sense of awe, as we sat together and waited – for what? In my heart of hearts I knew in whose name we were met together, and who was truly in the midst of us. Never before had his influence revealed itself to me with so much power as in those quiet assemblies.

And another result of the practice of silent waiting for the unseen presence proved to be a singularly effectual preparation of mind for the willing reception of any words which might be offered 'in the name of a disciple'. The words spoken were indeed often feeble, and always inadequate (as all words must be in relation to divine things), sometimes even entirely irrelevant to my own individual needs, though at other times profoundly impressive and helpful; but, coming as they did after the long silences which had fallen like dew upon the thirsty soil, they went far deeper, and were received into a much less thorny region than had ever been the case with the words I had listened to from the pulpit.

Caroline Stephen, 'Quaker Strongholds' (1890) in *Quaker Spirituality: Selected Writings*, ed. Douglas V. Steere (Paulist Press 1984).

A listening heart
5.13

Responsive listening is the form the Bible gives to our basic religious quest as human beings. This is the quest for a full human life, for happiness. It is the quest for meaning, for our happiness hinges not on good luck; it hinges on peace of heart. Even in the midst of what we call bad luck, in the midst of pain and suffering, we can find peace of heart, if we find meaning in it all. Biblical tradition points the way by proclaiming that God speaks to us in and through even the most troublesome predicaments. By listening deeply to the message of any given moment I shall be able to tap the very source of meaning and to realize the unfolding meaning of my life.

To listen in this way means to listen with one's heart, with one's whole being. The heart stands for that centre of our being at which we are truly 'together'. Together with ourselves, not split up into intellect, will, emotions, into mind and body. Together with all other creatures, for the heart is that realm where I am paradoxically not only most intimately myself, but most intimately united with all. Together with God, the source of life, the life of my life, welling up in the heart. In order to listen with my heart, I must return again and again to my heart through a process of centering, through taking things to heart. Listening with my heart I will find meaning. For just as the eye perceives light and the ear sound, the heart is the organ for meaning.

David Steindl-Rast, *A Listening Heart: The Art of Contemplative Listening* (Crossroad 1983), pp. 9–10.

The one and the many
5.14

Religion is not a purely individual matter. Nothing in human life is. We are social beings, and all elements of our life come to their full development only through social interchange and co-operation. A person working alone is an inefficient producer; by division of labour and co-operation the productive efficiency of all is multiplied. A person educating himself is at a great disadvantage compared with a student who has teachers and fellow-students to stimulate him. Our pleasures, our affections, our moral aspirations are all lifted to higher power and scope by sharing them with others. An isolated individual is to that extent a crippled person. We never realize all our powers and enthusiasms until we shout with others in a public meeting, or keep step with others to the drumbeat, and see the flag, which is the symbol of our common life, leading us forward.

It stands to reason that reason, too, demands social expression, and will come to its full strength and richness only when it is shared with others. And so in fact we find it. There is a sweetness in private prayer, but there is an additional thrill when we join in a heartfelt hymn and are swept on the wave-crest of a common emotion. Most of us have come to the great religious decision in life only under the influence of social emotion. With most of us the flame of religious longing and determination would flicker lower and lower in the course of the years, if it were not fanned afresh by contact with the experiences and the religious will-power of others. When Jesus said that where two or three are gathered in his name, he is in the midst of them, he expressed the profound truth that his presence is fully realized only in a Christian society; it may be a very small group, but it needs at least one other human heart next to ours to be fully sensible of the Christ.

Walter Rauschenbusch, 'Why I am a Baptist' in *The Colegate–Rochester
Divinity School Bulletin*, vol. XI, no. 2 (1938), pp. 94–95.

The treasure of scripture

5.15

Reading is the careful study of the scriptures, concentrating all one's powers on it. Meditating is the busy application of the mind to seek with the help of one's own reason for knowledge of hidden truth. Prayer is the heart's devoted turning to God to drive away evil and obtain what is good. Contemplation is when the mind is in some sort lifted up to God and held above itself, so that it tastes the joys of everlasting sweetness.

Reading seeks for the sweetness of a blessed life, meditation perceives it, prayer asks for it, contemplation tastes it. Reading, as it were, puts food whole into the mouth, meditation chews it and breaks it up, prayer extracts its flavour, contemplation is the sweetness itself which gladdens and refreshes.

Reading works on the outside, meditation on the pith, prayer asks for what we long for, contemplation gives us delight in the sweetness which we have found. To make this clearer, let us take one of many possible examples.

I hear the words read: 'Blessed are the pure in heart, for they shall see God.' This is a short text of scripture, but it is of great sweetness, like a grape that is put into the mouth filled with many senses to feed the soul. When the soul has carefully examined it, it says to itself, 'There may be something good here. I shall return to my heart and try to understand and find this purity, for this is indeed a precious and desirable thing...' So, wishing to have a fuller understanding of this, the soul begins to bite and chew upon this grape, as though putting it in a wine press, while it stirs up its power of reasoning to ask what this precious purity may be and how it may be had.

When meditation busily applies itself to this work, it does not remain on the outside, it is not detained by unimportant things, climbs higher, goes to the heart of the matter, examining each point thoroughly.

Guigo II, *The Ladder of Monks: A Letter on the Contemplative Life and Twelve Meditations*, tr. Edmund College OSA and James Walsh SJ (Cistercian Publications 1981).

Knowing God
5.16

With Christ, philosophers can tell me that I cannot 'know' Christ and so on. All right, but I can still say that I am very sorry, I just do know him.

Take a simple example. Hold your hand at arm's length and look at it, four fingers and a thumb and so on. Now, draw it slowly towards you. At first you can keep it in focus, and then gradually it is too close to be seen whole and clearly. Finally, it is right up against your face and you cannot see at all... everything is dark... but the contact is very real and very different. Though you cannot see, you are clear that there is something there up against your nose; you can no longer distinguish it as 'hand' or see the shape and so on. But it is very real.

Well, the same reaction occurs in relationship with God. The closer we approach, the more dark is our knowledge. It is neither easy to express this in words or to hold its credibility in life. When a person is set down before God, is trying hard to be recollected, is even trying to think of God and Christ, and all that happens is that there is a blank, an emptiness, a pain, it is not easy to get across to that person that all is well and this is as it should be! BUT IT IS AS IT SHOULD BE!

Michael Hollings, *Day by Day* (Mayhew–McCrimmon 1972), pp. 94–95.

The heart of intercession
5.17

The first step in intercession is to make a definite 'act' of union with this stream of God's love and power, which is flowing ceaselessly out of his heart, and back to him again...

Making a conscious effort to unite our wills and hearts with the ever-flowing river of the love of God will give us a restful energy. As we realize that the love of God is flowing through us and using us as it passes, all merely natural strain will disappear. If suffering comes to us in our time of intercession, we must accept it, and still remain tranquilly surrendered to God for his purpose. If we experience difficulty in 'getting going', it would be well to search our hearts to see whether after all we are praying that God will bless *our* efforts for his glory, rather than seeking to be united with *his* will. 'The greatest works wrought by prayer have been accomplished, not by human effort but by human trust in God's effort.' In prayer of this kind we are united with the very life of God, sharing in his work...

The essence and heart of intercession is self-offering. The deeper our surrender to God, the more true and powerful will be our intercession. Intercession is indeed a basic principle of human living: it expresses that corporate sense of community which is the real nature of human life and it expresses that instinct to give to the point of sacrifice which is one of the deepest elements in our nature, fulfilled once for all by Christ on the cross... Thus intercession covers the whole world: all the sins and cruelties and miseries of men; all the horrors of war; the sighing of prisoners and captives; the sufferings of the oppressed and the outcast; the despair of those who are far from God: 'Christian intercession is the completion and expression of self-giving.' We offer our poor imperfect love to God to be a channel of his perfect and redeeming love. We offer ourselves to be a way through which God will reach, and save and bless the whole world.

Olive Wyon, *The School of Prayer* (SCM Press 1943), p. 115.

Friend of silence
5.18

God is the friend of silence...

We need to find God and he cannot be found in noise and restlessness. See how nature, the trees, the flowers, the grass grow in perfect silence – see the stars, the moon and the sun, how they move in silence...

Silence gives us a new outlook on everything. We need silence to be able to touch souls. The essential thing is not what we say but what God says to us and through us. Jesus is always waiting for us in silence. In that silence he will listen to us, there he will speak to our soul, and there we will hear his voice. Interior silence is very difficult but we must make the effort. In silence we will find new energy and true unity. The energy of God will be ours to do all things well. The unity of our thought with his thoughts, the unity of our prayers with his prayers, the unity of our actions with his actions, of our life with his life. All our works will be useless, unless they come from within – works which do not give the light of Christ increase the darkness.

Mother Teresa of Calcutta, in *In the Silence of the Heart*, comp. Kathryn Spink
(SPCK 1983), p. 19.

Riding the wave
5.19

The surfer is my favourite example of the disciplined wild man, the man who has a perfectly balanced ascetical-mystical life. Check out his style. He gets up early in the morning. That's a tough ascetical act of self-denial. Then he attends carefully and reverently to his board, polishing and waxing it with love. Next he puts the board, this burden of love, this sacred tool, on his head and walks silently and solitary to the sea. There he faces a lonely and forbidding beach hardly perceptible in the fog. He then plunges into cold water, works his way out into the deeps against the waves, and now comes the keenest ascetical act of all: he waits; no impulsive action, no rush, no rash moves. He looks, listens, sees the distant waters, watching intently, contemplatively for the right wave, letting all the others go by. Finally, he sees the big wave coming. Deftly and adroitly he moves into position – timing is so important – not to master the wave, but to meet it and become one. They meet. He is caught up in the magnificent, mounting momentum of that majestic wave; his muscles relax, his spirits soar, he lets himself go, surrenders himself to the mighty swelling and roaring onslaught of that wave; and he rides and rides and rides in utter delight and sheer ecstasy. That is the mystical goal of a surfer's asceticism.

Such exquisite, abandoned delight in God's cascading glory, flowing through the parched human soul made ready for the pinnacle of all human achievements, spiritual matrimony with God, is the mystical goal of all human asceticism.

William McNamara, *The Human Adventure: The Art of Contemplative Living*
(Amity House 1974), pp. 160–61.

God all in all
5.20

But what are your delights to be? 'And they shall delight in abundance of peace': peace, your gold; peace, your silver; peace, your property; peace, your life; peace, your God. Peace will fulfil your every desire. For what is here gold cannot become your silver; what is wine cannot become your bread; your light cannot become your drink also. Your God shall be all to you. He will be your meat, that you hunger not; your drink, that you do not thirst; your enlightening, that you be not blind; your stay and support, that you do not falter. Himself whole and entire, he will possess you whole and entire. You will not feel cramped for space in possessing him with whom you possess all else besides. You shall have all and he shall have all, because you and he shall be one. This complete whole will be his who possesses you.

Augustine of Hippo, 'First Discourse on Psalm 36', 12 (V. 11),
St Augustine on the Psalms: Psalms 30–37, tr. and ed. Scholastica Hegbin and
Felicitas Corrigan (Newman Press/Longmans, Green and Co. 1961).

Change and decay
5.21

If the Fire has come down into the heart of the world it is, in the last resort, to lay hold on me and to absorb me. Henceforth I cannot be content simply to contemplate it or, by my steadfast faith, to intensify its ardency more and more in the world around me. What I must do, when I have taken part with all my energies in the consecration which causes its flames to leap forth, is to consent to the communion which will enable it to find in me the food it has come in the last resort to seek.

So, my God, I prostrate myself before your presence in the universe which has now become living flame: beneath the lineaments of all that I shall encounter this day, all that happens to me, all that I achieve, it is you I desire, you I await.

It is a terrifying thing to have been born: I mean, to find oneself, without having willed it, swept irrevocably along a torrent of fearful energy which seems as though it wished to destroy everything it carries with it.

What I want, my God, is that by a reversal of forces which you alone can bring about, my terror in face of the nameless changes destined to renew my being may be turned into an overflowing joy at being transformed into you...

My communion would be incomplete – would, quite simply, not be

Christian – if together with the gains which this new day brings me, I did not accept, in my own name and in the name of the world as the most immediate sharing in your own being, those processes, hidden or manifest, of enfeeblement, of ageing, of death, which unceasingly consume the universe, to its salvation or its condemnation. My God, I deliver myself up with utter abandon to those fearful forces of dissolution which, I blindly believe, will this day cause my narrow ego to be replaced by your divine presence.

Pierre Teilhard de Chardin, Hymn of the Universe (Collins 1965), pp. 31–32.

Sensing God
5.22

My love for you, Lord, is not an uncertain feeling but a matter of conscious certainty. With your word you pierced my heart, and I loved you. But heaven and earth and everything in them on all sides tell me to love you. Nor do they cease to tell everyone that 'they are without excuse' (Romans 1:20). But at a profounder level you will have mercy on whom you will have mercy and will show pity on whom you will have pity (Romans 9:15). Otherwise heaven and earth would be uttering your praises to the deaf. But when I love you, what do I love? It is not physical beauty nor temporal glory nor the brightness of light dear to earthly eyes, nor the sweet melodies of all kinds of songs, nor the gentle odour of flowers and ointments and perfumes, nor manna or honey, nor limbs welcoming the embraces of the flesh; it is not these I love when I love my God. Yet there is a light I love, and a food, and a kind of embrace when I love my God – a light, voice, odour, food, embrace of my inner man, where my soul is floodlit by light which space cannot contain, where there is sound that time cannot seize, where there is a perfume which no breeze disperses, where there is a taste for food no amount of eating can lessen, and where there is a bond of union that no satiety can part. That is what I love when I love my God.

Augustine of Hippo, Confessions X, vi (8), tr. Henry Chadwick
(Oxford University Press 1991), p. 183.

Passing over
5.23

Whoever looks upon the mercy seat and turns his face fully toward the Crucified, with faith, hope and love, with devotion, wonder and exultation, with delight, praise and joy, makes the passover, in the company of Christ. With the staff of the cross he enters the Red Sea on his way out of Egypt into the desert; there he tastes the hidden manna, and with Christ he lies in the tomb, apparently dead to the world, but all the while experiencing in himself, as much as is possible in this present state of wayfaring, what was said on the cross to the robber who confessed Christ: 'Truly I tell you, today you will be with me in Paradise.'

... If this passing over is to be perfect, all intellectual operations must be given up, and the sharp point of our desire must be entirely directed toward God and transformed in him. Such a motion as this is something mystical and very secret, and no one knows it except him who receives it, and no one receives it except him who desires it, and no one desires it unless the fire of the Holy Spirit, whom Christ sent to earth, inflames him to the very marrow. That is why the apostle attributes to the Holy Spirit the revelation of such mystical wisdom.

Since nature is powerless in this respect, and effort alone makes little progress, little importance should be attached to speculation, but much to affection; little to what is said aloud, but more to the heart's joy; little to words written down, but all to God's Gift, the Holy Spirit; little to the created world, but everything to the One who creates it, Father, Son and Holy Spirit.

Bonaventure, *The Journey of the Mind to God*, ch. 7, based on translation in *The Works of Bonaventure, I, Mystical Opuscula* (St Anthony Guild Press 1960), pp. 56–57.

Vision of God
A Meditation on Exodus 33:18
5.24

Moses was still dissatisfied: he wanted more. He was thirsty for the very thing with which he kept on filling himself; he asked for it as if he had never partaken of it, begging God to appear to him, not according to his own capacity to see God, but according to God's very being. This, it seems to me, is the sort of experience that befits the person who loves what is beautiful. Hope keeps on drawing them beyond the beauty they can see to that which is out of sight, keeps alight the longing for what is hidden by what is there to see. So the one who is in love with beauty, in spite of seeing the image of his desire in what is visible, still longs to be satisfied with the original of the image, the archetype itself.

So he goes up the mountain of desire boldly asking this: to enjoy beauty not just in reflected images as in a mirror, but face to face. And the voice of God granted what he asked precisely in what it denied him; in a few words it plumbed immeasurable depths of thought. God's boundless generosity agreed to the fulfilment of his desire, yet without promising that that desire would be satisfied or lessened.

If the sight of God could bring to an end the desire of the one who beheld God, then God would not have shown himself to his servant; for the true sight of God consists in this, that the person who looks towards God never ceases from his desire. For God says: You cannot see my face, for humankind cannot see me and live. By this, scripture does not mean that this causes the death of those who look at God – how could the face of life ever cause the death of those who draw near to it? Far from it: the divine is of its very nature life-giving. Yet the nature of the divine is to transcend all natures. So the person who thinks God is something to be known does not possess life: he has turned from real Being to what his own perceptions tell him about being.

Real Being is real life, and this Being is not accessible to our powers of knowing. So if the life-giving nature is beyond knowledge, what can be seen is certainly not life. In this way Moses' yearning was satisfied by the very things that left his desire dissatisfied. He learned from the divine word that the divine is by its very nature infinite, without boundaries. If it had boundaries, one would have to recognize that there must be something beyond those boundaries... We can give no credence to anything that would put bounds to that which is infinite. One cannot grasp that which has no boundaries; but every desire for that which is good, which is drawn to climb the mountain to find it, simply goes on expanding as one presses on towards the object of one's desire. And this truly is the vision of God: never to have one's desire for God satisfied, so that the more one looks towards what one can see, the more one is drawn on by the eager longing to see more. There is no limit that can be set to our growth in our Godward life, since the good has no limit, and the desire for the good is not brought to an end by being satisfied.

Gregory of Nyssa, *Life of Moses*, 230–236, 238–239
(compilers' version).

The Way of Contemplation

God present
5.25

The life of prayer, the life of contemplation, is simply to realize God's presence to us. It is not therefore a special way of life reserved for those few individuals who are called to get away from the world and to dwell in the deserts. Contemplation and prayer ought to be the very breath of every disciple of Christ.

But there remains the problem which troubles so many people: How can I remain always in prayer? There is even the preliminary question: How can I pray at all? We wonder, however, whether such problems do not arise mainly from the wrong conceptions of prayer that people generally have, and perhaps, even more basically, from the wrong conceptions they too often have of the mystery of God.

Most people actually imagine that in order to pray, and especially, in order to find themselves in the presence of God, they have to stop their minds from thinking of any creature whatsoever, and instead to form some mental picture or idea of God, or rather about God, and then to busy themselves mentally with that image or that concept. Yet is it not a fact that no image or idea which we may form of God is God himself, but remains inevitably and for ever simply *what we think of God*?

It is just the same with our ideas of God as it is with statues and icons which many Christians like to have in their churches or in their houses. A crucifix, or a picture of Christ, is not Christ himself; nor are icons of saints identical with the saints they represent. Their immediate function is to catch the eyes and hold the attention of the worshippers, which are always too inclined to run away towards worldly and temporal things, and to refresh their minds with the remembrance of the saints or of the Lord. It is true that they may also be something more than that, at least when they have been ritually blessed and consecrated; the faithful are then fully authorized to believe piously that they communicate some halo of the divine presence.

The same applies to the mental images and ideas of God which we form when we study or meditate. They are signs pointing to the reality they represent, but they are for ever unable to comprehend that reality, which stands in its aloneness far beyond the reach of any conception or imagination of man… The day in which we attempt to identify them with the reality they become simply idols; and mental idols are no less vanity and nothingness than stone or metal ones. The most perfect prayer necessarily makes use of signs, because the human mind has been created such by God, but it makes use of them with full liberty and sovereignty and it tends always towards the *beyond* where alone reality abides in the unfathomable silence of the Godhead.

… Do we say 'Let us first think of the air which surrounds us and then breathe'? Willingly, unwillingly, consciously, unconsciously, we breathe and go on breathing; continuously, too, air is entering our lungs. So it is also with the divine presence which is more essential to our life, to our very being, than the air itself which we breathe.

Abhishiktananda (Henri Le Saux), Prayer (SPCK 1967), pp. 3–5.

Pearl of eternity
5.26

This pearl of eternity is the church or temple of God within thee, the consecrated place of divine worship, where alone thou canst worship God in spirit and in truth. In spirit, because thy spirit is that alone in thee, which can unite and cleave unto God and receive the workings of his divine Spirit upon thee. In truth, because this adoration in spirit is that truth and reality, of which all outward forms and rites, though instituted by God, are only the figure for a time; but this worship is eternal. Accustom thyself to the holy service of this inward temple. In the midst of it is the fountain of living water, of which thou mayest drink and live for ever. There the mysteries of thy redemption are celebrated, or rather opened in life and power. There the supper of the Lamb is kept; the bread that came down from heaven, that giveth life to the world, is thy true nourishment: all is done and known in real experience, in a living sensibility of the work of God on the soul. There the birth, the life, the sufferings, the death, the resurrection and ascension of Christ are not merely remembered, but inwardly found and enjoyed as the real states of thy soul, which has followed Christ in the regeneration. When once thou art well grounded in this inward worship, thou wilt have learnt to live unto God above time and place. For every day will be Sunday to thee, and wherever thou goest thou wilt have a priest, a church and an altar along with thee.

William Law, The Spirit of Prayer, ch. II, in Selected Mystical Writings of William Law,
ed. Stephen Hobhouse (Rockliff 1948), p. 89.

'I look at him'
5.27

There was a simple peasant, a good father of a family, an unlettered husbandman, whose fervent piety was the joy of his pastor's heart. Whether going to his work or returning from it, never did that good man pass the church-door without entering it to adore his Lord. He would leave his tools, his spade, hoe, and pickaxe, at the door, and remain for hours together sitting or kneeling before the tabernacle. M. Vianney, who watched him with great delight, could never perceive the slightest movement of the lips. Being surprised at this circumstance, he said to him one day, 'My good father, what do you say to our Lord in these long visits you pay him every day and many times a day?' 'I say nothing to him,' was the reply; 'I look at him, and he looks at me.' 'A beautiful and sublime answer,' says M. Monnin. He said nothing, he opened no book, he could not read; but he had eyes – eyes of the body and eyes of the soul – and he opened them, those of the soul especially, and fixed them on our Lord. 'I look at him.' He fastened upon him his whole mind, his whole heart; all his sense, and all his faculties. There was an interchange of ineffable thought in those glances which came and went between the heart of the servant and the heart of the Master. This is the secret, the great secret, of attaining sanctity.

Alfred Monnin, *Life of the Blessed Cure D'Ars* (Burns & Oates 1907), p. 47.

Tiny pools of silence
5.28

Deserts, silence, solitudes are *not necessarily places but states of mind and heart*. These deserts can be found in the midst of the city, and in the every day of our lives. We need only look for them and realize our tremendous need for them. They will be small solitudes, little deserts, tiny pools of silence, but the experience they will bring, if we are disposed to enter them, may be as exultant and as holy as all the deserts of the world, even the one God himself entered. For it is God who makes solitude, deserts and silences holy.

Consider the solitude of walking from the subway train or bus to our home in the evening, when the streets are quieter and there are few passersby. Consider the solitude that greets you when you enter your room to change your office or working clothes to more comfortable, homey ones. Consider the solitude of a housewife, alone in her kitchen, sitting down for a cup of coffee before beginning the work of the day. Think of the solitudes afforded by such humble tasks as housecleaning, ironing, sewing.

One of the first steps towards solitude is a departure. Were you to depart to a real desert, you might take a plane, train or car to get there. But we're blind to the 'little departures' that fill our days. These 'little solitudes' are often right behind a door which we can open, or in a little corner where we can stop to look at a tree that somehow survived the snow and dust of a city street. There is the solitude of a car in which we return from work, riding bumper to bumper on a crowded highway. This too can be a 'point of departure' to a desert, silence, solitude.

Catherine de Hueck Doherty, *Poustinia: Christian Spirituality of the East for Western Man*
(Ave Maria Press 1975), pp. 21–22.

A praise of glory
5.29

In heaven every soul is established in pure love and no longer lives its own life, but the life of God. Then, says St Paul, 'I shall recognize God as he has recognized me' (1 Corinthians 13:12). In other words, 'a praise of glory' is a soul who abides in God, who loves him with a pure and unselfish love, without self-seeking in the pleasure of that love, who loves him for all his gifts, who would love him as much even if it had received nothing from him – and who desires good for God, except by doing his will, since that will orders all things to his greater glory? Such a soul, then, must give itself up completely and blindly to God's will, so that it can will only what he wills.

'A praise of glory' is a silent soul which rests like a lyre under the mysterious trials of the Holy Spirit, that he may bring forth divine harmonies. Knowing that suffering is a string which produces the most beautiful sound of all, this soul loves to see it on its own instrument, that it may move God's heart with great delight.

'A praise of glory' is a soul who gazes on God, in faith and simplicity. It reflects all that he is, and is like a fathomless abyss into which he can flow and outpour himself. It is a crystal through which he can shine and contemplate all his perfections and splendour. A soul who thus allows the divine being to satisfy within it his need to communicate all that he is and all that he has, is a true praise of glory of all his gifts.

Elizabeth of the Trinity, *Spiritual Writings*
(Geoffrey Chapman 1962), p. 152.

Beat upon the cloud of darkness
5.30

If you want to gather all your desire into one simple word that the mind can easily retain, choose a short word rather than a long one. A one-syllable word such as 'God' or 'love' is best. But choose one that is meaningful to you. Then fix it in your mind so that it will remain there come what may. This word will be your defence in conflict and in peace. Use it to beat upon the cloud of darkness above you and to subdue all distractions, consigning them to the cloud of forgetting beneath you. Should some thought go on annoying you demanding to know what you are doing, answer with the one word alone. If your mind begins to intellectualize over the meaning and connotations of this little word, remind yourself that its value lies in its simplicity. Do this, and I assure you these thoughts will vanish. Why, because you have refused to develop them with arguing...

As I have already explained to you, this simple work is not a rival to your daily activities. For with your attention centred on the blind awareness of your naked being united to God's, you will go about your daily rounds, eating and drinking, sleeping and waking, going and coming, speaking and listening, lying down and rising up, standing and kneeling, running and riding, working and resting. In the midst of it all, you will be offering to God continually each day the most precious gift you can make. This work will be at the heart of everything you do, whether active or contemplative.

The Cloud of Unknowing and the Book of Privy Counselling, ed. William Johnston SJ
(Doubleday 1973), pp. 56, 162–63.

Faith alone
5.31

All too easily when we talk about the interior life of prayer or contemplation we have in mind some sort of refined human activity going on within; it can be cultivated and grow to wonderful proportions.

But let us substitute the words 'interior life' for 'depth life' and we come nearer to what it means to be a contemplative. A contemplative lives below the surface, is present to what really is and not in the ephemeral, often illusory world of impressions.

Contemplation is based on faith. Only faith takes us behind appearances; only faith roots us in naked reality and keeps us there steadfastly, refusing to allow us to escape into pleasant fantasy, to make excursions into 'if only', into what our ego wants for its satisfaction and comfort.

Faith says: You are for God. You must abandon all desire to cling to boundaries, to your own limits, your own idea of things. You have to allow yourself all the time to be drawn up and away, or down and beyond, to God himself.

Ruth Burrows in *The Watchful Heart*, ed. Elizabeth Ruth Obbard
(Darton, Longman & Todd 1988), p. 15.

The goal
5.32

We like to look on the spiritual life as something very noble, very holy but also very peaceful and consoling. The word 'contemplation' easily tempts those who have not tried it to think that the mystical life consists in looking at the everlasting hills, and having nice feelings about God. But the world of contemplation is really continuous with the world of prayer, in the same way as the high Alps are continuous with the lower pastures. To enter it means exchanging the lovely view for the austere reality; penetrating the strange hill country, slogging up stony tracks in heavy boots, bearing fatigue and risking fog and storm, helping fellow climbers at one's own cost. It means renouncing the hotel-life level of religion with its comforts and conveniences, and setting our face towards the snows not for any personal ambition or enjoyment, but driven by the strange mountain love. 'Thou hast made us for thyself and our hearts shall have no rest save in thee.' Narrow rough paths, slippery shale, the glimpse of awful crevasses, terrible storms, cold, bewildering fog and darkness – all these wait for the genuine mountaineer. The great mystics experience all of them, and are well content so to do.

One of the best of all guides to these summits, St John of the Cross, drew for his disciples a picturesque map of the route. It starts straight up a very narrow path. There are two much wider and better paths going left and right; one of them is marked 'the advantages of this world' and the other 'the advantages of the next world'. Both must be avoided for both end in the foothills, with no road further on. The real path goes very steeply up the mountain, to a place where St John has written, 'After this there is no path at all' and the climber says with St Paul, 'Having nothing I possess all things.'

Here we are already a long way from the valley and have reached the stage which is familiar to all climbers, where we feel exhilarated because we think we see the top, but are really about to begin the true climb. This is the illuminative life; and here, says St John, on these levels, the majority of souls come to a halt. For the next thing he shows us is an immense precipice towering above us, and separating the lovely alpine pastures of the spiritual life from the awful silence of the Godhead, the mysterious region of the everlasting snows. No one can tell the climber how to tackle the precipice. Here he must be led by the Spirit of God, and his success must depend on his self-abandonment and his courage – his willingness to risk, to trust and to endure to the very end. Every one suffers on the precipice. Here all landmarks and all guides seem to fall, and the naked soul must cling as best it can to the naked rock of reality. This is the experience which St John calls in another place the dark night of the spirit. It is a rare experience, but the only way to the real summit; the supernatural life of perfect union with the self-giving and outpouring love of God. There his reality, his honour and his glory alone remain the very substance of the soul's perpetual joy. And that, and only that, is the mystic goal.

Evelyn Underhill, in *Collected Papers of Evelyn Underhill*
(Longmans, Green & Co. 1946), p. 118.

Relaxation in prayer
5.33

This [contemplative] prayer involves a search for peace, tranquillity and serenity. We seek to meet the lord of the Sabbath in his place of rest deep within us and, as we rest and relax in his presence, to give him the worship of our lives.

A major task, therefore, while we pray, is to let go of tension, to calm down, to accept his will, to surrender to him in faith so that at his word storms may cease. We become alert and attentive, not with a violent effort, but by gently letting go of all tension, excitement, anxiety, worries, the heat of desire, the venom of hatred, the weighing down of self pity.

The word 'concentration' is often used in connection with contemplative prayer. This concentration or attentiveness is not the result of a mighty and tense effort; it is a gentle letting go of things, a relaxing of our nervous grip on people and situations and the release from worry and anxiety.

While all these flow out of us, there remains only one thing: attention to the Lord, awareness of the presence of him who is the author and giver of all peace and strength… We can relax and let go of everything precisely *because* God is present. In his presence nothing really matters; all things are in his hands. Tension, anxiety, worry, frustration, all melt away before him, as snow before the sun.

Jim Borst, *Coming to God in the Stillness* (Eagle 1992),
pp. 20, 22.

Only listen

5.34

Should any thought arise and obtrude itself between you and the darkness, asking what you are seeking, and what you are wanting, answer that it is God you want: 'Him I covet, him I seek, and nothing but him.'

Should he (the thought) ask, 'What is this God?' answer that it is the God who made you and redeemed you, and who has, through his grace, called you to his love. 'And', tell him, 'you do not even know the first thing about him.' And then go on to say, 'Get down', and proceed to trample on him out of love for God; yes, even when such thoughts seem to be holy, and calculated to help you find God. Quite possibly he will bring to your mind many lovely and wonderful thoughts of his kindness, and remind you of God's sweetness and love, his grace and mercy. If you will but listen to him, he asks no more. He will go on chattering increasingly, and bring you steadily down to think of Christ's Passion. There he will show you the wonderful kindness of God, and he wants nothing so much that you should listen to him. For he will then go on to let you see your past manner of life, and as you think of its wretchedness your mind will be well away, back in its old haunts. Before you know where you are you are disintegrated beyond belief! And the reason? Simply that you freely consented to listen to that thought, and responded to it, accepted it and gave it its head.

And yet of course the thought was both good and holy, and indeed necessary, so that, paradoxically, no man or woman can hope to achieve contemplation without the foundation of many such delightful meditations on his or her own wretchedness, and our Lord's Passion, and the kindness of God, and his great goodness and worth. All the same, the practised hand must leave them, and put them away deep down in the cloud of forgetting if he is ever to penetrate the cloud of unknowing between him and God.

The Cloud of Unknowing, ch. 7, tr. Clifton Wolters (Penguin 1961), pp. 60–61.

The ocean of God's glory

5.35

One who stands beside the sea sees the infinite ocean of the waters, but cannot grasp the extent of them, beholding only a part. So it is with one who is judged worthy to fix his gaze in contemplation on the infinite ocean of God's glory and behold him with the intelligence: he sees not how great God is, but only what the spiritual eyes of his soul can grasp... Just as one who enters the waters of the sea up to his knees or his waist sees clearly what is outside the water, but if he plunges into the depths and is wholly covered by water, can no longer see anything outside the water, and knows nothing else than that he is in the depths of the sea, so it is with those who increase in spiritual progress and come to the perfection of knowledge and contemplation.

Symeon the New Theologian, Theological Centuries II, II, 14.

Take flight
5.36

But although that penetrating ray of contemplation is always suspended near something because of greatness of wonder, yet it operates neither always nor uniformly in the same mode. For that vitality of understanding in the soul of a contemplative at one time goes out and comes back with marvellous quickness, at another time bends itself, as it were, into a circle, and yet at another time gathers itself together, as it were, in one place and fixes itself, as it were, motionless. Certainly if we consider this rightly, we see the form of this thing daily in the birds of the sky. Now you may see some raising themselves up on high; now others plunging themselves into lower regions and often repeating the same manner of their ascent and descent. You may see some turning to the side, now to the right, now to the left, and while coming down a little ahead now in this part, now in that, or advancing themselves almost not at all, repeating many times with great constancy the same changes of their movements. You may see others thrust themselves forward in great haste. But next, with the same rapidity, they return to the rear, and moving themselves often they continue and prolong, with long-lasting repetition, the same going forth and returning. You may see how others turn themselves in a circle, and how suddenly and how often they repeat the same or a similar path – one time a little wider, another time slightly smaller, yet always returning to the same place. You may see how others suspend themselves for a long time in one and the same place with beating and rapidly vibrating wings and fix themselves motionless by means of agitated motion, as it were. And they do not depart at all from the place where they are suspended, clinging closely for a long time, as if by the performance of the work and of their constancy they might seem, by all means, to exclaim and say: 'It is good for us to be here' (Matthew 17:4).

Richard of St Victor, The Mystical Ark, Book I, ch. V, tr. Grover A. Zinn,
(Paulist Press 1979), pp. 158–59.

Spiritual wonder
5.37

Contemplation is the highest expression of man's intellectual and spiritual life. It is that life itself, fully awake, fully active, fully aware that it is alive. It is spiritual wonder. It is spontaneous awe at the sacredness of life, of being. It is gratitude for life, for awareness and for being. It is a vivid realization of the fact that life and being in us proceed from an invisible, transcendent and infinitely abundant source. Contemplation is, above all, awareness of the reality of that source. It *knows* the source, obscurely, inexplicably, but with a certitude that goes both beyond reason and beyond simple faith. For contemplation is a kind of spiritual vision to which both reason and faith aspire, by their very nature, because without it they must always remain incomplete. Yet contemplation is not vision because it sees 'without seeing' and knows 'without knowing'. It is a more profound depth of faith, a knowledge too deep to be grasped in images, in words or even in clear concepts. It can be suggested by words, by symbols, but in the very moment of trying to indicate what it knows the contemplative mind takes back what it has said, and denies what it has affirmed. For in contemplation we know by 'unknowing'. Or better, we know beyond all *knowing* or 'unknowing'.

Poetry, music and art have something in common with the contemplative experience. But contemplation is beyond aesthetic intuition, beyond art, beyond poetry. Indeed, it is beyond philosophy, beyond speculative theology. It resumes, transcends and fulfils them all, and yet at the same time it seems, in a certain way, to supersede and to deny them all. Contemplation is always beyond our own knowledge, beyond our own light, beyond systems, beyond explanations, beyond discourse, beyond dialogue, beyond our own self. To enter into the realm of contemplation one must in a certain sense die: but this death is in fact the entrance into a higher life. It is a death for the sake of life, which leaves behind all that we can know or treasure as life, as thought, as experience, as joy, as being.

Thomas Merton, *New Seeds of Contemplation* (Burns & Oates 1962), p. 1.

River's course
5.38

Nothing is more quiet and unobtrusive than the source of a river; it rises in solitary heights, and only a slight greenness among the moss and heather, or a slight trickle of water at the edge of the snowfield, shows where the stream has begun to flow. Fed from heaven, it trickles slowly down among rocks or heather, till it gathers strength, bores its way through rocky channels, wears down resistance, if necessary flowing underground till it emerges on the plain below, widening out into a broad stream, bringing life and fertility to a whole region. This is a picture of the life of prayer, in its origins, and its middle course. For many people it stops here.

But this is not all: the river seems placid, but all the time it is moving gently and steadily towards its goal. Presently it leaves the fertile fields behind, and flows under bridges, past the wharves and factories of great industrial towns. It has become a highway of trade, a place for the commerce of many nations. More than that: filth and rubbish, and worse, are thrown into its muddy waters. For the moment it seems as though the river, with its clear blue-green waters, has been hopelessly defiled. But it flows on undisturbed, its waters clear, and once more it refreshes and fertilizes the land through which it flows, till at last – it slips out to sea and loses itself in the infinite ocean, its goal. All along its course it has been moved by one steady purpose.

This is a picture-parable of the later stages of the life of prayer.

Olive Wyon, *The School of Prayer* (SCM Press [1943] 1962), p. 111.

Darkness and light
5.39

Mysticism in the proper sense is an intense realization of God within the self, and the self embraced within God in vivid nearness.

It is a phenomenon known in a number of religions, and in those religions very similar language is used in describing the experience. There is deep darkness, the darkness of not knowing, and there is light, with flashes in which the self knows the unknowable to be terribly near, and knows itself as never before.

Now, through the centuries Christian teaching has emphasized that the significant thing is not just the mystic experience in itself, but its place and context within the whole life of a Christian. The experience is given by God sometimes to one who seeks God in a life of humility and charity, turned towards righteousness as well as the beauty of God. And the effect of the experience of mystic union, sometimes described as 'passive contemplation', is not to cause the person to long to have the experience again, but to long to serve God, and to do his will.

Those who have had the mystic experience will not want to tell everyone about it: they will have a longing to serve God in daily life, for in his *will* is our peace.

Michael Ramsey, in *Through the Year with Michael Ramsey*, ed. Margaret Duggan
(Hodder & Stoughton 1975), p. 164.

The experience of loving
5.40

It is not only the experience of being loved that is therapeutic. The very response to love is therapeutic too. This answering love is not directed towards some abstraction but towards the living, risen, cosmic Christ who is in our friends and our enemies, who is in the poor and the sick and the afflicted. And the experience of loving him in himself and in others, no less than the experience of being loved, is therapeutic in its consequences because it purifies the whole person – mind and memory and unconscious. When one begins to love profoundly at a new level of awareness (as often happens in deep intimacy between a man and a woman) it may happen that latent or repressed forces rise to the surface of the mind: hatred, jealousy, fear, insecurity, anger, suspicion, anxiety, unbridled eroticism and the rest surge up from the murky depths of the unconscious. And all this, it is well known, can coexist with true love. This violence, unleashed in human relations, can be unleashed also in the divine – the two are not so distinct, and divine love is incarnate. And one is liberated only by continuing to love. By fixing one's heart on the cloud of unknowing with deep peace, one becomes detached from these turbulent uprisings; and then they wither and die, leaving only love. It is by loving at the ultimate point, by going beyond all categories to the deepest centre, that one is liberated from jealousy and hatred and the rest. But this is an agonizing purification.

William Johnston, *Silent Music* (Fontana Collins 1974), p. 120.

Contemplative transformation
5.41

We stand helpless, confused, and guilty before the insurmountable problems of our world. We dare not let the full import of the impasse even come to complete consciousness…

Today, instead of realizing that the impasse provides a challenge and concrete focus for prayer and drives us to contemplation, we give in to a passive sense of inevitability, and imagination dies. We do not really believe that if we surrender these situations of world impasse to contemplative prayer that new solutions, new visions of peace and equality, will emerge in our world. We dare not believe that a creative revisioning of our world is possible. Everything is just too complex, too beyond our reach. Yet it is only in the process of bringing the impasse to prayer, to the perspective of the

God who loves us, that our society will be freed, healed, changed, brought to paradoxical new visions, and freed for non-violent, selfless, liberating action, freed, therefore, for community on this planet earth. Death is involved here – a dying in order to see how to be and to act on behalf of God in the world.

This development suggests two questions: Do we really expect anything at all of the contemplative process of prayer in our world today? And how does the failure of imagination and creativity in our national life relate to the breakdown of the contemplative process of prayer and transformation in people's lives?

Constance Fitzgerald OCD, 'Impasse and Dark Night' in
Women's Spirituality: Resources for Christian Development,
ed. Joann Wolski Conn (Paulist Press 1986), pp. 300, 301.

God in the commonplace
5.42

I share the secret of the child, of the saints and sages, as well as of clowns and fools when I realize how wondrous and marvellous it is to carry fuel and draw water. Once the spiritual significance of such ordinary earthly acts dawns on me, I can skip the yoga and koans, the mantras and novenas.

One finds pain and pleasure, ecstasy and enstasy, God and humanity in the commonplace. All these good natural experiences usher us, if we let them, into the presence of God, into supernatural life. It's better to stay home and smell a flower, bake an apple pie, or sweep a floor than to have a spooky, spurious religious experience at a prayer meeting. It's better to simply enjoy the sunshine or a good show than to meddle curiously and conceitedly with the occult. It's better to romp with the dogs in the backyard than rap with the intellectuals on campus or at church, if the dogs in the yard help us to be less egotistic and more God-centred.

Ordinarily the best contemplative activities are those where contemplation is least emphasized. For instance, self-conscious, highly structured 'houses of prayer' are less conducive to contemplation than the average city dump. The higher experiences of the spiritual life are most desirable. But they are most likely to occur if we are at home with and are enjoying the daily things that fill our lives. They provide the only foundation we've got for sky-high peak experiences. If there's no foundation, there's nothing. How can we relish the higher things of God if we cannot enjoy some simple little thing like a glass of beer, a boat ride, a hot tub, a good kiss, a belly laugh, walking in the rain, lying in the sun – anything that comes along as a gift from God. The inner truth of these good things is always accessible. If we stay in touch and remain faithful to them, we will be ready when he comes.

William McNamara, *Mystical Passion: Spirituality for a Bored Society*
(Paulist Press 1977), pp. 56–57.

When Prayer is Hard

A spirituality for all weathers
5.43

I would be climbing a mountain where, off and on, I might be enveloped in mist for days on end, unable to see a foot before me. Had I noticed how mountaineers climb mountains? How they have a quiet, regular, short step – on the level it looks petty; but then this step they keep up, on and on, as they ascend, whilst the inexperienced townsman hurries along, and soon has to stop, dead beat with the climb. That such an expert mountaineer, when the thick mists come, halts and camps out under some slight cover brought with him, quietly smoking his pipe, and moving on only when the mist has cleared away…

How I was taking a long journey on board ship, with great storms pretty sure ahead of me; and how I must now select, and fix in my little cabin, some few but entirely appropriate things – a small trunk fixed up at one end, a chair that would keep its position, tumbler and glass that would do ditto: all this, simple, strong, and selected throughout in view of stormy weather. So would my spirituality have to be chosen and cultivated especially in view of 'dirty' weather…

I am travelling on a camel across a huge desert. Windless days occur, and then all is well. But hurricanes of wind will come, unforeseen, tremendous. What to do then? It is very simple, but it takes such practice to do well at all. Dismount from the camel, fall prostrate face downwards on the sand, covering your head with your cloak. And lie thus, an hour, three hours, half a day: the sandstorm will go, and you will arise and continue your journey as if nothing had happened…

You see, whether it be great cloud-mists on the mountainside, or huge, mountain-high waves on the ocean, or blinding sandstorms in the desert: there is each time one crucial point – to form no conclusions, to take no decisions, to change nothing during such crises, and especially at such times, not to force any particular religious mood or idea in oneself. To turn gently to other things, to maintain a vague, general attitude of resignation – to be very meek, with oneself and with others: the crisis goes by, thus, with great fruit.

Friedrich von Hügel, *Letters to a Niece* (J.M. Dent & Co. 1929), p. 85.

Darkness
5.44

The term 'darkness' is one which comes at different stages and has different meanings. It is, however, very much a part of growth in prayer, and needs to be looked at, if not fully understood. Why? Because if you are going to go on, you will need to go through it, and let it go through you.

In the beginning, there may be the darkness which is really blankness – unbelief. The soul can be shattered from God's light, not knowing how to begin to pray, not even wanting to, or thinking it possible. Faced with this impossibility, the impossible is demanded; you must 'Begin, all the same'… somehow, anyhow, however falteringly, however little.

When a person has set off in rather a different mood – filled with joy and eagerness, the honeymoon period which seems so full of light and promise gives way in most cases to loss of light, greyness and aridity. It is not quite dark, but it is like those days when a blight comes over the weather and nothing is quite so good or so worthwhile. The difficulty at that point is to avoid going back or trying to recapture the first taste of God which was so good. But this is the one thing you must not do, for it is necessary to go on through it – not back. Later there may be a deeper darkness as you move into the unknown – a loss of images, an intensification of aridity.

Again this, though difficult and even painful and tasteless, like eating sawdust while you pray, must be gone through. It is right, however wrong it feels; so keep on. You may be partly experiencing that God is immense – that is, too big for your mind to grasp or focus upon, and therefore everything blurs, becomes indistinct. Perhaps, too, in the greater penetrations of God's light into the soul there must ensue darkness, as happens with the naked eye moving from darkness to sudden sunshine.

There is another darkness (or is it part of the same? Who knows!). This is desolation. It can be a sense of the loss of God or of sin separating you from God; when it is really bad, it can seem that God is abandoning you. In some cases the intensity grows to the point where the horror and blackness of it stems from the idea that God hates you and appears to will your destruction. When God is lost, then faith is deeply tested. It is not at all unusual – in fact it is to be expected – that you seem no longer able to believe that God exists.

Needless to say, much of this is very painful and almost puts the soul into a panic. There is genuine need for a guide at these times – even if only to give support and encouragement to go on. It can appear to be a real agony. Only God fully knows the purpose of it. But the soul, which is humble enough to endure in faith, later glimpses what it is all about – but only later.

The message at these points is to live through, groan, let yourself be broken open or be ignored by God. Above all, trust.

Michael Hollings and Etta Gullick, The One Who Listens
(Mayhew–McCrimmon 1972), p. 144.

Distractions
5.45

When we consider with a religious seriousness the manifold weaknesses of the strongest devotions in time of prayer, it is a sad consideration. I throw myself down in my chamber, and I call in, and invite God, and his angels thither, and when they are there, I neglect God and his angels, for the noise of a fly, for the rattling of a coach, for the whining of a door; I talk on, in the same posture of praying, eyes lifted up, knees bowed down, as though I prayed to God; and, if God or his angels should ask me when I thought last of God in that prayer, I cannot tell: sometimes I find that I had forgot what I was about, but when I began to forget it, I cannot tell. A memory of yesterday's pleasures, a fear of tomorrow's dangers, a straw under my knee, a noise in mine ear, a light in mine eye, an anything, a nothing, a fancy, a chimera in my brain, troubles me in my prayer. So certainly is there nothing, nothing in spiritual things, perfect in this world.

John Donne, Eighty Sermons (1640), from Sermon LXXX (12 December 1626).

Dangerous prayer
5.46

The desert is a teacher. It offers an illustration of the danger of prayer. You hope to pass calmly through the prayer country. There are pleasant pauses. You admire spiritual landscapes which fill you with peace. Your itinerary is well planned. A few excursions into fresh territory, but care is taken to provide precise points of reference. And there is a camp base to receive you back into familiar surroundings.

You have obviously not taken seriously the sign which said, 'Danger! Prayer'. As soon as you leave the security of the oasis, you find yourself inevitably in the middle of a storm. Prayer does not spare you. In fact you do not walk into a storm. It is prayer that brutally crosses your path, shaking you, jolting you, disorienting you. You must realize that you are no longer at the wheel of your car. Your life is at the mercy of a force which you are unable to resist. Prayer plays havoc on your plans, upsets your itineraries, brings chaos into your ordered life, ruins your arrangements and destroys your camp base.

To start with, therefore, prayer is confusion, shock, abandonment. You have lost your familiar points of reference. You do not know anything any more. (St John of the Cross used to say, 'I no longer know what I know.') You understand nothing. You are literally disoriented. The guide maps offered by the most accredited spiritual masters prove useless.

Prayer invalidates all your previous knowledge, radically questions your experience, and ridicules the books which were indispensable to you.

After the experience of prayer you realize that nothing is as it was. Things have been stood on their heads. You have to come to terms with a new reality. You are forced to find a new equilibrium.

If before you were frightened because you had lost the way, now you are even more frightened because the road is impassable. No, prayer does not show you the way. Prayer obliges you to invent it. It would therefore be advisable to ensure that places of prayer have clear signs with the words: 'Danger! Prayer'.

Allessandro Pronzato, *Meditations on the Sand* (St Paul Publications 1982), pp. 9–10.

When God is absent
5.47

Oh, let not the Lord be angry, and I, who am but dust, will speak. Why dost thou withdraw thyself, and suffer me to pursue thee in vain? If I am surrounded with thy immensity, why am I thus unaware of thee? Why do I not find thee, if thou art everywhere present? I seek thee in the temple, where thou hast often met me; there I have seen the traces of thy majesty and beauty; but those sacred visions bless my sight no more. I seek thee in my secret retirements, where I have called upon thy name, and have often heard the whispers of thy voice; that celestial conversation hath often reached and raptured my soul, but I am solaced no more with thy divine condescension. I listen, but I hear those gentle sounds no more. I pine and languish, but thou fleest me. Still I wither in thy absence, as a drooping plant for the reviving sun.

Oh when wilt thou scatter this melancholy darkness? When shall the shadows flee before thee? When shall the cheerful glory of thy grace dawn upon my mind at thy approach? I shall revive at thy light; my vital spirits will confess thy presence. Grief and anxiety will vanish before thee, and immortal joys surround my soul.

Where thou art present, heaven and happiness ensue; hell and damnation fills the breast where thou art absent. While God withdraws I am encompassed with darkness and despair; the sun and stars shine with an uncomfortable lustre; the faces of my friends grow tiresome; the smile of angels would fail to cheer my languishing spirit. I grow unacquainted with tranquillity; peace and joy are empty sounds to me, and words without a meaning.

Tell me not of glory and pleasure – there are no such things without God. When he withdraws, what delight can these trifles afford? All that amuses mankind are but dreams of happiness, shadows and fantasies. What compensation can they make for an infinite good departed? All nature cannot repair my loss; heaven and earth would offer their treasures in vain. Not all the kingdoms of this world, nor the thrones of archangels, could give me a recompense for an absent God.

> Elizabeth Rowe, *Devout Exercises of the Heart*, VIII: 'Seeking after an Absent God'
> (Fowler and Russell 1798).

A scream for God
5.48

It is precisely as broken, poor and powerless that one opens oneself to the dark mystery of God in loving, peaceful waiting. When the pain of human finitude is appropriated with consciousness and consent, and handed over in one's own person to the influence of Jesus' spirit in the contemplative process, the new and deeper experience gradually takes over, the new vision slowly breaks through, and the new understanding and mutuality are progressively experienced.

At the deepest level of night, in a way one could not have imagined it could happen, one sees the withdrawal of all one has been certain of and depended upon for reassurance and affirmation. Now it is a question, not of satisfaction, but of support systems that give life meaning: concepts, systems of meaning, symbolic structures, relationships, institutions. All supports seem to fail one, and only the experience of emptiness, confusion, isolation, weakness, loneliness and abandonment remains. In the frantic search for reassurance, one wonders if anyone – friend or spouse or God – is really 'for me', is trustworthy. But no answer is given to the question.

The realization that there is *no* option but faith triggers a deep, silent, overpowering panic that, like a mighty underground river, threatens chaos and collapse. This 'scream of suffering contains all the despair of which a person is capable, and in this sense every scream is a scream for God', writes Dorothee Soelle. In this experience of the cross of Jesus, what the 'soul feels most', John [of the Cross] explains, 'is that God has rejected it and with abhorrence cast it into darkness'... Yet it is the experience of this abandonment and rejection that is transforming the human person in love. This is a possession, a redemption, an actualizing and affirmation of the person that is not understood at the time. Its symbolic expression is dispossession and death.

Constance Fitzgerald OCD, 'Impasse and Dark Night' in *Women's Spirituality: Resources for Christian Development*, ed. Joann Wolski Conn (Paulist Press 1986), pp. 297–98.

Good for you
5.49

I recommend to you prayer, because it is good for everybody, and our Lord tells us to pray. As to method, do what you can do, and what suits you. It seems obvious that most spiritual reading and meditation fails to help you; and the simplest kind of prayer is the best. So use that.

But prayer, in the sense of union with God, is the most crucifying thing there is. One must do it for God's sake; but one will not get any satisfaction out of it, in the sense of feeling 'I am good at prayer,' 'I have an infallible method.' That would be disastrous, since what we want to learn is precisely our own weakness, powerlessness, unworthiness. Nor ought one to expect 'a sense of the reality of the supernatural' of which you speak. And one should wish for no prayer, except precisely the prayer that God gives us – probably very distracted and unsatisfactory in every way!

On the other hand, the only way to pray is to pray; and the way to pray well is to pray much. If one has no time for this, then one must at least pray regularly. But the less one prays, the worse it goes. And if circumstances do not permit even regularity, then one must put up with the fact that when one does try to pray, one can't pray – and our prayer will probably consist of telling this to God.

As to beginning afresh, or where you left off, I don't think you have any choice! You simply have to begin wherever you find yourself. Make any acts you want to make and feel you ought to make; but do not force yourself into *feelings* of any kind.

As to religious matters being 'confused and overwhelming', I daresay they may remain so – in a sense – but if you get the right simple relation to God by prayer, you have got into the centre of the wheel, where the revolving does not matter. We can't get rid of the worries of this world, or of the questionings of the intellect; but we can laugh at and despise them so far as they are worries.

Dom John Chapman, in *The Spiritual Letters of Dom John Chapman*, ed. Roger Hudleston (Sheed & Ward 1946), pp. 52–53.

Not without variations
5.50

Dryness is perhaps the most common difficulty [in prayer]. Whether one week, one month, or one year after initial conversion or renewal, it is almost certain to come. Dryness consists in not experiencing the presence of God or the desire to pray. God may seem absent or distant; we may feel we are talking to ourselves. It becomes more difficult to persist in prayer under such circumstances; yet if understood correctly, these can be special times of grace.

Experience of God is intended to be a normal part of the Christian life. It is not, however, without its variations. Sometimes our failure to experience God in a sensible manner comes through no fault of our own, but is a normal stage in God's purification of our desire and intention to serve and follow him. When we experience his presence in a satisfying way, our feelings may well become the motive for our love of him. Love will not mature or deepen unless it reaffirms its choice of the beloved when the consolation of experience is not there.

Some dry times are caused by normal fluctuations in our human nature. Our psychological and physical wellbeing will inevitably affect our experience of God. Lack of sleep or food (or too much) can affect our prayer times, as can the psychological drain of long, sustained effort. We should not be alarmed at these effects but should seek God for the wisdom we need to deal with the root problems.

God's plan for us is ultimate union with him. Our experience of God will deepen as our fidelity through dry times remains steady. Temptations to shorten our prayer times during these periods, or to drop them altogether, should be resisted. Getting out of the habit of regular prayer prolongs the dry time, and makes it more difficult to respond to the next prompting of the Holy Spirit.

Ralph Martin, *Hungry for God* (Fontana 1976), pp. 93–94.

Weary flats
5.51

And who will venture to say that the highest insight of the spirit is even half as constant as the highest action of the mind? Ask the saintliest men and women of this world, whether their holy watch was continuous, and their faith and love as reliable as their thought; and they will tell you how long, even when they went up to be with the Saviour on the mount, have been the slumbers of unconsciousness, compared with the priceless instants when they were awake and beheld his glory. In every earnest life, there are weary flats to tread, with the heavens out of sight – no sun, no moon – and not a tint of light upon the path below; when the only guidance is the faith of brighter hours, and the secret hand we are too numb and dark to feel. But to the meek and faithful it is not always so. Now and then, something touches the dull dream of sense and custom, and the desolation vanishes away; the spirit leaves its witness with us; the divine realities come up from the past and straightway enter the present; the ear into which we poured our prayer is not deaf; the infinite eye to which we turned is not blind, but looks in with answering mercy on us. The mystery of life and the grievousness of death are gone; we know now the little from the great, the transient from the eternal; we can possess our souls in patience; and neither the waving palms and scattered flowers of triumph can elate us, nor the weight of the cross appear too hard to bear. Tell me not that these undulations of the soul are mere instability of enthusiasm and infirmity. Are they not found characteristically in the greatest and deepest men – Augustine, Tauler, Luther? Nay did not the Son of God himself, the very type of our humanity, experience them more than all?

Did he not quit the daily path, now for a transfiguration, and now for a Gethsemane? Did not his voice burst into the exclamation, 'I beheld Satan as lightning fall from heaven,' yet also confess, 'Now is my soul troubled'? and had he not his hours on the mountain all night? And what, think you, passed beneath those stars? Ah no! Those intermittent movements are the sign of divine gifts, not of human weakness. God has so arranged the chronometry of our spirits that there shall be thousands of silent moments between the striking hours.

James Martineau, *Hours of Thought on Sacred Things*, vol. 1
(Longmans, Green, Reader & Dyer 1880), p. 10.

God never forsakes us

5.52

'My God, my God, why have you forsaken me?'

He is not forsaken, but Christ does feel the pain and anguish that our hearts must sometimes suffer.

It's the psychology of suffering: to feel alone, to feel that no one understands, to feel forsaken...

God is not failing us when we don't feel his presence.

Let's not say: God doesn't do what I pray for so much, and therefore I don't pray any more.

God exists, and he exists even more, the farther you feel from him.

God is closer to you when you think he is farther away and doesn't hear you.

When you feel the anguished desire for God to come near because you don't feel him present, then God is very close to your anguish.

When are we going to understand that God is not only a God who gives happiness but that he tests our faithfulness in moments of affliction?

It is then that prayer and religion have most merit: when one is faithful in spite of not feeling the Lord's presence.

Let us learn from that cry of Christ that God is always our Father and never forsakes us, and that we are closer to him than we think.

Archbishop Oscar Romero, from a homily given on Good Friday,
13 April 1979, *The Church is All of You: Thoughts of Archbishop Oscar Romero*,
comp. and tr. James R. Brockman SJ (Winston Press 1984), p. 75.

Why no answer to prayer?
5.53

Again, we pray and pray, and no answer comes. The boon does not arrive. Why? Perhaps we are not spiritually ready for it. It would not be a real blessing. But the persistence, the importunity of faith, is having a great effect on our spiritual nature. It ripens. A time comes when we are ready for an answer. We then present ourselves to God in a spiritual condition which reasonably causes him to yield. The new spiritual state is not the answer to our prayer, but it is its effect; and it is the condition which makes the answer possible. It makes the prayer effectual. The gift can be a blessing now. So God resists us no more. Importunity prevails, not as mere importunity (for God is not bored into answer), but as the importunity of God's own elect, that is, as obedience, as a force of the kingdom, as increased spiritual power, as real moral action, bringing corresponding strength and fitness to receive. I have often found that what I sought most I did not get at the right time, not till it was too late, not till I had learned to do without it, till I had renounced it in principle (though not in desire). Perhaps it had lost some of its zest by the time it came, but it meant more as a gift and a trust. That was God's right time – when I could have it as though I had it not. If it came, it came not to gratify me, but to glorify him and be a means of serving him.

P.T. Forsyth, *The Soul of Prayer* (Independent Press [1916] 1966),
pp. 84–85.

A common experience
5.54

It would be wrong to assume that what John of the Cross speaks of as 'dark night' has nothing in common with ordinary, non-religious human experience. The image is not alien.

How many pages of literature, how many paintings and songs, have as their theme a dark night when what once had meaning now has none – when life's light has been extinguished, the heart bruised, the mind bewildered.

Bereavement, disappointment, failure, old age and, on the wider scene, the threat of atomic destruction; these and countless other common experiences engulf us in night.

All of them confront us with our finitude, raise fundamental questions on human existence and contain a challenge to accept our human vocation, whether we know the shape of that vocation or not.

Every human being is for God and an openness for God. It is not only around us who know his name but around every single person that the sun is shining, seeking an entrance. He uses every occasion to illuminate us and his illumination is most often perceived as darkness.

Ruth Burrows, *Ascent to Love*, ed. Elizabeth Ruth Obbard
(Darton, Longman & Todd 1988), p. 48.

Praying eccentrics
5.55

These days there is a great deal of talk about the 'rediscovery of one's identity'. But they seem to be talking about an identity which is imposed on the individual by society. It is predetermined and unalterable. You have found your identity if you 'resemble' the model which has already been decided for you. The search for one's identity then ends in slavery, not freedom. For you do not become what you are called to be, but what society wants you to be.

In the context of the search for identity, prayer is a subversive factor rather than a consolidating element. The individual passes from a *concentric* mode of living to an *eccentric* one. Eccentric not in the bizarre sense of the word, but meaning that the individual in question has the centre of his being outside himself. For he allows himself to be acted upon by God's grace.

People who pray are eccentric because they go outside the circles of brainwashing and conformism. They transcend the circles of plans and possibilities and enter the sphere of God's influence. All this, however, can only happen through the painful process of an exodus. It is their desert, fascinating and frightening at the same time, with its dark nights and its promised land.

Allessandro Pronzato, *Meditations on the Sand* (St Paul Publications 1982), p. 57.

Light in prison
5.56

And so the time passed in darkness and uncertainty. My solitude was complete; apart from the few necessary words exchanged between me and my guards I was completely silent. Each morning, at midday, and in the evening, meals were brought to me; this was all the contact between my cell and the outside world. I had no watch; I hadn't a scrap of paper for writing or reading; only the four bare walls of the cell; that was all. I realized that I must gather up all my mental and spiritual forces, in order not to go to pieces; I had no contact with the outside world at all.

And yet the consolation of God did not fail. One of his lesser consolations was the fact that one day when I was looking out of my window I saw a falcon flying round in the sky. The sky was absolutely cloudless, and the sun shone down into the grey bare quadrangle of the prison courtyard, which seemed devastatingly empty under the summer sky. Suddenly, the falcon rose into the light blue above us and wheeled around with his glorious wings – a wonderful picture of freedom. There was nothing in this empty prison courtyard to attract him, so far as I could see, so I had the impression that God had sent him; and the words of Calvin on the 104th Psalm flashed into my mind with a deep sense of consolation: 'Status mundi in Dei laetitia fundatus est' [The stability of the world is founded on the joy of God]. When the supernatural world is a present reality and more powerful than that of our external world, then even the smallest ray of its glory illumines our path, and lights up our life with a ray of eternal significance.

Hanns Lilje, *The Valley of the Shadow*, tr. Olive Wyon (SCM Press n.d.).

The Touch of God

Sound of silence

5.57

Creative silence is a necessary part of prayer. Pascal once commented that 'most of man's troubles come from his not being able to sit quietly in his chamber'. St Isaac of Nineveh, who wrote in Syriac towards the end of the seventh century, spoke of the place of silence in prayer:

> Many are avidly seeking, but they alone find who remain in continual silence... Every man who delights in a multitude of words, even though he says admirable things, is empty within. If you love truth, be a lover of silence. Silence, like the sunlight, will illuminate you in God, and will deliver you from the phantoms of ignorance. Silence will unite you to God himself...

In silence we first come to listen. Bodily composure and meditation will help in this work. But the essential element in silence is the turning inwards towards 'the still point of the turning world'...

Through deepening our experience of inner silence, there grows within us a stillness in the midst of turmoil, an emptiness and poverty of spirit. Eckhart calls this positive emptiness 'the central silence, the pure peace and abode of the heavenly birth'. The point at which silence becomes prayer is the point at which God fills the emptiness with himself. In Eckhart's words, 'Here he meets God without intermediary. And from out the Divine Unity there shines into him a simple light: and this light shows him Darkness and Nakedness and Nothingness.'

So we have come to the point at which, through discipline and silent waiting, prayer *happens*. We do not create prayer, but merely prepare the ground and clear away obstacles. Prayer is always a gift, a grace, the flame which ignites the wood; the Holy Spirit gives prayer. The human response is one of adoring love.

Kenneth Leech, *True Prayer: An Introduction to Christian Spirituality*
(Sheldon Press 1980), pp. 58–59.

Sovereignty of the Spirit
5.58

The Spirit of God falls like the dew, in mystery and power, but it is in the spiritual world as in the natural: certain substances are wet with the celestial moisture while others are always dry. Is there not a cause? The wind blows where it lists; but if we desire to feel a stiff breeze we must go out to sea, or climb the hills. The Spirit of God has his favoured places for displaying his might. He is typified by a dove, and the dove has chosen haunts: to the rivers of water, to the peaceful and quiet places, the dove resorts; we meet it not upon the battlefield, neither does it alight on carrion. There are things congruous to the Spirit, and things contrary to his mind. The Spirit of God is compared to light, and light can shine where it wills, but some bodies are opaque, while others are transparent; and so there are those through whom God the Holy Ghost can shine, and there are others through whom his brightness never appears.

> Charles Haddon Spurgeon, 'The Holy Spirit in Our Ministry',
> *Lectures to My Students* (American Tract Society n.d.).

Intercession
5.59

In 1938 a man died on Mount Athos. He was a very simple man, a peasant from Russia who came to Mount Athos when he was in his twenties and stayed for about fifty years… For a long time he was in charge of the workshops of the monastery. The workshops of the monastery were manned by young Russian peasants who used to come for one year, for two years, in order to make some money, really farthing added to farthing, in order to go back to their villages with a few pounds, perhaps, at the utmost to be able to start a family by marrying, by building a hut and by buying enough to start their crops.

One day other monks, who were in charge of other workshops, said 'Father Silouan, how is it that the people who work in your workshops work so well while you never supervise them, while we spend our time looking after them and they try continuously to cheat us in their work?' Father Silouan said 'I don't know. I can only tell you what I do about it. When I come in the morning, I never come without having prayed for these people and I come with my heart filled with compassion and with love for them, and when I walk into the workshop I have tears in my soul for love of them. And then I give them the task they have to perform in the day and as long as they will work I will pray for them, so I go into my cell and I begin to pray about each of them individually. I take my stand before God and I say "O Lord, remember Nicholas. He is young, he is just twenty, he has left in his village his wife, who is even younger than he, and their first child. Can you imagine the misery there is there that he has had to leave them because they could not survive on his work at home? Protect them in his absence. Shield them against every evil. Give him courage to struggle through this year and go back to the joy of a meeting, with enough money, but also enough courage, to face the difficulties."' And he said 'In the beginning I prayed with tears of compassion for Nicholas, for his young wife, for the little child, but as I was praying the sense of the divine presence began to grow on me and at a certain moment it grew so powerful that I lost sight of Nicholas, of his wife, his child, his needs, their village, and I could be aware only of God, and I was drawn by the sense of the divine presence deeper and deeper, until of a sudden, at the heart of this presence, I met the divine love holding Nicholas, his wife, and his child, and now it was with the love of God that I began to pray for them again, but again I was drawn into the deep and in the depths of this I again found the divine love. And so', he said, 'I spend my days, praying for each of them in turn, one after the other, and when the day is over I go, I say a few words to them, we pray together and they go to their rest. And I go back to fulfil my monastic office.'

Anthony Bloom, *School for Prayer* (Darton, Longman & Todd 1970).

Little things
5.60

Only he who gives thanks for little things receives the big things. We prevent God from giving us the great spiritual gifts he has in store for us, because we do not give thanks for daily gifts. We think we dare not be satisfied with the small measure of spiritual knowledge, experience and love that has been given to us, and that we must constantly be looking forward eagerly for the highest good. Then we deplore the fact that we lack the deep certainty, the strong faith and the rich experience that God has given to others, and we consider this lament to be pious. We pray for the big things and forget to give thanks for the ordinary, small (and yet really not small) gifts. How can God entrust great things to one who will not thankfully receive from him the little things? If we do not give thanks daily for the Christian fellowship in which we have been placed, even where there is no great experience, no discoverable riches, but much weakness, small faith and difficulty; if on the contrary we only keep complaining to God that everything is so paltry and petty, so far from what we expected, then we hinder God from letting our fellowship grow according to the measure and riches which are there for us all in Jesus Christ.

Dietrich Bonhoeffer, *Life Together* (SCM Press 1963), p. 19.

The book that reads me
5.61

On my desk stands a small wood sculpture, the work of an unknown Tanzanian artist. It portrays an African woman on her knees. What captures one's eyes is her tattooed face, where a big smile is beginning to break through her otherwise severely symmetrical features. It is as if she is going to reveal a great secret which has given her deep joy. The secret obviously relates to the book with the cross which she holds high above her head.

In this sculpture the artist wanted to capture the climax of a story often told in East Africa: A simple woman always walked around with a bulky Bible. Never would she part from it. Soon the villagers began to tease her: 'Why always the Bible? There are so many books you could read!' Yet the woman kept on living with her Bible, neither disturbed nor angered by all the teasing. Finally, one day she knelt down in the midst of those who laughed at her. Holding the Bible high above her head, she said with a big smile: 'Yes, of course there are many books which I could read. But there is only one book which reads me!'

This, in a nutshell, is the whole secret of Bible study. People start out by listening to an old message, by analyzing ancient texts, by reading – naively or critically – the biblical documents of antiquity. They experience this exercise as dull or instructive, as something Christians ought to do or something they have been led to do by their own historical, literary or theological interests. Yet a mysterious change of roles can then occur. Listening, analyzing and reading, students of the Bible meet a living reality which begins to challenge them. Out of the biblical stories, texts and documents a person comes to life, the God of Abraham, Isaac and Jacob, and even more intimately Jesus of Nazareth in whom the biblical God chose to be present among us. This divine presence starts to question, judge and guide us. Perhaps gradually, perhaps quite suddenly, the book which was the object of our reading and study becomes a subject which reads us.

There are no methods to guarantee such a mysterious change of role. It does not come from the power of human scholarship or clever teaching and know-how. It is a change worked by the power of the Holy Spirit.

Hans-Rudi Weber, *Experiments with Bible Study* (WCC 1981), p. vii.

Channels of God's love
5.62

We may be certain that… the believer indeed, drawing the depth and fullness of the divine life from Christ by the Spirit, shall in his wholly subordinate way, yet in a way most real, be wonderfully used in the conveyance of that life around him. He shall not be an original fountainhead; only one can be that. But he shall be a *living watercourse*; a living secondary cause in others of living faith, and hope, and love, by the Holy Ghost. He shall not merely speak truth about Christ and the Spirit; he shall speak it as living by it, as living it; he shall speak by 'the power that worketh in him'; he shall touch his brother's conscience, and will, and love, with a contact whose power is not of him while yet it comes through him.

If I may quote my own words written elsewhere, the Lord

> will use the man, or the woman, who is really drinking the heavenly water from the Rock, who is really filled for life's needs with the supplies of life eternal, in a mysterious way, and yet a way all the while profoundly natural. Through that personality the Spirit shall be pleased to work special blessings, for he will have made it fit to be so used. It shall be a vessel unto honour, sanctified and serviceable to the Master. The believer in question may perhaps *know* that he is thus privileged and employed, or he may never know it at all. But that matters comparatively little.

What matters is the promise of the all-faithful Lord that we, even we, shall somehow be channels for the life-giving operation of the Eternal Spirit, on condition that we 'come unto him', for ourselves, 'and drink', and that we live 'believing', live by faith in the Son of God.

Blessed be he for such a promise, and for such a condition.

Handley Carr Glyn Moule, *Veni Creator* (Hodder & Stoughton 1890),
pp. 150–51.

The last shall be first
5.63

Isaac wanted to bless Esau, and Esau was eager to receive his father's blessing; but they failed in their purpose (cf. Genesis 27). For God in his mercy blesses and anoints with the Spirit, not necessarily those whom we prefer, but those whom he marked out for his service before creating them. Thus we should not be upset or jealous if we see certain of our brethren, whom we regard as wretched and insignificant, making progress in holiness. You know what the Lord said: 'Make room for this man, so that he can sit in a higher place' (cf. Luke 14:9). I am full of admiration for the judge, who gives his verdict with secret wisdom: he takes one of the humblest of our brethren and sets him above us. And though we claim priority on the basis of our asceticism and our age, God puts us last of all. For 'each must order his life according to what the Lord has granted him' (1 Corinthians 7:17). 'If we live in the Spirit, let us also walk in the Spirit' (Galatians 5:25).

John of Karpathos, 'Texts for the Monks in India', in *The Philokalia*, vol. I,
tr. G.E.H. Palmer, Philip Sherrard and Kallistos Ware (Faber & Faber 1979), p. 305.

Inertia
5.64

The world has lost vigour and the sustaining power *to do*; it can think, but it cannot bring its thinking into being, and perhaps that is the most terrifying of all our post-war neuroses, because inertia of any kind is the devil's own playground. Average men and women are magnificent when their backs are against the wall; they lapse into triviality and slackness immediately danger is over, because they have no inward dynamo to keep them going. The most stimulating literature is poured out these days, it is read more widely than it has ever been read before, yet so little happens! But here again is another miss, because to meet that we have a power – regenerative, reactive, redirective, refreshing and sustaining. Good news indeed. It was this power proceeding from God through Jesus Christ, residing in the Christian *koinonia* [fellowship] and falling upon many on their first contact with Christianity, that transformed St Paul, a divided and distracted man indeed, into one with clear-cut purpose, enormous vigour, and an inexhaustible inward sense of peace and joy.

But when the world looks at some churches and some Christians they see the withered, sapless branches of what those very same Christians are telling them should be a fruitful vine.

The Holy Spirit quickeneth. But a supernatural treasure is not got by anything tainted with slackness, and here we can only be faithful, often coldly, drearily, faithful, before that hot miracle comes to save us. And how can we expect a fitful, furtive, patchy praying to be of any use? Here truly is perpetual decision; here is the very core of dying and resurrection, because here, in praying, we must die to our comfortable slackness and casualness.

Florence Allshorn, *The Notebooks of Florence Allshorn* (SCM Press 1957),
pp. 20–21.

Sighs and groans
5.65

Friends, 'quench not the Spirit, nor despise prophesying' where it moves; neither hinder the babes and sucklings from crying Hosanna, for out of their mouths will God ordain strength. There were some in Christ's day that were against such, whom he reproved; and there were some in Moses' day, who would have stopped the prophets in the camp, whom Moses reproved, and said, by way of encouragement to them, 'Would God, that all the Lord's people were prophets!' [Numbers 11:29]. So I say now to you. Therefore you, who stop it in yourselves, do not quench it in others, neither in babe nor suckling; for the Lord hears the cries of the needy, and the sighs and groans of the poor. Judge not that, nor the sighs and groans of the Spirit, which cannot be uttered, lest you judge prayer; for prayer as well lies in sighs and groans to the Lord as otherwise. Let not the sons and daughters, nor the hand-maidens be stopped in their prophesyings, nor the young men in their visions, nor the old men in their dreams; but let the Lord be glorified in and through all, who is over all, God blessed for ever! So every one may improve his talents, every one exercise his gifts, and every one speak as the Spirit gives him utterance. Thus every one may minister as he has received grace, as a good steward to him that has given it him; so that all plants may bud and bring forth fruit to the glory of God; 'for the manifestation of the Spirit is given to every one to profit withal.'

George Fox, *The Journal of George Fox* (London 1852), vol. 1, pp. 311–12.

A vision of the world in God
5.66

The fact that we are present in a situation alters it profoundly because God is then present with us through our faith. Wherever we are, at home with our family, with friends when a quarrel is about to begin, at work or even simply in the underground, the street, the train, we can recollect ourselves and say, 'Lord, I believe in you, come and be among us.' And by this act of faith, in a contemplative prayer which does not ask to see, we can intercede with God who has promised his presence when we ask for it. Sometimes we have no words, sometimes we do not know how to act wisely, but we can always ask God to come and be present. And we shall see how often the atmosphere changes, quarrels stop, peace comes. This is not a minor mode of intercession, although it is less spectacular than a great sacrifice. We see in it again how contemplation and action are inseparable, that Christian action is impossible without contemplation. We see also how such contemplation is not a vision of God alone, but a deep vision of everything enabling us to see its eternal meaning. Contemplation is a vision not of God alone, but of the world in God.

Anthony Bloom and George LeFebvre, *Courage to Pray*, tr. Dinah Livingstone
(Darton, Longman & Todd 1973), p. 56.

Feeling the touch of God's hand
5.67

'O gentle hand! O delicate touch!'

This hand is... the merciful and omnipotent Father. We should understand that, since it is as generous and bountiful as it is powerful and rich, it gives, when opened to favour the soul, rich and powerful presents. For this reason the soul calls it a gentle hand. It is like saying: O hand, you are as gentle to my soul, which you touch by resting gently, as you would be powerful enough to submerge the entire world if you rested somewhat heavily, for by your look alone the earth trembles, the nations melt and faint, and the mountains crumble! Oh, then again, great hand, by touching Job somewhat roughly, you were as hard and rigorous with him as you are friendly and gentle with me; how much more lovingly, graciously, and gently do you permanently touch my soul! You cause death, and you give life, and no one flees from your hand. For you, O divine lie, never kill unless to give life, never wound unless to heal. When you chastise, your touch is gentle, but it is enough to destroy the world. When you give delight, you rest very firmly, and thus the delight of your sweetness is immeasurable. You have wounded me in order to cure me, O divine hand, and you have put to death in me what made me lifeless, deprived me of God's life in which I now see myself live. You granted this with the liberality of your generous grace, which you used in contacting me with the touch of the splendour of your glory and the figure of your substance, which is your only begotten Son, through whom, being your substance, you touch mightily from one end to the other. And your only begotten Son, O merciful hand of the Father, is the delicate touch by which you touched me with the force of your cautery and wounded me.

John of the Cross, 'The Living Flame of Love', Stanza 2.16 (Commentary),
tr. Keiran Kavanaugh and Otilio Rodriguez, in *The Collected Works of St John of the Cross*
(Institute of Carmelite Studies 1979), pp. 600–601.

PART 6

Journey of the Spirit

New Beginnings

'Today is the day'
A Meditation on Song of Songs 3:1

6.1

['I sought him whom my soul loves.']

Notice three reasons which occur to me why those who seek are disappointed; perhaps they seek at the wrong time, or in the wrong way, or in the wrong place. For if any time were the right time to seek, why does the prophet say… 'Seek the Lord while he may be found'? There must be a time when he will not be found. Then he adds that he should be called upon while he is near, for there will be a time when he will not be near. Who will not seek him then? 'To me,' he says, 'every knee shall bow.' Yet he will not be found by the wicked; the avenging angels will restrain them and prevent them from seeing the glory of God. In vain will the foolish virgins cry, for the door is shut and he will certainly not go out to them. Let them apply to themselves the saying 'You will seek me and you will not find me.'

But now is the acceptable time, now is the day of salvation. It is clearly the time for seeking and for calling, for often his presence is sensed before he is called. Now hear his promise: 'Before you call me,' he says, 'I will answer. See, I am here.' The psalmist, too, plainly describes the generosity of the bridegroom, and the urgency: 'The Lord hears the crying of the poor; his ear hears the movement of their hearts.' If God is to be sought through good works, then while we have time let us do good to all, all the more because the Lord says clearly that the night is coming when no one can work. Will you find any other time in ages to come to seek for God, or to do good, except that time which God has ordained, when he will remember you? Thus today is the day of salvation, because God our king before all ages has been working salvation in the midst of the earth.

Bernard of Clairvaux, *On the Song of Songs* IV, tr. Irene Edmonds
(Cistercian Publications 1980), pp. 100–101.

Life does care
6.2

Most of the time we tend to think of life as a neutral kind of thing, I suppose. We are born into it one fine day, given life, and in life itself is neither good nor bad except as we make it so by the way that we live it. We may make a full life for ourselves or an empty life, but no matter what we make of it, the common view is that life itself, whatever life is, does not care one way or another any more than the ocean cares whether we swim in it or drown in it. In honesty one has to admit that a great deal of the evidence supports such a view. But rightly or wrongly, the Christian faith flatly contradicts it. To say that God is spirit is to say that life does care, that the life-giving power that life itself comes from is not indifferent as to whether we sink or swim. It wants us to swim. It is to say that whether you call this life-giving power the Spirit of God or reality or the life force or anything else, its most basic characteristic is that it wishes us well and is at work toward that end.

Heaven knows terrible things happen to people in this world. The good die young, and the wicked prosper, and in any one town, anywhere, there is grief enough to freeze the blood. But from deep within, whatever the hidden spring is that life wells up from, there wells up into our lives, even at their darkest and maybe especially then, a power to heal, to breathe new life into us. And in this regard, I think, every person is a mystic because everyone at one time or another experiences in the thick of joy or pain the power out of the depths of life to bless. I do not believe that it matters greatly what name you call this power – the Spirit of God is only one of its names – but what I think does matter, vastly, is that we open ourselves to receive it; that we address it and let ourselves be addressed by it; that we move in the direction that it seeks to move us, the direction of fuller communion with itself and with one another. Indeed, I believe that for our sakes this Spirit beneath our spirits will make Christs of us before we are done, or, for our sakes, it will destroy us.

Frederick Buechner, *The Magnificent Defeat* (Chatto and Windus 1967), p. 114.

'My life suddenly changed'
6.3

Five years ago I came to believe in Christ's teaching and my life suddenly changed... It happened to me as it happens to a man who goes out on some business and on the way suddenly decides that the business is unnecessary and returns home. All that was on his right is now on his left and all that was on his left is now on his right; his former wish to get as far as possible from home has changed into a wish to be as near as possible to it. The direction of my life and my desires became different, and good and evil changed places...

I, like the thief on the cross, have believed Christ's teaching and been saved... I, like the thief, knew that I was unhappy and suffering... I, like the thief to the cross, was nailed by some force to that life of suffering and evil. And as, after the meaningless suffering and evils of life, the thief awaited the terrible darkness of death, so did I await the same thing.

In all this I was exactly like the thief, but the difference was that the thief was already dying while I was still living. The thief might believe that his salvation lay there beyond the grave but I could not be satisfied with that, because, besides a life beyond the grave, life still awaited me here. But I did not understand that life. It seemed to me terrible. And suddenly I heard the words of Christ and understood them, and life and death ceased to seem to me evil, and instead of despair I experienced happiness and the joy of life undisturbed by death.

Leo Tolstoy, *What I Believe,* tr. Constantine Popoff (Eliott Stock 1885).

Moment of believing
6.4

I went to bed and slept well. In the morning, I dreamed that the sweetest boy I ever saw came dancing up to my bedside; he seemed just out of leading-strings, yet I took particular notice of the firmness and steadiness of his tread. The sight affected me with pleasure, and served at least to harmonize my spirits so that I awoke for the first time with a sensation of delight on my mind. Still, however, I knew not where to look for the establishment of the comfort I felt; my joy was as much a mystery to myself as to those about me. The blessed God was preparing me for the clearer light of his countenance by this first dawning of that light upon me.

... Having risen with somewhat of a more cheerful feeling, I repaired to my room, where breakfast waited for me. While I sat at table, I found the cloud of horror which had so long hung over me was every moment passing away, and every moment came fraught with hope... The happy period which was to shake off my fetters and afford me a clear opening of the free mercy of God in Christ Jesus was now arrived. I flung myself into a chair near the window and, seeing a Bible there, ventured once more to apply to it for comfort and instruction. The first verse I saw was the 25th of the third chapter of Romans: 'Whom God hath set forth to be a propitiation through faith in his blood, to declare his righteousness for the remission of sins that are past, through the forbearance of God.'

Immediately I received strength to believe it, and the full beams of the sun of righteousness shone upon me. I saw the sufficiency of the atonement he had made, my pardon sealed in his blood, and all the fullness and completeness of his justification. In a moment I believed, and received the gospel... Unless the almighty arm had been under me, I think I should have died with gratitude and joy. My eyes filled with tears, and my voice choked with transport, I could only look up to heaven in silent fear, overwhelmed with love and wonder. But the work of the Holy Ghost is best described in his own words: it is 'joy unspeakable and full of glory'. Thus was my heavenly Father in Christ Jesus pleased to give me the full assurance of faith, and out of a strong, stony, unbelieving heart, to raise up a child unto Abraham.

William Cowper, *Memoir of the Early Life of William Cowper Written by Himself* in *A Burning and Shining Light: English Spirituality in the Age of Wesley*, ed. David L. Jeffrey (Eerdmans 1987).

Sacred space
6.5

In Rio a group of Christians was working with street children, of whom there are twenty-five million in Brazil. Every day boys from the street got together at one spot to chat, to discuss their problems and to share their fears and anger with one another. Many came regularly. The church people consisted of a Catholic priest, a Methodist, a priest of the Umbanda cult, a Presbyterian and a young Lutheran pastor.

One day one of the boys said: 'I would like to be baptized.'

'In which church, then?' asked the Catholic.

'Which church? In ours here, of course.'

'But to which church building would you like to go?'

'Building? No, to our church, here on the street. I want to be baptized here among us.'

The Methodist said he couldn't issue a certificate. The Catholic thought it wouldn't be possible to perform jointly with the man from the Umbanda religion. The boy stuck by his wish. Finally the pastor organized the necessary things: he laid a board over two crates and filled an old boot with water for flowers, which the children provided. The Catholic brought along a candle. The baptism took place on the street, in the name of Jesus Christ.

Dorothee Soelle, *Celebrating Resistance: The Way of the Cross in Latin America*,
tr. Joyce Irwin (Mowbray 1993), p. 78.

'I felt my heart strangely warmed'
6.6

In the evening I went very unwillingly to a society in Aldersgate Street, where someone was reading Luther's preface to the Epistle to the Romans. About a quarter before nine, while he was describing the change which God works in the heart through faith in Christ, I felt my heart strangely warmed. I felt I did trust in Christ, Christ alone, for salvation; and an assurance was given me that he had taken away my sins, even mine, and saved me from the law of sin and death.

I began to pray with all my might for those who had in a more especial manner despitefully used me and persecuted me. I then testified openly to all there that what I now first felt in my heart. But it was not long before the enemy suggested, 'This cannot be faith; for where is your joy?' Then was I taught that peace and victory over sin are essential to faith in the captain of our salvation; but that, as to the transports of joy that usually attend the beginning of it, especially in those who have mourned deeply, God sometimes gives, sometimes withholds them, according to the counsels of his own will.

After my return home, I was much buffeted with temptations; but I cried out, and they fled away. They returned again and again. I as often lifted up my eyes, and he 'sent me help from his holy place'. And I found the difference between this and my former state chiefly consisted in this. I was striving, yes, fighting with all my might under the law, as well as under grace. But then I was sometimes, if not often, conquered; now, I was always conquered.

Thursday 25. The moment I awoke, 'Jesus, master' was in my heart and in my mouth; and I found all my strength lay in keeping my eye fixed on him, and my soul waiting on him continually.

John Wesley, *The Journal of the Rev. John Wesley*, 24–25 May 1738 (J. Kershaw 1827).

Excuses
6.7

No sinner under the light of the gospel lives a single hour in sin, without some excuse, either tacit or avowed, by which he justifies himself. It seems to be a law of our intelligent nature that when accused of wrong, either by our conscience or any other agent, we must either confess or justify. The latter is the course taken. It is so hard to abandon all excuses and admit the humbling truth that we ourselves are all wrong and God all right. Thus it becomes the great business of a gospel minister to search out and expose the sinner's excuses; to demolish if possible their refuge of lies, and lay open their heart to the shafts of truth.

I can recollect very well the year I lived on excuses, and how long it was before I gave them up. I had never heard a minister preach on the subject. I found, however, by my experience that my excuses and lies were the obstacles in the way of my conversion. As soon as I let these go utterly, I found the gate of mercy wide open. And so would you.

Charles Grandison Finney, 'The Excuses of Sinners Condemn God',
Sermons on Gospel Themes (New York 1876).

Conviction of sin
6.8

One morning, while I was walking as usual in a solitary place, I at once saw that all my contrivances and projections to effect or procure deliverance and salvation for myself were utterly in vain. I was brought quite to a stand as finding myself totally lost. The tumult that had been before in my mind was now quieted, and I was something eased of that distress which I felt while struggling against a sight of myself and of the divine sovereignty. I had the greatest certainty that my state was forever miserable, for all that I could do. I wondered that I had never been sensible of it before.

In the time I remained in this state, my notions respecting my duties were quite different. Before this, the more I did in duty, the more I thought God was obliged to me. But now, the more I prayed, the more I saw I was indebted to God for allowing me to ask for mercy; for I saw it was self-interest that had led me to pray, and that I had never once prayed from any respect to the glory of God. I saw that I had been heaping up my devotions before God, fasting, praying, pretending; whereas I never once truly intended to aim at the glory of God, but only my own happiness. I saw that, as I had never done anything for God, I had no claim to lay to anything from him.

David Brainerd, *The Diary and Journal of David Brainerd* (London 1902).

Rock bottom
6.9

We are to *die* to sin. What does it mean to die? It means that we are to accept the absolutely inescapable, the utterly unavoidable, and go down into it – we have to face it in its final reality. When we die to sin, therefore, we are to confront our sin, look it in the face, recognize it utterly without flinching. We cannot deal with it any other way: we dare not hide from it, pretend it is other than it is, run from it, the way we run from the knowledge of death. We are not to dream up excuses, or develop ways of explaining it away, or blame it on someone else. We are to face up to it and its certainty. Only then, only at that rock-bottom point of penitence, can we hear the word that raises us to a new and joyful life. At the very moment of hopelessness, when we confront, possibly for the first time, what we really are, that very moment is the resurrection now!

And the same is true in our relationships with each other. Nothing is sadder than broken relationships and the suspicion, hatred and malice that result. And nothing is worse for the Christian or the Christian community than that. But here again, there is to be no superficial healing or patching up. Here, too, we must die, must really face what we have done, what we have become, how we have handled others, abused them, ignored them, exploited them, taken them for granted, taunted and tortured them in ways both blatant and subtle. And what a dying it is to recognize all that: to climb out from behind all our protective fortifications and see the havoc we have wrought; to have our eyes really forced to look long and honestly at what we are, without benefit of that professional advocate who is always there to leap in to our defence and explain it all away. There is no dying like that dying, but there is no substitute for it, no escape from it, if we would have honest and healthy relationships that are not built on pretence or on tyranny. Think of the marriages that are collisions of strangers. Think of the working relationships that are snarling cockpits of hatred and tension. Think of the congregations that are war zones of feuding interest groups, or, which is almost as bad, little bands of friends who freeze out any hapless stranger who inadvertently wanders into their midst. We cannot know the healing of any of these relationships, we cannot live the resurrection life, until we have faced unflinchingly the reality of what we are. We must die if we would rise again.

Richard Holloway, *The Way of the Cross* (Fount 1986), pp. 118–19.

Does it matter?
6.10

We are always in need of repentance, of the willingness to acknowledge our state of forgiveness; we are always being forgiven, transfigured and forgiving, and thus being part of God's transfiguration of creation.

Sin both matters terribly and matters not at all: matters terribly as a vehicle for evil, and matters not at all because it can be transformed in the love of God. Sin, which we cannot avoid, and the acknowledgment of sin, can be a balancing factor, not a morbid preoccupation. It is rather a knowledge that adds reality to the assessment of decisions we are about to make, and brings us to a kind of self-knowledge that surpasses gladness because of the fire in the dark, and the fire in our tears.

And because we are one organism our tears cannot stop with ourselves; our responsibility cannot stop with a narcissistic perception of where our sin leaves off and another's begins. The more we participate in transfiguration, the less we fear, the less we feel we have to control. Thus the boundaries between ourselves and others become less defined and finally disappear altogether, not because we are finding ourselves by testing ourselves against the actions and reactions of others, but precisely because we are being found in God and thus need less self-reflection.

We come to a knowledge of our selves and, at the same time, who we are no longer matters. Thus our acknowledgment of our responsibility is not the devouring, passionate, neurotic assumption of responsibility that is false guilt, but rather a recognition of the dynamic process of being privileged to acknowledge membership in the human race, and thus be a bearer of responsibility.

Maggie Ross, *The Fountain and the Furnace: The Way of Tears and Fire*
(Paulist Press 1987), p. 121.

Brought to the Father
6.11

When a sinner is brought to Christ, he is brought to the Father. Jesus gave himself for us, 'that he might bring us to God'. Oh! what a sight breaks in upon the soul – the infinite, eternal, unchangeable God! I know that some of you have been brought to see this sight. Oh! praise him, then, for what he is. Praise him for his *pure, loving holiness*, that cannot bear any sin in his sight. Cry, like the angels, 'Holy, holy, holy, Lord God Almighty.' Praise him for his *infinite wisdom* – that he knows the end from the beginning. In him are hid all the treasures of wisdom and knowledge. Praise him for his *power* – that all matter, all mind, is in his hand. The heart of the king, the heart of saint and sinner, are all in his hand. Hallelujah! for the Lord God omnipotent reigneth. Praise him for his *love*; for God is love. Some of you have been at sea. When far out of sight of land, you have stood high on the vessel's prow, and looked round and round – one vast circle of ocean without any bound. Oh! so it is to stand in Christ justified, and to behold the love of God – a vast ocean all around you, without a bottom and without a shore. Oh! praise him for what he is. Heaven will be all praise. If you cannot praise God, you never will be there.

Robert Murray M'Cheyne, 'Thanksgiving Obtains the Spirit' (1839) in *Sermons* (Banner of Truth Trust 1960).

To be naked
6.12

Physical nakedness has a profound significance, or rather when it has significance at all it is profound. In many cultures it has none, it is simply the way people are, and there is an unconsciousness and 'innocence' about this which provokes guilty envy in more conscious people. But in such a culture there is really no such thing as nakedness. There has to be differentiation before there can be union. To be naked does not mean simply to be unclothed, it means to remove (or to have stripped off) the normal defences and disguises of common life, by which sinful people protect themselves from too much knowledge of themselves or others. It means to be defenceless, intensely vulnerable. Lovers delight to be naked to each other because it expresses their joy in mutual giving, without reserve, but violently to strip off a person's clothes is a recognized means of humiliating and degrading a human being. In Christianity, with its awareness of the significance of the physical, for good or evil, it is not surprising that nakedness has always had a peculiarly strong symbolism. (The anti-physical prudery of some Christian traditions is merely a perversion of the truthful awareness of the fact that bodies are where sin, as well as holiness, resides.) Nakedness, in Christian iconography, has symbolized equally the erotic and the innocent, the extreme of penitent love and the extreme of brazen seduction. Francis Bernardone stripped naked and handed his worldly clothes back to his father, and many religious orders and sects have initiated new members by stripping and reclothing them, though not necessarily in public. For the Christian, unclothing is a word of penitence, renunciation and love, and the stripping of the baptismal candidate was a very powerful means of preparing the moment of breakthrough. In a sense, it represents the edge of that gap, the entrance into the darkness of unknowing, which is the way of passionate love.

Rosemary Haughton, *The Passionate God* (Darton, Longman & Todd 1982), pp. 218–19.

God's mysterious ways
6.13

Conversion is a great and glorious work of God's power, at once changing the heart, and infusing life into the dead soul, though the grace then implanted displays itself more gradually in some than in others. There are very many who do not know, even when they have it, that it is the grace of conversion, and sometimes do not think it to be so till a long time after. The manner of God's work on the soul is very mysterious.

Persons after their conversion often speak of religious things as seeming new to them; that preaching is a new thing; that it seems to them they never heard preaching before; that the Bible is a new book; they find there new chapters, new psalms, new histories, because they see them in a new light. Many have spoken much of their hearts being drawn out in love to God and Christ. I have seen some, and conversed with them, who have certainly been perfectly sober, and very remote from anything like enthusiastic wildness. And they have talked of the glory of God's perfections, the wonderfulness of his grace in Christ, and their own unworthiness, in such a manner as cannot be perfectly expressed after them.

Many, while their minds have been filled with spiritual delights, have as it were forgot their food. Their bodily appetite has failed, while their minds have been entertained with 'meat to eat that others knew not of'. The light and comfort which some of them enjoy give a new relish to their common blessings, and cause all things about them to appear as it were beautiful, sweet and pleasant. All things abroad, the sun, moon and stars, the clouds and sky, the heavens and earth, appear as it were with a cast of divine glory and sweetness upon them.

Jonathan Edwards, 'A Faithful Narrative of the Surprising Work of God in Northampton',
in *The Works of Jonathan Edwards*, rev. and corrected by Edward Hickman
(Banner of Truth Trust [1834] 1974).

Masks
6.14

May I be quite honest with you? We both know your life is masked, and there is a terrible split within it. One part of you wants a different life, while another part refuses to change. So you exist on a see-saw.

I know there is a key, somewhere, to the puzzle of you. I have not been able to find it, which is my own shortsightedness and failure. If you could only venture forth from the deep recesses in which that frantic, frightened child dwells, and crouch in a safe place to watch the dawn. I have seen, in your eyes, the child. The child is emaciated, hungry, longing and very pale for a lack of sun. Liberate the child who wants to become an adult.

Liberation is not 'easy'. It takes a single moment of dying. The child wants to be liberated (I know this). The child must either try to become free, or it must ask – cry out – for help. What you must do is draw closer to others. Healing occurs when it is least sought or anticipated. It occurs, in fact, when one has forgotten about being healed, and has simply entered into the human condition more fully to be with others, and, if possible, serve them.

No matter how tight the mask you place on your face, you can't hide the child's eyes.

Malcolm Boyd, *Malcolm Boyd's Book of Days* (Heinemann/SCM Press 1968), p. 135.

Change of direction
6.15

We see that we cannot partake deeply of the life of God unless we change profoundly. It is therefore essential that we should go to God in order that he should transform and change us, and that is why, to begin with we should ask for conversion.

Conversion in Latin means a turn, a change in the direction of things. The Greek word *metanoia* means a change of mind. Conversion means that instead of spending our lives in looking in all directions, we should follow one direction only. It is turning away from a great many things which we value solely because they were pleasant or expedient for us. The first impact of conversion is to modify our sense of values. God being at the centre of all, everything acquires a new position and a new depth. All that is God's, all that belongs to him, is positive and real. Everything that is outside him has no value or meaning. But it is not a change of mind alone that we can call conversion. We can change our minds and go no farther; what must follow is an act of will and unless our will comes into motion and is redirected Godwards, there is no conversion; at most there is only an incipient, still dormant and inactive change in us.

Anthony Bloom, *Living Prayer* (Darton, Longman & Todd 1966), p. 65.

A time to die
6.16

Another thing that happened on that two-week retreat was that I began to toy with the notion of becoming a Christian. It was not a very pleasant notion. To act on it, I felt, would require a kind of death on several levels. For one, there was this old business of me being in the driver's seat of *my* time. It seemed to me that if I were to become a Christian my time would no longer belong to me, that it would have to belong to Christ/God and to the mystical 'Body of Christ'. My ownership of my time would have to die, and that very much felt like having to die myself.

No one likes to die, and so I dragged my feet as long as I could. I used every rationalization in the book to avoid being baptized. The best was that I couldn't decide whether I wanted to be baptized as an Eastern Orthodox, or Roman Catholic, or Episcopalian, or Presbyterian or Lutheran or Methodist or Baptist. Since this complex, intellectual denominational decision was obviously going to take at least thirty years of research, I didn't have to get on with it. But then it hit me that I didn't have to choose a denomination, that, in fact, baptism is not a denominational celebration. So when I was finally drowned March 9, 1980, it was by a North Carolina Methodist minister at the chapel of a New York Episcopal convent in a deliberately non-denominational party. And I have very jealously guarded my non-denominational status ever since. For one thing, it is good for business. But the more compelling reason is that, on a certain deep level, I don't believe in denominations. I do believe there should be different flavours of worship for different folk, but the idea of one denomination denying Communion to another – or to any individual at all – is anathema to me. As far as I am concerned, I feel free to walk into a Christian church of whatever denomination because I belong there.

M. Scott Peck, *Further Along the Road Less Travelled* (Simon & Schuster 1993).

'Become as little children'

6.17

When Jesus urged people to repent, he was urging them to become as little children. He wasn't asking them to eat the dust. He was confronting them with the necessity of a radical change of outlook, a fundamental reorientation of their lives, so that they would no longer trust for security in the persona they had built up – the drama of being me which I continuously stage for my own benefit – so that they would no longer trust that, but have the courage to become as receptive as little children, with all the openness to life, the taking down of the shutters and the throwing away of the armour which that entails...

That is what repentance means: discovering that you have more to you than you dreamt or knew, becoming bored with being only a quarter of what you are and therefore taking the risk of surrendering to the whole, and thus finding more abundant life...

It is obvious how important repentance is for the Christian. It was part of the basic message of Jesus. He began his ministry by telling people to repent and believe in the gospel.

Unless, therefore, we are willing to repent, we cannot be his disciples.

H.A. Williams, *True Wilderness* (Collins 1983), pp. 72, 76, 78.

Our fundamental decision
6.18

Conversion is our fundamental decision in regard to God. It marks nothing less than the ending of the old and the emergence of the new. 'When anyone is united to Christ, there is a new world; the old has gone, and a new order has already begun' (2 Corinthians 5:17, New English Bible). Heart, mind and soul, being, thinking and doing – all are remade in the grace of God's redeeming love. This decision to allow ourselves to be remade, this conversion, is neither a static nor a once-and-finished event. It is both a moment and a process of transformation that deepens and extends through the whole of our lives. Many think conversion is only for non-believers, but the Bible sees conversion as also necessary for the erring believer, the lukewarm community of faith, the people of God who have fallen into disobedience and idolatry.

The people of God are those who have been converted to God and to God's purpose in history. They define their lives by their relationship to the Lord. No longer are their lives organized around their own needs or the dictates of the ruling powers. They belong to the Lord and serve God alone. Transformed by God's love, the converted experience a change in all their relationships: to God, to their neighbour, to the world, to their possessions, to the poor and dispossessed, to the violence around them, to the idols of their culture, to the false gods of the state, to their friends and to their enemies. The early church was known for these things. In other words, the early Christians were known for the things their conversion wrought. Their conversion happened in history; and, in history, the fruits of their conversion were made evident.

Jim Wallis, *The Call to Conversion* (Lion 1986), pp. 7–8.

True religion
6.19

As our faith, so our devotion should be lively. Cold meat won't serve at those repasts. It's a coal from God's altar must kindle our fire; and without fire, true fire, no acceptable sacrifice. 'Open thou my lips, and then', said the Royal Prophet, 'my mouth shall praise God' [Psalm 51:15]. But not till then.

The preparation of the heart, as well as answer of the tongue, is of the Lord. And to have it, our prayers must be powerful, and our worship grateful. Let us choose, therefore, to commune where there is the warmest sense of religion; where devotion exceeds formality, and practice most corresponds with profession; and where there is at least as much charity as zeal. For where this society is to be found, there shall we find the church of God.

It is a sad reflection that many hardly have any religion at all, and most have none of their own. For that which is the religion of their education, and not of their judgment, is the religion of another, and not theirs. To have religion upon authority and not upon conviction, is like a finger watch, to be set forward or backward as he pleases that has it in keeping.

William Penn, *The Fruits of Solitude* (1693).

Longing for salvation
6.20

'Yet I trust in your word.'

The word in which David put his trust was that word which, according to prophecy, was still to come. We can take this as referring to the Word of God. Believing as he did in that heavenly Word, there is no doubt that the prophecy upon which David's hope was set was either the promised coming of our Lord Jesus Christ or the prediction of his glory. Himself a prophet, David reflected upon the scriptural texts and realized that as long as he was living in the flesh he was, as it were, bound by the chains of this present life and far removed from the salvation of God. Consequently he was filled with great hunger for this salvation, wearing himself out with longing and consumed with desire to possess the object of his yearning. His own words are: 'I pour out my prayer before him.' His spirit fainted within him; and indeed it can be said that those who totally deny themselves in order to belong to Christ experience this kind of ecstasy of spirit.

Truly, for those who seek God, Christ is the way. We too must long for that eternal happiness, the salvation God offers us in him. Do not let us set our hearts on money as misers do. Worn out and exhausted with longing, our souls must raise themselves up to cling to the salvation of God which is in Christ Jesus our Lord, for he is our healing, our fidelity, our strength, and our wisdom.

Ambrose, from a commentary on Psalm 118 [119], in *A Word in Season* I, ed. Friends of Henry Ashworth (St Bede's Publications & Exordium Books 1981), p. 81.

A difficult choosing
6.21

The difficulty of conversion is a difficulty of choosing. A choice must be made to enter into life and share in other's search for life.

Inasmuch as conversion is a matter of choice, it entails conflict. When one possesses a certain socioeconomic position, a break is inevitable if there is to be a conversion. Gustavo Gutiérrez says: 'To wish to accomplish conversion without conflict is to deceive oneself and others.'

Almost all who have written on the subject of conversion are in agreement on this point. It has been said that a conversion must be radical to the point 'of confronting death in order to achieve a resurrection'. Jon Sobrino claims that the exhortation 'repent, and believe in the gospel' has an element of intimidation in it. 'Now is the time to make a decision, and it will entail a conversion... a radical change in one's form of existence.'

This inescapable break takes the form of a rejection of the present, in which death is at work or, in other words, the oppression exercised by the socioeconomic conditions in which we are caught. If conversion is what we say it is – a change of outlook that impels us inexorably to hasten the process of liberation (so that the masses may have the right to life) – then conflict is inevitable. For conversion brings with it an identification of opposites and a definitive confrontation.

Conversion is a gift of God because it shows us the way and invites us to enter the world of freedom, the world of life. But at the same time conversion is a human task, because it demands of us an individual and collective commitment to the building of that world.

Elsa Tamez, *Bible of the Oppressed*, tr. Matthew J. O'Connell
(Orbis Books 1982), pp. 80–81.

Wake up!
6.22

Seeking workers in a multitude of people, God calls out and says again: 'Is there anyone here who yearns for life and desires to see good days?' If you hear this and your answer is 'I do', God then directs these words to you: if you desire true and eternal life, 'keep your tongue free from vicious talk and your lips from all deceit; turn away from evil and do good; let peace be your quest and aim.' Once you have done this, my 'eyes will be upon you and my ears will listen for your prayers; and even before you ask me, I will say' to you: 'Here

I am.' What is more delightful than this voice of the Holy One calling to us? See how God's love shows us the way of life. Clothed then with faith and the performance of good works, let us set out on this way, with the gospel for our guide, that we may deserve to see the Holy One 'who has called us to the eternal presence'.

> Benedict of Nursia, Prologue to the Rule of Benedict, in *The Rule of Benedict: Insights for the Ages*, ed. Joan Chittister (St Pauls 1992), p. 23.

The Struggle of Faith

Gracious uncertainty

A Meditation on 1 John 3:2

6.23

'It doth not yet appear what we shall be.'

Naturally, we are inclined to be so mathematical and calculating that we look upon uncertainty as a bad thing. We imagine that we have to reach some end, but that is not the nature of spiritual life. The nature of spiritual life is that we are certain in our uncertainty, consequently we do not make our nests anywhere. Common sense says – 'Well, supposing I were in that condition…' We cannot suppose ourselves in any condition we have never been in.

Certainty is the mark of the common-sense life: gracious uncertainty is the mark of the spiritual life. To be certain of God means that we are uncertain in all our ways; we do not know what a day may bring forth. This is generally said with a sigh of sadness; it should be rather an expression of breathless expectation. We are uncertain of the next step, but we are certain of God. Immediately we abandon to God, and do the duty that lies nearest; he packs our life with surprises all the time. When we become advocates of a creed, something dies; we do not believe God, we only believe our belief about him. Jesus said 'Except ye… become as little children.' Spiritual life is the life of a child. We are not uncertain of God, but uncertain of what he is going to do next. If we are only certain in our beliefs, we get dignified and severe and have the ban of finality about our views; but when we are rightly related to God, life is full of spontaneous, joyful uncertainty and expectancy.

'Believe also in Me,' said Jesus, not – 'Believe certain things about Me.' Leave the whole thing to him; it is gloriously uncertain how he will come in, but he will come. Remain loyal to him.

Oswald Chambers, *My Utmost for His Highest*
(Marshall Simpkin 1926), p. 120.

The friendly night
6.24

I shall never forget the nights under the Saharan stars. I felt as if I were wrapped around by the blanket of the friendly night, a blanket embroidered with stars.

Yes, a friendly night, a benevolent darkness with restful shadows. In them the movement of my soul is not hindered. On the contrary, it can spread out, be fulfilled, grow and be joyful.

I feel at home, safe, fearless, desirous only of staying like this for hours; my only worry that of the shortness of the night, so avid am I to read within and outside myself the symbols of divine language.

The friendly night is an image of faith, that gift of God defined, 'The guarantee of the blessings we hope for and proof of the existence of the realities that at present remain unseen' (Hebrews 11:1). I have never found a better metaphor for my relationship with the eternal: a point lost in infinite space, wrapped round by the night under the subdued light of the stars. I am this point lost in space: the darkness, like an irreplaceable friend, is faith; the stars, God's witness.

When my faith was weak, all this would have seemed incomprehensible to me. I was afraid as a child is of the night. But now I have conquered it, and it is mine. I experience joy in night, navigating upon it as upon the sea. The night is no longer my enemy, nor does it make me afraid. On the contrary, its darkness and divine transcendence are a source of delight.

Sometimes I even close my eyes to see more darkness. I know the stars are there in their place, as a witness to me of heaven. And I can see why darkness is so necessary.

The darkness is necessary, the darkness of faith is necessary, for God's light is too great. It wounds.

I understand more and more that faith is not a mysterious and cruel trick of a God who hides himself without telling me why, but a necessary veil. My discovery of him takes place gradually, respecting the growth of divine life in me.

Carlo Carretto, *Letters from the Desert* (Darton, Longman & Todd 1972),
pp. 139–41.

Waiting in faith
6.25

Sometimes the person seeking the guidance of God has to put up with the fact that it may be God's will, perhaps for reasons known only to him, that this trusting Christian should be in uncertainty. Often the sense of certainty comes as we approach the time when action is necessary. Before that point we simply have to wait in faith.

God's guidance is not an interruption of the normal flow of life, a special occasion. It is with us all the time because his presence is with us all the time. His present guidance is generally clear.

We can generally know now what he wants us to do *now*. We cannot always know now what he will want us to do in the future. If we are thinking out a problem and light does not come, it is right to regard that as present guidance. Having done all the thinking we fruitfully can about the matter, we have clearly to endure the obscurity of the situation, and we had better leave the perplexing issue and give ourselves to the immediate duty or pleasure that is in front of us. There is always something God wants us to do *now*. It must always be one thing. It must always be something that we can do.

We should not assume that, because we believe in the guidance of the Spirit and have prayed and thought about the problem, the decision we finally come to will be the most prudent we could have reached and must be successful. God is wisdom and truth. We perceive this wisdom and truth imperfectly. Our conscience may be ill-informed and immature. The decision to which our minds finally come may be the wrong one. We may not always know what is the will of God in the sense of that which he wants done in this particular situation, but it is always God's will that we do that which in an attitude of prayer and extensive thought and faith we believe to be the best course. And when we have done that, we can say that we have done God's will. But we say it in faith and humility, already asking for forgiveness, because we know that somewhere in it all there will be failure on our part – and leaving the issue to that fatherly providence which eternally directs and redirects the movement of life, and can, without invading their freedom, make the mistaken insights of men serve his purpose as long as they love him and want his will to prevail.

Our prayer for the guidance of the Spirit does not expect that the situation will be changed into some form more in accordance with our wishes or our strength. It is a means of expressing our Christian outlook, providing words for our deeper intention, and can be seen as the Holy Spirit bringing to our remembrance the things of Christ. One of the 'things of Christ' is the conviction that though life continually eludes calculation and manipulation there is always something for love to do. As we dwell on this we find ourselves defining the situation in new terms, some of our original wishes concerning it are seen to be quite irrelevant and it becomes clear that there is in fact a way forward and a grace to be relied on.

J. Neville Ward, *Five for Sorrow, Ten for Joy*
(Epworth Press 1971), p. 117.

Faith and love
6.26

We must not separate faith from love. Evangelicals have always emphasized faith. *Sola fide*, 'by faith alone', was one of the great watchwords of the Reformation, and rightly so. 'Justification', or acceptance with God, is not by good works which we have done or could do; it is only by God's sheer unmerited favour ('grace'), on the sole ground of the atoning death of Jesus Christ, by simple trust in him alone. This central truth of the gospel cannot be compromised for anything. But, although justification is by faith alone, this faith cannot remain alone. If it is living and authentic, it will inevitably issue in good works, and if it does not, it is spurious. Jesus himself taught this in his 'sheep and goats' description of Judgment Day. Our attitude to him, he said, will be revealed in, and so judged by, our good works of love to the least of his brothers and sisters. The apostles all lay the same emphasis on the necessity of good works of love. We all know that James taught it: 'faith by itself, if it is not accompanied by action, is dead... I will show you my faith by what I do' (2:17, 18). So does John: 'If anyone has material possessions and sees his brother in need but has no pity on him, how can the love of God be in him?' (1 John 3:17). And so does Paul. Christ died to create a new community who would be 'eager to do what is good' (Titus 2:14). We have been recreated in Christ 'to do good works, which God prepared in advance for us to do' (Ephesians 2:10). Again, 'the only thing that counts is faith expressing itself through love... Serve one another in love' (Galatians 5:6, 13). This, then, is the striking sequence – faith, love, service. True faith issues in love, and true love issues in service.

John Stott, *Issues Facing Christians Today*
(Marshall Morgan & Scott 1984), pp. 23–24.

Untimely zeal
6.27

Some persons, as soon as they begin to find further light dawning upon their minds and are let into the knowledge of some doctrine or perception which they had not previously understood, immediately set their zeal to work. Their zeal is all on fire to propagate and promote this new lesson of truth before their own hearts are established in it upon solid understanding and before they have considered whether it is a doctrine of great importance or merits such a degree of zeal. How common it is among Christians, too often among ministers of the gospel, to give free rein to their emotions at the first glimpse of some pleasing opinion or some fresh discovery of what they call truth! They compensate for the weakness of the proof by the strength of their emotions, and by the pleasure they take in the opinion they have embraced. This confirms their assent too soon, and they grow deaf to arguments that are brought to oppose it. They construe every text in scripture to support this doctrine; they bring in the prophets and apostles to maintain it. They fancy they see it in a thousand verses of their Bibles and they pronounce all that dare maintain contrary opinions heretics. Their conduct in this matter is as vehement as if every gleam of light were sufficient to determine their faith, because it happens to fire their emotions. They grow warm about it as if every opinion in spiritual life were fundamental, every mistake deserved the severest censures…

There are too many who take up most of their articles of faith initially without due examination and without sufficient argument. Their veneration for great names or their affection for a particular party has determined their opinions long before. Their passions and other prejudices have formed their schemes of doctrine to the neglect or abuse of their understanding, and yet they pronounce as positively upon truth and error as though they were infallible. Happy are those whose faith is built on better foundations!

Isaac Watts, *Abuse of the Emotions in Spiritual Life* (1746).

Attitude of a believer
6.28

Methinks there be not impossibilities enough in religion for an active faith; the deepest mysteries ours contains have not only been illustrated, but maintained, by syllogism and the rule of reason. I love to lose myself in a mystery, to pursue my reason to an *O altitudo!* [see Romans 11.33]. 'Tis my solitary recreation to pose my apprehension with those involved enigmas and riddles of the Trinity, with incarnation, and resurrection. I can answer all the objections of Satan and my rebellious reason with that odd resolution I learned of Tertullian, *Certum est, quia impossibile est* [it is certain because it is impossible]. I desire to exercise my faith in the difficultest point; for to credit ordinary and visible objects is not faith, but persuasion. Some believe the better for seeing Christ's sepulchre; and, when they have seen the Red Sea, doubt not of the miracle. Now, contrarily, I bless my self and am thankful that I lived not in the days of miracles, that I never saw Christ nor his disciples. I would not [like to] have been one of those Israelites that pass'd the Red Sea, nor one of Christ's patients on whom he wrought his wonders; then had my faith been thrust upon me, nor should I enjoy that greater blessing pronounced to all that believe and saw not. 'Tis an easy and necessary belief, to credit what our eye and sense hath examined. I believe that he was dead, and buried, and rose again, and desire to see him in his glory, rather than to contemplate him in his cenotaph or sepulchre.

Thomas Browne, *Religio Medici*, I.9 (1636).

Marks of the Christian
6.29

What is the distinguishing mark of a Christian? Faith working by love. What is the mark of faith? Unhesitating conviction of the truth of the inspired words, unshaken by any argument either based on the plea of physical necessity or masquerading in the guise of piety.

What is the mark of a believer? To hold fast by such conviction in the strength of what scripture says and to dare neither to set it at nought nor to add to it. For if what is not of faith is sin, as the apostle says, and faith comes from hearing and hearing through the word of God, then everything that is outside inspired scripture, being not of faith, is sin.

What is the mark of love towards God? Keeping his commandments with a view to his glory. What is the mark of love towards our neighbour? Not to seek one's own good, but the good of the loved one for the benefit of his soul and body.

What is the mark of a Christian? To be born anew in baptism of water and Spirit. What is the mark of the one who is born of water? As Christ died to sin once, that he should thus be dead and unmoved by any sin... What is the mark of the one who is born of the Spirit? That he should be, according to the measure given him, that very thing of which he was born...

What is the mark of the one who is born again? To put off the old man with his doings and lusts, and to put on the new man, which is being renewed unto knowledge after the image of him that created him...

What is the mark of those who eat the bread and drink the cup of the Lord? To keep in perpetual memory him who died for us and rose again. What is the mark of those who keep such a memory? To live for themselves no longer, but unto him who died for them and rose again...

What is the mark of the Christian? To love one another, even as Christ also loved us.

Basil of Caesarea, *Morals*, 80.22.

The practice of faith
6.30

What, then, do we mean by spirituality? At its simplest spirituality is the practice of faith. All religions have some place for myth, ritual, meditation, mysticism, devotion and social action – all of which are ways of coping with the fundamental human desire to come to terms with the ultimate mystery of existence. Such basic practical attitudes are expressions of the fundamental conviction at the heart of all religion, that life ultimately makes sense. In this sense spirituality is prior to the great world religions as they actually exist. If faith informs practice, then practice establishes the communities of faith.

The faith which forms such communities is enormously powerful. This power is expressed not just in the intellectual coherence of a system, nor in some mysterious hold over the imagination which somehow supports people in times of crisis, but in the way a religion can motivate people to challenge and change the structures, both personal and institutional, of their lives. In the day-to-day life of a religious community liturgy, ritual and myth come first; doctrines, creeds and theology second. To argue for the value of religion on the basis of the latter alone implies that religions are like philosophies. They may appeal to the head and make for a good late-night argument when friends are ready for a game of verbal fisticuffs, but few religious founders – certainly neither Christ nor Buddha – would recognize what passes for religious feeling, let alone commitment, in smoke-filled pubs and common-rooms.

What makes for a religious commitment? Theologians talk about the 'leap of faith', and no doubt there are many for whom commitment comes at the end of a long and largely intellectual search. Many more, however, commit themselves to the creed of a particular faith because they have first managed to identify with a church or community or group of people who meet together for prayer and worship. The symbols of faith, the celebrations and the social cohesion which mark the group have an authority which impresses itself on people, a power which makes them feel 'at home'. Commitment comes when the heart, not just the head, feels right. Spirituality is a way of expressing this commitment of the heart.

To put it another way, all spirituality is about the right ordering and challenging of the deepest of human desires.

Michael Barnes SJ, *God East and West*
(SPCK 1991), p. 13.

Responding to crisis
6.31

How do we prepare ourselves to enter conflict? Our true human stature is measured by our response to crisis. Spiritually too, our capacity for a faithful response is revealed when we are put to the test. In some ways, daily living with its multiple demands and stresses prepares us for the time of battle. But there are particular experiences that ready our spirits for the day of conflict.

Radicalizing experiences, that is, moments of risk, plunge us into deeper waters than we currently know. All of us accept the importance of such moments in the life of every human being. Bearing a child, undergoing surgery, losing a loved one, necessary separations, marriage itself, require risk and upset our usual routine and patterns. Those involved in the formation of youth try to provide radicalizing experiences (sometimes called initiation rites). For some of us a bus trip into our inner cities alters our perspective. Or a conversation with a Buddhist or a Muslim. A woman who had never known poverty or discrimination was shocked into action when her son was jailed for theft. A college student changed his academic direction and became a community organizer after a summer in the slums of Mexico City. For me, the day of my arrival in Bombay provided as much radicalization as I could then bear.. My first encounter with stark poverty and overwhelming misery. I had quickly to come to terms with my Western identity and my personal inner resources. Unforgettable markings on my spirit, unseasoned and over-protected.

Such are the effects of entering radically different realms, realms that open our eyes, jar our habitual mindsets and values and force us to re-evaluate our attitudes and our actions. They put into the balance what is familiar and acceptable to us and challenge us to go deeper, to enlarge our narrow ideas and our reluctant hearts. We break with our clean, orderly, intellectual arguments and enter unthought-of and undescribed realities. We are never again quite the same. We lose some of our complacency and we are humbled by our inability to adapt and our limited understanding of life. We are also forever opened to further risk and further adventure. Radicalizing experiences are baptisms of the spirit, preparation for living in new ways, closer to the fragile humanity we share with our remotest neighbours.

Joan Puls OSF, *Every Bush is Burning*
(WCC 1985), pp. 51–52.

With burning patience
6.32

You keep on asking me, 'How can I find fulfilment?' If only I could lay my hand on your shoulder and go with you along the way. Both of us together, turning towards him who, recognized or not, is your quiet companion, someone who never imposes himself. Will you let him plant a source of refreshment deep within you? Or will you be so filled with shame that you say, 'I am not good enough to have you near me'?

What fascinates about God is his humility. He never punishes, domineers or wounds human dignity. Any authoritarian gesture on our part disfigures his face and repels. As for Christ, 'poor and humble of heart' – he never forces anyone's hand. If he forced himself upon you, I would not be inviting you to follow him.

In the silence of the heart, tirelessly he whispers to each of us, 'Don't be afraid; I am here.' Wait for him, even when body and spirit are dry and parched. Wait, too, with many others for an event to occur in our present day. An event which is neither marvel nor myth, nor projection of yourself. The fruit of prayerful waiting, it comes concretely in the wake of a miracle from God.

In prayer, prayer that is always poor, like lightning rending the night, you will discover the secret: you can find fulfilment only in the presence of God... and also you will awaken others to God, first and foremost, by the life you live.

With burning patience, don't worry that you can't pray well. Surely you know that any spiritual pretension is death to the soul before you begin. Even when you cannot recognize him, will you stay close to him in long silences when nothing seems to be happening? There, with him, life's most significant decisions take shape. There the recurring 'what's the use?' and the scepticism of the disillusioned melt away. Tell him everything, and let him sing within you the radiant gift of life. Tell him everything, even what cannot be expressed and what is absurd. When you understand so little of his language, talk to him about it. In your struggles, he brings a few words, an intuition or an image to your mind... And within you grows a desert flower, a flower of delight.

Roger Schutz (Brother Roger of Taizé), *The Wonder of a Love: Journal 1974–1976*
(Mowbray 1981), pp. 105–106.

The spring of moral fruitfulness
6.33

Christianity, when it is true to its own genius, is able to believe in humanity recklessly, despite all that saddens and discourages, because it has seen the vision of God, the eternal source of all worth and wonder – lifting us up to become sons and daughters of God. That is the spring of all creative effort, sureness of touch and mastery in life. On the whole and in the long run those men and women have been most effective in changing and remodelling the present world, who have realized that goodness, in whatever form, is not in the end something that we produce, but something that claims us and is imparted to us by the eternal and unchanging goodness. The vision of God is the spring of moral fruitfulness. The source of all creative conviction is the vision of one who is 'Faithful and True', unchanged in underived perfection.

F.R. Barry, *The Relevance of Christianity* (James Nisbet & Co. 1932), p. 130.

'Where could I go from thy spirit?'
A Meditation on Psalm 139
6.34

God is inescapable. He is God only *because* he is inescapable, and only that which *is* inescapable is God.

There is no place to which we could flee from God which is outside of God. 'If I ascend to the heavens, thou art there.' It seems very natural for God to be in heaven, and very unnatural for us to wish to ascend to heaven in order to escape him. But that is just what the idealists of all ages have tried to do. They have tried to leap towards the heaven of perfection and truth, of justice and peace, where God is not wanted. That heaven is a heaven of man's making, without the driving restlessness of the divine spirit and without the judging presence of the divine face. But such a place is a 'no place'; it is a 'utopia', an idealistic illusion. 'If I make hell my home, behold, thou art there.' Hell or Sheol, the habitation of the dead, would seem to be the right place to hide from God. And that is where all those who long for death, in order to escape the divine demands, attempt to flee. I am convinced that there is not one amongst us who has not at some time desired to be liberated from the burden of his existence by stepping out of it. And I know that there are some amongst us for whom this longing is a daily temptation. But everyone knows in the depth of his heart that death would not provide an escape from the inner demand made upon him. 'If I take the wings of the dawn and dwell in the midst of the sea, thy hand would even fall upon me there, and thy right hand would grasp me.' To fly to the ends of the earth would not be to escape from God... To flee into darkness in order to forget God is not to escape him. For a time we may be able to hurl him out of our consciousness, to reject him, to refute him, to argue convincingly for his non-existence, and to live very comfortably without him. But ultimately we know that it is not he whom we reject and forget, but that it is rather some distorted picture of him. And we know that we can argue against him, only because he impels us to attack him. There is no escape from God through forgetfulness.

Paul Tillich, *The Shaking of the Foundations* (SCM Press 1949), pp. 40–41.

Life is opportunity
6.35

Let us try to get a right thought about life. In any young life that is unspoilt, that of the kitten and the child, the first outlook on life is a beautiful world, full of flowers and sunshine and kind people. This, of course, is a superficial view, a real view but not the whole truth. Then perhaps there is some great cruelty or disappointment or pain, and then the temptation is to become a pessimist. The danger is, when the weeds appear among the flowers to see only the weeds. The pessimist counts the sick people, the failures, the frauds, till he begins to declare that there is no health, no success, no honesty anywhere. 'Who will do us any good?' he cries. He sees a real view of life but again it is a superficial view. Like the first view of life it is true, but not the whole truth. There are weeds, but there are flowers. There are dark nights, but there are stars. There is a third outlook, something more profound than lamentation over the sin and misery of life. There is the recognition of the power of life by its contacts and occasions to educate the soul and develop the character.

So there is first the thought of life as a success because the world is beautiful and the skies are bright, then the thought of life as a failure, because every joy is in danger of disappointment and every confidence in danger of disillusionment. Then the thought of life as a success again, though of a different order, because we see that all these things have educational value. The man who first delighted in outside pleasures, and then bowed down in misery because he despaired, rises up now and stands upon his feet. A sense of self-respect and loyal obedience to a heavenly call takes the place of pessimism and despair. Life is an opportunity of co-operation with God.

Father Andrew, *Light of the World* (A.R. Mowbray and Co. 1957), pp. 64–65.

The wager
6.36

'Either God exists, or he does not.' But which side shall we take? Reason cannot decide for us one way or the other; we are separated by an infinite gulf.

A game is on, at the other side of this infinite distance, where either heads or tails will turn up. Which will you gamble on?...

Let us weigh the gain and the loss in betting that God exists... If you win, you win everything; if you lose, you lose nothing. Do not hesitate, then: gamble on his existence...

You want to come to faith, but you do not know the way. You would like to cure yourself of unbelief, and you ask for remedies. Learn from those who were once bound and gagged like you, and who now stake all that they possess. These are the people who know the road you wish to follow; they are cured of the disease of which you wish to be cured. Follow the way by which they set out: by acting as though they already believed...

Now what harm will come to you if you follow this course? You will be faithful, honest, humble, grateful, generous, a sincere friend, truthful. Certainly you will not enjoy those poisonous pleasures, ambition and luxury. But will you not have others? I tell you that you will gain in this life, and that at every step you take along this road you will see so great an assurance of gain, and so little in what you risk, that you will finally realize you have gambled on something certain and infinite, which has cost you nothing.

Blaise Pascal, *Pensées*, tr. W.F. Trotter (J.M. Dent & Sons 1941).

On the train to heaven
6.37

An old church member says, 'I have so many dark days. I do want to get to heaven.'

Keep your seat! The train goes through. If you want to get to the good world, get on God's excursion train, and you will run in under the old car shed of heaven. Some of you will have children there to take hold of your hand and welcome you to the city of God. We will get there, thank God! Sister, keep your seat, it will go through. Brother, keep your head in at the window; the train is in safe hands. I have quit troubling myself. I have turned it all over to God.

Another says, 'I am waiting for faith.' Yes, you have been waiting forty years for faith. How much have you saved up? Like the fellow who had ten bushels of wheat, and was waiting till more grew before he would sow what he had. Sow it, and you will have a hundredfold. By keeping it, you will not get any more, but the rats will eat up what you have.

... 'I want to be a blacksmith as soon as I get muscle.' Why don't you go at it? There he stands until at last he has not muscle enough to lift the hammer. He is 'getting it' with a vengeance. How did you get faith? By using what you had. I tell you what tickles me – to hear fellows down praying for faith. 'Lord, give me faith.' The next time you get any in that way, bring it over and let me see it. That ain't scriptural, that talk you are doing now. Christ rebuked those who prayed for faith. The trouble with you is not that you need more faith. You use the faith you have, and then you will get more. I would as soon pray for sweet potatoes as for faith.

Samuel P. Jones, 'Waiting and Hoping', in *Sermons and Sayings, by the Rev. Sam P. Jones*, ed. W.M. Leftwich (Nashville 1885).

Radical faith

6.38

To be radical means to seize a matter at its roots. More radical Christian faith can only mean committing oneself without reserve to the 'crucified God'. This is dangerous. It does not promise the confirmation of one's own conceptions, hopes and good intentions. It promises first of all the pain of repentance and fundamental change. It offers no recipe for success. But it brings a confrontation with the truth. It is not positive and constructive, but is in the first instance critical and destructive. It does not bring man into a better harmony with himself and his environment, but into contradiction with himself and his environment. It does not create a home for him and integrate him into society, but makes him 'homeless' and 'rootless', and liberates him in following Christ who was homeless and rootless. The 'religion of the cross', if faith on this basis can ever be so called, does not elevate and edify in the usual sense, but scandalizes; and most of all it scandalizes one's 'co-religionists' in one's own circle. But by this scandal, it brings liberation into a world which is not free. For ultimately, in a civilization which is constructed on the principle of achievement and enjoyment, and therefore makes pain and death a private matter, excluded from its public life, so that in the final issue the world must no longer be experienced as offering resistance, there is nothing so unpopular as for the crucified God to be made a present reality through faith. It alienates alienated men, who have come to terms with alienation. And yet this faith, with its consequences, is capable of setting men free from their cultural illusions, releasing them from the involvements which blind them, and confronting them with the truth in the midst of untruth. In this pain we experience reality outside ourselves, which we have not made or thought out for ourselves. The pain arouses a love which can no longer be indifferent, but seeks out its opposite, what is ugly and unworthy of love, in order to love it. This pain breaks down the apathy in which everything is a matter of indifference, because everything one meets is always the same and familiar.

Jürgen Moltmann, *The Crucified God* (SCM Press 1974), p. 39.

Do you want...?
6.39

Freedom is complete obedience to the element for which we were designed... Complete obedience to the pursuit of truth. Not the truth of facts or of science, but the truth that is wholeness and integrity. And complete obedience to the calls and demands of love. For there is in each of us a potential nurturer and healer and tender lover and faithful friend. Freedom is complete obedience to the *special* elements for which we were designed. For some, the element of listening. For others, of being a bridge-builder, or bone-grafter, or a community-catalyst. Of fashioning meaning out of words or musical sounds, or out of movement. Of gardening or teaching or translating or pastoring. Just as discovering our element is the focus of our search and the key to our vocations, so is obedience to our element the entrance into freedom.

The question becomes for us: how far do we want to go into freedom? How serious are we about its bold discoveries and its perilous pitfalls? How free do we want to become? Jesus asked this question many times in different words. 'What are you looking for?' he asked his first novices (John 1:38). 'Do you want to be healed?' (John 5:6) and 'What do you want me to do for you?' (Mark 10:51) were his questions to those seeking help. His parables and stories also posed the question: do you want to go as far as the good Samaritan? Are you more serious than the brother of the prodigal son? Can you take lessons from the flowers of the field and the birds of the air? Do you want to go as far as praying for your enemies, and being consecrated in the truth? And what about the cup of suffering and the undeserved insults and the weight of the cross? Is your desire for freedom that wide and deep?

Joan Puls OSF, *Every Bush is Burning* (WCC 1985), pp. 74–75.

Cat's eyes
6.40

The courage needed to obey, to step out in faith, never changes. In fact, as the years go by, it seems we are often trusted with longer stretches of fog-bound road than in the earlier days, when sunshine frequently breaks through with exhilarating encouragement. To return to a place or circumstance of known danger or harassment may require even greater courage than when the danger was unknown and the harassment unexperienced. The courage to return to overwhelming problems that have already crushed; to accept a task already known to be too great and beyond our natural training or experience; to go back in the face of increasing opposition; all these can make it harder and harder to be sure of guidance and the Lord's clear direction. Yet throughout, cat's eyes do appear, and courage is given to take the next step, and faith holds on to believe for further cat's eyes, confirming the first.

Some have continued long years in a straight line of duty, yearning for a word of direction to move out into new fields. Some have nursed and cared for loved ones, doing a routine job at home, with their hearts burdened for some special corner of the overseas missionary field. Silence seems to answer their prayers for guidance, and yet the cat's eyes are there, quietly, consistently, one after another. Then when the basic situation changes, suddenly there is a corner, and the eyes momentarily disappear, only to reappear in a new direction: but by faithful obedience, one can move off confidently along the new way.

Helen Roseveare, *Living Faith* (Hodder & Stoughton 1980), p. 127.

Acceptance, not resignation
6.41

Acceptance is not resignation, which is a dead end in the sense that it has no life about it and nothing comes from it. Christian acceptance is a beginning. It is the taking up of a position preliminary to action, and the best possible position, since it is the concurring of the will with things as they are at the moment, preparatory to attempting to find what God wants us to do with the situation. The concurring of the will means that the mind will be free, not tightly organized by resentment or fear but able to put the whole of itself into the fight or the work, able to use what it has already learned about life, and adaptable too, open to guidance, ready to change habitual attitudes that will not work this time, as it feels its way to discernment of the right course.

It is often harder to bear with oneself than with any frustrations in one's circumstances, though this may be simply a matter of turning against ourselves the disapproval of life that for some reason we cannot express. More often we find ourselves a burden through our unacknowledged wish to be rather successful spiritually; we are driven to exasperation with ourselves through the shame of being continually tripped up by contemptibly ordinary failures in tolerating people and putting up with life's frictions. We may then resort to hopelessness and cynicism about the life of faith, or we become sanctimonious Christians, unpleasantly ready to wear our spiritual inadequacy on our sleeve, or we externalize in good works in which the love of God has completely disappeared in the agitated service of our unfortunate neighbours, or we throw in the towel and quit.

Everyone has to cope with the self's need to expand and gain power, with its variable success and its consequent fantasies of importance and inferiority. We need reassurance as keenly as the body needs food. For this reason much of the time our egocentricity or our immaturity is showing, and we have to live with this fact. It is part of the Christian life to get used to being a rather unsatisfactory self. It is all never really going to come right in time.

Neville Ward, *Five for Sorrow, Ten for Joy* (Epworth Press 1971),
pp. 75–76.

Finding God in all things
6.42

One of the hardest battles in the spiritual life, perhaps I should say the hardest, is the struggle to see God in our trivial human happenings. How often we have to renew our act of faith! At first we are tempted to see only ourselves, to believe only in ourselves to value only ourselves. Then gradually we perceive that the thread of life has a rationale, a mysterious unity, and we are led to think that we meet God in its basic stages. Then again, as our religious experience grows, we begin to realize that we meet God not only in the big events of our lives but in all the events, however small and apparently insignificant. God is never absent from our lives. He cannot be, because 'in him we live, and move, and exist' (Acts 17:28). But it requires so much effort to turn this truth into a habit!

We need repeated acts of faith before we learn to sail with confidence on the 'immense and endless sea' which is God (St Gregory of Nazienzen), knowing that if we founder we do so in him, the divine, eternal, ever-present God. How fortunate we are if we can learn to navigate our frail craft on the sea and remain serene even when the storm is raging!

Carlo Carretto, *Love is for Living*, tr. Jeremy Molser
(Darton, Longman & Todd 1976), p. 109.

Keep moving
6.43

'Darkness' in the spiritual life may be due to several causes. It may be 'psycho-physical' – that is, the result of illness or overstrain. Here common sense, rest and refreshment, coupled with quiet confidence in God, is the only line to take. It may be due to sin: to self-will or to lack of love or truth. This cause can soon be discovered by one who is sensitive to the voice of the Spirit; the only way back is through repentance, followed by the humble effort to wait for God, to follow at his pace, and not to try to force ours. But the 'darkness' of which writers like St John of the Cross speak with such authority is a normal experience, and must be patiently endured... In the words of St John of the Cross:

> The soul makes greatest progress when it travels in the dark, not knowing the way. The truth is that the nearer the soul comes to him it perceives that the darkness is deeper and greater because of its own weakness... So the further a penitent advances, the further from himself he must go – walking by faith and not seeing.

In such darkness there is nothing to fear. The trial is severe, it is true, and there is no getting away from the fact that the darkness is real, and the way seems hard. Often we feel as though we were travelling in the wrong direction; but by faith we know that we are not alone; that God is with us, leading and sustaining us all the time. Gradually, as we learn to adjust ourselves to this new way of living, we begin to understand why God must work in us in this secret way: he has to do so, because if we could see what he was doing we might become far too much interested in the process, and then we would spoil his work by looking at ourselves instead of at him. All we are asked to do is to keep moving: 'Some run swiftly; some walk; some creep painfully; but everyone who keeps on will reach the goal.'

Olive Wyon, *On the Way* (SCM Press 1958), p. 63.

The abyss of faith
6.44

Normally, perhaps, the word 'faith' suggests something definite to be believed in, something with a shape, that inspires confidence. But here, to envisage the act of faith in terms of the vertiginous experience of standing on the edge of a cliff and deliberately looking down into a bottomless gully, proposes quite new meanings for what faith might be. Not only is fear, and the need to face that fear, paramount, but it is implied that it is precisely that which challenges any sense of confidence ('solid ground') that must be the focus of faith. In one sense, 'faith' loses all definite shape, since an abyss is that kind of gulf where no contours or limits can be detected; at the same time, there is a sickening *precision* about the image. Faith is the act of contemplating steadily something (or, perhaps, an *absence* of something) that you would much rather not. Thus, it may well be that our inclination to view faith, and the language of faith that we use in our liturgies, as something rock-solid and reliable, may need to be subverted. I want to suggest that at least one of the functions of liturgy is to keep returning us to the abyss of faith, from which we would prefer to escape; and that if there is an appropriate 'safety' that must be retained, it is no more than that of a container which makes it just safe enough to contemplate the fearfulness of God.

> Janet Morley, 'Liturgy and Danger' in *Mirror to the Church*,
> ed. Monica Furlong (SPCK 1988), p. 27.

Discerning God's Will

'What good work?'
6.45

A brother asked an old man: 'What thing is so good that I may do it and live by it?' And the old man said: 'God alone knows what is good. Yet I have heard that one of the Fathers asked the great Abba Nesteros, who was a friend of Abba Anthony and said to him "What good work shall I do?". And Anthony replied "Cannot all good works please God equally? Scripture says, Abraham was hospitable and God was with him. And Elijah loved quiet, and God was with him. And David was humble and God was with him. So whatever you find your soul wills in following God's will, do it, and keep your heart."'

Sayings of the Fathers, in Owen Chadwick, *Western Asceticism* (1958), pp. 39–40, no. 11.

A family idol?
6.46

How terrible, how continuous, how besetting, is the temptation to get religion taped, and make of Christ a family idol! We lose reality, because we are not open to movement. No sooner has Christ brought us to know him, than his eyes are looking through us at those who are next to us, and then at those that are beyond; to keep his love we must go with his love. We must abandon ourselves to the will of Christ if we are to be his disciples. The secret of it is always to do cheerfully what the manifest will of God calls us to do. Let no one ask, Where is the will of God? Pray with your heart, and ask him the question. You will quickly be reminded of what he wants you to do. Your mother likes to have your letters: do you write? There is a not very successful person who wants a share of your company: do you brush him off? If you are to do good work, you must sleep: why don't you keep proper hours? How do you employ your imagination when you are alone? Couldn't you employ it better? I am talking of everyone's omissions, everyone's careless ways, merely to remind you that there is always a road along which you can put your good foot foremost in the doing of God's manifest will. The trouble about us may not so much be that we are ill-natured or vicious, but that we are just bad disciples. We do not do the things we are called to do, or we do them late, and with reluctance. When Peter found he could not keep Christ in his house, at least he did follow him; Christ did not keep having to go back to Capernaum, to fetch Peter out again: and if he had needed to do so, would he have done it? And how many times? Would he, perhaps, have left Peter to his own devices, and found another apostle? I do not know. But we think Christ should come back for us again and again: his will for us never becomes a path that runs steadily on, for we keep falling back to the beginning.

Austin Farrer, *The Brink of Mystery*, ed. Charles C. Conti (SPCK 1976), p. 90.

Scripture's magnitude
6.47

Who is capable of comprehending the extent of what is to be discovered in a single utterance of yours [Christ]? For we leave behind in it far more than we take from it, like thirsty people drinking from a fountain.

The facets of his word are more numerous than the faces of those who learn from it. God depicted his word with many beauties, so that each of those who learn from it can examine that aspect of it which he likes. And God has hidden within his word all sorts of treasures, so that each of us can be enriched by it from whatever aspect he meditates on. For God's word is the tree of life which proffers to you on all sides blessed fruits; it is like the rock which was struck in the wilderness, which became a spiritual drink for everyone on all sides: 'They ate the food of the Spirit and they drank the draft of the Spirit.'

Anyone who encounters scripture should not suppose that the single one of its riches that he has found is the only one to exist; rather, he should realize that he himself is only capable of discovering that one out of the many riches which exist in it.

Nor, because scripture has enriched him should the reader impoverish it. Rather, if the reader is incapable of finding more, let him acknowledge scripture's magnitude. Rejoice because you have found satisfaction, and do not be grieved that there has been something left over by you. A thirsty person rejoices because he has drunk: he is not grieved because he proved incapable of drinking the fountain dry. Let the fountain vanquish your thirst, your thirst should not vanquish the fountain!

Ephrem the Syrian, *Commentary on the Diatessaron*, tr. Sebastian Brock in *The Luminous Eye: The Spiritual World Vision of St Ephrem* (Cistercian Publications 1992), pp. 50–51.

Every hour the hour of God's will
6.48

Our continual mistake is that we do not concentrate upon the present day, the actual hour, of our life; we live in the past or in the future; we are continually expecting the coming of some special moment when our life will unfold itself in its full significance. And we do not notice that life is flowing like water through our fingers, sifting like precious grain from a loosely fastened bag.

Constantly, each day, each hour, God is sending us people, circumstances, tasks, which should mark the beginning of our renewal; yet we pay them no attention, and thus continually we resist God's will for us. Indeed, how can God help us? Only by sending us in our daily life certain people, and certain coincidences of circumstance. If we accepted every hour of our life as the hour of God's will for us, as the decisive, most important, unique hour of our life – what sources of joy, love, strength, as yet hidden from us, would spring from the depths of our soul!

Let us then be serious in our attitude towards each person we meet in our life, towards every opportunity of performing a good deed; be sure that you will then fulfil God's will for you in these very circumstances, on that very day, in that very hour.

Alexander Elchaninov, *The Diary of a Russian Priest* (Faber & Faber 1967), p. 157.

'Test the spirits'
6.49

Judge not therefore of yourself by considering how many of those things you do which divines and moralists call virtue and goodness, nor how much you abstain from those things which they call sin and vice.

But daily and hourly, in every step that you take, see to the spirit that is within you whether it be heaven or earth that guides you. And judge everything to be sin and Satan in which your earthly nature, own love, or self-seeking has any share of life in you; nor think that any goodness is brought to life in you but so far as it is an actual death to the pride, the vanity, the wrath and selfish tempers of your fallen, earthly life.

Again, here you see where and how you are to seek your salvation, not in taking up your travelling staff, or crossing the seas to find out a new Luther or a new Calvin to clothe yourself with their opinions. No. The oracle is at home that always and only speaks the truth to you because nothing is your truth but that good and that evil which is yours within you. For salvation or damnation is no outward thing that is brought into you from without, but is only that which springs up within you as the birth and state of your own life. What you are in yourself, what is doing in yourself, is all that can be either your salvation or damnation.

For all that is our good and all that is our bad has no place nor power but within us. Again, nothing that we do is bad but for this reason, because it resists the power and working of God within us; and nothing that we do can be good but because it conforms to the Spirit of God within us.

William Law, *The Spirit of Love* (1754), Part II, The First Dialogue,
ed. Paul G. Stanwood (Paulist Press 1978), p. 411.

Actors without a script
6.50

We are actors in a drama with no book of words. It has not pleased God to provide us with the book of words. He has brought us into the light, but he has also left us in the dark. 'O ye light and darkness, bless ye the Lord.' He has given us sufficient light to know what is the aim and object of our life. He has given us a sufficient clue to the meaning of the great drama in which he has assigned us a part. But he has not laid down in advance exactly what we are each to do. He has given us the responsibility of co-operating with him in actually working out the drama. Further, he has not given us a book of words which would make it possible for us to understand what is going on over the whole course of human history. He has given us enough light to play our own parts worthily; but we continue to be in the dark about many questions to which we should dearly like to know the answers.

Alec R. Vidler, *Windsor Sermons* (SCM Press 1963), p. 29.

A promise and a threat
6.51

Be afraid of being wise in your own eyes, lest you should approach the character of those from whom the righteous God sees fit to hide the knowledge of those truths without which they cannot be saved. The gospel is not proposed to you to ask your opinion of it, that it may stand or fall according to your decision, but it peremptorily demands your submission. If you think yourselves qualified to judge and examine it by that imperfect and depraved light which you call your reason, you will probably find reasons enough to refuse your assent. Reason is properly exercised in the ordinary concerns of life, and has a place in religious inquiries in so much as none can or do believe the gospel without having sufficient reasons for it. But you need a higher light, the light of God's Spirit, without which the most glorious displays of his wisdom will appear foolishness to you. If you come simply, dependent and teachable, if you pray from your heart with David, 'Open thou mine eyes, that I may see wondrous things in thy law' (Psalm 119:18), you will be heard, and answered. You will grow in the knowledge and grace of our Lord Jesus Christ. But if you neglect this, and trust in yourselves, supposing this promised assistance of the Holy Spirit unnecessary, the glorious light of the gospel will shine upon you in vain, for Satan will maintain such hold of you by this pride of your heart that you will remain in bondage and darkness, that you shall neither see it nor desire to see it.

John Newton, from a sermon preached at Olney on 'The Small Success of the Gospel Ministry' (1767) in *A Burning and a Shining Light: English Spirituality in the Age of Wesley*, ed. David L. Jeffrey (Eerdmans 1987), pp. 398–99.

The way of love
6.52

I was still being tormented by this question of unfulfilled longings and it was a distraction in my prayer, when I decided to consult St Paul's epistles in the hopes of getting an answer. It was the twelfth and thirteenth chapters of First Corinthians that claimed my attention. The first of these told me that we can't all of us be apostles, all of us be prophets, all of us doctors, and so on; the Church is composed of members which differ in their use; the eye is one thing and the hand is another. It was a clear enough answer, but it didn't satisfy my aspirations, didn't set my heart at rest… Reading on to the end of the chapter, I met this comforting phrase: 'Prize the best gifts of heaven. Meanwhile, I can show you a way which is better than any other.'

What was it? The Apostle goes on to explain that all the gifts of heaven, even the most perfect of them, without love, are absolutely nothing; charity is the best way of all, because it leads straight to God. Now I was at peace; when St Paul was talking about the different members of the mystical body I couldn't recognize myself in any of them; or rather I could recognize myself in all of them. But charity – that was the key to my vocation. If the Church was a body composed of different members, it couldn't lack the noblest of all; it must have a heart, and a heart burning with love. And I realized that this love was the true motive force which enabled the other members of the Church to act; if it ceased to function the Apostles would forget to preach the gospel, the Martyrs would refuse to shed their blood. Love, in fact, is the vocation which includes all others; it's a universe of its own, comprising all time and space – it's eternal. Beside myself with joy, I cried out; 'Jesus, my Love! I've found my vocation, and my vocation is love.'

> Thérèse of Lisieux, *Story of a Soul*, tr. Ronald Knox, in *Autobiography of a Saint*
> (Harvill Press 1958), pp. 234–35.

Wilderness and vineyard
6.53

Part of the circle of interpretation is to see how Christians view the same question or doctrine from their different economic and social experiences. In the Bible there is an interplay between the wilderness and the vineyard experiences of the people of God. The wilderness is the place of vision; the Law is given. There are no ifs or buts. There are no grey areas. Right and wrong are utterly clear. God leads in a pillar of cloud by day and a pillar of fire by night. Then the people of God are to go into the land; the symbol of Israel is the vineyard. They are to stop wandering, settle down and build a civilization. A vineyard is a place of organizations and structures; its success is measured by its productivity. The settled life of Israel in the vineyard brings with it complicated structures, choices between two evils. But the vineyard people are to listen to the wilderness people, whom God keeps sending to remind them of that clear vision.

Today many of us are called to be vineyard people; to take a more complex society than ever, and make it work for the good of people and to the glory of God. Wilderness people are very important to us. They sit loose to the materialistic demands, which seem so important to us. They may be young people looking for alternative styles of life, or the elderly holding on to values which have been tested through generations. They may be members of religious orders or Christians who sit very loose to Church structures. They may be those who are specially vulnerable to mental stress, who see some truths with blinding clarity. They may be the poor and powerless, who can see society and its values very differently from the way it appears to vineyard people.

> David Sheppard, *Bias to the Poor* (Hodder & Stoughton 1983),
> pp. 224–25.

A tradition of experience
6.54

If we want to do justice to the word 'tradition' and above all to its reality, we must be careful to remember that this is a tradition of *experience*: in other words a handing down of what the Christian communities have experienced and done from and with Jesus, above all in and through their praxis of solidarity with a God concerned for humanity, moreover a God who wants a people of God concerned with humanity. Fundamentally that is tradition, and we cannot dispense with such a tradition without exhausting our resources.

In general human terms, quite apart from religious traditions, social and personal identity is inconceivable without tradition. No society, not even the most revolutionary one, starts from nothing; it finds inspiration in dangerous recollections. Therefore tradition really has a constructive significance: it can also teach us what we must change and what we must revive at any price as a value which has been acquired once and for all.

Therefore all cultural traditions express themselves in some basic stories which are told time and again; they also express themselves in rites the heart of which is laid down, and even in rarefied formulae. If a society no longer believes in the tradition which supports it, not only does its tradition die but the society itself becomes aimless, without a direction and chaotic, and general disquiet arises. Not to know the tradition is not to know one's own society and ultimately not to know oneself. Any person, any society, any culture is as it were a crossroads where on the basis of the past the present takes an inventive attitude towards the future. The whole structure of the Old and New Testaments is built on this connection of past, present and future. No mortal is creative from nothing. To neglect or underestimate one of these three elements mutilates a person, his or her society and religion; it then leads either to pure traditionalism, which kills and throttles; to pure opportunism, arbitrary actualism which does not see the blind spots in its own time and its own eye, or pure futurism, a blind undirected concern for change.

Edward Schillebeeckx, *For the Sake of the Gospel* (SCM Press 1989), pp. 171–72.

The wilderness of faith
6.55

Today in our uneasy culture of casual brutality, nuclear intimidation, and the cheapness of life, we are constantly faced with outward and visible signs of an immense inward and spiritual grace, a gift of the Holy Spirit, which is to *let go*.

The various processes of letting go can also be thought of as holocaust, of letting go of the familiar and therefore safe concepts of self, of how things ought to be and never will, of how they have been – so we can bring about the genuinely new order, which is the only means by which the earth will survive; of going out, like Abram, from all that is familiar, from the illusion of security into the desert where fire falls from heaven.

For all the world has become this desert. Here, in our wanderings, we are called to make each place, like Little Gidding, a place where prayer can be valid. And then to let it go; to make each step, each moment, a holocaust of prayer, praise, and thanksgiving, and then let it go. And this letting go is itself the heart of prayer: the cry of the heart that has emptied itself of everything that is most precious to it – even its own idea of itself – so that it may be filled with the fire of the living God.

We are all journeying into the wilderness of faith, and we are all, though it may remain completely hidden, given one of the greatest gifts God gives of himself: the gift of Abraham – to go into the Promise, into the vows we have made by our baptism, knowing that we are called out of all that is familiar, to bless God for it, to bless the unknown, to bless, finally, even our own death.

The future is always unknown, but in these latter days there are no longer even any inklings of what will be asked of us, whether city-dweller or woodland hermit. One thing only is sure: that we will be asked to accept, thank, offer and repent in the midst of constant flux.

Maggie Ross, *The Fire of Your Life: A Solitude Shared* (Paulist Press 1983), p. 92.

All are theologians
6.56

Each of us has a theological work to do. We may think we haven't but we can't help it, because every time we make a decision, or refuse to make one, we are showing whether we are with Jesus or against him. We are saying something about what we think Christianity is. There never has been a time when even the most passive could really allow a Church to make all their moral decisions for them, because the decision to obey is itself a moral decision and can have as many varied motives, from cowardice to true humility, as any other decision. Nor are the most emancipated present-day believers making their moral decisions in a vacuum. The cloud of witnesses from all ages and places surrounds them. They choose with the Church, or against it, in some sense or other, and there are many senses. So also our decisions form part of the tradition, and create the material from which others draw in making their decisions, and all these decisions depend on the kind of notions we have about what God is doing, to us and around us. Our practical decisions display theological premises, whether we like it or not. To say 'I'm not interested in theology,' is to display an ignorance as gross as that betrayed by people who smugly disclaim interest in politics, not knowing that every day is crammed with political acts, from greeting certain people and not others in the street, to posting letters, or buying a newspaper. Each of these acts springs from a given political doctrine, however unperceived it may be. A person may not even know the meaning of the word theology, but there is scarcely a conscious act which does not express a theological position of some kind, and even unconscious motivations often grow from the theological views of our forebears.

Rosemary Haughton, *The Knife Edge of Experience*
(Darton, Longman & Todd 1972), pp. 31–32.

Follow your own light
6.57

One of the hardest but one of the most absolutely necessary things is to follow our own particular line of development, side by side with souls who have quite a different one; often one opposed to our own. It is natural for youth to hesitate between an attitude which it fears may be presumptuous and a candid admission of inferiority to everything around it. But this hesitation must cease or we shall never grow up. We must be ourselves and not try to get inside someone else's skin. David could have done nothing in the armour of Saul; he refused it and ran to fetch his sling and some pebbles from the brook. It was with these he slew Goliath, the symbol of the devil as the Holy Fathers taught. Still less must we look for approval and appreciation as a sign that we are on the right path. There are not so many good judges as all that, and the judgment of common opinion is far from being common sense. Good judges are so rare that St François de Sales could declare, 'It is said that only one in a thousand is a true spiritual director. I say only one in ten thousand!' We must therefore free ourselves absolutely of this anxious desire to be at one with other souls, however virtuous or wise they may be; just as we must never expect them to see through our eyes. We must follow our own light as though we were alone in the world, save as regards charity to others. In purely private matters, we must never be deflected from our own path.

Henri de Tourville, *Letters of Direction*, ch. V, tr. Lucy Menzies
(Dacre Press 1939), pp. 34–35.

Spiritual Growth

Arise and shine
6.58

'Arise, shine' (Isaiah 60:1).

We have to take the first step as though there were no God. It is no use to wait for God to help us, he will not; but immediately we arise we find he is there. Whenever God inspires, the initiative is a moral one. We must do the thing and not lie like a log. If we will arise and shine, drudgery becomes divinely transfigured.

Drudgery is one of the finest touchstones of character there is. Drudgery is work that is very far removed from anything to do with the ideal – the utterly mean, grubby things; and when we come in contact with them we know instantly whether or not we are spiritually real. Read John 13; we see there the incarnate God doing the most desperate piece of drudgery, washing fishermen's feet, and he says – 'If I then, your Lord and master, have washed your feet, ye also ought to wash one another's feet.' It requires the inspiration of God to go through drudgery with the light of God upon it. Some people do a certain thing, and the way in which they do it hallows that thing for ever afterwards. It may be the most commonplace thing, but after we have seen them do it, it becomes different. When the Lord does a thing through us, he always transfigures it. Our Lord took on him our human flesh and transfigured it, and it has become for every saint the temple of the Holy Ghost.

Oswald Chambers, *My Utmost for His Highest* (Marshall Simpkin 1926), p. 50.

'Common things'
6.59

Religion consists, not so much in doing spiritual or sacred acts, as in doing secular acts from a sacred or spiritual motive… A life spent amidst holy things may be intensely secular; a life the most of which is passed in the thick and throng of the world, may be holy and divine. A minister, for instance, preaching, praying, ever speaking holy words and performing sacred acts, may be all the while doing actions no more holy than those of the printer who prints Bibles, or the bookseller who sells them; for, in both cases alike, the whole affair may be nothing more than a trade. Nay, the comparison tells worse for the former, for the secular trade is innocent and commendable, but the trade which traffics and tampers with holy things is, beneath all its mock solemnity, 'earthly, sensual, devilish'... To spiritualize what is material, to Christianize what is secular – that is the noble achievement of Christian principle... It is a great thing to love Christ so dearly as to be 'ready to be bound and to die' for him; but it is often a thing not less great to be ready to take up our daily cross, and to live for him.

John Caird, sermon, 14 October 1855.

A time for everything
6.60

Ecclesiastes declares that there is a time for everything under heaven (cf. Ecclesiastes 3:1), and 'everything' may be taken to refer to our spiritual life. If this is so, then we ought to examine the matter; and we should do everything in proper season. For those entering the struggle... there is a time for dispassion and a time for passion. There is a time for tears and a time for hardness of heart, a time for obedience and a time for command, a time for fasting and a time for eating, a time for the battle against the body our enemy and a time for quiet in our flesh. There is a time for the soul's upheaval and a time for calm in the mind, a time for heart's sorrow and a time for joy of spirit, a time for teaching and a time for listening, a time for pollutions, perhaps on account of conceit, and a time for cleaning by humility, a time for effort and a time for secure rest, a time for stillness and a time for undistracted distraction, a time for unceasing prayer and a time for honest service. Proud zeal must therefore never be allowed to deceive us and we should never strain from what will come in its own good time, since winter is not the time for summer's goods nor seed-time the proper season for the harvest. There is a time for the sowing of labours and a time to reap the astounding fruits of grace; and if it were otherwise we would not receive in due time whatever was proper to the season.

God in his unspeakable providence has arranged that some received the holy reward of their toils even before they set to work, others while actually working, others again when the work was done, and still others at the time of their death. Let the reader ask himself which one of them was made more humble.

John Climacus, *The Ladder of Divine Ascent*, Step 26,
tr. Colm Luibhead and Norman Russell (Paulist Press 1992), p. 241.

Struggle with memory
6.61

Remembering is an important part of the process of growth. We often get caught on the treadmill of repeated acts. Every confessor knows the agony of people who are tormented by a 'besetting sin'. The treadmill of repetition can only be stopped by a process of remembering, which is often painful. From the point of view of the believer, memory plays another important role in the work of healing. We are not only urged to remember our own past, but to enter contemplatively into a corporate memory that guards healing stories of salvation.

The medieval writers called such an entry into the corporate memory 'meditation'. It was a matter of hard chewing and digestion. The Latin word to describe this was *ruminare*, to ruminate, to chew the cud. As the old collect has it with regard to the Bible: we are to 'read, mark, learn and inwardly digest' the saving stories. Another significant word associated with meditation was *parturire*, to bring forth to birth something new. Thus we are to struggle with our own memories and the corporate memory in order, by the grace of God, to give birth to ourselves. Our own history has, in some way, wounded us. Our neuroses spring from the hurts we received as children. Salvation history (which, for the believer, is rehearsed in the Bible and the Liturgy) provides the antidote for those hidden early hurts that continue to wield great influence over us in adult life. 'By his stripes we are healed.' From the point of view of the believer, this means that my history and salvation history are inextricably bound together in the love of God.

Alan Jones, *Soul Making* (SCM Press 1986), p. 51.

Given or earned?
6.62

I have been writing of spiritual growth as if it were an orderly, predictable process. It has been implied that spiritual growth may be learned as one might learn a field of knowledge through a PhD programme; if you pay your tuition and work hard enough, of course you will succeed and get your degree. I have interpreted Christ's saying 'Many are called but few are chosen' to mean that very few choose to heed the call of grace because of the difficulties involved. By this interpretation I have indicated that whether or not we become blessed by grace is a matter of our choice. Essentially, I have been saying that grace is earned. And I know this to be true.

At the same time, however, I know that that's not the way it is at all. We do not come to grace; grace comes to us. Try as we might to obtain grace, it may yet elude us. We may seek it not, yet it will find us. Consciously we may avidly desire the spiritual life but then discover all manner of stumbling blocks in our way. Or we may have seemingly little taste for the spiritual life and yet find ourselves vigorously called to it in spite of ourselves. While on one level we do choose whether or not to heed the call of grace, on another it seems clear that God is the one who does the choosing. The common experience of those who have achieved a state of grace, on whom 'this new life from heaven' has been bestowed, is one of amazement at their condition. They do not feel that they have earned it. While they may have a realistic awareness of the particular goodness of their nature, they do not ascribe their nature to their own will; rather, they distinctly feel that the goodness of their nature has been created by hands wiser and more skilled than their own. Those who are the closest to grace are the most aware of the mysterious character of the gift they have been given.

M. Scott Peck, *The Road Less Travelled: A New Psychology of Love, Traditional Values and Spiritual Growth* ([1978], Hutchinson 1983), pp. 307–308.

The pilgrim's hope

6.63

The Christian hope – a combination of responsive faith and responsive love – is, in the end, what makes our pilgrimage possible at all. Knowing that God is vulnerable but indestructible, we know that the journey will be strenuous and full of suffering, but that it is not absurd: that it will bring us to the water's edge in the end. It seems to me that I have learnt that the journey itself has its own value, for it shows me that I am not alone and that I cannot expect to leapfrog over the heads of my fellow pilgrims and arrive at the Celestial City by private plane, cleared by the spiritual immigration authorities. Christian faith is the Christian's response to life.

'After this,' says Bunyan, Mr Ready-to-Halt called for his fellow pilgrims and told them, saying, 'I am sent for, and God shall surely visit you also.' So he desired Mr Valiant to make his will. And because he had nothing to bequeath to them that should survive him but his crutches and his good wishes, therefore thus he said: 'These crutches I bequeath to my son that shall tread in my steps, with an hundred warm wishes that he may prove better than I have been.' Then he thanked Mr Great-Heart for his conduct and kindness, and so addressed himself to his journey. When he came to the brink of the river, he said: 'Now I shall have no more need of these crutches, since yonder are chariots and horses for me to ride on.' The last words he was heard to say were: 'Welcome life!' So he went his way.

Gerald Priestland, *Priestland's Progress: One Man's Search for Christianity Now*
(quoting from John Bunyan, *The Pilgrim's Progress*) (BBC 1981), p. 215.

Transformation
6.64

Concentration, whether in meditation or in prayer, can only be achieved by an effort of will. Our spiritual life is based on our faith and determination, and any incidental joys are a gift of God. St Seraphim of Sarov, when asked what it was that made some people remain sinners and never make any progress while others were becoming saints and living in God, answered: 'Only determination.' Our activities must be determined by an act of will, which usually happens to be contrary to what we long for; this will, based on our faith, always clashes with another will, our instinctive one. There are two wills in us, one is the conscious will, possessed to a greater or lesser degree, which consists in the ability to compel ourselves to act in accordance with our convictions. The second one is something else in us, it is the longings, the claims, the desires of all our nature, quite often contrary to the first will. St Paul speaks of the two laws that fight against each other (Romans 7:23). He speaks of the old and new Adam in us, who are at war. We know that one must die in order that the other should live, and as we must realize that our spiritual life, our life as a human being taken as a whole, will never be complete as long as these two wills do not coincide. It is not enough to aim at the victory of the good will against the evil one; the evil one, that is the longings of our fallen nature, must absolutely, though gradually, be transformed into a longing, a craving, for God. The struggle is hard and far-reaching.

Anthony Bloom, *Living Prayer*
(Darton, Longman & Todd 1966), p. 63.

Lantern to our feet
6.65

The scripture of God is the heavenly meat of our souls: the hearing and keeping of it maketh us blessed, sanctifieth us, and maketh us holy; it turneth our souls; it is a light lantern to our feet; it is a sure, steadfast, and everlasting instrument of salvation; it giveth wisdom to the humble and lowly hearts; it comforteth, maketh glad, cheereth, and cherisheth our conscience; it is a more excellent jewel, or treasure, than any gold or precious stone; it is more sweet than honey or honeycomb...

Let us hear, read, and know these holy rules, injunctions and statutes of our Christian religion, and upon that we have made profession to God at our baptism. Let us with fear and reverence lay up, in the chest of our hearts, these necessary and fruitful lessons. Let us night and day muse, and have meditation and contemplation in them. Let us ruminate, and, as it were, chew the cud, that we may have the sweet juice, spiritual effect, marrow, honey, kernel, taste, comfort and consolation of them. Let us stay, quiet, and certify our consciences with the most infallible certainty, truth and perpetual assurance of them. Let us pray to God, the only author of these heavenly studies, that we may speak, think, believe, live and depart hence, according to the wholesome doctrine and verities of them. And, by that means, in this world we shall have God's defence, favour and grace, with the unspeakable solace of peace and quietness of conscience.

Thomas Cranmer, 'A Fruitful Exhortation to the Reading and Knowledge of Holy Scripture' in *The Book of Homilies* (1547).

Living on God's word
6.66

I was sitting, one day, in the New Forest, under a beech tree. I like to look at the beech, and study it, as I do many other trees, for every one has its own peculiarities and habits, its special ways of twisting its boughs, and growing its bark, and opening its leaves, and so forth. As I looked up at that beech, and admired the wisdom of God in making it, I saw a squirrel running round and round the trunk, and up the branches, and I thought to myself, 'Ah! this beech tree is a great deal more to you than it is to me, for it is your home, your living, your all.' Its big branches were the main streets of his city, and its little boughs were the lanes; somewhere in that tree he had his house, and the beech-mast was his daily food, he lived on it. Well, now, the way to deal with God's word is not merely to contemplate it, or to study it, as a student does; but to live on it, as that squirrel lives on his beech tree. Let it be to you, spiritually, your house, your home, your food, your medicine, your clothing, the one essential element of your soul's life and growth.

Charles Haddon Spurgeon, sermon preached at the Tabernacle, London,
Autobiography (revised edn Banner of Truth Trust 1973), p. 218.

Hastening to God
6.67

Have you become disenchanted about the half-hearted religiosity you see about you? Has there gnawed around the margin of your conscience a feeling of disloyalty to a heavenly vision? Have you stilled that disquieting thought of complete and awful and irrevocable commitment to God beyond any degree that is commonly found? Have you said, 'Other people take their religion wildly, I must be more balanced and use common sense'? Have you said, 'If I followed out my God-hunger *absolutely*, people would think me crazy, and I'd do harm, by my fanaticism, to the cause of religion'? For shame! How much religious zeal is killed by so-called 'common sense'... Better to run the risk of fanaticism by complete dedication to God than to run the certain risk of mediocrity by twenty per cent dedication. Better to run the risk of being examined by a psychiatrist, as [George] Fox was taken to a surgeon to have his excess blood drawn off, than to measure our lives by our mediocre fellow, and, achieving respectable security in religion, be satisfied if we strike the average...

Hasten unto God. Woo him. Pursue him. Yet he, the hound of heaven, has been pursuing us through the years, baying ever on our track. It was we who needed to give assent to his presence, not he who had to be attracted and come to us. And when he enters in and sups with us and we with him, what unspeakable joy! At last we are home. We are on the rock. Life's end is in God, as its beginning and middle is in God. Such was Jesus' passion – the Father. Such is ours, if we prodigals find we have wandered into a far country. Is God your passion? Do you long for him and rejoice in him and find life meaningful only to the degree you are in his presence and he is in your life? Do you keep close to the divine centre, the inner principle, counting all else but loss? For a depth of commitment such as mild men do not know, I speak in order that you may hear *him* speak in you the same message. Out of such lives will the world be reborn, will the church be reborn. Hasten unto God, all you zealous pearl-merchants, and peace, and joy unspeakable and full of glory.

Thomas Kelly, *The Eternal Promise* (Hodder & Stoughton 1967), pp. 114–15.

All one
6.68

Lonely is not a synonym for *alone*. The word *lonely* connotes isolation and dejection, a missed absence of companions when it is applied to persons. The root of *alone*, however, is in two words: *all one*. This means the opposite of isolation and dejection. The emphasis is not on the *one* but on the *wholly* one. It means complete by oneself. How many of us can actually feel that way? It is not easy to be full in oneself, to respect oneself, and to self-develop to such a degree that a person looks forward to long periods of being alone. For some who enjoy this oneness, they realize that because of their relationship with Christ they are never lonely. They cultivate the chances to be alone so that they can actually savour the moments with God alone, the moments when their unity with the creator can be both enjoyed and developed. This implies quite a special human being. Too often we are frantic for companionship – for the team or the club or the class or the party or the movie or the TV. Immersion in such activities will free us from having to face the basic issues of existence. Such trivial busyness will keep us from intimate contact with ourselves. The kingdom of heaven is within each of us, yet how seriously do we try to make contact with it? Not only is there no need to go 'out there' in most instances, but rather it is spiritually harmful to look outside of ourselves while ignoring what is by nature within us. The woman or man who can be alone – can be *together* in the self – is the kind of person we can admire, can hold as a model. The quest for wholeness for individual unity is one of the great journeys a life can make, indeed should make. There is no easy route to being properly alone. But making the trip is learning to find what the meaning of life is.

Harry James Cargas, *Encountering Myself* (SPCK 1978), p. 108.

Memories surface
6.69

Part of the movement towards acceptance of basic worth is the business of becoming reconciled with my past. My past, with its mixture of pain and joy, of failure and success, of selfishness and love, is composed of everything that has brought me to this point now. Issues for forgiveness arise in prayer because my relationships with self and others are intrinsic to my relationship with God. Issues for reconciliation arise in prayer for I am vulnerable in prayer to any resistances to reality. Can I forgive myself for the shape I have put on my life? Can I accept that my growth was necessarily a zigzag course as I strayed to the left and the right and endeavoured to keep moving forward…? Can I accept my own particularity and the circumstances which have shaped me? Can I say 'yes' to God's world, which is in all respects limited, imperfect and in process? This reconciliation is a deep prayer stance, and its fruit is a growing appreciation, beyond mere acceptance, of all those persons – parents and others – who have influenced my life…

Memories surface from the past throughout life, asking to be faced and felt and integrated, and mature age is no exception. The love and affirmation experienced in prayer opens our defences and lets the pain of the past come through to be seen and understood from a new viewpoint and to be accepted; what we ran from originally can now be befriended because of the assurance of God's love for who we are. A 'yes' to one's past becomes a 'yes' to one's present, and leads one closer to a contemplative stance of living in the present moment, able to receive the awareness of God's presence, and to appreciate life as it is.

Finbarr Lynch, 'Ageing and Praying' in *The Way*, vol. 36, no. 2
(April 1996), pp. 116–17.

Signs of life
6.70

'Grace is never apparent and sensible to the soul, except when it is in action': therefore want of action must needs cause want of assurance: habits are not felt immediately, but by the freeness and facility of their acts; of the very being of the soul itself, nothing is felt or perceived but only its acts. The fire that lies still in the flint is neither seen nor felt: but when you smite it, and force it into act, it is easily discerned. The greatest action forces the greatest observation, whereas the dead and inactive are not remembered or taken notice of. Those that have long lain still in their graves, are out of people's thoughts as well as their sight; but those that walk the streets, and bear rule among them, are noted by all; it is so with our graces. That you have a habit of love or faith, you can know by no other way than as a consequence of reasoning: but that you have acts, you may know by feeling. If you see a man lie still in the street, what will you do to know whether he is drunk, or fainted, or dead? Will you not try to rouse him, or speak to him, to see whether he can move? Or feel his pulse, or observe his breath? Knowing that where there is life, there is some kind of movement? I earnestly beg and beseech you, Christian, observe and practise this excellent rule: you do not know now whether you have repentance, or faith, or love, or joy; but if you turn to acting them out, you will easily know it: take an object for godly sorrow, or faith, or love, or joy: put your heart into it, and take pains to provoke it into suitable action; and then see whether you have these graces or not. As Dr Sibbs observes, 'There is sometimes grief for sin in us when we think there is none': it only wants stirring up by some quickening word: he says the same of love; and it may be said of every other grace. You may go seeking for the hare or partridge many hours, and never find them while they lie close and do not stir; but when once the hare betakes itself to its legs, and the bird to its wings, then you see them at once. So long as a Christian has his graces in lively action, so long, for the most part, is he assured of them. How can you doubt whether you love God in the act of loving? Or whether you believe in the very act of believing? If therefore you want to be assured that this sacred fire is kindled in your heart, blow on it; get it into a flame, and then you will know: believe till you feel that you do believe: and love till you feel that you love.

Richard Baxter, *The Saints' Everlasting Rest*, part 3, ch. 8 (slightly modernized).

Please be patient
6.71

The struggle with self-acceptance is complicated by the fact that it cannot be selective. It is futile to conduct an inventory of ourselves, claiming some parts as good and discarding others as undesirable. Psychologically speaking, healthy self-acceptance cannot be based on denial and projection. Maturity will elude us as long as we try to disown unattractive parts of ourselves and project them onto others. As a popular retreat master used to put it, 'Maturity comes when we stop blaming God for making us the way we are!' Only by embracing the totality of who we are as people uniquely fashioned by the Lord can we progress spiritually. Paradoxically, this self-acceptance, instead of leading to self-complacency, can be the beginning of growthful change. Acceptance allows the wall of self-defensiveness to crumble and permits the pentecostal winds of conversion to blow freely throughout the self. Energies formerly wasted on battling the truth of who we are can be converted to peaceful reconstruction of the self under the guidance of God's spirit. Factored into the reality of Christian self-acceptance is the humble acknowledgment that at every point in our lives we are called to conversion. The Lord's creative power is continually at work in us, with stunning grace. Our personhood is oriented to completions that are received rather than achieved. Capturing the spirit of this truth, a popular poster states, 'Please be patient. The Lord is not finished with me yet!'

Wilkie Au, *By Way of the Heart: Toward a Holistic Christian Spirituality*
(Geoffrey Chapman 1990), p. 28.

The image remade
6.72

At rock-bottom we are made in the image of God, and this stripping is very much like the cleaning of an ancient, beautiful wall painting, or of a painting by a great master that was painted over in the course of the centuries by tasteless people who had intruded upon the real beauty that had been created by the master. To begin with, the more we clean, the more things disappear, and it seems to us that we have created a mess where there was at least a certain amount of beauty; perhaps not much, but some beauty. And then we begin to discover the real beauty which the great master has put into his painting; we see the misery, then the mess in between, but at the same time we have a preview of the authentic beauty. And we discover that what we are is a poor person who needs God; but not God to fill the gap – God to be met.

Anthony Bloom, *Living Prayer*
(Darton, Longman & Todd 1966), p. 115.

God's work
6.73

The designs of God, the good pleasure of God, the will of God, the operation of God and the gift of his grace are all one and the same thing in the spiritual life. It is God working in the soul to make it like unto himself. Perfection is neither more nor less than the faithful co-operation of the soul with this work of God, and is begun, grows, and is consummated in the soul unperceived and in secret. The science of theology is full of theories and explanations of the wonders of this state in each soul according to its capacity. One may be conversant with all these speculations, speak and write about them admirably, instruct others and guide souls; yet, if these theories are only in the mind, one is, compared with those who, without any knowledge of these theories, receive the meaning of the designs of God and do his holy will, like a sick physician compared with simple people in perfect health. The designs of God and his divine will accepted by a faithful soul with simplicity produce this divine state in it without its knowledge, just as a medicine taken obediently will produce health, although the sick person neither knows nor wishes to know anything about medicine. As fire gives out heat, and not philosophical discussions about it, nor knowledge of its effects, so the designs of God and his holy will work in the soul for its sanctification, and not speculations of curiosity as to this principle and this state. When one is thirsty one quenches one's thirst by drinking, not by reading books which treat of this condition. The desire to know does but increase this thirst. Therefore when one thirsts after sanctity, the desire to know about it only drives it further away. Speculation must be laid aside, and everything arranged by God as regards actions and sufferings must be accepted with simplicity, for those things that happen at each moment by the divine command or permission are always the most holy, the best and the most divine for us.

> Jean Pierre de Caussade, *Abandonment to Divine Providence*, Book I, ch. I, sec. IV, ed. Rev. J. Ramiere SJ (Sydney Lee Ltd 1921).

Wounds of life
6.74

Much later in life, in a release of my adolescent experience, I began to reinterpret the crucifixion. I began to see it in terms of the wounds in my own life. I had been brought up to see Jesus as God in disguise, like one of the Greek gods assuming human form, so there was a sense in which the suffering had never been real or painful. Now, the crucifixion came to have far more to do with entry into the depths of desolation that are a part of human living as we go through feelings of non-being: of only existing through others as a wife or a mother but not as an autonomous human being with a sense of self. The crucifixion became a symbol for the presence of God who is present to me directly, rather than mediated through others.

Jesus, stripped of all the trappings with which my church had surrounded him, became a human being like me: all the perspectives changed. At that time I was reading *On Being a Christian* by Hans Küng, and there I found the external validation that gave me the courage to trust my own thoughts and feelings. The spiritual life became one of liberation into life. God ceased to be remote and became the life that creates, sustains and moves through all life, and the resurrection the symbol of all that gives and nurtures life. I began to move away from images for God. Religious experience and spirituality became associated with the pool at the centre of my being: a wellspring that gurgled and bubbled away and sometimes sent up sparkling fountains.

> Barbara Harrison in Barbara and Penelope Harrison, 'Conversation Piece' in *Life Cycles: Women and Pastoral Care*, Elaine Graham and Margaret Halsey (SPCK 1993), p. 24.

A new language
6.75

The concentration which we bring to bear on our interior conduct is like that which we bring to the learning of a new language. In your case it is now time for this intensity to cease and give place to interior simplicity, leaving the soul with great freedom of movement, in the same way that after we have spoken a foreign language for some time we leave our words to look after themselves. Is there not a stage when we are very careful about the details of grammar, and a later stage when we need to think of nothing but of speaking freely and easily? It is the same with the growth of the spirit. After having studied ourselves deeply, we must then forget all about it, go straight ahead and do our best, trusting only to that simple instinct of straightforward wisdom which is the natural side, the truth of the Christian life. What perfection of good we reach in this way without realizing it! Just as, after our grammar lessons, we acquire a surprising fluency without thinking about it as soon as we aim at nothing but speaking naturally.

Henri de Tourville, *Letters of Direction*, ch. XI, tr. Lucy Menzies (Dacre Press 1939), p. 65.

Maturity
6.76

Spiritual maturity shows itself in the ability to transcend not only repeated frustrations but the mood of despair which repeated frustrations can engender. The spiritually mature are not impervious to disappointment, but are perhaps more keenly sensitive to it than most. The point is that they are not governed by it, do not sink into self-pity because of it, are not fatalistic about it. They accept the cross and even, without being morbid or superstitious about it, expect the cross; they do not make it their whole preoccupation. With an awareness of Christ's promise about the yoke being sweet and the burden light when endured with him, Christian sufferers aim as far as possible at self-forgetfulness in their sufferings. The protesting self, the resentful and potentially embittered self, will be sickened. The reaction to every trial will be St Paul's 'I have learned in whatsoever state I am to be content therewith.' Such an attitude is a degree of personal fulfilment not often attained by men and women of considerable ability and position. In any age when achievement counts far more than motive, efficiency is often mistaken for maturity.

Achievement is not the lot of all, so the Christian would be wise to cultivate the disposition of being content to do without it.

Hubert van Zeller, *Leave Your Life Alone* (Sheed & Ward 1973), p. 101.

A doorway to slander
6.77

Talkativeness is the throne of vainglory on which it loves to preen itself and show off. Talkativeness is a sign of ignorance, a doorway to slander, a leader of jesting, a servant of lies, the ruin of compunction, a summoner of despondency, a messenger of sleep, a dissipation of recollection, the end of vigilance, the cooling of zeal, the darkening of prayer.

Intelligent silence is the mother of prayer, freedom from bondage, custodian of zeal, a guard on our thoughts, a watch on our enemies, a prison of mourning, a friend of tears, a sure recollection of death, a painter of punishment, a concern with judgment, servant of anguish, foe of licence, a companion of stillness, the opponent of dogmatism, a growth of knowledge, a hand to shape contemplation, hidden progress, the secret journey upward. For those who recognize their sins have taken control of their tongue, while the chatterers have yet to discover themselves as they should.

John Climacus, *The Ladder of Divine Ascent*, Step 11,
tr. Colm Luibhead and Norman Russell (slightly adapted)
(Paulist Press 1992), pp. 158–59.

Accepting what comes
6.78

It is a luxury to be able to complete one job before starting the next. All our good intentions to give ourselves totally to the task in hand can be shattered by interruptions. Sometimes the first interruption is in turn interrupted by something else, so that we entirely lose the thread of where we were and what we were trying to do. Surrounded by unfinished tasks, we feel as if we are running up an escalator which is going downwards. It is a struggle to hang on to inward peacefulness in the frustration of seeing all our plans blown out of the window. At such moments my prayer is, 'Lord, help me to find your wholeness in the middle of incompleteness.'

We have to find a way of prayerful acceptance as each interruption comes. We must let go of what we were doing, leaving it firmly in God's hands for the moment, so that we are free to turn our whole attention to the person who has come into the office, or the child who has lost his teddy, or the caller on the telephone. By giving ourselves to the need in front of us, we can regain our inner surrender and stillness and respond as if there were nobody else and nothing else at that moment. In our rising frustration we have to entrust to

256

God the jobs we haven't even started yet, as well as the unfinished ones. This is an act of faith. If we have given ourselves to God in everything, we can trust him to see us through everything.

Angela Ashwin, *Heaven in Ordinary* (McCrimmon 1991), p. 46.

People are like rivers
6.79

You will observe that some rivers move gravely and slowly, and others with greater velocity; but there are rivers and torrents which rush with frightful impetuosity, and which nothing can arrest. All the burdens which might be laid upon them, and the obstructions which might be placed to impede their course, would only serve to redouble their violence. It is thus with souls. Some go on quietly towards perfection, and never reach the sea, or only very late, contented to lose themselves in some stronger and more rapid river, which carries them with itself into the sea. Others, which form the second class, flow on more vigorously and promptly than the first. They even carry with them a number of rivulets; but they are slow and idle in comparison with the last class, which rush onward with so much impetuosity, that they are utterly useless: they are not available for navigation, nor can any merchandise be trusted upon them, except at certain parts and at certain times. These are bold and mad rivers, which dash against the rocks, which terrify by their noise, and which stop at nothing. The second class are more agreeable and more useful; their gravity is pleasing, they are all laden with merchandise, and we sail upon them without fear and peril.

Madame Guyon, *Spiritual Torrents*, Part I, ch. I, tr. A.W. Marston
(H.R. Allenson 1908).

Yours in love
6.80

May God be God for you in truth, in which he is God and love at once!

If he is yours in love, you must live for him, by yourself being love. In that expectation, abandon yourself to the truth that he himself is. Live thus exclusively for holy love out of pure love, not because of the satisfaction you might find by communing with his love in your devout exercises, but in order to devote yourself to God himself in the works that content love. And whatever God bestows on you, however beautiful it is, do not give your kiss before the day when you know it will last eternally.

Behave yourself wisely where you now are; this is certainly needful for you. Above all things I counsel you to withhold yourself there very prudently from eccentricities, which are there very numerous; yield they pain or pleasure, have nothing to do with them. Always and in every way be humble, yet not so humble that you become foolish and neglect truth and justice wherever you can put them into practice. For verily I say to you: he who tells a lie for the sake of humility shall be punished for it. In this respect they are capable of almost everything. Look after yourself, spend your time well, be faithful and grow with us. They would gladly draw you away from us and attach you to themselves; their hearts suffer from our exceptional fidelity. Do not let yourself now be too greatly engrossed in anything. Do everything with reliance on love. Live in the same fervour as we; and let us live in sweet love. Live for God; let his life be yours, and let yours be ours.

Hadewijch, in *Hadewijch: The Complete Works*, Letter 23, tr. Mother Columba Hart OSB
(Paulist Press 1981), pp. 102–103.

Power from on high
6.81

The only purpose of the Pentecostal Blessing is to manifest Jesus in us as Saviour, in order that he may manifest his saving power in and through us to the world. The Spirit did not come instead of Jesus, but only and wholly in order to make the disciples more intimately and perfectly in relationship with the Lord than they had been when he was on earth. The power from on high did not come as a power which they could consider as their own: that power was bound inseparably to the Lord Jesus and the Spirit. Every action of the power was an immediate action of Jesus in them. All the aspects of the relationship which the disciples had had with Jesus when he was on the earth – following him, receiving his teaching, doing his will, sympathising with his suffering – were to continue even more powerfully, since through the Spirit the life of Jesus was now inside them. And it is the same with us. The Spirit in us will always glorify Jesus, always show that he alone must be Lord, that everything that is beautiful comes only from him.

Andrew Murray, *The Promise of the Spirit*
(Marshall Pickering 1990).

Opportunity in little things
6.82

There are often great opportunities in the little things of life. An ordinary life may be quite extraordinarily romantic, because beneath the conventional clothes of the local tailor, and the daily progress along the pavement of the same dull streets, is going on all the while the spiritual movement of a soul, accepting or rejecting the beckoning of the divine ideal...

When the greatest of all created beings, the Blessed Virgin Mary, first looked upon the face of God, what she saw was just a little child, born of her own travail; when the boys and girls came down the street of Nazareth on their way home from school, and passed the carpenter's shop, the divine life was there amongst the sawdust and the shavings; and when the thief on the gallows turned an eye of admiration upon the courage and undefeated love of his fellow-sufferer, there, in the very place of common execution, was the grandest of all sacrifices being enacted.

Little things bring great opportunities for a great love, and have been the steps of a heavenly ladder to the greatest of lives. A convent comes into being because some good women see how wonderful a thing silence can be; a children's home grows about the idea of the joy of guiding developing lives. All quiet housework and care and arrangement of the garden may have their inspiration from Nazareth, ministry to the sick and courage in growing old find their hallowing and help from Calvary, and the patience of prayer its radiant fortitude from the vision of the Saviour on the Holy Mount.

Father Andrew SDC, *Meditations for Every Day*
(A.R. Mowbray 1941), p. 255.

Begin today ·
6.83

Some believe in and rely on prayer, others think of it as mumbo jumbo. But we should not allow the word prayer to divide us. Whenever we express our dearest wishes, that is praying.

Let us open our eyes. Let us begin at once to fight our selfishness and come out of ourselves, to dedicate ourselves once and for all, whatever the sacrifices, to the non-violent struggle for a juster and more human world.

Let us not put off the decision till tomorrow. Let us begin today, now, intelligently and firmly.

Let us look about us and recognize our brothers and sisters who are called like us to give up their ease and join all those who hunger for the truth and who have sworn to give their lives to make peace through justice and love.

Let us not waste time discussing who shall be our leader. What is important is for us to unite and go forward, remembering that time too is our enemy.

Let us give the best of ourselves to helping create moral pressure for freedom to bring about the necessary structural changes.

Let us gather information on the situations we wish to change.

Let us spread this information by all reasonable means at our disposal. And let the information be truthful, able to stand up to criticism and disturb the consciences of all good people.

Let us through all things stand firm without falling into hatred, let us be understanding without conniving at evil.

Helder Camara, *The Desert is Fertile*, tr. Dinah Livingstone
(Sheed and Ward 1974), pp. 59–60.

Black spirituality
6.84

Do we [Black South Africans] need the type of meditation and spiritual training that is being used in our seminaries and convents? I put this question because attitudes developed in so-called spiritual training come to the surface in the liturgy. I mean the type of meditation in which one is supposed to go into oneself to exercise one's memory, one's imagination and one's sentiments, especially in trying to call up scenes from the life of Jesus and then trying to express one's sentiments about all this. Now, this is supposed to be the kind of exercise that helps to increase one's moral excellence, one's spiritual perfection; for my part, I think this kind of practice to be foreign to our traditions.

I cannot remember in any of the traditional practices of the black people that anyone was encouraged to cultivate high moral excellence or self-perfection by 'entering into himself'. A sensible person in our society was supposed to be one who knew and performed his or her duties towards ancestors and members of the community. The faithful performance of these duties and the development of correct attitudes also towards natural objects was not supposed to imbue such a person with any kind of halo of sanctity or holiness. It was supposed to make him or her a sensible and well-adjusted member of society and the universe.

Since spirituality is a basic element in our worship, I would advocate that black people should also question and challenge the traditional methods and aims of present spirituality. We do not believe that withdrawal into self can result in any kind of moral excellence, sanctity of holiness, or whatever you call it. We believe in developing correct attitudes towards things and towards people. These pave the way towards fuller communion between the individual and nature and human society. This fuller communion is in itself a healthy state and not any kind of mysterious sanctity or holiness.

Mongameli Mabona, 'Black People and White Worship' in *Black Theology:*
The South African Voice, ed. Basil Moore (C. Hurst & Co. 1973), pp. 107–108.

Other 'christs'
6.85

The countless lamps which are burning were all lit at the same fire, that is to say they were all lighted and are all shining through the action of one and the same substance. Thus Christians shine brilliantly through the action of the divine fire, the Son of God. Their lamps that have been lit are in the depth of their heart and they shine in his presence during the time they spend on earth, just as he himself shines brilliantly. Does not the Spirit say, 'God, your God, has anointed you with the oil of gladness'? (Psalm 45:7). He was called Anointed (*Christos*) in order that we might receive the unction of the same oil with which he was anointed, and might thereby become 'christs' also, being of the same nature as he and forming a single body with him. It is written likewise: 'He who sanctifies and those who are sanctified have all one origin' (Hebrews 2:11).

Pseudo-Macarius, 'Great Letter', tr. Theodore Berkeley and Jeremy Hummerstone in
Olivier Clément, *The Roots of Christian Mysticism* (New City 1993).

Watching
6.86

Our Lord says 'Watch!' Now I consider this word *watching* a remarkable word; remarkable because the idea is not so obvious as might appear at first sight... We are not simply to believe, but to watch; not simply to love, but to watch; not simply to obey, but to watch; to watch for what? Most of us have a general idea what is meant by believing, fearing, loving and obeying; but perhaps we do not contemplate or apprehend what is meant by watching.

And I conceive it is one of the main points, which, in a practical way, will be found to separate the true and perfect servants of God from the multitude called Christians. I am speaking of two *characters*, the true and consistent character, and the inconsistent; and these I say will be found in no slight degree discriminated and distinguished by this one mark – true Christians, whoever they are, watch, and inconsistent Christians do not. Now what is watching?

Do you know the feeling in matters of this life, of expecting a friend, expecting him to come, and he delays? Do you know what it is to be in unpleasant company, and to wish for the time to pass away, and the hour strike when you may be at liberty? Do you know what it is to be in anxiety lest something should happen which may happen or may not, or to be in suspense about some important event, which makes your heart beat when you are reminded of it, and of which you think the first thing in the morning? Do you know what it is to have a friend in a distant country, to expect news of him, and to wonder from day to day what he is now doing, and whether he is well? Do you know what it is so to live upon a person who is present with you, that your eyes follow his, that you read his soul, that you see all its changes in his countenance, that you anticipate his wishes, that you smile in his smile, and are sad in his sadness, and are downcast when he is vexed, and rejoice in his successes? To watch for Christ is a feeling such as all these; as far as feelings of this world are fit to shadow out those of another.

He watches for Christ who has a sensitive, eager, apprehensive mind; who is awake, alive, quick-sighted, zealous in seeking and honouring him; who looks out for him in all that happens, and who would not be surprised, who would not be over-agitated or overwhelmed, if he found that he was coming at once.

John Henry Newman, 'Watching', in *Parochial and Plain Sermons*,
vol. IV (1875) (abridged).

Serving the Lord
6.87

That the devil tries to draw us into a false and noxious humility is evident from your own words… You do not dare to say outright, 'I want to serve our Lord', or 'Our Lord has given me the desire to serve him', but only that you *think* you desire this. Now if you just reflect, you will see that those desires of serving Christ our Lord are not from you but from him, and when you say boldly that he has given them to you, you publish his praise and glorify him, not yourself… We must, then, be very careful, and if the Enemy exalts us straightaway humble ourselves, counting our sins and miseries; if he lowers and depresses us, we must at once lift up our hearts in true faith and hope, counting the blessings which we have received from our Lord and remembering with how much love and eager desire he waits upon us so as to save us... Bear well in mind how the martyrs when arraigned before their pagan judges proclaimed that they were the servants of Christ. You should do likewise when confronted by the Enemy of human nature, anxious to deprive you of the courage which our Lord bestows upon you, and to render you weak and fearful by his snares and deceits. Do not merely venture to say that you are desirous of serving the Lord, when you ought to proclaim and confess boldly that you *are* his servant, and that you would sooner die than desert his service.

> Ignatius Loyola, letter to Teresa Rejadella, in James Brodrick,
> *Saint Ignatius Loyola: The Pilgrim Years* (Burns & Oates 1956),
> p. 331, slightly adapted.

PART 7

Living With Each Other

Justice and Peace

The right kind of fasting?

7.1

If you have fasted for two days, do not think yourself better than the one who is not fasting. You fast and are bad-tempered; the other person eats and has a cheerful face. You work off your irritability of mind and your belly's emptiness by picking quarrels, while the other person eats moderately and is grateful to God. Hence Isaiah proclaims every day: 'This is not the sort of fast I have chosen, says the Lord,' and again,

> In the day when you fast you will be seeking your own pleasure and oppressing those who work for you. You fast for strife and quarrelsomeness and beat up the poor labourer! Is *that* the sort of fast I want?

What sort of fast is that, when not even the full moon puts an end to your bad mood, much less the ending of the day? Look to yourself and your own state, and do not be self-satisfied when others fall, only when you yourself truly achieve something – if you do achieve anything.

Jerome, *Letters*, 22, tr. Jennifer Wild.

'Where is my brother or sister?'

7.2

The crucial question ringing out through history – as humans heedlessly and needlessly go on destroying life – is this: 'Where is your brother/sister?' The message of Jesus shows clearly that both men and women are indeed responsible to nurture, foster and help life to blossom out in this world. In this way women and men co-operate with God not only in bringing new life into the world, but also in strengthening that life and in being a solid foundation for it to grow in wisdom and age. God has placed life in our hands and life has become very vulnerable in human hands in this age of sophisticated arms and unsatiated human greed for perishable and transitory things; such as wealth, power and prestige. Yet, could we ever forget that it is our sacred duty, and that we are answerable for life? 'Where is your sister/brother?'

In the gospels, too, there is the same insistence and urgency on behalf of life. In the attitude of Jesus we see this great regard for life, especially for that of the poor, the outcast and those considered by society to be sinners. Jesus moves with them, he heals them and they are transformed by his presence and by his touch. A new life springs in them.

A certain young man asked Jesus, 'What must I do to receive eternal life?' Jesus answered him, 'What do the scriptures say? How do you interpret them?' The man answered him, 'You must love the Lord your God with all your heart, with all your soul and with all your strength and with all your mind; and you must love your neighbour as yourself.' 'Your answer is correct,' replied Jesus. 'Do this and you shall live.' There is no side-stepping it. Our lives are intimately bound with that of others. The command of Jesus that we should love our neighbour as ourselves challenges us to protect his or her life as we would our very own. So if we are to really live, we need to have respect, love and concern for life by actively sponsoring all that defends, protects and fosters life, and shunning all that is against life.

Marlene Perera, 'Where is Your Sister/Brother?' (Genesis 4:1–16) in *Women of Courage: Asian Women Reading the Bible*, ed. Lee Oo Chung et al. (Asian Women's Resource Centre for Culture and Theology 1992), pp. 15–16.

Loving God and neighbour
7.3

When our Lord says: *You shall love your God with all your heart, and with all your soul, and your neighbour as yourself*, let the faithful soul receive the unfading love of its creator and ruler, and submit itself entirely to his will. For his works and decrees are never lacking in the truth of justice and the mercy of kindness. And if anyone should be burdened with great labours and countless difficulties, they will find a good reason to bear with them if they understand that they are either set right by obstacles, or tested by them. But our devotion to this love will never be perfect unless our neighbour is also loved. And by this word *neighbour* we are to understand not only those who are bound to us by ties of friendship or blood, but absolutely every human being with whom we share a common nature, whether they be enemies or companions, free or enslaved. For one maker made us, and one creator breathed life into us. We all have the benefit of the same sky and air, the same days and nights. And, although some are good and some are bad, some upright and others not, the wideness of Christian grace has given us even stronger reasons for loving our neighbour. Stretching out to every part of the entire world, it despairs of no one, and teaches that no one should be passed over.

Leo the Great, Homily 8 on the Gospel (Christmas Day), tr. Aelred Squire, in
Fathers Talking (Cistercian Publications 1986), pp. 11–12.

How many faithful?
7.4

'Who, then, is the man that fears the Lord? He will instruct him in the way chosen for him.' Sovereign Lord! Your way is the way of peace, and blessed is the person who walks there. For mercy, love, justice, humility, obedience and patience are found along this way. Such a person clothes the naked, feeds the hungry, satisfies the thirsty, comforts the needy, and reproves, warns, consoles and admonishes. Such a person is sober, honest, modest, upright and just. Such a person gives no reason for offence and walks towards eternal life. But there are very few who find this way. I fear, beloved Lord, that hardly ten in a thousand find this way, and of those, hardly five really walk it. So it has been from the beginning. For when there were only four people on earth, the scripture says that three were disobedient and the fourth was killed by his brother. There were only eight righteous ones who were saved from the flood, and one of those was disrespectful to his father. In Sodom and Gomorrah and the surrounding area, there were only four righteous ones, and one of those turned back to look and was turned into a pillar of salt. More than 600,000 fighting men came out of Egypt, among whom only two were able to enter into the promised land. Not, beloved Lord, that all who died along the way were damned. But it was due to their unbelief that their way into the promised land of Canaan was delayed.

Menno Simons, 'A Meditation on the Twenty-fifth Psalm' (1537), in *Early Anabaptist Spirituality*, tr. and ed. Daniel Liechty (Paulist Press 1994), pp. 257–58.

An active kind of God
7.5

This act of saving a rabble of slaves, this highly political act called the Exodus in the Bible, came to be seen as the founding event of the people of God, what constituted them his people, and other divine events were described in the light of this event, as the Christians later were to describe everything in their salvation history in the light of the death and resurrection event of Jesus Christ. God showed himself there as a saving God, as a doing, an active kind of God, not one who was fond of delivering eloquent speeches, as a gracious God (they did not deserve to be saved, they could not merit being saved); and he showed himself to be a God of liberation, the great Exodus God, who took the side of the oppressed, the exploited ones, the downtrodden, the marginalized ones. He was no fence-sitter. He took sides against the powerful on behalf of the widow, the orphan and the alien – classes of people who were often at the back of the queue, at the bottom of the pile.

The God of Abraham, Isaac and Jacob, the God of our Fathers, the Father of our Lord Jesus Christ was known then first as the God of the Exodus, the liberator God, and the theme of setting free, of rescuing captives or those who have been kidnapped, is one that runs through the Bible as a golden thread.

Desmond Tutu, *Hope and Suffering*
(Collins Fount 1984), pp. 79–80, 81.

Reconciling love
7.6

Reconciling love is patient and persevering, for its ministry is daily, routine, never-ending. It is riddled with complications and complexities. It takes an enduring hope to tutor in a drug-rehabilitation centre, to visit people in prison, to pray for judges and lawmakers and corporation executives. The disciple comes soon to acknowledge that his or her own limits and frailty prepare the ground for the forgiveness and acceptance of others.

Reconciliation is a responsibility that we cannot delegate. Each of us is part of a pattern of relationships that demand respect and non-violence. Our spirit will be tested at critical moments: when the funds for our poverty project are cut, when someone else is awarded the honour we deserve, when we are shunned or rejected. And by the wearying tasks of maintaining an honest, caring, community. 'While we live we are constantly being delivered to death for Jesus' sake, so that the life of Jesus may be revealed in our mortal flesh' (2 Corinthians 4:11).

The ministry of reconciliation has no defined or definable limits. All of life belongs to God and all brokenness awaits healing: distorted and destructive political systems, damaged personal relationships of all manner and making, our own failed covenants with ourselves and with God.

Healing is needed in the caste systems of India, the capitalist systems of the West, the places where patriarchalism and militarism stunt life and where people suffer the consequences of greed and oppression. Healing is needed in the delicate systems of renewal and rebirth within our larger sacred community, the earth. The wounds of broken-hearted mothers, marginalized Indians, excommunicated mavericks, cry for healing, as do those of isolated and alienated psyches and spirits starved for dignity and affection.

Joan Puls OSF, *Hearts Set on the Pilgrimage: In Search of a Common Spirituality*
(Lamp Press 1989), p. 60.

Possessiveness

7.7

Christians have to be clear where they stand with regard to property and goods. They should not condemn them, since they are good things. But they should be ruthless and radical towards the possessive instinct in themselves. There Christ asks for everything and rejects any compromise – surely because the facts of the case themselves reject compromise. If I do not act ruthlessly against my possessiveness, I will be possessed by it. It will lead me and govern me. I will be caught up in an unending spiral of desire, fulfilment and greater desire and soon both my surrender to God and my openness to my neighbour will have been thrown aside. In fact these two gospel commands of love presuppose an attitude of poverty and detachment from self which are incompatible with the acquisitive spirit. Perhaps the reason we so often fail to love as we should is not because of a defect of loving in us, but because we are unwilling to conquer our spirit of greed and so, inevitably, put ourselves before others. When it comes to a final count we cling to our own self's needs and put our neighbour second. This is true of families as well as individuals.

The surrender to God in adoration and to one's neighbour in availability imply a 'letting go' which is the opposite of the acquisitive 'hanging on'. We have to be very honest with ourselves about the possessive instinct. Unless we root it out from the depths, it will take charge and oust every fine feeling in our hearts and leave only selfish concern. Jesus really meant it when he said 'You cannot serve God and Mammon.'

John Dalrymple, *Costing Not Less than Everything*
(Darton, Longman & Todd 1975), pp. 106–107.

Filling the void
7.8

Gluttony at first sight looks like a survival from our animal ancestry. Certainly the urgent drive to search for food is one of the most powerful of animal instincts. But in fact excessive eating such as is common to man is rarely if ever found among animals, except those domesticated by men and so influenced by him. Men and women commonly overeat, at least in countries where there is an abundance of food, to fill the void caused by loneliness or boredom. This is even truer of excessive drinking. 'The gin shop is the quickest way out of Manchester.' Eating and drinking, despite excess, are clearly good and necessary. This is seen conspicuously when food and drink are shared in a meal between friends or in a family. It is not without reason that heaven has been likened to a feast.

Covetousness is an undue desire to possess. It gives to money or possessions, which are essentially only means to living, the value of ends, of objects to be clung to for their own sake. It can be powered by more than one motive. Avarice, like pride can be an attempt to escape from the painful sense of insignificance and of dependence on the whim of others. The power which money gives and the wealth which surrounds a rich man can help a person to maintain the image of his superiority. But like lust, the urge to possess may have as its underlying motive the desire to escape from loneliness, from the fear of being unloved or even of being unlovable. Money, it is felt, can buy friendship, though in fact it is singularly unsuccessful in doing this. For the rich, though they can buy the company of their fellows, become painfully aware that their so-called friends love their money and the comfort it can obtain more than themselves. Wealth, especially when sought diligently and acquired with effort, tends to separate those who have it from those who have not. It makes the poor envious and the rich defensive. Covetousness has been called idolatry, for it has a unique power of blinding men to their dependence on God and their need to love and to be loved by their fellows. The splash of wealth can distract the rich from the needs of the poor and make them forget their humanity. Wealth also appears to be a source of perpetual anxiety. Our Western world has been called an acquisitive society because its economic system, for its efficient working, seems to require the constant stimulation, by means of advertising for example, of the desire to possess more and more. Nevertheless, despite all that can be said against either human avarice or the capital system, both possessions and money are means to the enhancement of human life. Seen as servants of human welfare they are to be valued. But recognized as powerful servants, ever liable to usurp the position of master, they need to

271

be kept firmly in their subordinate place. We live at a time when science and technology have together enabled men to create immense wealth. It may be that the future of human life on this planet depends on the wisdom and determination really to subordinate the new-found wealth to the well-being of the race.

Christopher Bryant SSJE, *The Heart in Pilgrimage*
(Darton, Longman & Todd 1980), p. 40.

Prayer and politics
7.9

Without prayer and its grounding in faith, the human city and its politics remain irredeemable. Selfishness and the corruption of sectional interests are too strong. But without politics prayer becomes a selfish ego-trip, an escape from that burden of secular reality for which every one of us is inherently responsible. A way to God which is not a way back hour by hour to our neighbour on the streets of Sarajevo is the way to a God who does not deserve either to be worshipped or to exist. He deserves rather to be abolished like so many other gods of the human past – abolished because in their strange attributes they never did exist, though some glimmer in their images may still have witnessed to what does and must exist beyond us all.

Every time prayer is detached from the politics of the market place, leaving the marketeers free to proclaim a God concerned with the spiritual only, the core element of the specifically Christian is lost. Public things are material things; things that are spiritual only are private things. A religion of pure spirituality is a privatized religion with a privatized God, and a privatized God cannot or should not exist. God is the God of everything or of nothing, but of everything seen through the image of the crucified. Without such a God and without the human prayer that makes us conscious of such a God there can be no absolute critique of evil government and corrupt politics, no tradition of prophecy...

We can only prophesy out of an objectivity of truth and of goodness. If love is absolutely preferable to hate, truth to lies, whatever an individual chooses to think or do, then there exists over and above us a moral order, unchangeable, objective, absolute. That, as Aquinas would say, is what we call God. By prayer, in silence and meditation, we can open mind and heart to the overwhelming importance of the good and true, and realize the petty criminality of preferring the criteria of ethnic, party or commercial advantage. Out of prayer comes prophecy. Moreover in Christ we discover that the God who is truth and goodness is none other than our neighbour in need. Prayer leads us to politics while politics can only be saved from itself by the prophecy which has come out of prayer.

Adrian Hastings, *The Shaping of Prophecy* (Geoffrey Chapman 1995), pp. 19–20.

A common vision
7.10

The dream of the mighty for more power, of the rich for more wealth, is the nightmare of the powerless and poor. But the dream of the oppressed and poor for liberation is the nightmare of the powerful and rich. It has always been so in a world which is unwilling to share resources and to discern them as gifts not possessions. The dream of the oppressed is utopian, it is a vision of a better world. It is this vision which enabled the first Christians to face persecution. 'Then I saw a new heaven and a new earth.' It is the same vision which has motivated the prophets throughout the centuries, the vision of the kingdom of God inaugurated in Jesus Christ but yet to come in its fullness. This vision threatens those who possess everything except the ability to share with others. The powerful and privileged fear the dreams of the poor and the visions of the prophets because they derive from the coming kingdom of God, God's purpose for his world. They are dreams and visions which are just and right, and will come true.

A nation needs a common vision, a shared dream. A dream which is no one's nightmare because it promises hope and life in a new way for all. The message of Pentecost is that all people, young and old, Jew and Gentile, black and white, rich and poor, are brought within the scope of God's action through the Spirit. All people may be transformed and so transcend the barriers of race and class which divide nations and turn the dreams of some into the nightmares of others. This is the promise of the gospel in our land, a vision of righteousness and justice. Without such a shared vision the people will perish, and all our dreams will become a nightmare.

John de Gruchy, *Cry Justice* (Collins 1986).

Justice coming home
7.11

The spiritual growth of persons is intimately linked to the problem of lifestyles, for that is where the option for social justice comes home to a person, a family, a group. Social justice requires a rethinking of the lifestyle of families, especially of the affluent. Action for justice can lead persons to situations in which they may have to suffer loss of employment, imprisonment or other dire consequences. Then the whole family is affected. Action for justice thus requires a common reflection among the members of a family. This brings to the fore a dimension of social concern that may be generally absent from or neglected by families. Groups of families may have to pool their resources in order to cope with the calamities that affect them. Such sharing of risks and securities will bring families closer to each other.

Change in lifestyle requires awareness, conviction, and courage. It is as difficult to opt for a simpler, poorer, and more authentic way of life as it is to give up other areas of personal selfishness. A person, family or group going through the process will therefore need the help of friends and associates. For a certain period of time, individuals may have to be supported by others financially and psychologically.

Tissa Balasuriya, *Planetary Theology*
(SCM Press 1984), pp. 267–68.

No right of purchase
7.12

The Lord God gave us a material world – like this material Mass, with its material cup that we raise in our toast to Christ the Lord. A material world for all, without borders. That's what Genesis says. I'm not the one saying it. 'I'll buy half of El Salvador. Look at all my money. That'll give me the right to it.' No! There's no 'right' to talk about! 'It's called right of purchase. I've got the right to buy half of El Salvador.' No! That's denying God! There is no 'right' against the masses of the people! A material world for all, then, without borders, without frontiers. A common table, with broad linens, a table for everybody, like this Eucharist. A chair for everybody. And a table setting for everybody. Christ had good reason to talk about his kingdom as a meal. He talked about meals a lot. And he celebrated one the night before his supreme sacrifice. Thirty-three years old, he celebrated a farewell meal with his closest friends. And he said that this was the great memorial of the redemption: a table shared in brotherhood, where all have their position and place. Love, the law code of the kingdom, is just one word, but it is the key word that sums up all of the codes of ethics of the human race, exalting them and presenting them in Jesus. This is the love of a communion of sisters and brothers that smashes and casts to the earth every sort of barrier and prejudice and that one day will overcome hatred itself.

Rutilio Grande SJ, in Jon Sobrino, *Jesus in Latin America*
(Orbis Books 1987), pp. 96–97.

National greed
7.13

To our shame, the world is tumbling down in ruins all round us, but our sins are not included in the downfall… There is no country in the world without its asylum-seekers. Buildings once regarded as sacred have fallen in dust and ashes, and yet we still set our hearts on 'value for money'. We live as though we were going to die tomorrow, and yet we build houses as though we were going to be here for ever. Our walls, ceilings, entrance porches are lavishly luxurious, while Christ is dying at our doors naked and starving in the persons of his poor.

… God said to Moses, 'Let me alone and I will wipe out this people.' That 'let me alone' shows that he can be held from carrying out his threats; for the prayers of the servant of God stood in the way of the power of God. But now, who do you think there is under heaven who can face God's wrath, go to meet the flames and say with the apostle, 'I wish that I myself were cursed for the sake of my fellows'?

Flocks and shepherds are perishing together, because as the people are, so is the priest. Moses, with love and compassion, said, 'If you will, forgive the sin of this your people; if not, then blot my name out of your book.' He wanted to perish with the perishing, and was not satisfied with winning salvation for himself alone. Indeed it is true that 'the honour of rulers lies with the mass of the people'.

Jerome, *Letters*, 128 (a contemporary reading, tr. Jennifer Wild).

Cheerful giving
7.14

Our Lord encourages us to put our money, our treasure, where our hearts are; the question has to be asked – are our hearts really committed? The view is also held that money is evil, it is dirty, and that Christians should not be concerned with it or about it. But that is not to live in the real world; money *is* part of the real world in which we live, and therefore is to be used responsibly. As part of this responsible use of money the gospel encourages us to give to those in need… I am constantly amazed by the begrudging nature of those who on the one hand affirm their indebtedness to God who has given them so much and so generously, yet render back to him so little. 'The Lord loves a cheerful giver' is heard in our churches. Yet I have seen few of these cheerful givers! But this is precisely what we need if the church itself is to be that authentic sign in the world of the costly giving and service which is so much part of the life of Christ and of the gospels. Furthermore, let it not be a drudge but rather a joy as we recall the words of St Francis: 'It is in giving that we receive.' Here the saint echoes the words of the New Testament; in Acts (20:35) as part of Paul's farewell, it is written 'remembering the words of the Lord Jesus, how he said it is more blessed to give than to receive' – and Paul had been called upon to give to the uttermost, to the shedding of his blood for the sake of the gospel.

David Hope, *Friendship with God* (Fount 1989), pp. 36–37.

No coexistence

7.15

Christians have a responsibility for making peace. We believe nature, as well as humanity, has been created by God, and that we are entrusted to manage all natural resources responsibly, not only for our own self-interest in this generation, but also for those who come after us. We also acknowledge that the love of God for us, God's creatures, gives immense value and dignity to the life of every person. If we are to respond to this love of God, we must seek to protect the integrity of nature and defend the lives and dignity of all people. In this spirit, one of the most urgent current issues in which we Christians should be involved is the matter of nuclear power, both in its military use as a weapon of mass destruction and in its peaceful use as a source of energy. We human beings cannot coexist with nuclear power.

The peace movement is becoming a giant wave in Europe, America, and Asia. People are extending their hands and banding together across the boundaries that separate East and West. Voices for peace, coming from the grassroots people in the marginalized areas of the world, have been raised more and more wherever oppression has become dominant. Today more people believe that their small actions for peace can become a cornerstone for peacemaking and have realized the importance of solidarity among people for uniting their power together for peace. We have to commit ourselves to the world peace movement and give effect to our determination to save succeeding generations from the scourge of war and destruction of our earth.

Reiko Shimado, 'War and Peace: A Japanese Perspective' in *Justice as Mission*, ed. Terry Brown and Christopher Lind (Trinity Press 1985), pp. 225–26.

Christian giving
7.16

If ten per cent of all Western Christians adopted the graduated tithe, huge sums of money would become available for kingdom work. Where would that money do the most good?... Here are some general criteria for deciding where to channel your giving for development in hungry lands:

1. Do the funds support holistic projects in the Third World working simultaneously at an integrated programme of evangelism, social change, education, agricultural development and so on?

2. Do the funds support truly indigenous projects? That involves several issues: (a) Are the leaders and most of the staff of the projects in the developing nations indigenous persons? (They should be.) (b) Do the projects unthinkingly adopt Western ideas, materials and technology or do they carefully develop material suited to their own culture? (c) Did the project arise from the felt needs of the people rather than from some outside 'expert'?

3. Are the projects primarily engaged in long-range development (that includes people development), or in brief emergency projects only?

4. Are the programmes designed to help the poor masses understand that God wants sinful social structures changed and that they can help effect that change?

5. Do the programmes grow out of and foster Christian community?

6. Are the programmes potentially self-supporting after an initial injection of seed capital? And do the programmes from the beginning require commitment and a significant contribution of capital or time (or both) from the people themselves?

7. Do the programmes aid the poorest people in the poorest developing countries?

8. Is agricultural development involved? (It need not always be, but in a majority of cases it should be.)

9. Is justice rather than continual charity the result?

10. Several important questions can be asked of the agency through which one channels funds. How much is spent on administration and fund raising? Are the board and staff persons of known integrity? Is the board paid? (It should not be.) Are Third World and other minority persons and women represented among the board and top staff? Are staff salaries consistent with biblical teaching on economic relationships amongst the people of God? Did the organization object to answering these questions?

Ronald J. Sider, <i>Rich Christians in an Age of Hunger</i>
(Hodder & Stoughton 1978), pp. 159–60.

Salvation: individual *and* social
7.17

Conservative religion has often produced a cultural theology that fosters an acceptance or at least an acquiescence to the cultural and political status quo. Jesus is proclaimed as saviour, but the implications of his lordship over all of life are not drawn out, or are spiritualized into irrelevance. The influence of individualism and the ethic of success in evangelism has resulted in a depreciation of Jesus' call for public discipleship. Thus the offer of grace without discipleship has come to characterize the evangelistic proclamations of conservative religion.

An individualistic world view, adopted from secular culture, has fostered a misunderstanding of both sin and the gospel, which in scripture are seen as having individual and corporate dimensions. When this occurs, evil is viewed for the most part in personal terms and is not connected to the infliction of evil by social systems and institutional arrangements. Salvation, too, is wrongly viewed as an exclusively private and personal affair and is thus separated from its social and political meaning. There has been a marked tendency in conservative religious circles to put religion and politics into dichotomy, which invariably results in conformity with the status quo either by intent or by default.

In contrast to biblical thought, personal realities are divorced from institutional and social realities, and the vital connections between them are not made. Such practice narrows the scope and meaning of the gospel and causes ethical blindness and insensitivity. Our lives are lived either in support of present social and political realities or in opposition to them, but never in neutrality.

Jim Wallis, <i>Agenda for Biblical People</i> (Triangle 1986), pp. 30–31.

The Community of Love

The magic ritual of a dinner party
7.18

A dinner party is a magical ritual. Its purpose is to realize the dream of the alchemist: the universal transubstantiation of things. It starts with the magical powers of digestion. Onions, peppers, beans, potatoes, tomatoes, bread, beef, chicken, fish, lobsters, oysters, sweets, cheese, wine, beer... They are all different entities. They have different names. They have different properties. And yet, through the alchemic operations of the body they lose their identity. They cease to be what they were. They are assimilated. They become like the body (from the Latin *assimilare*, to be made like; *ad*, to, and *similis*, like). They are incorporated: they become one with the body (Latin *corpus*, body). A meal is a triumph of the body over food. All differences become sameness.

But another transformation takes place, when the etiquette is added to the food. Just as in a vegetable soup many different vegetables are cooked into one single broth, so the different guests become one single soup. They eat together, they become 'companions'. The meaning of this word is very suggestive. It comes from the Latin *com*, with, and *panis*, bread. Companions are those who eat bread together. The purpose of a dinner party is not the pragmatical end of nourishment and not only the pleasure of eating. It is hoped that eating together will become an occasion of companionship, friendship. The guests assimilate the food. The ritual assimilates the guests.

Rubem A. Alves, *The Poet, The Warrior, The Prophet*
(SCM Press/Trinity Press International 1990), pp. 11–12.

Children of God
7.19

The Christian gospel declares that people are of inestimable value because they are the children of God, the concern of his love, created for an eternal destiny;

not just people in general, but individual men, women and children, each with a name, each having priceless worth. This was made startlingly plain by Jesus when he told his disciples 'the very hairs of your head are all numbered': an extravagant piece of imagery to drive home what he was saying. When we take his words seriously, we begin to realize how far-reaching their significance is. If they are true, if that is how things really are, if God really does care for every single man, woman and child in the teeming millions that inhabit the globe, not to speak of the countless generations of the past and those as yet unborn, we cannot dismiss anyone as of no consequence; nor are we entitled to suppose that some are more important than others or that any should be sacrificed to serve some interest which takes precedence over their inherent worth. The consequences of accepting this basic presupposition are shattering, calling in question not only the way in which we commonly behave towards many of our fellow human beings, but the international, military, political, economic and social policies which have been and still are considered reasonable by those who are responsible for them.

Paul Rowntree Clifford, *Government by the People?* (SCM Press 1986).

Universal love
7.20

Our power of doing external acts of love and goodness is often very narrow and restrained. There are, it may be, but few people to whom we can contribute any worldly relief.

But though our outward means of doing good are often thus limited, yet if our hearts are but full of love and goodness we get, as it were, an infinite power because God will attribute to us those good works, those acts of love and tender charities, which we sincerely desired and would gladly have performed had it been in our power.

You cannot heal all the sick, relieve all the poor; you cannot comfort all in distress nor be a father to all the fatherless. You cannot, it may be, deliver many from their misfortunes or teach them to find comfort in God.

But if there is a love and tenderness in your heart that delights in these good works and excites you to do all that you can, if your love has no bounds but continually wishes and prays for the relief and happiness of all that are in distress, you will be received by God as a benefactor to those who have had nothing from you but your good will and tender affections.

William Law, *A Serious Call to a Devout and Holy Life*, ch. 20,
ed. Paul G. Stanwood (Paulist Press 1978), pp. 291–92.

Hear our prayer
7.21

[One evening] I was part of the volunteer staff of an overnight shelter for street women. It was a very cold night and the women began to arrive early in the evening. The rooms reserved for them were behind the sanctuary of the church and were used for other purposes during the day. Foam rubber mats were laid out over the entire area in one room. Many of the women chose a mat as soon as they arrived. Some had very little with them, though most of them had the bags that had given them the name of bag ladies. One carried her possessions in a child's wagon, and another, more affluent, had hers piled dangerously high in a supermarket cart. The conversation was disconnected, but the atmosphere was warm and peaceful. Each one was given a bowl of stew, bread and tea…

When morning came the peaceful atmosphere inside the shelter turned hostile. Distraught women – some of them old and sick – could not comprehend why they were once more being 'pushed out' into the streets. We who had received them so warmly the night before were the very ones hurrying them along, benefactors so soon to become enemies.

In the narrow hall where the women were having breakfast, an old woman with a gentle face kneeled to pray. She was in the way of another woman who taunted her, 'Get up woman. God don't hear your prayer.' The praying woman did not respond and her taunter said again, 'God don't hear your prayer, woman. God don't hear your prayer.'

I asked myself, 'Does God hear her prayer?' Then I remembered. God is in me and where I am God is. The real question was, 'Did I hear her prayer?' What would it mean to hear her prayer?

Elizabeth O'Connor, *Cry Pain, Cry Hope* (The Servant Leadership School n.d.).

Jesus the outsider
7.22

There are many ways of being marginalized. One may be an outsider economically, politically, religiously, sociologically or sexually, to mention a few. The gospels contain many examples of each of these categories. Jesus himself exemplifies outsider status in a number of ways. He was marginal as regards his origins in national and world history, as regards his death as an outsider, as regards his departure from work and village and his place in the urban setting of Jerusalem, as regards the non-traditional source of his teaching and ideas, and as regards his anti-establishment role as a poor person who had no power base and was not integrated into the dominant culture. Finally, in some sense Jesus marginalized himself, choosing to remain within his outsider position where he perceived and evaluated the world from a different standpoint.

Jesus draws others who are marginalized into his inclusive community, but they never entirely lose their marginal status because they do not become a part of the established power base in society. Whether the people Jesus invites into his circle of friends are marginalized because of illness, poverty, occupation or social status, he helps them discover personal and social values that transcend the standards of worth set in the larger society. He integrates them into a community that is prophetic and that functions as a continuing challenge to the larger community when that populace fails to recognize and do something to include the marginalized.

At times the marginality of Jesus seems to set up an opposition between God and 'the world'. The apparent dualism that results has sometimes been interpreted as a power struggle between God and world. Rather than separating him from others, Jesus' marginality puts him more deeply into the world by highlighting his vulnerability. That vulnerability becomes more apparent as we examine his relationship with other outsiders.

Jane Kopas, 'Outsiders in the Gospels: Marginality as a Source of Knowledge',
The Way, vol. 33, no. 2 (April 1993), pp. 118–19.

Christined in us

7.23

Christ in us knows both the loneliness of the outsider and the crabbed lives of the insider. He experiences in us the full diversity of the human condition. The meeting of Christ in us with the Christ in others will mean that we shall be willing to expose ourselves in openness to others without fear, seeing each person we meet as having a significance because both of us are accepted and loved by God...

To have a prayerful approach to people is to have eyes to see, a mind intent upon seeing, a heart hopeful of seeing the image of God in each person I meet, to see them in themselves and in God.

It is only when this significance has been given by us in our approach to people, when we have freed ourselves of the need to assess blame and responsibilities, that we can take them on to the next step on the road to redemption, namely, to be aware of their true selves and that which is blocking the potentialities which lie within them. It is this kind of freedom which the

Christ in us brings in our personal approach: the Christ who revealed to the Samaritan woman the truths she was concealing from herself, who enabled the blind not only to see physically but to see spiritually, who enabled the prostitute to realize the real love which lay within her...

This will mean that in our encounters with people we shall do a great deal of listening in order that we may learn how people see themselves. By sensitivity to what is heard, and by insight into the right kind of questions to be put, we may be able both to build up the fearful and insecure and rightly disturb and undermine the complacent – those who are 'too much at ease in Zion'.

Douglas Rhymes, *Prayer in the Secular City* (Lutterworth Press 1967), p. 68.

Our neighbour
7.24

It may be possible for each to think too much of his own potential glory hereafter; it is hardly possible for him to think too often or too deeply about that of his neighbour. The load, or weight, or burden of my neighbour's glory should be laid daily on my back, a load so heavy that only humility can carry it, and the backs of the proud will be broken. It is a serious thing to live in a society of possible gods and goddesses, to remember that the dullest and most uninteresting person you talk to may one day be a creature which, if you saw it now, you would be strongly tempted to worship, or else a horror and a corruption such as you now meet, if at all, only in a nightmare. All day long we are, in some degree, helping each other to one or other of these destinations. It is in the light of these overwhelming possibilities, it is with the awe and the circumspection proper to them, that we should conduct all our dealings with one another, all friendships, all love, all play, all politics. There are not *ordinary* people. You have never talked to a mere mortal. Natures, cultures, arts, civilizations – these are mortal, and their life is to ours as the life of a gnat. But it is immortals whom we joke with, work with, marry, snub, and exploit – immortal horrors or everlasting splendours. This does not mean that we are to be perpetually solemn. We must play. But our merriment must be of that kind (and it is, in fact, the merriest kind) which exists between people who have, from the outset, taken each other seriously – no flippancy, no superiority, no presumption. And our charity must be a real and costly love, with deep feeling for the sins in spite of which we love the sinner – no mere tolerance or indulgence which parodies love as flippancy parodies merriment. Next to the Blessed Sacrament itself, your neighbour is the holiest object presented to your senses. If he is your Christian neighbour he is holy in almost the same way, for in him also Christ – the glorifier and the glorified, Glory himself, is truly hidden.

C.S. Lewis, 'The Weight of Glory' in *Transposition and Other Addresses* (Geoffrey Bles 1949), pp. 32–33.

Absolute standard?
7.25

We are afraid of religion and of the community that goes hand in hand with it. It is difficult to control. We are afraid of the emotions that religion helps to articulate. We do not object to emotions so long as they are private and restrained. Nor do we object to a group dynamic that is totally wrapped up in itself. But the kind of religious emotions that are expressed in ways critical of the world are regarded as dangerous. For us such emotions are as much taboo as was conversation about sexual matters to our grandparents. To pray, to experience common aspirations, to share with one another our fears as well as our hopes – such acts we find constricting and not bourgeois, indeed quite unappealing. Prayers and songs and rituals such as lighting candles, distributing bread, kneeling and embracing, are quickly disparaged. The intellectual can easily dismiss them with a contemptuous smile and the observation that religion, even when practised to a small extent, is a fraud.

We are afraid of the kind of experiences that challenge our sense of security. We are afraid to allow the petty bourgeois individual we were and are to be shaken and disturbed by such experiences. And that is precisely what religion does. We want to prevent religion from doing this. We do not want religion to do what its most radical critic says it has done and in spite of his criticism still does – protest and comfort. We are afraid of religion's inherent radical protest against the death-ridden life we live and cultivate. We do not want to hear the protest and outcry that religion raises. So we say that religion is not an outcry of protest but the babbling of addicts or, as Marx put it, the opiate of the masses. Actually, however, Marx knew full well that religion is an outcry of protest. And we can know that we are afraid of religion because we are afraid of the absolute demands religion lays upon us. We refuse to recognize any absolute standard for our lives. In fact, the very word 'absolute' is suspect and unleashes thoughts of relativity. We can look at anything from a number of points of view. We can even look at the effect of horrible weapons upon the flesh of children from several points of view. We refuse to accept any absolute standards for our lives because if we did life would be unendurable for us.

Dorothee Soelle, *The Inward Road and the Way Back*, tr. David L. Scheidt (Darton, Longman & Todd 1979), pp. 21–22.

Love's work
7.26

I believe that our world is on the verge of self-destruction and death because the society as a whole has so deeply neglected that which is most human and most valuable and the most basic of all the works of love – the work of human communication, of caring and nurturance, of tending the personal bonds of community. This activity has been seen as women's work and discounted as too mundane and undramatic, too distracting from the serious business of world rule. Those who have been taught to imagine themselves as world builders have been too busy with master plans to see that love's work *is* the deepening and extension of human relations. This urgent work of love is subtle but powerful. Through acts of love – what Nelle Morton has called 'hearing each other to speech' – we literally build up the power of personhood in one another. It is within the power of human love to build up dignity and self-respect in each other or to tear each other down. We are better at the latter than the former. However, literally through acts of love directed to us, we become self-respecting and other-regarding persons, and we cannot be one without the other. If we lack self-respect we also become the sorts of people who can neither see nor hear each other.

Beverly Wildung Harrison, *Making the Connections: Essays in Feminist Social Ethics*
(Beacon Press 1985), p. 12.

A life that is shared
7.27

My spiritual life is not something specialized and intense; a fenced-off devotional patch rather difficult to cultivate, and needing to be sheltered from the cold winds of the outer world. Nor is it an alternative to my outward, practical life. On the contrary, it is the very source of that quality and purpose which makes my practical life worthwhile. The practical life of a vast number of people is not, as a matter of fact, worthwhile at all. It is like an impressive fur coat with no one inside it. One sees many of these coats occupying positions of great responsibility. Hans Andersen's story of the king with no clothes told one bitter and common truth about human nature; but the story of the clothes with no king describes a situation just as common and even more pitiful.

Still less does the spiritual life mean a mere cultivation of one's own soul; poking about our interior premises with an electric torch. Even though in its earlier stages it may, and generally does, involve dealing with ourselves, and that in a rather drastic way, and therefore requires personal effort and personal choice, it is also intensely social; for it is a life that is shared with all other spirits, whether in the body or out of the body, to adopt St Paul's words. You remember how Dante says that directly a soul ceases to say mine and says ours, it makes the transition from the narrow, constricted, individual life to the truly free, truly personal, truly creative spiritual life; in which all are linked together in one single response to the Father of all spirits, God. Here, all interpenetrate, and all, however humble and obscure their lives may seem, can and do affect each other. Every advance made by one is made for all.

Only when we recognize all this and act on it, are we fully alive and taking our proper place in the universe of spirits; for life means the fullest possible give and take between the living creature and its environment: breathing, feeding, growing, changing. And spiritual life, which is profoundly organic, means the give and take, the willed correspondence of the little human spirit with the Infinite Spirit, here where it is.

Evelyn Underhill, *The Spiritual Life* (Hodder & Stoughton [1937] 1955), pp. 24–26.

Divine pity

7.28

Why, people ask, are the Christians no better than the non-Christians, if all that they claim for their faith is true? And the answer, in so far as the accusation is a true one, must be that we are influenced far more deeply than we know by the individualism we inherit and the selfish materialism with which we are surrounded. We are busy with the defence of people's right to property, as so we must be; but only if we remember that we are advocating no absolute right, only if we take care that in opposing one error we do not fall into a worse one. We have a right to property, yes; but every right implies a corresponding duty. The right to property implies a duty to the common good – and the more we have, the greater our responsibility for that common good. We have a right to property, but only within the life of charity. We have a right to a house, a home; but it must be, not a fortress from which all are excluded, but a home where all can find a welcome.

And as with material possessions of every sort, so with all that we have and are, the gift enables us to be humbly and royally lavish, and above all with the gift of pity itself. You must be lavish, first of all, to those nearest to you, those you love most; but you must be lavish, too, to those who are most in need; you must be lavish to your enemies – or rather to those who think themselves your enemies, for it takes two to make an enemy. You must have pity for all, and the greatest pity for those who have greatest need of it. But humbly, reverently, not conferring a gift but asking to be given one; otherwise you will have not pity but the terrifying vulgarity of condescension and all the ugliness of pride.

(Think for a moment of whether you are ever 'shocked' in the colloquial sense of the word: if you are it is a lack of wisdom, for you ought to know more about human nature, including your own; it is a lack of humility, for you are presupposing that the thing that shocks you is something far below your own moral level – and if that is the way you think you will never have the gift of divine pity.)

Gerald Vann, *The Divine Pity: A Study in the Social Implications of the Beatitudes*
(The Catholic Book Club 1946), pp. 110–11.

'No more mourning, no more sadness'
7.29

One reading of John's famous prologue is that, in the life of Jesus, the word *started* to become flesh and that it will take a whole world responding to him to complete the incarnation. Some hope, one might say, looking at a world torn and twisted, largely deaf to Jesus' message from God of the love that can fill the emptiness and eventually unite creation.

And yet, we are occasionally granted the faintest glimpses of what the incarnation ultimately means. One of the most tangible visions, if you like, of hope for the future struck me on the day of the Live Aid concert in 1985. With the God-given gift of high technology and satellite television – not to mention the glorious sunshine – it was suddenly possible to have a perception of the world as a community of love (and not least among the young). For one day nations were united in the fight against famine. It wasn't the money raised that was so impressive, but the few precious moments of universal communion in one common purpose, with no motivation other than goodness and generosity. There were tears for a suffering world, yes, but also joy and celebration in sharing a hope for the future.

When the incarnation, like leaven in the dough, has worked its way all through the human race, the global village or world community will no longer be a dream but a reality. When love reigns there will be no more famine, 'no more mourning, no more sadness. The world of the past has gone' (Revelation 21:4).

Delia Smith, *A Journey into God* (Hodder & Stoughton 1988), p. 118.

Blessed are the meek
7.30

At the present time when violence, clothed in life, dominates the world more cruelly than it ever has before, I still remain convinced that truth, love, peaceableness, meekness, and kindness are the violence which can master all other violence. The world will be theirs as soon as ever a sufficient number of people with purity of heart, with strength, and with perseverance think and live out the thoughts of love and truth, of meekness and peaceableness...

All ordinary violence produces its own limitations, for it calls forth an answering violence which sooner or later becomes its equal or its superior. But kindness works simply and perseveringly; it produces no strained relations which prejudice its working; strained relations which already exist it relaxes. Mistrust and misunderstanding it puts to flight, and it strengthens itself by calling forth unswerving kindness. Hence it is the furthest-reaching and the most effective of all forces.

All the kindness which a person puts out into the world works on the heart and thoughts of humankind, but we are so foolishly indifferent that we are never in earnest in the matter of kindness. We want to topple a great load over, and yet will not avail ourselves of a lever which would multiply our power a hundredfold.

There is an unmeasured depth of truth in that strange saying of Jesus: 'Blessed are the meek, for they shall inherit the earth' (Matthew 5:5).

Albert Schweitzer, *Memoirs of Childhood and Youth* (George Allen & Unwin 1924), p. 102.

Structures for freedom
7.31

Neither authoritarian individualism nor communal fascism can ever be a structure for freedom. They are static structures for control. But freedom can never be a state; it is a process, for it involves the continual movement within ourselves to be in our uniqueness and to be in our community. If ever there is to be freedom it has to allow for this movement. It demands a tremendously high evaluation of human beings to allow them to *be* – both in their desire to be themselves and in their desire for acceptance into a living community.

This does not mean that there are not structures which can give greater life to this mobility and other structures that can destroy it. Our task is to look for the structures that can support freedom, though the structures themselves are not freedom. But they will be structures which are as flexible and adaptable as the human beings they are designed to serve. Within such structures no one will be given a position of power to control the lives of others, and there will be no rigid 'policy' decisions by which people will be judged. Instead, all those involved will share in taking the decisions that affect them. And while no one will be free to harm any other, those who wish to disagree or to opt out will be free to do so. What structures there are will be there simply as servants of people or as servants of any function or project. No structure should exist to perpetuate itself. It should exist only to achieve a certain purpose or to enable people as much as possible to explore the ever-increasing horizon of their freedom in their uniqueness and desire for community.

Ananias Mpunzi, 'Black Theology as Liberation Theology' in *Black Theology: The South African Voice*, ed. Basil Moore (C. Hurst & Co. 1973), p. 133.

At the weak places
7.32

The ability of people to move to a new place tomorrow depends on the love and acceptance they feel today. We live so close together that it is hard not to know everything that is wrong with each other, including the sins and mistakes of the past. With this awareness comes a choice: we can complain and judge the other person, or we can love him or her the way Jesus loved the woman at the well. The only thing greater than our awareness of each other's sins is our awareness of God's love for us and God's desire to see us healed and made whole. This is the kind of love that deepens conversion in community. Conversion begins with turning, and forgiveness invites that turning. For most people, the experience of God's forgiveness occurs most directly through the forgiveness of their brothers and sisters. Only out of that forgiveness are people enabled to move from their past into God's future for their lives. Communities that develop a habit of forgiving and loving also tend to develop an overflowing reservoir of forgiveness and love, something they cannot help but offer to a world full of pain and suffering.

The principal lesson of community is a principal lesson of the kingdom – namely, that God breaks in at the weak places. God's spirit is active in the most unlikely places – the poor, broken and humble places. The power of God is most realized at the point of our vulnerability, our risk-taking, and our letting go. To be vulnerable means to be available to the power of God's love. Community brings us to the point where God's love can break in.

Jim Wallis, *The Call to Conversion* (Lion 1986), p. 126.

Taking tea
7.33

Professor Tadakazu Uwoki encouraged the development of a Christian *koinonia*, fellowship, through the tea ceremony. He helped to form a group called Migiwa-kai (the fellowship beside still waters) among those Christians who were interested in the tea ceremony. He formulated the following nine articles to indicate a Christian expression of the meaning of the tea ceremony.

The spirit in which to share a tea-koinonia

1. Christ loved the household of Mary and Martha and enjoyed their friendship and the relaxed family atmosphere. It is an invitation to us to share a cup of tea (Luke 10:38–42).

2. One of the blessings of the tea ceremony is that it enables us to appreciate the gifts of nature. This reminds us of the teachings of Christ, especially those where he refers to the flowers in the field and the birds of the air (Matthew 6:26–30).

3. The circle of friendship in the tea room reminds us of the fellowship of two or three gathered together in his name (Matthew 18:20).

4. Informal ritual and warm fellowship reflect the beauty of the communion of the saints (Psalm 133).

5. The attentive concern to find goodness in incompleteness reminds us of his grace in forgiving the sinner (1 Corinthians 1:26–31).

6. It reminds us how God can bring an abundant life out of poverty (2 Corinthians 6:10).

7. The taste of bitter tea helps us to understand grace in the midst of suffering (Matthew 26:39).

8. The master of the tea ceremony trains him- or herself in the art of tea through the way of servanthood (Romans 5:3–5).

9. Here in the tea ceremony there is no formal teaching, only a mutual sharing, a joyful discipline, and life with a formal arrangement (John 3:7–8).

Masao Takenaka, *God is Rice: Asian Culture and Christian Faith* (WCC 1986), pp. 81–82.

With people all over the world
7.34

On our own, what can we do to give the voiceless their say, and to promote a society without castes?

With the whole people of God, collectively, it is possible to light a fire on the earth. One of Christ's questions hits home. When the poor person was hungry, did you recognize him? Where were you when I was sharing the life of the utterly destitute? Have you been the oppressor of even one single human being? When I said 'Woe to the rich' – rich in money, or rich in dogmatic certainties – did you prefer the illusions of wealth?

Your struggle cannot be lived out in the ideas that fly from pillar to post and never become reality.

Free from oppression the poor and the exploited, and to your astonishment you will see signs of resurrection springing up, here and now.

Share all you have for greater justice.

Roger Schutz (Brother Roger of Taizé), *Parable of Community* (Mowbray 1984), p. 51.

Mother Mary
7.35

I remember having a very romantic idea of Mary... I remember the occasion which forced me to analyze the position of Mary in our Catholic thinking.

Pedro, aged five and ever cheerful, was humming and singing all day. He was going through his school repertoire and, like a record stuck in a groove, he was repeating over and over again the line, 'The little Lord Jesus, no crying he makes.' In between the singing we had tears and quarrels. Bianca was fed up with Pedro's cheerfulness. She mucked up his game of cars. I got cross. More tears. As the day wore on the idea of a perfect, non-crying baby Jesus and a composed mother Mary really annoyed me. What a mother needs to know is that all children are the same and that other mums lose patience. As a Catholic mother exhorted to look to Mary as a model for motherhood, I want her, in fact I need her to have experienced the same tiredness and frustrations. It makes no sense that Jesus didn't cry as a baby. If he didn't, he wasn't human.

Is he supposed never to have thrown a two-year-old tantrum? Never to have stamped a three-year-old's foot and shouted 'No'? Never to have whined and wanted his own way *now* as a four year old? If Mary was spared our common mother experiences of the more painful kind, I don't think she can be our example. When I walk around a supermarket and see a mother dragging an unwilling youngster round or losing patience with an insistent 'wanting, wanting' child, I feel very close to that mum. I know exactly how tired she feels. I now presume that Mary is close to us in this same way and joins in the sense of community that I feel with all mothers. She has been there too.

Clare Richards, *From Nun to Mum* (Triangle 1991).

Love your neighbour
7.36

[God speaking] I would have you know that every virtue of yours and every vice is put into action by means of your neighbours. If you hate me, you harm your neighbours and yourself as well (for you are your chief neighbour), and the harm is both general and particular.

I say general because it is your duty to love your neighbours as your own self. In love you ought to help them spiritually with prayer and counsel, and assist them spiritually and materially in their need – at least with your good will if you have nothing else. If you do not love me you do not love your neighbours, nor will you help those you do not love. But it is yourself you harm most, because you deprive yourself of grace. And you harm your neighbours by depriving them of the prayer and loving desires you should be offering to me on their behalf. Every help you give them ought to come from the affection you bear them for love of me.

In the same way, every evil is done by means of your neighbours, for you cannot love them if you do not love me... You harm your neighbours by not giving them the pleasure of the love and charity you owe them, the love with which you ought to be helping them by offering me your prayer and holy desire on their behalf. Such is the general help that you ought to give to every reasoning creature.

Catherine of Siena, in *Catherine of Siena: The Dialogue*,
tr. Suzanne Noffke OP (Paulist Press 1980).

Do you believe in Jesus Christ?
7.37

If persons and communities follow Jesus and proclaim the kingdom of God to the poor; if they strive for liberation from every kind of slavery; if they seek, for all human beings, especially for that immense majority of men and women who are crucified persons, a life in conformity with the dignity of daughters and sons of God; if they have the courage and forthrightness to speak the truth, however this may translate into the denunciation and unmasking of sin, and steadfastness in the conflicts and persecution occasioned by this forthrightness; if, in this discipleship of Jesus, they effectuate their own conversion from being oppressors to being men and women of service; if they have the spirit of Jesus, with the bowels of mercy and the pure heart to see the truth of things, and refuse to darken their hearts by imprisoning the truth of things in injustice; if in doing justice they seek peace and in making peace they seek to base it on justice; and if they do all this in the following and discipleship of Jesus because he did all this himself – then they believe in Jesus Christ.

If, in the following of Jesus the ultimate problems of existence and history arise, and they have the courage to respond as Jesus has, citing and invoking the name of God; if they have the courage to stand before this God in prayer, the prayer of jubilee when the kingdom is revealed to the poor and the prayer of the agony in the garden when the mystery of iniquity rears its head; if they have found in this discipleship the pearl of great price and the way to God, to whom they give themselves over whole and entire and the heavy burden of the gospel becomes light; if they abide with God in the cross of Jesus and in the numberless crosses of history; and if in spite of all this their hope is mightier than death – then they believe in the God of Jesus.

If they discover in this discipleship and this faith more happiness in giving than in receiving; if they are prepared to give of their own lives, and life itself, that others may have life; if they surrender their lives instead of keeping them for themselves – then they are bearing witness to the greatest love. They are responding, in love for their sisters and brothers, to the God who has loved us first; they are living in the Spirit of God, who has been poured forth into our hearts; they are living the gift of God, and God as gift – before whom the last word, despite and through the horrors of history, is a word of thanksgiving.

Jon Sobrino, *Jesus in Latin America* (Orbis Books 1987), pp. 53–54.

From death to resurrection

7.38

A community is only a community when the majority of its members is making the transition from 'the community for myself' to 'myself for the community', when each person's heart is opening to all the others, without any exception. This is the movement from egoism to love, from death to resurrection; it is the Easter, the passover of the Lord. It is also the passing from a land of slavery to a promised land, the land of interior freedom.

A community isn't just a place where people live under the same roof; that is a lodging house or an hotel. Nor is a community a work-team. Even less is it a nest of vipers! It is a place where everyone – or, let's be realistic, the majority! – is emerging from the shadows of egocentricity to the light of a real love. 'Do nothing from selfishness of conceit, but in humility count others better than yourselves. Let each of you look not only to his own interests, but also to the interests of others' (Philippians 2:3–4).

Love is neither sentimental nor a passing emotion. It is an attraction to others which gradually becomes commitment, the recognition of a covenant, of a mutual belonging. It is listening to others, being concerned for them and feeling empathy with them. It means answering their call and their deepest needs. It means feeling and suffering with them – weeping when they weep, rejoicing when they rejoice. Loving people means being happy when they are there, sad when they are not. It is living in each other, taking refuge in each other. 'Love is a power for unity,' says Denys the Areopagite. And if love means moving towards each other, it also and above all means moving together in the same direction, hoping and wishing for the same things. Love means sharing the same vision and the same ideal. So it means wanting others to fulfil themselves, according to God's plan and in service to other people. It means wanting them to be faithful to their own calling, free to love in all the dimensions of their being.

There we have the two poles of community: a sense of belonging to each other and a desire that each of us goes further in our own gift to God and to others, a desire that there is more light in us, and a deeper truth and peace.

Jean Vanier, *Community and Growth* (Darton, Longman & Todd 1979), pp. 10–11.

Loving defiance
7.39

Christ's calling is to a radical alternative society which will, by its existence and values, profoundly challenge the existing society of today. 'The church should consist of communities of loving defiance. Instead it consists largely of comfortable clubs of conformity' [Ronald J. Sider]. No one will bother to persecute dull conformity. But as soon as we adopt a lifestyle of 'loving defiance' which challenges the status quo concerning covetousness, oppression or self-centredness, there is likely to be some strong and bitter opposition. Fellowship for those first Christians 'meant unconditional availability to and unlimited liability for the other brothers and sisters – emotionally, financially and spiritually'. This striking statement exposes the superficiality of many church fellowships today. It is interesting that the word for fellowship (*koinonia*) in the New Testament occurs more frequently in the context of sharing money or possessions than in any other. If the church is to become a community of God's people in the way that Christ demonstrated with his own disciples, it means much more than singing the same hymns, praying the same prayers, taking the same sacraments, and joining in the same services. It will involve the full commitment of our lives, and of all that we have, to one another. Yet it is only when we lose our lives that we will find them, so bringing the life of Jesus to others. In fact, this practical expression of love will speak more powerfully of the living God than anything else.

David Watson, *Discipleship* (Hodder & Stoughton 1983), pp. 42–43.

The power of anger
7.40

It is my thesis that we Christians have come very close to killing love precisely because we have understood anger to be a deadly sin. Anger is not the opposite of love. It is better understood as a feeling-signal that all is not well in our relation to other persons or groups or to the world around us. Anger is a mode of connectedness to others and it is always a vivid form of caring. To put the point another way: anger is – and it always is – a sign of some resistance in ourselves to the moral quality of the social relations in which we are immersed. Extreme and intense anger signals a deep reaction to the action upon us or toward others to whom we are related.

To grasp this point – that anger signals something amiss in relationship – is a critical first step in understanding the power of anger in the work of love. Where anger rises, there the energy to act is present. In anger, one's body-self is engaged, and the signal comes that something is amiss in relation. To be sure, anger – no more than any other set of feelings – does not lead automatically to wise or humane action... We must never lose touch with the fact that all serious human moral activity, especially action for social change, takes its bearings from the rising power of human anger. Such anger is a signal that change is called for, that transformation in relation is required.

Beverly Wildung Harrison, *Making the Connections: Essays in Feminist Social Ethics*
(Beacon Press 1985), pp. 14–15.

The good news
7.41

The proclamation of the good news is important for its relevance to the Christian grasp of meaning. If the content of this meaning is good news, the way of grasping it is gratuitousness. According to the New Testament the good news is not something invented or discovered by humankind, but something given; for this reason it must be spoken. The fact that the good news must be spoken does not mean that something which has always been known needs further clarification, but rather that something by no means evident in a world of sin and wretchedness needs to be proclaimed. It does not mean that what we grasp in hope needs further explanation, but rather that the present partial reality of what we hope for needs to be asserted.

Through this proclamation the hearers of the good news experience meaning, because they find their lives being drawn back again into the ambit of an Other who liberates them from their self-centredness. The meaning of their lives derives from an Other, and in Christianity (which perhaps differs in this from other ideologies) the experience of this derivation is an integral part of the experience of meaning.

If evangelization is to be Christian, the element of proclamation may not be forgotten, for it gives expression to the concrete historical character of God's will for the world; it states the positive content of this will; and because of it human beings will be those whose existence gets its meaning through reference to an Other who is different from and greater than they. For all these reasons proclamation is not merely something said but something that has to be said.

Jon Sobrino, *The True Church and the Poor* (SCM Press 1985), pp. 270–71.

Alliance of the spirit
7.42

Community requires alliance of the spirit. It cannot exist apart from the sense of ultimate commitment to a common future. And how beautiful it is when this discovery takes place! Words become unnecessary. Even silence communicates. Because in our silence our eyes and hearts are set on a common horizon. Love which takes place only in the immediacy of the present is a lie; it cannot endure. This is one of the great falsities of the traditional idea of Christian love. And this is the drama of the pastor who desperately struggles to keep his congregation together. He discovers that the price of this nice fellowship is avoidance of the critical issues that actually and unavoidably separate people from each other. People remain together to the extent that they hide from each other the real values to which they are committed. The price of fellowship which does not grow out of a true alliance of the heart is hypocrisy.

Rubem A. Alves, *Tomorrow's Child: Imagination, Creativity, and the Rebirth of Culture* (SCM Press 1972), pp. 171–72.

Age and youth
7.43

We hear a great deal about the rudeness of the rising generation. I am an oldster myself and might be expected to take the oldsters' side, but in fact I have been far more impressed by the bad manners of parents to children than by those of children to parents. Who has not been the embarrassed guest at family meals where the father or mother treated their grown-up offspring with an incivility which, offered to any other young people, would simply have terminated the acquaintance? Dogmatic assertions on matters which the children understand and their elders don't, ruthless interruptions, flat contradictions, ridicule of things the young take seriously – sometimes of their religion – insulting references to their friends, all provide an easy answer to the question 'Why are they always out? Why do they like every house better than their home?' Who does not prefer civility to barbarism?

If you asked any of these insufferable people – they are not all parents of course – why they behaved that way at home, they would reply, 'Oh, hang it all, one comes home to relax. A chap can't be always on his best behaviour. If a man can't be himself in his own house, where can he? Of course we don't want Company Manners at home. We're a happy family. We can say *anything* to one another. No one minds. We all understand.'

It is so nearly true yet so fatally wrong. Affection is an affair of old clothes, and ease, of the unguarded moment, of liberties which would be ill-bred if we took them with strangers. But old clothes are one thing; to wear the same shirt till it stank would be another. There are proper clothes for a garden party, but the clothes for home must be proper too, in their own different way. Similarly there is a distinction between public and domestic courtesy. The root principle of both is the same: 'that no one give any kind of preference to himself'. But the more public the occasion, the more our obedience to this principle has been 'taped' or formalized. There are 'rules' of good manners. The more intimate the occasion, the less the formalization; but not therefore the less need of courtesy. On the contrary, affection at its best practises a courtesy which is incomparably more subtle, sensitive and deep than the public kind. In public a ritual would do. At home you must have the reality which that ritual represented, or else the deafening triumphs of the greatest egoist present.

C.S. Lewis, *The Four Loves* (Fount 1977),
pp. 42–43.

Cross and community
7.44

The power of God that was shown forth in the cross is made manifest in Christian community. What is that power in community? Here Paul is explicit: it is the power to 'build one another up', to enhance the well-being of others based on their concrete reality. The presence of the risen Christ in community makes possible not only a rich relationship with God but also a love that involves commitment to the well-being of the other. It provides the insight and the motivation to treat others with respect and to be responsive to their needs.

Paul does not recommend self-sacrifice as the model for human behaviour, though the needs of the other are to count as much as one's own needs. Rather, time and time again in his letters he exhorts Christians to understand first that the power of God is available to them as they change from a way of life that was concerned with being better than others to a way of life that was concerned with loving others. Second, he insisted that the well-being of each Christian depends on the well-being of the whole community, for it is in the attitudes and behaviour of the community that the power of God is manifest. The incarnation of God in the world is deeply relational, and Paul's relational theology is deeply incarnational.

The power of the cross, then, functions as a kind of organizing principle for Christian community. It is not power that dominates or manipulates, though it may call persons to task for harming others (and in this radically communal vision, what harms one harms all). It is power that enables loving in concrete ways, taking account of the actual needs of the other and the actual needs of oneself. It is a power that values unity, harmony, and fairness more than impressive behaviour by some individuals with the effect of intimidating others.

Sally B. Purvis, *The Power of the Cross* (Abingdon Press 1993), p. 53.

PART 8

Gifts of the Spirit

Compassion

Prayer of compassion

8.1

One of the things I found hardest to accept during the trauma [of remembering being raped as a child] was my own feeling of helplessness. I was continually on the receiving end, constantly asking other people for help. And no sooner had they given it than I was asking for more: 'Listen to me, explain it to me, tell me what to do now.'

I felt I had nothing to give, nothing worthwhile that I could offer, nothing that I could do for anyone else. This began to undermine my fragile sense of self-worth still further.

Then I read the results of a MORI survey of 2,019 adults in Britain: ten per cent of them had had at least one sexually abusive experience before the age of sixteen. 'That must be an underestimate,' I said to myself. 'What about people like me who have repressed the memory? If they had asked me, just a short time ago, I would have said no, I have never been abused.'

So I realized there was something I could do: I could pray for these others who had repressed all memory of their abuse. They were even more helpless than I was: they were still suffering the long-term damage, but did not know the cause and so could not even ask for help.

It was only a little thing, but it was something I could manage, and it was a small movement out of the self-centredness the trauma had pushed me into. It is not possible to do much for anyone else in the midst of a trauma, nor is it a good idea to try. But little things, like writing a prayer, and using it, can help…

As a result of using this prayer over a period of time, I began to feel compassion for adult survivors of child sexual abuse. I could not feel compassion for myself: I hated and blamed the 'child within' for what she had been involved in, and despised the adult I had become. But expressing compassion for others who had suffered in a similar way was a first step in having compassion for myself and the child I had once been.

Jesus, our brother and friend,
look with kindness and compassion
on those who are sexually abused.
You see the lost child within
still crying alone in the darkness
where the hidden wounds of childhood
still hurt, and make them afraid.
When they feel abandoned, give them hope,
when they feel ashamed, give them comfort,
when they feel unloved, give them faith,
when they feel betrayed, give them peace.
In the power of your resurrection
may love triumph over fear,
light shine in the darkness,
and the long reign of terror be ended.

Tracy Hansen, *Seven for a Secret: Healing the Wounds of
Sexual Abuse in Childhood* (Triangle 1991), pp. 38–40.

Kiss of life
8.2

A colleague has recently described to me an occasion when a West Indian woman in a London flat was told of her husband's death in a street accident. The shock of grief stunned her like a blow, she sank into a corner of the sofa and sat there rigid and unhearing. For a long time her terrible tranced look continued to embarrass the family, friends and officials who came and went. Then the schoolteacher of one of her children, an Englishwoman, called and, seeing how things were, went and sat beside her. Without a word she threw an arm around the tight shoulders, clasping them with her full strength. The white cheek was thrust hard against the brown. Then as the unrelenting pain seeped through to her the newcomer's tears began to flow, falling on their two hands linked in the woman's lap. For a long time that is all that was happening. And then at last the West Indian woman started to sob. Still not a word was spoken and after a little while the visitor got up and went, leaving her contribution to help the family meet its immediate needs.

That is the embrace of God, his kiss of life. That is the embrace of his mission, and of our intercession. And the Holy Spirit is the force in the straining muscles of an arm, the film of sweat between pressed cheeks, the mingled wetness on the backs of clasped hands. He is as close and as unobtrusive as that, and as irresistibly strong.

John V. Taylor, *The Go-Between God: The Holy Spirit and the Christian Mission* (SCM Press 1972), p. 243.

The mark of pain
8.3

The fellowship of those who bear the mark of pain. Who are the members of this fellowship? Those who have learnt by experience what physical pain and bodily anguish mean, belong together all the world over; they are united by a secret bond. One and all they know the horrors of suffering to which human beings can be exposed, and one and all they know the longing to be free from pain. He who has been delivered from pain must not think he is now free again, and at liberty to take life up just as it was before, entirely forgetful of the past. He is now a 'man whose eyes are open' with regard to pain and anguish, and he must help to overcome those two enemies (so far as human power can control them) and to bring to others the deliverance which he has himself enjoyed. The man who, with a doctor's help, has been pulled through a severe illness, must aid in providing a helper such as he had himself, for those who otherwise could not have one. He who has been saved by an operation from death or torturing pain, must do his part to make it possible for the kindly anaesthetic and the helpful knife to begin their work, where death and torturing pain still rule unhindered. The mother who owes it to medical aid that her child still belongs to her, and not to the cold earth, must help, so that the poor mother who has never seen a doctor may be spared what she has been spared. Where a person's death agony might have been terrible, but could fortunately be made tolerable by a doctor's skill, those who stood around the deathbed must help, that others, too, may enjoy that same consolation when they lose their dear ones.

Albert Schweitzer, *On the Edge of the Primeval Forest*, tr. C.T. Campion (A. & C. Black 1953), p. 116.

Courage

Martyrdom today
8.4

It is all too easy to consign the age of the martyrs, the church of the martyrs, to the past, to that period of time with its gladiatorial contests and amphitheatre sports, which came to a conclusion around the beginning of the fourth century. The term 'martyr' has come to mean only this. But as we all must know and recognize, martyrdom did not suddenly cease in the fourth century; in our own times the mention of but two names must serve to remind us that the twentieth century is a century of martyrdom, an age of martyrs just as that past age was. For many Anglicans the vicious death of Archbishop Janani Luwum, during the ghastly period when Amin was president of Uganda, brought home the fact that Christian believing and commitment can still lead to murder and death. Likewise in Central America, the sudden shooting down of Archbishop Oscar Romero in his own church as he celebrated the Eucharist brought shock and sadness to many Roman Catholics and other Christians.

These two deaths only focused what is presently happening in this century of the church's existence, no more nor less than it did in the first four centuries or indeed in any age – the fact that there are many people in our world who have given their lives unto death for the sake of Jesus Christ and his gospel. We live in an age of martyrdom; for those of us who live in areas where our profession of faith is not a direct threat to our lives, we should do well to reflect that within the same family and fellowship – that body of believers throughout the world – there are those who face such a possibility daily.

David Hope, *Friendship with God* (Fount 1989), pp. 75–76.

Calmness in crisis
8.5

As I travelled through markets, fairs and divers places, I saw death and darkness in all people, where the power of the Lord God had not shaken them.

As I was passing on in Leicestershire, I came to Twycross, where there were excise men. I was moved by the Lord to go to them, and warn them not to oppress the poor; as many poor people were afflicted by them. There was in that town a great man, that had long lain sick, and was given up by the doctors; and some Friends in the town wanted me to go to see him. I went up to him in his bedroom, and spoke the word of life to him, and was moved to pray by him; and the Lord was entreated, and restored him to health.

But when I was come downstairs, into a lower room, and was speaking to the servants, and to some people that were there, a serving-man of his came raving out of another room, with a naked rapier in his hand, and set it just to my side. I looked steadfastly on him, and said, 'Alack for you, poor creature! What will you do with your carnal weapon? It is no more to me than a straw.' The bystanders were much troubled, and he went away in a rage, and full of wrath. But when the news of it came to his master, he turned him out of his service. Thus the Lord's power preserved me, and raised up the weak man, who afterwards was very loving to Friends; and when I came to that town again, both he and his wife came to see me.

George Fox, *The Journal of George Fox*, vol. 1 (London 1852), p. 79.

Confidence in God
8.6

When we pray 'thy kingdom come' we are inviting God to come and do in us all he wants to do. We are affirming that we want him to be our God and Father, to love us into fullness of life. We are praying that his great plan of love for his creation be accomplished. Nothing else can satisfy the human hearts he has made for himself...

We are utterly confident that the Father wants to give us his kingdom (Luke 12:32) and that he will leave no stone unturned to do so. There is therefore no need for strain or anxiety. There is no mysterious art to be mastered, it is all there before us at each moment. What God asks of us we can always accomplish. There is nothing to be afraid of. It is not a chancy thing that might not come off.

Be happy to feel that you cannot control your life, that there is so much in you that you seem unable to cope with. Trust yourself to him, take each moment as it comes, for each moment holds him. Let him have the say, let him take charge, even though you are left feeling no one is in charge.

Dispossession of self is the reverse side of God-possession.

Ruth Burrows, *Living Love and Our Father* (Darton, Longman & Todd 1990), p. 130.

Facing fears
8.7

We do not need a lecture on psychology to tell us that courage is not the virtue of those 'who do not know what fear is'. I do not believe there are such people. Jesus was in an agony of fear in the garden and those hours come to us all. Courage is possessed by the person who estimates the fear-causing situation, but summons all his resources and meets it. Courage comes by doing courageous things when we want to run away, and let us remember that a little child going upstairs to bed in the dark, and imagining all sorts of bogeys and horrors, often shows as much courage as a soldier whose impulsive dash during some peak of mental excitement wins him a medal for bravery.

So let us, fifty times a day if need be, set before us a picture of *the real God*, utterly loving, whatever we have done, infinitely strong, resourceful and purposeful, finding this way for us when that way is closed for whatever reason, who will not allow us to be lost and defeated if we trust him, and who is generous beyond all thoughts of generosity. Let us commit ourselves to him every morning, for the real God is to be trusted, and whatever happens to us – called, as it may be by others, failure, catastrophe or defeat – we shall know that eternal love still bears us on its bosom, and that we shall find our way home without regret.

Leslie D. Weatherhead, *Prescription for Anxiety* (Hodder & Stoughton 1956), p. 51.

I will not be robbed
8.8

As a result of Beyers Naudé's opposition to apartheid in South Africa he suffered rejection by the Dutch Reformed Church and eventually banning, or house arrest, imposed by the South African government.

There was also the practical side of a banning order. It has to do with facing one's feelings of anger, frustration, and vindictiveness which inevitably arise. I soon discovered that I had to make a crucial decision with regard to these feelings: would I allow these feelings to take root in my life, or would I do everything in my power to ensure that no such feelings would corrode my inner life and freedom? I requested my wife, Ilse, to be on the outlook for any signs of such expression of anger or bitterness and to help me to discover this immediately she became aware of such expressions. This she faithfully did, and for this I thank God, and as far as I know both of us have been able to live through this period and to conquer any feelings of bitterness, hatred or revenge which otherwise could have destroyed us. I consciously refused to allow the banning order to accomplish its intended goal.

It would not rob me of the opportunity to think, reflect and plan the future.

It would not prevent me from sharing and passing on my insights, analyses, discovering of new values to other people – even if this could only be done one at a time. Such discovery of precious thoughts and new truths were like small seeds which I was sowing all the time, certain in my faith that the explosive power of truth would let it take root and grow in the heart and minds of many of those with whom I associated during this period.

It would not stop me loving people and trying to understand them better, deepening my concern for their hopes, their joys and their suffering, and therefore becoming more sensitive to such joys and suffering.

It would not stop me from growing as a human being and as a Christian.

It would not rob me of my inner freedom, my peace of mind, my joy of living and sharing.

All of this brought me to the firm conclusion: through God's grace I would never allow this banning to break my spirit, to distort my freedom of mind, or my concern for justice. It would never rob me of the deep conviction... that freedom will come to our land, that the system of apartheid will eventually crumble and disappear, and that our country and our people will be free.

C.F. Beyers Naude, 'My Seven Lean Years', *Journal of Theology for Southern Africa*, no. 51 (June 1985), pp. 10–11.

Another body on the bus
8.9

My indignation was kindled long before my intellect caught up. My intellect kept busy for a long time when my conscience remained conveniently dormant. I did not have to commit myself at all. Then indignation, intellect, conscience and commitment finally had a head-on collision while I was sitting on a freedom bus ride. We learn more from experience than from anything else. All the thought and moral processes that went into my boarding the freedom ride bus were not nearly so important as just my being on it.

I had now thrown away all roadmaps. I had no idea where I was going, in the next hour or the next five years, but I was damned well committed to the going. It is refreshing to tear down all the assumed security. One can get down to the core of what one's life is all about.

Mine was another body on the bus. It didn't seem so important at that moment whose body it was. It was one of twenty-seven bodies pledged to be there. Meaning took over when strategy did. It matters in the total war if a bridge is captured; it matters in the total war that twenty-seven men got on a bus instead of twenty-three, and that the bus moved along the highway to a particular destination. One wished, sitting on the bus, to say this to the people who have a way of asserting that nothing matters.

Malcolm Boyd, *Malcolm Boyd's Book of Days* (Heinemann/SCM Press 1968), p. 106.

Discipline

Exercising the gift
8.10

The spiritual life is a gift. It is the gift of the Holy Spirit, who lifts us up into the kingdom of God's love. But to say that being lifted up into the kingdom of love is a divine gift does not mean that we wait passively until the gift is offered to us. Jesus tells us to set our hearts on the kingdom. Setting our hearts on something involves not only serious aspiration but also strong determination. A spiritual life requires human effort. The forces that keep pulling us back into a worry-filled life are far from easy to overcome. Here we touch the question of the other side of discipleship. The practice of a spiritual discipline makes us more sensitive in the small, gentle voice of God. The prophet Elijah did not encounter God in the mighty wind or in the earthquake or in the fire, but in the small voice...

Through a spiritual discipline we prevent the world from filling our lives to such an extent that there is no place left to listen. A spiritual discipline sets us free to pray or, to say it better, allows the Spirit of God to pray in us.

Henri J.M. Nouwen, in *Circles of Love*, ed. John Garvey
(Darton, Longman & Todd 1990), p. 41.

Self-knowledge
8.11

As a theory we are ready enough to admire self-knowledge; yet when the practice comes in question we are as blindfold as if our happiness depended on our ignorance. To lay hold on a religious truth, and to maintain our hold, is no easy matter. Our understandings are not more ready to receive than our affections to lose it. We like to have an intellectual knowledge of divine things, but to cultivate a spiritual acquaintance with them cannot be effected at so cheap a rate. We can even more readily force ourselves to believe that which has no affinity with our understanding, than we can bring ourselves to choose that which has no interest in our will, no correspondence with our passions.

One of the first duties of a Christian is to endeavour to conquer this antipathy to the self-denying doctrines against which the human heart so sturdily holds out. The learned take incredible pains for the acquisition of knowledge. The philosopher cheerfully consumes the midnight oil in his laborious pursuits; he willingly sacrifices food and rest to conquer a difficulty in science. Here the labour is pleasant, the fatigue is grateful, the very difficulty is not without its charms. Why do we feel so differently in our religious pursuits? Because in the most laborious human studies there is no contradiction to self, there is no opposition to the will, there is no combat of the affections. If the passions are at all implicated, if self-love is at all concerned, it is rather in the way of gratification than of opposition.

Hannah More, 'Self-Love', *Practical Piety* (c. 1800), in
Collected Works (London 1830).

Inner stillness
8.12

Inner stillness is necessary if we are to be in perfect control of our faculties and if we are to hear the voice of the Spirit speaking to us.

There can be no stillness without discipline, and the discipline of external silence can help us towards that inner tranquillity which is at the heart of authentic religious experience.

In meditation we take steps to achieve this stillness. We quieten our bodies and our emotions, then gradually allow the mind to become single-pointed.

Stillness within one individual can affect society beyond measure.

Bede Griffiths OSB in *The Universal Christ*, ed. Peter Spink
(Darton, Longman & Todd 1993), p. 31.

The old lie
8.13

The old lie about self-denial still keeps spooking around in the psyches of many Christians. It says that Christianity is about squashing your feelings, doing your duty and soldiering on regardless. It leads eventually to chronic exhaustion, cynicism, depression or drink – or all four. That is a well-recognized condition known as burn-out, grey-faced and driven, and when we get into that, no matter how virtuous or good the work itself may be, it will not convey good news to anyone. To use St Paul's words, it is to be under the law.

Do not misunderstand me. There is nothing wrong with self-denial; but we do need to exercise some care in defining what is meant by the first of those two words. I am at some pains… to explain that God calls you to discover your true self, that greater self that you could become, and to let it flower generously in some specific activity at his gracious invitation. To deny yourself does *not* mean nipping this process in the bud. But allowing this flowering may mean forgoing popularity, or status, or your good name, or money, or power, or security; the kind of things that advertisers try to persuade us are essential. In other words, it *will* mean denying the self that runs after or clings to these things; that part of our nature that we call our ego *will* need to be subdued and crushed – a painful process, very painful, but not a destructive one. It is the grain of wheat falling to the ground and dying (John 12:24), that it may bear a rich harvest. To the extent that our ego is not subjugated it will blight both the flowering and the fruitfulness.

Francis Dewar, *Invitations* (SPCK 1996), p. 29.

What good will means
8.14

Nothing can be offered to God more precious than good will. Good will means to experience fear for the adversities of another as if they were our own, to give thanks for a neighbour's prosperity as for our own advancement, to believe another's loss is our own, to count another's gain our own, to love a friend not in the world but in God, to bear even with an enemy by loving him, to do to no one what you do not wish to suffer yourself, to deny no one what you rightly desire for yourself, to choose to help a neighbour in need not only to the extent of your ability but even to assist him beyond your means. What is richer and more substantial than this whole burnt offering, when what the soul is offering to God on the altar of its heart is a sacrifice of itself?… Holy preachers, in order to be able to love their neighbours completely, have been eager to love nothing in this world, to seek nothing ever, to possess and even to desire nothing.

Isaiah admired such people and said: *Who are they that fly like clouds, and like doves at their windows?* He sees them despising earthly things, approaching heavenly things in their hearts, raining words, flashing miracles. Those whom holy preaching and a noble life had lifted above earthly contact he calls flying doves and clouds. Your eyes are windows, since the soul looks through them at what it craves outside. Doves are guileless animals, unacquainted with bitterness and malice. Those who crave nothing in this world, who look at everything without guile, whom eager greed does not draw to what they see, are like doves at their windows. But on the other hand, one who pants with desire to snatch what he observes with his eyes is a hawk, and not a dove at its windows.

Gregory the Great, Homily 5 [Migne], tr. David Hurst, in *Gregory the Great: Forty Gospel Homilies* (Cistercian Publications 1990), pp. 12–13.

Forgiveness

'Settle it in your heart'
8.15

A brother was vexed with another brother who, when he learned of it, came to ask pardon, but he did not open the door to him. So the other went to an old man and told him of the matter, and the old man replied, 'See if there is not a motive in your heart, such as blaming your brother, or thinking it is he who is responsible. You want to justify yourself, and that is why he is not moved to open the door to you. In addition I tell you this, even if it is he who has sinned against you, go, settle it in your heart that it is you who have sinned against him and think your brother is right, then God will move him to reconcile himself with you.' Convinced, the brother did thus; then he went to knock at the brother's door and almost before he heard the sound the other was first to ask pardon from inside. Then he opened the door and embraced him with all his heart. So there was deep peace between them.

The Wisdom of the Desert Fathers, tr. Benedicta Ward (SLG Press 1975), no. 187.

Are you perfect?
8.16

Charity does not demand of us that we should not see the faults of others; we must, in that case, shut our eyes. But it commands us to avoid attending unnecessarily to them, and that we be not blind to the good, while we are so clear-sighted to the evil, that exists. We must remember, too, God's continual kindness to the most worthless creature, and think how many causes we have to think ill of ourselves; and, finally, we must consider that charity embraces the very lowest human being. It acknowledges that, in the sight of God, the contempt that we indulge for others has, in its very nature, a harshness and arrogance opposed to the spirit of Jesus Christ. The true Christian is not insensible to what is contemptible – but he bears with it.

Because others are weak, should we be less careful to give them their due? You who complain so much of what others make you suffer, do you think that you cause others no pain? You who are so annoyed at your neighbour's defects, are you perfect?

How astonished you would be, if those whom you cavil at should make all the comments that they might upon you. But even if the whole world were to bear testimony in your favour, God, who knows all, who has seen all your faults, could confound you with a word; and does it never come into your mind to fear, lest he should demand of you why you had not exercised towards your brother a little of that mercy which he who is your master so abundantly bestows upon you?

François de la M. Fénelon, in *Selections from the Writings of Fénelon*,
tr. 'Mrs Follen' (Edward T. Whitfield 1850), p. 232.

Blocks to change
8.17

I asked an American the secret of his firm's obviously successful development policy. He looked me straight in the eye. 'Forgiveness,' he said. 'We give them big jobs and big responsibilities. Inevitably they make mistakes, we can't check them all the time and don't want to. They learn, we forgive, they don't make the same mistake again.'

He was unusual. Too many organizations use their appraisal schemes and their confidential files to record our errors and our small disasters. They use them to chastise us with, hoping to inspire us, or to frighten us to do better. It might work once but in future we will make sure that we do not venture far enough from the beaten track to make any mistake. Yet no experiment, no test of new ideas, means no learning and no change. As in organizations, so it can be in families.

The evidence is quite consistent; if you reward the good and ignore or forgive the bad, the good will occur more frequently and the bad will gradually disappear. A concern over trouble in the classroom led to research into the way teachers allocated praise and blame. About equally, it seemed, except that all praise was for academic work and all blame was for behaviour. The teachers were coached to *only* give praise, for both academic work and good behaviour and to *ignore* the bad. It worked. Within a few weeks unruly behaviour had almost disappeared.

More difficult than forgiving others is to forgive oneself. That turns out to be one of the real blocks to change. We as individuals need to accept our past but then to turn our backs on it. Organizations often do it by changing their name, individuals by moving house, or changing spouses. It does not have to be so dramatic. Scrapbooks, I believe, are useful therapy – they are a way of putting the past to bed, decorously. Then we have to move forward.

Charles Handy, *The Age of Unreason*
(Arrow Books 1995), pp. 60–61.

Power makes no noise
8.18

Why do I forgive anyone? Ordinary ethics say, because I feel sympathy with him. They allow people to seem to themselves, when they pardon others, frightfully good, and allow them to practise a style of pardoning which is not free from humiliation of the other. They thus make forgiveness a sweetened triumph of self-devotion.

The ethic of reverence for life does away with this unpurified view. All acts of forbearance and of pardon are for it acts forced from one by veracity toward oneself. I must practise unlimited forgiveness because, if I did not, I should be wanting in veracity to myself, for it would be acting as if I myself were not guilty in the same way as the other has been guilty towards me. Because my life is so liberally spotted with falsehood, I must forgive falsehood which has been practised upon me. Because I myself have been in so many cases wanting in love, and guilty of hatred, slander, deceit or arrogance, I must pardon any want of love, and all hatred, slander, deceit or arrogance which have been directed against myself. I must forgive quietly and without drawing attention to it; in fact, I do not really pardon at all, for I do not let things develop to any such act of judgment. Nor is this any eccentric proceeding; it is only a necessary widening and refinement of ordinary ethics.

The struggle against the evil that is in humankind we have to carry on not by judging others, but by judging ourselves. Struggle with oneself and veracity towards oneself are the means by which we work upon others. We quietly draw them into our efforts after the deep spiritual self-assertion which springs out of reverence for one's own life. Power makes no noise. It is there, and works. True ethics begin where the use of language ceases.

Albert Schweitzer in George Seaver, *Albert Schweizer: Christian Revolutionary*
(James Clarke & Co. 1944), p. 91.

Love your enemies
8.19

It was at a church service in Munich that I saw him, the former SS man who stood guard at the shower room door in the processing centre at Ravensbruck. He was the first of our actual jailers that I had seen since that time. And suddenly it was all there – the roomful of mocking men, the heaps of clothing, Betsie's pain-blanched face.

He came up to me as the church was emptying, beaming and bowing. 'How grateful I am for your message, Fraulein,' he said. 'To think that, as you say, he has washed my sins away.'

His hand was thrust out to shake mine. And I, who had preached so often to the people in Bloemendaal the need to forgive, kept my hand at my side.

Even as the angry, vengeful thoughts boiled through me, I saw the sin of them. Jesus Christ had died for this man; was I going to ask for more? Lord Jesus, I prayed, forgive me and help me to forgive him.

I tried to smile, I struggled to raise my hand, but I could not. I felt nothing, not the slightest spark of warmth or charity. And so again I breathed a silent prayer. Jesus, I cannot forgive him. Give me your forgiveness.

As I took his hand the most incredible thing happened. From my shoulder along my arm and through my hand a current seemed to pass from me to him, while into my heart sprang a love for this stranger that almost overwhelmed me.

And so I discovered that it is not on our forgiveness, any more than on our goodness, that the world's healing hinges, but on his. When he tells us to love our enemies, he gives, along with the command, the love itself.

Corrie ten Boom, *The Hiding Place*
(Hodder & Stoughton/Christian Literature Crusade 1972).

The hope of the hopeless
8.20

The Church of God has to be the salt and light of the world. We are the hope of the hopeless, through the power of God. We must transfigure a situation of hate and suspicion, of brokenness and separation, of fear and bitterness. We have no option. We are servants of the God who reigns and cares. He wants us to be the alternative society; where there is harshness and insensitivity, we must be compassionate and caring; where people are statistics, we must show they count as being of immense value to God; where there is grasping and selfishness, we must be a sharing community now.

In the early Church people were attracted to it not so much by the preaching, but by the fact that they saw Christians as a community, living a new life as if what God had done was important, and had made a difference. They saw a community of those who, whether poor or rich, male or female, free or slave, young or old – all quite unbelievably loved and cared for each other. It was the lifestyle of the Christians that was witnessing.

We witness too, by being a community of reconciliation, a forgiving community of the forgiven. We need it in the world today, don't we? But how can we say we offer the remedy to the world's hatreds and divisions, if we ourselves as Christians are divided into different Churches, if we are unforgiving, if we don't greet or speak to certain people? People will be right to say 'Physician heal thyself!' We must not only speak about forgiveness and reconciliation – we must act on these principles.

Desmond Tutu, *Crying in the Wilderness*, ed. John Webster
(Mowbray 1990), pp. 6–7.

Generosity

Greatheartedness
8.21

Our hearts are the size of a gooseberry, where God is concerned. We want a big heart, which he is only too ready to give… But there is something that stops us. If you don't get rid of this big stone in the way, you'll never get far forward. Don't think anything hopeless: there is no spiritual disease without a remedy. We sometimes expect too much of ourselves – sometimes too little. We are apt to lose heart on looking back to our former efforts and the resolutions we made. This desolation of mind belongs to persons who expect too much. What God likes us to say is that we have made a step in advance; he will then take us up and plant us a mile further on. Some, if they have not done everything, think they have done nothing. Checking the tongue, checking conceit – don't let us ever tire of thanking God for helping us in what seem small matters… Many might be heroic if they would only *believe* God is calling them to higher things. As long as we feel that we are going to get better, we do get better.

Daniel Considine, *Words of Encouragement*
(Catholic Truth Society 1933), pp. 12–13.

With all my love
8.22

One woman who exemplified the commitment to defending life was Mary Barreda, who together with her husband was murdered by the Contras (Nicaraguan rebels) after they were kidnapped during the coffee harvest in 1982. As a woman who played leadership roles in the liberation of the people, she could not stand back, but decided she had to engage in practice alongside the least and the poorest. At that moment, such a practice alongside the people meant going out to harvest coffee, knowing that her contribution would become foreign exchange that would contribute to changing the life of the people. Before going out with the harvest brigade, she wrote the following letter to members of her basic ecclesial community in one of the poorest neighbourhoods of Esteli:

To my dear brothers and sisters in Omar Torrijos neighbourhood:

You can't imagine how much Don Ramon and I have been waiting for this moment. From the time we began to share our lives with one another, you have been a part of us, and we love your streets, your houses, your children and, indeed, everything about you. As far as I am concerned, the best gift the Lord was going to give me would be sharing this moment with you. I was also thinking that I had to give you a good present, but I couldn't come up with anything. But suddenly I've been given the chance to give you a good gift, although it means I won't be with you physically, and that is a chance to go harvest coffee these next ten days. That is why I am writing this brief note, to tell you that this is my gift for all of you: the little I shall be able to harvest will be translated, or rather, converted, into health care, clothing, shelter, roads, education, food, etc. That is why I am going to harvest coffee with all the love and enthusiasm I am capable of, and you can be assured that in every coffee bean I harvest, each one of your faces, those of your children, and even those of people I don't know, will be present. Because of this love I have toward you, I know that the Lord will multiply what we harvest.

I want to ask you that you also make a gift to the Lord this Christmas, in a smile, in taking better care of your wives, husbands and children.

Wherever I may be, I am thinking about you at this moment while Don Ramon is reading you these few lines.

Greetings to all and a big hug. I love you very much.

Mary

Luz Beatriz Arellano, 'Women's Experience of God in Emerging Spirituality' in *With Passion and Compassion: Third World Women Doing Theology*, ed. Virginia Fabella and Mercy Amba Oduyoye (Orbis Books 1988), pp. 143–44.

Hospitality
8.23

Hospitality brings us back to the theme of acceptance, accepting ourselves and accepting others, in a most immediate and practical situation which we cannot evade. There is a knock at the door and I have to respond; as I lay four extra places for supper I know that soon four people will be sitting round the table sharing the meal. If I am actually afraid and defensive (or aggressive, which is much the same), anxious and insecure about the impression that I shall be making, I may offer a glass of sherry or a bowl of soup but any real hospitality of the heart will be lacking; I shall have merely fulfilled the social expectation. I cannot become a good host until I am at home in my own house, so rooted in my centre (as stability has taught) that I no longer need to impose my terms on others but can instead afford to offer them a welcome that gives them the chance to be completely themselves. Here again is the paradox, that by emptying myself I am not only able to give but also to receive. Filled with prejudice, worry, jealousy, I have no inner space to listen, to discover the gift of the other person, to take down my defences and be open to what they have to offer.

But there is another danger, and that is that I may be so welcoming and so ready to give that I give too much of myself. The cheerful greeting is right and St Benedict is insistent that the porter is always ready with his warm response... [But] a proper care and love of myself is something I must preserve at all costs, even in the face of the subversive claims that I hear so many other people making about how they never spare themselves and how they never count the cost in what they do for others. Endless people encountered, a mass of entertaining, constant coming and going, countless numbers of people and at the end of all this activity St Benedict faces us with two very simple questions: Did we see Christ in them? Did they see Christ in us?

Esther de Waal, *Seeking God: The Way of St Benedict*
(Collins Fount Paperbacks 1984), pp. 120–21.

Measuring progress
8.24

When people ask how they can tell if they are making progress since they are not supposed to analyze or assess their actual periods of meditation, the answer is usually self-evident.

A greater rootedness in self, a deeper emotional stability, a greater capacity to centre in others and away from self are the signs of spiritual growth.

If you want to ask the question, 'Am I making progress?' do not look at your meditation. There is only one way we can judge our progress and that is by the quality of our love.

As the mantra leads us ever further from self-centredness we turn more generously to others and receive their support in return. Indeed, our love for others is the only truly Christian way of measuring our progress on the pilgrimage of prayer.

If we try to force the pace or to keep a constant self-conscious eye on our progress we are, if there is such a word, non-meditating because we are concentrating on ourselves, putting ourselves first, thinking about ourselves.

John Main OSB, in *The Joy of Being*, selected by Clare Hallward
(Darton, Longman & Todd 1989), p. 37.

Sacrifice is...

8.25

It is a help to think of the life and death of Jesus as sacrifice, but the word needs to be used with care. In the world of religion a sacrifice is either an offering to the ultimately holy or the giving up of something in devotion to the holy. The two ideas can blend in a single instance but it is wise to keep them apart because the first meaning is infinitely important, the second infinitely dangerous. To give is at once expressive and liberating. To give up suggests reluctance; it implies that one needs or is perhaps particularly identified by this thing which is to be surrendered for some laudable reason. There was nothing about Jesus that he wanted to keep. He found his identity in giving.

People who do not want to give think it is more blessed to give than to receive because giving is painful. There are others who actually sense the enjoyment of existence through giving, through spending and being spent. For these it is more blessed to give than to receive not because there is virtue in it but because there is happiness in it.

Jesus was this kind of giver. He is the great sign to us that life need not be dreary, need not be saved, but can be, must be, entirely spent. It is fear that makes us hold on to life or to what represents life's meaning for us. The cross marked the place in history where a superb victory over fear was won, the public fear in religion and politics, the private fear within the individual's insecurities. The proof of that is simply the verdict of time, that at the cross it is clear that life is represented by the man who died there and death by the people who put him there.

And he is still with us, after all these years, still making a huge difference to the life of the world.

Neville Ward, *Five for Sorrow, Ten for Joy*
(Epworth Press 1971), pp. 87–88.

The Liberty Bell
8.26

We desperately need economists deeply immersed in biblical faith who will fundamentally rethink economics as if poor people mattered. I have only an incomplete idea of what a modern version of the year of Jubilee would look like. But at the heart of God's call for Jubilee is a divine demand for regular, fundamental redistribution of the means for producing wealth. We must discover new, concrete models for applying this biblical principle in our global village. I hope and pray for a new generation of economists and political scientists who will devote their lives to formulation, developing and implementing a contemporary model of Jubilee.

The Liberty Bell which was made in Great Britain and now hangs in historic Philadelphia could become a powerful symbol for Western citizens working to share our resources with the poor of the world. The inscription on the Liberty Bell, 'Proclaim liberty throughout the land', comes from the biblical passage on Jubilee (Leviticus 25:10)! These words promised freedom and land to earn a living to Hebrews enslaved in debt. Today poverty enslaves hundreds of millions. The God of the Bible still demands institutionalized mechanisms which enable everyone to earn a just living. The Jubilee inscription on the Liberty Bell issues a ringing call for international economic justice. Do Christians have the courage to demand and implement the structural changes needed to make that ancient inscription a contemporary reality?

Ronald J. Sider, *Rich Christians in an Age of Hunger: A Biblical Study*
(Hodder & Stoughton 1977), p. 195.

Gratitude

Widen your horizon
8.27

Thank God for all he has done for you, and ask him to do still more. Try to widen your horizon. Expect great things from God, and he will give them to you. In your relations with him be always happy, joyous and trusting. Be very careful to avoid deliberate faults. There must be no persistence in anything, however small in itself, that displeases our Lord, but don't be upset by faults of surprise. Try to do all your work well for God, and keep peaceful and happy.

You are not going back because you feel his presence less. The real test of advance is not feeling, but the soul deepens. It tries more earnestly to please God, and is more sorry, though peacefully sorry, when it has displeased him.

Do you think our Lord is taking less pains with you now than he did before? Have more confidence in him. You are nearer to him than before.

You need not be always imploring God to come back to you. He can see into your heart that you want him. Do you think you will be giving him any information?

Daniel Considine, *Delight in the Lord* (Burns, Oates & Washbourne 1924),
pp. 14–15.

Accepting a gift
8.28

Why is it so difficult to acknowledge a gift as a gift? Here is the reason. When I admit that something is a gift, I admit my dependence on the giver. This may not sound that difficult, but there is something within us that bristles at the idea of dependence. We want to get along by ourselves. Yet a gift is something we simply cannot give to ourselves – not as a gift, at any rate. I can buy the same thing or even something better. But it will not be a gift if I procure it for myself. I can go out and treat myself to a magnificent treat. I can even be grateful later for the good time I had. But can I be grateful to myself for having treated myself so well? That would be neck-breaking mental acrobatics. Gratefulness always goes beyond myself. For what makes something a gift is precisely that it is given. And the receiver depends on the giver.

This dependence is always there when a gift is given and received. Even a mother depends on her child for the smallest gift. Suppose a little boy buys his mother a bunch of daffodils. He is giving nothing that he has not already received. His mother gave him not only the money he spent, but his very life and the upbringing that made him generous. Yet his gift is something that she depends on his giving. There is no other way she could receive it as a gift. And she finds more joy in that dependence than in the gift itself. Gift giving is a celebration of the bond that unites giver and receiver. That bond is gratefulness.

David Steindl-Rast, *Gratefulness, Heart of Prayer*
(Paulist Press 1984), pp. 15–16.

Different kinds of tears
8.29

There are tears of personal suffering, purely and simply, in all their reality of bitterness and oppression. Actual suffering, physical and psychological, can be ugly and disfiguring. Here are the people from whom we gladly turn our eyes, that we don't like to think about very much. These are the people that appeal to God's compassion; all these Lazaruses, with their stinking sores, will be found in the kingdom of heaven when the final reordering comes, the judgment of God and the reign of his just mercy and eternal love. The last shall be first.

There are also tears that are not bitter. They are like the dew of the morning, gentle, silent, springing from the depths of the heart, we know not why. They do not have a name; they have no cause. Sometimes these are tears of joy, a quiet joy, from the depths, far deeper than our superficial feelings, tears born from the silence of solitude when suddenly the life of stillness takes on a luminous intensity – or rather, we become aware of the intense reality of the life in which we are immersed. Why weep? I do not know. Perhaps it is because of the utter gratuitousness of life, of being, which we experience in such moments, like the occasions when we know what it is to be loved, truly, deeply, for ourselves. Such a gift is so beautiful, so grand! They are tears of gratitude, of wonder, of love.

A Carthusian monk, *The Way of Silent Love*
(Darton, Longman & Todd 1993), p. 30.

Holiness

Essential goodness
8.30

The goodness of the saint is a peculiar goodness. It flames with the numinous. It is a goodness which unconsciously proclaims itself. One feels it as an aura around its possessor. It is incandescent. It is *essential* goodness: goodness 'in the inward parts'; it is white with a whiteness 'no fuller on earth can whiten'.

If a person came near to this goodness in a saint and did not feel it, there is nothing one could do about it. It is spiritually discerned. Yet its radiations are so powerful that it may be doubted whether anyone could be near it and quite unaware of it.

W.E. Sangster, *The Pure in Heart* (Epworth Press 1954), p. 140.

'To the pure all things are pure'
8.31

When all were seated, the bishops asked my lord Nonnus to speak to them, and at once the holy bishop began to speak words for the edification and salvation of all. Now while we were marvelling at his holy teaching, lo, suddenly there came among us the chief actress of Antioch, the first in the chorus in the theatre, sitting on a donkey. She was dressed in the height of fantasy, wearing nothing but gold, pearls and precious stones, even her bare feet were covered with gold and pearls... When the bishops saw her bareheaded and with all her limbs shamelessly exposed with such lavish display, there was not one who did not hide his face in his veil or his scapular, averting their eyes as if from a very great sin.

But the most blessed Nonnus gazed after her very intently for a long space of time. And after she had gone by, he turned round and still gazed after her. Then he turned towards the bishops sitting round him and said, 'Were you not delighted by her great beauty?' Still they did not answer, so 'Indeed', he said,

I was very greatly delighted and her beauty pleased me very much. See, God will place her before his awful and tremendous judgment seat and he will judge her on her gifts, just as he will judge us on our episcopal calling.

Life of Pelagia the Harlot, ed. and tr. Benedicta Ward in
Harlots of the Desert (Mowbray 1987), p. 67.

Responding with love and creativity
8.32

You whose loving wisdom fashions my being out of all the forces and all the hazards of earth, teach me to adopt here and now, however clumsily, an attitude the full efficacy of which will be plain to me when I am face to face with the powers of diminishment and death: grant that having desired I may believe, and believe ardently, believe above all things, in your active presence.

Thanks to you, this faith and this expectancy are already full of effective power. But how am I to show you, and prove to myself, through some visible endeavour, that I am not of those who, with their lips only, cry to you 'Lord, Lord'? I shall co-operate with that divine power through which you act upon me and anticipate my initiatives; and I shall do so in two ways.

First, to that profound inspiration whereby you impel me to seek the fullness of being I shall respond by striving never to stifle or distort or squander my powers of loving and making. And then, to your all-embracing providence which at each moment shows me, through the events of the day, the next step I must take, the next rung I must climb, I shall respond by striving never to miss an opportunity of rising up towards the realm of spirit.

Pierre Teilhard de Chardin, *Hymn of the Universe* (Collins 1965), p. 112.

Holiness God's gift
8.33

The persons on whom the blessing of sanctification is bestowed are those who are justified. Holiness is a wonderful blessing of the new covenant, not a condition for our entry into that covenant. Holiness, too, is a gift of God's grace. To explain this more clearly, let me show that only a justified person can do good and holy deeds.

For an act to be a 'good deed' in God's sight, it must be done with a right motive, in a right manner and with a right aim; it must be done out of love for God; it must be done in the manner God commands; it must have only God's glory as its aim. No ungodly person can act with the right motive and aim, even if he acts in a right manner.

The good deeds the believer does are not to earn his salvation. He has been given that salvation as a gift of God's grace. But he loves to keep God's laws now out of gratitude and love to this gracious God. So we do not dismiss God's law as irrelevant. Indeed, as Jesus said, 'He who has my commandments and keeps them, it is he who loves me' (John 14:21). True obedience comes from love to God; true love is obedient to God.

Holiness in believers is the result of their being united to Christ. And the Spirit uses the Bible to influence believers to produce holiness in heart and life. As Jesus prayed: 'Sanctify them by your truth; your word is truth' (John 17:17). And since the Bible is the basis of faith, the clearer we understand its truth, the more will the fruit of holiness be produced in our lives.

> Abraham Booth, *The Reign of Grace* (1768), 'an easier-to-read and abridged version' prepared by H.J. Appleby (Grace Publications Trust 1983), pp. 48–49.

Blessed are the pure in heart
8.34

'Blessed are the pure in heart: for they shall see God.'

If we are to take part in the kingdom, there must be singleness of purpose. Purity of heart is, of course, continually taken in its narrower meaning of absence of sensual defilement and pollution. That is an important part of purity; and may I say a word about the pursuit of purity in this narrower sense? A great many people are distressed by impure temptations, and they very frequently fail to make progress with them for one reason, namely, that while they are anxious to get rid of sin in this one respect, they are not trying after goodness as a whole. Uncleanness of life and heart they dislike. It weighs upon their conscience and destroys their self-respect. But they have no similar horror of pride, or irreverence, or uncharity. People very often say that it is impossible to lead a 'pure' life. The Christian minister is not pledged to deny this, if a person will not try to be religious all round, to be Christ-like altogether. For the way to get over uncleanness is, in innumerable cases, not to fight against that only, but to contend for positive holiness all round, for Christ-likeness, for purity of heart in the sense in which Christ used the expression, in the sense in which in the fifty-first psalm a clean heart is coupled with a 'right spirit' – that is, a will set straight towards God, or simplicity of purpose. There is an old Latin proverb – 'Unless the vessel is clean, whatever you pour into it turns sour.' It is so with the human will. Unless the human will is directed straight for God, whatever you put into the life of religious and moral effort has a root of bitterness and sourness in it which spoils the whole life. Our Lord means 'Blessed are the single-minded,' for they, though as yet they may be far from seeing God, though as yet they may not believe a single article of the Christian creed, yet at last shall attain the perfect vision; yes, as surely as God is true, they shall be satisfied in their very capacity for truth and beauty and goodness; they shall behold God.

Charles Gore, *The Sermon on the Mount* (John Murray 1896), p. 40.

Holy people
8.35

Holiness is a complex concept. In particular it involves two almost contradictory strands – something (someone) holy is something that has been 'set apart', but also and simultaneously something that channels the transcendent back into the mundane. It is in this sense a liminal state and therefore necessarily hard to categorize. It seems to me helpful to some extent to recognize that the word 'holy' derives from the same root as the words 'whole' and 'health'. When such a concept is applied to persons (as opposed to buildings, costumes or vessels, for example) there is an immediate conflict between contemporary ideas of psychological integrity and Christian ideals of self-denial. It is easier then to reduce the concept of the holy from the mysterious to the ethical, and make it refer solely to moral goodness, usefulness, lovability, than to address the inevitable destabilization of psychological wellbeing involved in the decentralized location of the liminal.

But the liminal is a key value here. A holy person, in Christian terms, has to have an 'owned self', an autonomy, a rigorous ego, in order to give it away. Holiness has been described to me as 'a person with a strong enough sense of their own ego to be able to make themselves available to others without loss.' The process of annihilation of self requires a self to annihilate. Or, in contemporary terms, a saint has to be a bit crazy.

Sara Maitland, 'Saints for Today' in *The Way*, vol. 36, no. 4 (October 1996), pp. 275–76.

What makes a saint?
8.36

It is not being *virtuous* that makes a saint: the Pharisees were very virtuous, and they and their virtues needed conversion. It is not *doing good* that makes a saint; he often does do good, but so do many people whom we would never call saints. It is not the practice of *religion* which makes a saint. I expect you and I are pretty religious, but our religion, like every part of us, needs converting. No, the saint is one who has a strange nearness to God and makes God real and near to other people.

A saint embodies the parable of the corn of wheat that falls into the earth and dies. His virtues do not make him proud, for he is reaching out towards a perfection far beyond them and is humbled by the quest. His sins and failings, which may be many and bitter, do not cast him down, for the divine forgiveness humbles him and humbles him again. He shares and bears the griefs of his fellows, and he feels the world's pains with a heightened sensitivity; but with that sensitivity he has an inner serenity of an unearthly kind which brings peace and healing to other people.

This strange blending of humility, sorrow and joy is the mark of a saint, and through him God is real and near.

Michael Ramsey, in Through the Year with Michael Ramsey,
ed. Margaret Duggan (Hodder & Stoughton 1975), p. 38.

The truly godly
8.37

We sometimes call people irreligious; and, surely, to be irreligious is bad enough: but to be religious is not good enough. A person may be religious, yet not be godly. There are many who are religious; as touching the law outwardly they are blameless: Hebrews of the Hebrews, Pharisees of the straitest sect. They neglect no rubric, they break no law of their church, they are exceedingly precise in their religion; yet, notwithstanding this, they may rank under the class of the ungodly; for to be religious is one thing, and to be godly is quite another. To be godly, then – to come at once to the mark – to be godly is to have a constant eye to God, to recognize him in all things, to trust him, to love him, to serve him. And the ungodly person is one who does not have an eye to God in his daily business, who lives in this world as if there were no God; while he attends to all the outward ceremonies of religion, he never goes to their core, never enters into their secret heart and their deep mysteries. He sees the sacraments, but he sees not God therein; he hears the preaching, he comes up to the house of prayer, into the midst of the great congregation, he bows his head, but there is no present deity to him, there is no manifest God. There is no hearing of his voice, there is no bowing before his throne... Why, you have been the last six days about your business, occupying all your time – and quite right is it to be diligent in business – but how many of you have forgotten God all the while? You have been trading for yourselves, not for God. The righteous man does everything in the name of God, at least, this is his constant desire. Whether he eats or drinks, or whatsoever he does, he desires to do all in the name of the Lord Jesus. But you have not recognized God in your shop. You have not acknowledged him in your dealings with your fellow men. You have acted towards them as if there had been no God whatever.

Charles Haddon Spurgeon, 'The Chaff Driven Away',
Sermons of C.H. Spurgeon of London (Funk and Wagnalls n.d.).

Willing to learn
8.38

The uneducated and foolish regard instruction as ridiculous and do not want to receive it, because it would show up their uncouthness, and they want everyone to be like themselves. Likewise those who are dissipated in their life and habits are anxious to prove that everyone else is worse than themselves, seeking to present themselves as innocent in comparison with all the sinners around them. The lax soul is turbid and perishes through wickedness, since it contains within itself profligacy, pride, insatiate desire, anger, impetuosity, frenzy, murderousness, querulousness, jealousy, greed, rapacity, self-pity, lying, sensual pleasure, sloth, dejection, cowardice, morbidity, hatred, censoriousness, debility, delusion, ignorance, deceit and forgetfulness of God. Through these and suchlike evils the wretched soul is punished when it is separated from God.

Those who aim to practise the life of virtue and holiness should not incur condemnation by pretending to a piety which they do not possess. But like painters and sculptors they should manifest their virtue and holiness through their works, and should shun all evil pleasures as snares.

Antony the Great (attributed), in *On the Character of Men*, The Philokalia, tr. G.E.H. Palmer, Philip Sherrard and Kallistos Ware (Faber & Faber 1981), pp. 330–31.

A rich minister?
8.39

When you have a rich, well-fed priest – what I am going to say now is terrible, but it is true – you can be sure that there are whole pages of the gospel which he will never preach, because he can't. There are things in the gospel which, if he says them as they are, will make everyone smile and say: 'Quite so. That's a sermon, of purely literary value; but we know very well how he lives, he never denies himself anything. So he can tell us as much as he likes that that's the gospel…'

A priest *must* love poverty, because it is only then that people will believe him when he says that he loves God; for God is love, and love consists in sharing with those who suffer. You cannot pretend that you are loving when you share the condition of those who have a superabundance of everything and are not struggling to serve those who suffer; that is being not a lover, but an accomplice. Love means sharing with those who suffer.

… Love those who are the least, and the poorest, and the most unhappy. There you can be sure of making no mistake. However much you are sinners, however hopeless characters you may be, it is impossible that God will not be with you. If you are always amongst those who love the poor, who live with the poor, who are in communion with those who suffer most, it is not possible that you will not be in communion with God. He said it a hundred times, in different ways, in the gospel. The best way of knowing if we are in communion with God is to see whether we are in communion with the sufferings of humanity.

> Henri Antoine Grouès, sermon, in *Abbè Pierre Speaks*, speeches collected by
> L.C. Repland, tr. Cecily Hastings and George Lamb
> (The Catholic Book Club 1956), pp. 120, 122.

Aim high
8.40

Abba Lot came to Abba Joseph and said: 'Father, according as I am able, I keep my little rule, and my little fast, my prayer, meditation and contemplative silence; and according as I am able I strive to cleanse my heart of thoughts: now what more should I do?' The elder rose up in reply and stretched out his hands to heaven, and his fingers became like ten lamps of fire. He said: 'Why not be totally changed into fire?'

> *The Sayings of the Desert Fathers.*

Hope

The awakening of life
8.41

When hope does awaken, an entire life awakens along with it. One comes fully to life. It begins to seem indeed that one has never lived before. One awakens to a life that is eternal in prospect, a life that opens up before one all the way to death and beyond, a life that seems able to endure death and survive it. Wherever hope rises, life rises. When one first enters upon the spiritual adventure, hope rises where there was no hope before, where there was a life of 'quiet desperation', and life rises too, the life of the spiritual adventure, the sense of being on a journey in time. There is *something to live for* where before there was nothing. Yet it proves not to be enough. One's heart is kindled, and yet there is a residue of darkness in it that remains unkindled. That dark residue is touched only when one discovers a new and unknown life in another person. Where one finds the other, a new hope rises and one seems now to have *someone to live for*, but that hope is disappointed. The dark residue in one's heart has been heated but not to the kindling point, the 'fire point' after which it will burn by itself. It reaches the kindling point only 'when we dead awaken', when one discovers a life that is able to live through death and loss. When the hope of living through death arises, then a life arises within one that appears to be the very life one is hoping for, the life that is spoken of in the words of promise 'and whoever lives and believes in me shall never die'.

John S. Dunne, *The Reasons of the Heart* (SCM Press 1978), p. 120.

Hope is realistic
8.42

Hope alone is to be called 'realistic', because it alone takes seriously the possibilities with which all reality is fraught. It does not take things as they happen to stand or to lie, but as progressing, moving things with possibilities of change. Only as long as the world and the people in it are in a fragmented and experimental state which is not yet resolved, is there any sense in earthly hopes. The latter anticipate what is possible to reality, historic and moving as it is, and use their influence to decide the processes of history. Thus hopes and anticipations of the future are not a transfiguring glow superimposed on a darkened existence, but are realistic ways of perceiving the scope of our real possibilities, and as such they set everything in motion and keep it in a state of change.

Jürgen Moltmann, Theology of Hope (SCM Press 1967), p. 25.

Thy kingdom come
8.43

What is our hope concerning this world in which we are now living? Certainly Christ encourages us to have hope concerning it. We are to pray, 'Thy kingdom come on earth', and so to hope that God's rule may become apparent in the world everywhere.

Thus we hope to see races free from injustice to one another, for racial strife is a denial of the divine image in man. We hope to see nations so using the earth's resources and economic structures that all may have enough to eat, instead of some being affluent while others starve. We hope to see war, and the possibility of war, banished. We hope to see family life everywhere secure and stable, happy and unselfish, with sex fulfilling its true use in lifelong marriage. We hope to see chastity, honesty and compassion prevail. We hope to see these things happen as part of a deep reconciliation between man and God through Jesus Christ. We hope to see people brought everywhere into fellowship with God through him. In all this we hold in one our hope about earth and our hope about heaven. A Christian can scarcely separate these hopes, as Jesus is the Lord of both earth and heaven.

Michael Ramsey, in Through the Year with Michael Ramsey
ed. Margaret Duggan (Hodder & Stoughton 1975), p. 205.

Doña Francisca's story
8.44

In the market at Santa Tecla, a small city six miles west of San Salvador, Doña Francisca sells yucca roots toasted on her earthen griddle. Four of her grandchildren, all malnourished, run around her, fighting over an old mango seed.

I was born in 1950. When I was a little girl, my mother worked as a servant. She had a room in the house where she worked and I lived there with her. I had to stay in the room all day.

My first child, Elvin, was born when I was 15. I made a little money selling food in a jail. That's where I met the father of my last three children – Maria, Yanira and Rigoberto. I've suffered a lot trying to raise them. Maria is sick and lives with me. Yanira goes out with me to sell in order to feed her children. Elvin can't find work, but he makes little things to sell. He doesn't like just sitting around doing nothing.

Life is difficult these days. Money hardly buys anything. If I don't sell anything I end up in debt. I owe 150 *colones* [about $20] now. How am I ever going to repay that amount? How will I ever get out of debt? I sell mangoes and toasted yucca outside the schools, but I haven't sold anything today or yesterday. I'm desperate. I sell so that we can eat. No sales, no food. There is no other way to survive. So we keep trying to sell toasted yucca; that's our whole life.

When there is no food, like now, we don't know what to do. Sometimes we help the cooks at the market, running errands for them. When that doesn't work, we wash clothes at the river. Somehow we keep going. Often I feel like crying because I know that my grandchildren Carlitos, Chon, Maria and Paquita are hungry. Poor things. Every morning they ask for bread, but we don't always have any. I ask God to give us food to eat.

I never went to school. With a lot of sacrifice my children completed third grade. It's hard for a mother to see her children suffer. I wonder what my grandchildren would be like if they could go to school. What would it be like if one of them was educated or somehow prepared to make his way in this life?

Doña Francisca, in *El Salvador: A Spring Whose Waters Never Run Dry*,
ed. Scott Wright, Minor Sinclair, Margaret Lyle, David Scott (Ecumenical Program
on Central America and the Caribbean (EPICA) 1990), pp. 28–29.

Humility

Vision of the glory
8.45

Humility, therefore, does not consist in forever trying to abase ourselves and renounce the dignity which God gives us and demands of us because we are his children not his slaves. Humility as we see it in his saints is not born solely of their awareness of sin, because even a sinner can bring to God a broken and contrite heart and a word of forgiveness is enough to blot out all evil from the past and the present.

The humility of the saints comes from the vision of the glory, the majesty, the beauty of God. It is not even a sense of contrast that gives birth to their humility, but the consciousness that God is so holy, such a revelation of perfect beauty, of love so striking that the only thing they can do in his presence is to prostrate themselves before him in an act of worship, joy and wonder. When the great experience of the overwhelming love that God has for us came to St Teresa, she was struck to her knees, weeping in joy and wonder; when she arose she was a new person, one in whom the realization of God's love left her 'with a sense of unpayable debt'. This is humility – not humiliation.

Anthony Bloom, *Meditations on a Theme* (A.R. Mowbray 1972), p. 68.

A tree
8.46

[God speaking] Discernment and charity are engrafted together and planted in the soil of that true humility which is born of self-knowledge.

Imagine a circle traced on the ground, and in its centre a tree sprouting with a shoot grafted into its side. The tree finds its nourishment in the soil within the expanse of the circle, but uprooted from the soil it would die fruitless. So think of the soul as a tree made for love and living only by love. Indeed, without this divine love, which is true and perfect charity, death would be her fruit instead of life. The circle in which this tree's root, the soul's love, must grow is true knowledge of herself, knowledge that is joined to me, who like the circle have neither beginning nor end. You can go round and round within this circle, finding neither end nor beginning, yet never leaving the circle. This knowledge of yourself, and of me within yourself, is grounded in the soil of true humility, which is as great as the expanse of the circle (which is the knowledge of yourself united with me, as I have said). But if your knowledge of yourself were isolated from me there would be no full circle at all. Instead, there would be a beginning in self-knowledge, but apart from me it would end in confusion.

So the tree of charity is nurtured in humility and branches out in true discernment. The marrow of the tree (that is, loving charity within the soul) is patience, a sure sign that I am in her and that she is united with me.

Catherine of Siena, in *Catherine of Siena: The Dialogue*,
tr. Suzanne Noffke OP (Paulist Press 1980).

Frail people
8.47

Whereas years ago I thundered eloquently from platform and pulpit about the needs of the Third World, I now sit and talk more gently of the yawning gulf between my ideals and the actual reality of how I live my life. I have learned to laugh at myself in public and share my weaknesses with others so that they may be encouraged, rather than impressed.

More than anything I have learned that we are all frail people, vulnerable and wounded: it is just that some of us are more clever at concealing it than others! And of course the great joke is that it is OK to be frail and wounded because that is the way the almighty transcendent God made people. The world is not divided into the strong who care and the weak who are cared for. We must each in turn care and be cared for, not just because it is good for us, but because that is the way things are. The hardest thing for those of us who are professional carers is to admit that we are in need, peel off our sweaty socks and let someone else wash our dirty blistered feet. And when at last we have given in and allowed someone to care for us, perhaps there is a certain inertia that makes us want to cling to the role of patient, reluctant to take up the task of serving once more. It is easy to forget that so much caring, so much serving is done by people who are weary and in some way not quite whole. Because we want our carers to be strong and invulnerable, we project onto them qualities which in fact they do not have. But again, perhaps that is the way things are because that is the way people are and we must learn to be strong for those who need us most urgently and relax and lower our guard with those who are able to accept our weakness and to cherish us.

Sheila Cassidy, *Sharing the Darkness: The Spirituality of Caring*
(Darton, Longman & Todd 1988), pp. 78–79.

Single-mindedness
8.48

Humility means that you feel yourself, as a distinct person, out of count, and give your whole mind and thought to the object towards which they are directed, to God himself in worship and to the fulfilment of his will in Christian love; and humility, in that sense, is quite plainly a source of effectiveness. The humility which consists in being a great deal occupied about yourself, and saying you are of little worth, is not Christian humility. It is one form of self-occupation and a very poor and futile one at that; but real humility makes for effectiveness because it delivers a person from anxiety, and we all know that in all undertakings, from the smallest to the greatest, the chief source of feebleness is anxiety. If you once begin to wonder whether you are going to catch the ball you will drop it, but if you just catch it without thinking about anything but catching it – not, above all, of what other people are going to think of you – probably you will hold it. That goes through everything from such a simple act to the greatest. But there is nothing big enough to hold a person's soul in detachment from the centre of himself through all the occupations of life except the majesty of God and his love; and it is in worship, worship given to God because he is God, that humanity will most learn the secret of real humility.

William Temple, *Christ in His Church* (Macmillan 1925).

A fine humility
8.49

Avoid being bashful with God, as some people are, in the belief that they are being humble. It would not be humility on your part if the King were to do you a favour and you refused to accept it; but you would be showing humility by taking it, and being pleased with it, yet realizing how far you are from deserving it. A fine humility it would be if I had the Emperor of heaven and earth in my house, coming to it to do me a favour and to delight in my company, and I were so humble that I would not answer his questions, nor remain with him, nor accept what he gave me, but left him alone. Or if he were to speak to me and beg me to ask for what I wanted, and I were so humble that I preferred to remain poor and even let him go away, so that he would see I had not sufficient resolution.

Have nothing to do with that kind of humility, but speak with him as with a father, a brother, a Lord and a spouse – and, sometimes in one way and sometimes in another, he will teach you what you must do to please him. Do not be foolish; ask him to let you speak to him... Remember how important it is for you to have understood this truth – that the Lord is within us and that we should be there with him.

> Teresa of Avila, *The Way of Perfection*, ch. 28, tr. E. Allison Peers, in
> *Complete Works of St Teresa*, vol. 2 (Sheed and Ward 1972), pp. 114–15.

Humour

The way to healing
8.50

The casting off of slavery to fear, slavery to the world, slavery to self-destruction; the healing of our selves, our society, the nations, will come through weeping, silence and laughter.

We must learn the ultimate honesty of self-knowledge that no longer seeks to blame others, or looks solely at self-aggrandizement, but which has been cleansed by tears that carry us through despair, and magnify the face of God in those we call enemy. In the mingling of tears for each tragedy of chance or human making we will begin to touch reality. We need to come to the knowledge of being God's nation of priests in which each person, each nation, is both offerer and offering, mirroring God's self-emptying, and co-creating with it.

It is only in the silence at the bottom of these tears that new possibility will arise: in so many of our works – relief of hunger, establishment of human dignity, efforts toward equality of exodus and jubilee, working for world peace – we have exhausted the possibility of our own thoughts and ways. From the silence of the first spark and the first drop of the abyss, from the primordial silence of creation; from hearts hushed in the dark flame of the tears of God who is silence comes the possibility we seek, and without which we will die.

And the vision of reality that emerges from this silence brings us to laughter: blessed laughter that reveals; laughter that heals; laughter that appreciates; laughter that rejoices in barriers broken; laughter that adores; laughter with tears that leaves us willingly helpless to do aught but be drawn into the abyss of God's joy.

Maggie Ross, *The Fountain and the Furnace:*
The Way of Tears and Fire (Paulist Press 1987),
p. 298.

All things bright and beautiful
8.51

It's always nice to know you're making some kind of impression on the world, which is why a friend of mine, a vicar's wife, was delighted when a member of the congregation came up to her after a service to tell her what an inspiration she was to the women in the church. Jo positively glowed with pleasure and tried to decide which of her many gifts and talents she had so selflessly and hitherto so thanklessly employed for the good of the church were at last bearing fruit. Was it perhaps her prayer life? Her leadership gifts? Her occasional preaching, or confidence as a woman? On the other hand it may well have been her counselling skills; the loving, pastoral care she was always at pains to provide; the patient way she dealt with the constant stream of callers and telephone calls. The possibilities seemed endless. She could hardly contain her curiosity as she waited in anticipation to discover what it was about her ministry that was so appreciated.

'In what way am I an inspiration?' she asked.

'No one', came the enthusiastic reply, 'until you came to the church, was wearing coloured tights. You've given us all permission to go out and buy some.'

Michele Guinness, *Tapestry of Voices: Meditations on Women's Lives*
(Triangle 1993), p. 180.

A good story
8.52

The Pope invited the Chief Rabbi to the Vatican. He was delighted to accept. When he was shown into the Pope's inner 'sanctum' – not the Latin! – he was particularly intrigued by the gold telephone on his desk. 'What's that?' he asked. 'Oh,' said the Pope, 'it's just my private line to God.' 'May I try it?' asked the Chief Rabbi. 'Of course; of course,' said the Pope. When he put the receiver down, the Chief Rabbi asked courteously: 'How much was the call?' 'To you,' said the Pope with a smile, 'just 10,000 Italian lira.'

The Chief Rabbi was anxious to return the Pope's hospitality, and invited him to meet him in Jerusalem. The Pope gladly accepted, but was equally intrigued when he saw a golden telephone on the Chief Rabbi's desk. 'What's that?' he asked. 'Oh,' said the Chief Rabbi, 'just my private line to God.' 'May I try it?' asked the Pope. 'Certainly, certainly,' said the Chief Rabbi. When he put the receiver down, the Pope asked, somewhat anxiously: 'And how much was the call?' 'Oh, nothing, nothing,' said the Chief Rabbi, putting an affectionate hand on the shoulder of the Pope. 'It was just a local call.'

Eric James, *Collected Thoughts* (Christian Action 1990), p. 19.

Company of laughter
8.53

The following is a story from a missionary in China.

Our visitors were mainly townsfolk escorting relatives and friends from the country, who had come to see the sights of town, amongst which we, our cuckoo clock and the gramophone ranked high.

One old, white-haired lady, who came from a village six miles away, was a Christian.

'My sons don't know I have come,' she said, as she beamed upon us. 'They said I could not walk six miles, but I knew I could; and I did want to hear those English songs, the one where the birds sing in the trees ['In a Monastery garden'], and I wanted to see the bird come out of the clock, and say "Cuckoo".'

And she did, dear old lady, and hear!

A record they always appreciated was a most infectious laughing one. No one could stand out against it for long and the company soon became hilarious.

'This is the sort of religion we need, a nice cheerful one,' one of them said one day as they wiped their eyes.

Cuckoo clocks and gramophone records were not all they heard in that room, and by and by many of them learned the true sources of Christian joy.

Edith Couche, *Lighting Chinese Lanterns*
(Church of Zenana Missionary Society n.d.), pp. 40–41.

Joy

Joy dwells with God
8.54

Joy belongs not only to those who have been called home, but also to the living, and no one shall take it from us. We are one with them in this joy, but never in sorrow. How shall we be able to help those who have become joyless and fearful unless we ourselves are supported by courage and joy? I don't mean by this something fabricated, compelled, but something given, free. Joy dwells with God; it descends from him and seizes spirit, soul and body, and where this joy has grasped a man it grows greater, carries him away, opens closed doors. There is a joy which knows nothing of sorrow, need and anxiety of the heart; it has no duration, and it can only drug one for the moment. The joy of God has been through the poverty of the crib and the distress of the cross; therefore it is insuperable, irrefutable. It does not deny the distress where it is, but finds God in the midst of it, indeed precisely there; it does not contest the most grievous sin, but finds forgiveness in just this way; it looks death in the face; yet finds life in death itself.

Dietrich Bonhoeffer, *True Patriotism* (William Collins 1965), p. 189.

Praising God
A Meditation on Psalm 150:6
8.55

Let not any of you say, this employment is not for me: for it is the duty of 'every thing that hath breath'. There is no creature in the universe so afflicted, but he has encouragement to pray, and scope for praise – some have an idea, that nothing but sighing and mourning are suited to their condition; and that the voice of praise and thanksgiving is for those only who have attained a fuller assurance of their acceptance with God. But they might as well say that gratitude was not their duty, as, that they were not called upon to express their gratitude in the language of praise. Know, brethren, that 'whosoever offereth God praise, glorifieth him'; and, his desire is, that every mourning soul should 'put off his sackcloth, and gird him with gladness'. I would not discourage humiliation; for I well know that it should ever be an associate of our sublimest joys; but this I would say to all: that Christ came to 'give unto them the oil of joy for mourning, and the garment of praise for the spirit of heaviness'; and that, in the experience of this, they shall approve themselves 'trees of righteousness, the planting of the Lord, in whom he will be glorified'. To every creature then, without exception, whether high or low, rich or poor, old or young, I would say with David in a foregoing psalm, 'Praise the name of the Lord'; yea, begin and close your every service with 'Hallelujah, hallelujah'.

Charles Simeon, 'The Duty of Praising God (Psalm 150:6)',
Discourses on the Old and New Testaments, *Works* vol. VI (1832), p. 752.

Creative work

8.56

I want you to think earnestly of the witness which joy on the one hand, and its antithesis, boredom, on the other, bear to the duty and happiness of creative work, that is to say, real work, on however small a scale. The happy people are those who are producing something; the bored people are those who are consuming much and producing nothing... God punishes the useless by giving them pleasure without joy; and very wearisome they find it...

Joy will be ours, in so far as we are genuinely interested in great ideas outside ourselves. When we have once crossed the charmed circle and got outside ourselves, we shall soon realize that all true joy has an eternal and divine soul and goal. We are immortal spirits, set to do certain things in time; were it not so, our lives would lack any rational justification. The joy of achievement is the recognition of a task understood and done. It is done, and fit to take its place – however lowly a place – in the eternal order.

W.R. Inge, *Personal Religion and the Life of Devotion*
(Longmans, Green & Co 1924), p. 64.

Kindness

Remnant of God's image
8.57

Kindness is the overflowing of self upon others. We put others in the place of self. We treat them as we would wish to be treated ourselves. We change places with them. For the time self is another, and others are self. Our self-love takes the shape of complacence in unselfishness. We cannot speak of the virtues without thinking of God. What would the overflow of self upon others be in him the ever-blessed and eternal? It was the act of creation. Creation was divine kindness. From it as from a fountain, flow the possibilities, the powers, the blessings of all created kindness. This is an honourable genealogy for kindness. Then, again, kindness is the coming to the rescue of others, when they need it and it is in our power to supply what they need; and this is the work of the attributes of God towards his creatures…

Moreover kindness is also like divine grace; for it gives us something which neither self nor nature can give us. What it gives us is something of which we are in want, or something which only another person can give, such as consolation; and besides this, the manner in which this is given is a true gift itself, better far than the thing given: and what is all this but an allegory of grace? Kindness adds sweetness to everything. It is kindness which makes life's capabilities blossom, and paints them with their cheering hues, and endows them with their invigorating fragrance.

Last of all, the secret impulse out of which kindness acts is an instinct which is the noblest part of ourselves, the most undoubted remnant of the image of God, which was given us at the first.

F.W. Faber, *Spiritual Conferences*
(Thomas Richardson & Son 1859), p. 2.

343

The right to know?
8.58

To carry ourselves through the treacherous straits of this life demands that we all the time keep our hand on the wheel of our own craft. While we all have a mission of kindness to others, we have no time to waste in doing that which is damaging to others.

... Gadders about town, with hands in pockets and hats set far back on their heads, waiting to hear baleful news, are failures now or will be failures. Christian men and women who go around with mouth and looks full of interrogation points to find how some other church member is given to exaggeration or drinks or neglects his home for greater outside attractions, have themselves so little grace in their hearts that no one suspects they have any. In proportion as people are consecrated and holy and useful, they are lenient with others and disposed to say, 'Wait until we hear the other side of that matter. I cannot believe that charge made against that man or woman until we have some better testimony than that given by these scandal-mongers. I guess it is a lie.'

If God had given us whole weeks and months and days with nothing to do but gauge and measure and scrutinize the affairs of others, there might be some excuse for such employment, but I do not know anyone who has such a surplus of time and energy and qualification that he can afford much of the time to sit as a coroner upon the dead failures of others... A successful man was asked how he had accumulated such a fortune. He replied, 'I have accumulated about one-half of my property by attending strictly to my business, and the other half by letting other people's alone.'

T. De Witt Talmage, 'The Busybody', in *500 Selected Sermons of T. De Witt Talmage*,
vol. 19 (Baker Book House 1957), pp. 188–89.

The grace of kind listening
8.59

There is also a grace of kind listening, as well as a grace of kind speaking. Some listen with an abstract air, which shows that their thoughts are elsewhere. Or they seem to listen, but by wide answers and irrelevant questions show that they have been occupied with their own thoughts, as being more interesting, at least in their own estimation, than what you have been saying. Some listen with a kind of importunate ferocity, which makes you feel that you are being put upon your trial, and that your auditor expects beforehand that you are going to tell him a lie, or to be inaccurate, or to say something which he will disapprove, and that you must mind your expressions. Some interrupt, and will not hear you to the end. Some hear you to the end, and then forthwith begin to talk to you about a similar experience which has befallen themselves, making your case only an illustration of their own. Some, meaning to be kind, listen with such a determined, lively, violent attention, that you are at once made uncomfortable, and the charm of conversation is at an end. Many persons, whose manners will stand the test of speaking, break down under the trial of listening. But all these things should be brought under the sweet influences of religion. Kind listening is often an act of the most delicate interior mortification, and is a great assistance towards kind speaking.

F.W. Faber, *Spiritual Conferences*
(Thomas Richardson & Son 1859), p. 40.

Patience

Bearing with another
8.60

Aelred:… It is difficult for one subject to the frenzy of anger not to rise up sometime against his friend, as it is written in Ecclesiasticus: 'There is a friend that will disclose hatred and strife and reproaches.' Therefore scripture says: 'Be not a friend to an angry man, and do not walk with a furious man, lest he become a snare for your soul.' And Solomon: 'Anger rests in the bosom of a fool.' And who does not think it impossible to preserve friendship for long with a fool?

Walter: But we have seen you, if we are not mistaken, with deep devotion cultivate a friendship with a very irascible man, and we have heard he was never hurt by you even to the end of his life, though he often offended you.

Aelred: There are some individuals who have a natural bent toward anger, yet who are accustomed so to restrain and overcome this passion that they never give way to those vices which scripture testifies dissolve and break friendship. However they may occasionally offend a friend by a thoughtless word or act or by a zeal that fails in discretion. If it happens that we have received such men into our friendship, we must bear with them patiently. And since their affection toward us is established with certainty, if then there is any excess in word or action, this ought to be put up with as being in a friend, or at least our admonition of his fault ought to be administered painlessly and even pleasantly.

Aelred of Rievaulx, *Spiritual Friendship* (Cistercian Publications 1977), pp. 94–95.

Self's guardian angel
8.61

To be patient with self is an almost incalculable blessing, and the shortest road to improvement, as well as the quickest means by which an interior spirit can

346

be formed within us, short of that immediate touch of God which makes some souls interior all at once. It breeds considerateness and softness of manner towards others. It disinclines us to censoriousness, because of the abiding sense of our own imperfections. It quickens our perception of utterest dependence on God and grace, and produces at the same time evenness of temper and equality of spirits, because it is at once an effort, and yet a quiet sustained effort. It is a constant source of acts of the most genuine humility. In a word, by it we act upon self from without, as if we were not self, but self's master, or self's guardian angel. And when this is done in the exterior life as well as the interior, what remains in order to perfection?

F.W. Faber, *Growth in Holiness* (Thomas Richardson and Son 1855), p. 140.

The way to life
8.62

Just as there is a wicked zeal of bitterness which separates from God and leads to hell, so there is a good zeal which separates from evil and leads to God and everlasting life. This, then, is the good zeal which members must foster with fervent love: 'They should try to be the first to show respect to the other' (Romans 12.10), supporting with the greatest patience one another's weaknesses of body or behaviour, and earnestly competing in obedience to one another. None are to pursue what they judge better for themselves, but instead, what they judge better for someone else. Among themselves they show the pure love of sisters and brothers; to God, reverent love, to their superior, unfeigned and humble love. Let them prefer nothing whatever to Christ, and may Christ bring us all together to everlasting life.

Benedict of Nursia, *Rule of St Benedict* ch. 72, ed. Joan Chittister
(Crossroad/St Pauls 1992).

Perseverance

The blood of martyrs is the seed of the church
8.63

What did the contemporaries of the early martyrs think about the events of their time? Perhaps the complexity of the factors in an historical situation, their own closeness to the events, and even their lack of personal courage prevented them from seeing the significance of occurrences that today seem so clearly to have been heroic testimonies to faith in the Lord. It is a fact that a consensus with regard to what is happening before our eyes is always more difficult to reach; this is because present events, unlike those of the past, are not situated in a world that we regard as idyllic and that we envelop in golden legends. Present events form part of our own universe and demand of the individual a personal decision, a rejection of every kind of complicity with executioners, a straightforward solidarity, an uncompromising denunciation of evil, a prayer of commitment.

But the poor are not fooled; they see the truth and speak out when others remain silent. They see in the surrender of these lives a profound and radical testimony of faith; they observe that in a continent where the powerful spread death in order to protect their privileges, such a testimony to God often brings the murder of the witness; and they draw nourishment from the hope that sustains these lives and these deaths. According to the very earliest Christian tradition the blood of martyrs gives life to the ecclesial community, the assembly of the disciples of Jesus Christ. This is what is happening today in Latin America. Fidelity unto death is a wellspring of life. It signals a new, demanding and fruitful course in the following of Jesus.

The new way is, of course, not entirely new. The present-day Latin American experience of martyrdom bids us all turn back to one of the major sources of all spirituality: the blood-stained experience of the early Christian community, which was so weak in the face of the imperial power of that day.

Gustavo Gutiérrez, *We Drink from Our Own Wells:*
The Spiritual Journey of a People (Orbis Books/SCM Press 1984), p. 23.

Bearing oneself
8.64

People who love themselves aright, even as they ought to love their neighbour, bear charitably, though without flattery, with self as with another. They know what needs correction at home as well as elsewhere; they strive heartily and vigorously to correct it, but they deal with self as they would deal with someone else they wished to bring to God. They set to work patiently, not exacting more than is practicable under present circumstances from themselves any more than from others, and not being disheartened because perfection is not attainable in a day. Such people judge their most trivial failings unsparingly, but endure all the mortification and humiliation involved. They neglect no means of amendment, but they are not fretful while so doing. They do not heed the pettishness of pride and self-esteem, which so often mingles with that quiet resolution wherewith grace inspires us for the correction of our faults. That sort of irritable pettishness only discourages a man, makes him self-absorbed, repels him from God's service, wearies him in his way, makes him seek unworthy consolations, dries him up, distracts, exhausts him, fills him with disgust and despair of ever reaching his end. Nothing so hinders souls as this inward peevishness when it is encouraged; but if endured without consenting to it, it may be turned to good, like all other trials by which God purifies and perfects us. The only thing to be done is to let such troubles pass away, like a headache or a feverish attack, without doing anything to prolong them.

Meanwhile, it is well to go on with your interior practices and your exterior duties as far as possible. Prayer may be less easy, the presence of God less evident and less comforting, outward duties may be harder and less acceptable, but the faithfulness which accomplishes them is greater, and that is enough for God. A boat which makes a quarter of a mile against wind and tides requires greater power on the part of the rowers than when it makes a mile with both favourable. The vexations of self-esteem should be treated as some men treat their nervous fancies, taking no notice of them any more than if they did not exist.

François Fénelon, in *Fénelon's Letters to Men and Women*, tr. H.L. Sidney Lear, sel. and intro. Derek Stanford (Peter Owen 1957), pp. 66–67.

A narrow way
8.65

The path of discipleship is narrow, and it is fatally easy to miss one's way and stray from the path, even after years of discipleship. And it is hard to find. On either side of the narrow path deep chasms yawn. To be called to a life of extraordinary quality, to live up to it, and yet to be unconscious of it is indeed a narrow way. To confess and to testify to the truth as it is in Jesus, and at the same time to love the enemies of that truth, his enemies and ours, and to love them with the infinite love of Jesus Christ, is indeed a narrow way. To believe the promise of Jesus that his followers shall possess the earth, and at the same time to face our enemies unarmed and defenceless, preferring to incur injustice rather than to do wrong ourselves, is indeed a narrow way. To see the weakness and wrong in others, and at the same time refrain from judging them; to deliver the gospel message without casting pearls before swine, is indeed a narrow way. The way is unutterably hard, and at every moment we are in danger of straying from it. If we regard this way as one we follow in obedience to an external command, if we are afraid of ourselves all the time, it is indeed an impossible way. But if we behold Jesus Christ going on before step by step, if we only look to him and follow him, step by step, we shall not go astray. But if we worry about the dangers that beset us, if we gaze at the road instead of at him who goes before, we are already straying from the path. For he is himself the way, the narrow way and the strait gate. He, and he alone, is our journey's end. When we know that, we are able to proceed along the narrow way through the strait gate of the cross, and on to eternal life, and the very narrowness of the road will increase our certainty.

Dietrich Bonhoeffer, *The Cost of Discipleship*, tr. R.H. Fuller
(SCM Press 1956), p. 162.

No such difference
8.66

While Mr Sackville was commending us and our course and telling how much it was esteemed by men of judgment among the cardinals at Rome, Father Minister, who was present, answered: 'It is true – while they are in their first fervour, but fervour will decay and when all is done, they are but women.'

I would know what you all think he meant by this speech of his 'but women', and what fervour is. Fervour is a will to do well, that is a preventing [i.e. prevenient] grace of God and a gift given freely by God, which we could not merit. It is true that fervour doth many times grow cold, but what is the cause? Is it because we are women? No, but because we are imperfect women. There is no such difference between men and women.

Therefore, it is not because we are women but, as I said before, because we are imperfect women and love not verity but seek after lies. 'The verity of the Lord remains for ever.' It is not the verity of men, nor the verity of women, but 'the verity of the Lord', and this verity women may have as well as men. If we fail, it is for want of this verity, and not because we are women.

... This is verity: to do what we have to do well. Many think it nothing to do ordinary things. But for us it is. To do ordinary things, to keep our Constitutions, and all other things that be ordinary in every office or employment whatsoever it be. To do it well: this is for us, and this by God's grace will maintain fervour.

Mary Ward, in *Till God Will: Mary Ward through Her Writings*
(Darton, Longman & Todd 1985), pp. 56–57.

Faithfulness in the daily round
8.67

It is quite easy to found a community. There are always plenty of courageous people who want to be heroes, are ready to sleep on the ground, to work hard hours each day, to live in dilapidated houses. It's not hard to camp – anyone can rough it for a time. So the problem is not in getting the community started – there's always enough energy for take-off. The problem comes when we are in orbit and going round and round the same circuit. The problem is in living with brothers and sisters whom we have not chosen but who have been given to us, and in working ever more truthfully towards the goals of the community.

A community which is just an explosion of heroism is not a true community. True community implies a way of living and seeing reality; it implies above all fidelity in the daily round. And this is made up of simple things – getting meals, using and washing the dishes and using them again, going to meetings – as well as gifts, joy and celebration.

A community is only being created when its members accept that they are not going to achieve great things, that they are not going to be heroes, but simply live each day with new hope, like children, in wonderment as the sun rises and in thanksgiving as it sets. Community is only being created when they have recognized that human greatness is to accept our insignificance, our human condition and our earth, and to thank God for having put in a finite body the seeds of eternity which are visible in small and daily gestures of love and forgiveness. The beauty of humanity is in this fidelity to the wonder of each day.

Jean Vanier, *Community and Growth*
(Darton, Longman & Todd 1979), pp. 67–68.

Shaken by the wind?
8.68

Let us listen to [Jesus'] words to the crowds about John after John's disciples had been sent away. *What did you go out into the wilderness to see? A reed shaken by the wind?* He did not expect assent to this, but a denial. As soon as a slight breeze blows on a reed it bends away. What does the reed represent if not an unspiritual soul? As soon as it is touched by approbation or slander, it turns in every direction. If a slight breeze of approbation comes from someone's mouth, it is cheerful and proud, and it bends completely, so to speak, toward being pleasant; but if a wind of slander comes from the source from which the breeze of praise was coming, it is quickly turned in the opposite direction, toward raving anger.

John [the Baptist] was no reed, shaken by the wind. No one's pleasant attitude made him agreeable, and no one's anger made him bitter. Prosperity could not elevate him nor adversity bring him down. This was no reed shaken by the wind! No change in events bent him from his upright state. Let us learn not to be a reed shaken by the wind, dearly beloved; let us steady our minds before the breezes of opinion. No slander should provoke us to anger, and no favour make us revel in foolish pleasure. Prosperity should not make us proud nor adversity trouble us. We who are firmly established in faith should not be moved at all by the vicissitudes of passing events.

Gregory the Great, Homily 6 [Migne], tr. David Hurst, *Gregory the Great: Forty Gospel Homilies* (Cistercian Publications 1990), p. 30.

Heroes of the ordinary
8.69

Everyone from childhood upwards has to learn to take monotony if they would get anywhere. It seems an inescapable part of human existence, inescapable that is if we are true to our human condition. There must come a time for each responsible person when options are closed, a way of life is chosen and perseverance in that way of life will be the actual expression of our dedication to God. Perhaps earlier generations did not feel the same irksomeness in monotony; nowadays there seems a resentment against it as though it should not be, as though our interest and enjoyment must be catered for at every turn, and as if when work becomes boring we were justified in abandoning one field of action for another. All that matters is our fulfilment, our satisfaction in what we do and accomplish. We may call it other names but honesty should make us admit that we are crassly self-seeking. It looks as if many... calmly accept this attitude to monotony. It is only those who can persevere for a long time who will come to maturity. 'A rolling stone gathers no moss.' No matter how much we enjoy our work, and surely this is desirable, there will be elements in it that test our endurance and patience over a long period.

... It is amazing to what heroic heights ordinary people attain in time of crisis. But does this tell us much about the moral stamina of those involved? People who show up splendidly in crises can prove self-centred and childish in the ordinary rough and tumble of life. If we are looking for real heroism, the sort of heroism Jesus displayed, then we are likely to find it in some very ordinary man or woman, getting on with the job of living, totally unaware that they are doing anything remarkable and completely without pretension.

Ruth Burrows, *To Believe in Jesus* (Sheed & Ward 1978), pp. 74–75.

Keep going
8.70

Perseverance is not merely the crown and stamp of perfection, it must accompany every step in the growth of every grace; just as the texture of the tree must be woven firm in every stage of its growth, so perseverance has to watch over the growth of each virtue day by day; every day in which it fails, the graces which are under its care begin to droop and lose their bloom.

Thus perseverance is not only a virtue in itself, but it is one without whose constant presence and assistance no other virtue can develop one step in its growth. If charity, then, be the soil into which all must spread their roots, perseverance is the cohesive force that gives form and consistency to all over whose development it presides. And thus temptation will often leave all the graces that the soul is trying to form unassailed, and attack the one grace of perseverance; for it knows well that if it can destroy this, all else must fail with it. We often meet with people with very high aspirations and the beginnings of many graces and with great possibilities, but nothing in them matures, nothing attains its full bloom, for they are lacking in the one grace which is the guardian and protector of all – they have no perseverance.

Now perseverance having so great a work to do, having to watch over every good thing that the soul would develop, cannot work alone – it has not only to keep everything under its protection, but it must live both in the present and future; it must look forward, but it must not for a moment forget the present. It knows indeed that many a promising virtue has been killed because the soul in which it was trying to grow could not look forward and wait and hope, recognizing the law of its organic growth and rejoicing, as it saw the blade, in the thought of the full-grown ear.

Therefore perseverance needs the aid of two fellow-workers: it needs, as it were, eyes with which to look forward, and hands with which to toil. It must keep ever before it the ideal towards which it presses, and it must never cease to work towards that ideal. Perseverance is not a mere dogged plodding on toward an unseen end, it is full of inspiration and enthusiasm; in all its endeavours, therefore, it is assisted by the two fellow-workers, hope and patience.

B.W. Maturin, *Some Principles and Practices of the Spiritual Life*
(Green & Co. 1899), p. 195.

Service

Serving God in all things
8.71

For the fulfilment of his purpose God needs more than priests, bishops, pastors and missionaries. He needs mechanics and chemists, gardeners and street sweepers, dressmakers and cooks, tradesmen, physicians, philosophers, judges and shorthand typists... I do not serve God only in the brief moments during which I am taking part in a religious service, or reading the Bible, or saying my prayers, or talking about him in some book I am writing, or discussing the meaning of life with a patient or a friend. I serve him quite as much when I am giving a patient an injection, or lancing an abscess, or writing a prescription, or giving a piece of good advice. Or again, I serve him quite as much when I am reading the newspaper, travelling, laughing at a joke or soldering a joint in an electric wire. I serve him by taking an interest in everything, because he is interested in everything, because he has created everything, and has put me in his creation so that I may participate in it fully. 'It is a great mistake', wrote Archbishop William Temple, 'to suppose that God is interested only, or even primarily, in religion.'

Paul Tournier, *The Adventure of Living* (SCM Press 1960).

Authority is a moral force
8.72

Authority is not an uncontrolled force; it is the right to rule according to reason. Therefore it derives its power to command from the moral order which is founded on God, its first principle and its last end.

Authority which is based mainly or only on the threats and fear of punishment, or on the promise and expectation of reward, is not an effective means of making human beings work for the common good. Even if it were to succeed the result would not be consonant with the personal dignity of the subject, that of a free and reasonable being. Authority is essentially a moral force; therefore it must make its appeal primarily to the conscience, the sense of duty which everyone must willingly obey as his contribution to the good of all. Human beings are all equal in their natural dignity: none may penetrate to the interior life of another. This only God can do, because he alone sees and judges the intentions of our innermost soul.

Human authority can therefore be a moral obligation only if it is intrinsically in harmony with the authority of God and has a share in this. In this way the personal dignity of citizens is safeguarded, since their obedience to the public authorities is not the subjection of one man to another but, in its true significance, an act of homage to God, our provident creator, who has decreed that the conditions of social life shall be regulated according to an order he himself has instituted. There is no humiliation in rendering homage to God; in fact this raises and ennobles us, for 'to serve God is to reign'.

Pope John XXIII, *Scritti e Discorsi di S.S. Giovanni XXIII*, ed. Cantagalli (Siena 1963), vols I–II, p. 285 in *Prayers and Devotions from Pope John XXIII*, ed. Rev. John P. Donnelly, tr. Dorothy White (Burns & Oates 1967), pp. 183–84.

The service of all
8.73

In the Christian understanding of mission there has to be a spirituality that integrates different dimensions in a wholistic vision. Proclamation, witness, dialogue with other faiths and ideologies, inculturation, struggles for societal justice and personal purification need to be correlated in one spiritual thrust within us. The planetary theology of the kingdom of God, the gospel of Jesus of Nazareth, the presence of the cosmic Christ, the indwelling of the Holy Spirit within each and all of us, and the return of all beings to the Creator God can inspire such a wholistic integration in us, in the churches and among peoples.

In this total mission we meet Jesus the Christ more fully. The more deeply we are committed to the human cause and the care of nature, the more truly we are identified with Jesus the Christ, who gave his life in service to others. The churches too will grow to maturity insofar as they die to themselves in service to all.

This is the same spirituality of the emptying of ourselves as person and groups in courageous service to others in today's world situation, but always beginning with our local context. The churches and their institutions will live only in dying to self for others – for this is the law of the gospel. It is the poor, the weak, the marginalized, and defenceless nature that may point the churches to the way of the cross – the unique path to the resurrection.

Tissa Balasuriya, *Planetary Theology* (SCM Press 1984), p. 274.

Simplicity

Silence of the heart
8.74

There is more to stillness than the silence of the tongue. There is, for instance, the silence of 'we don't know what to say' like the vapid silence we call 'angels passing by'. Everyone is embarrassed, frantically searching for something to say. There is no stillness in anyone's heart! Silence can also be condemning. We can reprove a person without saying a word. When we do not speak to a person for a number of days, we hurt them more than words can do. That is not stillness, because our hearts are in turmoil. A story from Zen Buddhism gives us a good example of this. One day two monks set out on their journey to another monastery in a heavy downpour of rain. The road is quite muddy. All of a sudden, in the bend of the road, they see a beautiful young woman who is dressed in a silk kimono with a wide sash and carrying an umbrella to protect herself from the rain. And there she stands! Tanzan immediately understands. The girl wants to cross the road but she cannot because of the mud. Her dress will be stained. So Tanzan goes to the girl, picks her up in his arms, carries her over the muddy road, and puts her down. The two monks continue on their journey. Ekido doesn't say a word for the rest of the day. When they arrive at their destination, Ekido cannot restrain himself any longer. He says, 'What you did was dangerous. Why did you do that? We monks stay away from women especially when they are young and pretty.' And Tanzan replies, 'I left that girl there. Do you still carry her?' Ekido's disturbance is not stillness of heart.

Peter G. van Breemen, *As Bread that is Broken* (Dimension Books 1974), pp. 131–32.

Life at the centre
8.75

Within all of us is a whole conglomerate of selves. There is the timid self, the courageous self, the business self, the parental self, the religious self, the literary self, the energetic self. And all of these selves are rugged individualists. No bargaining or compromise for them. Each one screams to protect his or her vested interests. If a decision is made to spend a relaxed evening listening to Chopin, the business self and the civic self rise up in protest at the loss of precious time. The energetic self paces back and forth impatient and frustrated, and the religious self reminds us of the lost opportunities for study or evangelistic contact. If the decision is to accept an appointment on the human services board, the civic self smiles with satisfaction, but all the excluded selves filibuster. No wonder we feel distracted and torn. No wonder we overcommit our schedules and live lives of frantic faithfulness. But when we experience life at the centre, all is changed. Our many selves come under the unifying control of the divine arbitrator. No longer are we forced to live by an inner majority rule which always leaves a disgruntled minority. The divine yes or no settles all minority reports. Everything becomes oriented in this new centre of reference. The quiet evening can be enjoyed to the fullest because our many selves have been stilled by the holy within. The business self, the religious self, the energetic self, all are at peace because they know we are living in obedience. There is no need to wave the flag of self-interest, since all things good and needful will be given their proper attention at the appropriate time. We enter a refreshing balance and equilibrium in life.

Richard Foster, *Freedom of Simplicity*
(Harper & Row/Triangle 1981), pp. 80–81.

The example of a good life
8.76

When Francis was staying in Siena he was visited by a doctor of theology from the Order of Preachers, a man who was both humble and sincerely spiritual. When he had discussed the words of our Lord with blessed Francis for some while, this doctor asked him about the passage in Ezekiel: *When I threaten the sinner with doom of death, it is for thee to give him word and warn him.* And he said, 'Good Father, I know many people who are in mortal sin, and do not warn them of their wickedness. Will their souls be required at my hand?' Blessed Francis humbly answered that he was no scholar, so that it would be more profitable for him to receive instruction from his questioner than to offer his own opinion on scripture. The humble doctor then added, 'Brother, although I have heard this passage expounded by various learned men, I would be glad to know how you interpret it.' So blessed Francis said, 'If the passage is to be understood in general terms, I take it to mean that a servant of God should burn and shine in such a way by his own life and holiness that he rebukes all wicked people by the light of his example and the devoutness of his conversation; in this way the brightness of his life and the fragrance of his reputation will make all aware of their own wickedness.'

Greatly edified, the doctor went away, and said to the companions of blessed Francis, 'My brothers, this man's theology is grounded on purity and contemplation, and resembles a flying eagle; but our knowledge crawls along the ground on its belly.'

'The Mirror of Perfection', 53, in *S. Francis of Assisi:*
His Life and Writings as Recorded by His Contemporaries,
tr. Leo Sherley-Price (A.R. Mowbray 1959), pp. 63–64.

Such trifling things!
8.77

We see many who have given up very great wealth not only in terms of money but in land as well – and still they get very upset over a knife, a scraper, a needle, a pan. If they had kept their gaze unwaveringly on the goal of purity of heart they would never have got wrapped up in such trifling things and indeed would reject them in the same way that they have rejected lands and wealth. There are some people who guard a book so jealously that they can hardly bear to have anyone else touch it. Far from leading them to the prize of love and gentleness, this sort of thing becomes for them an occasion for impatience, even sometimes to the point of death. Out of love for Christ they have given away all their great possessions, and yet they cling to their old passion for things that have no importance, and even give way to anger because of such things. They are like those of whom Paul spoke, in whom love is lacking, so that their lives become completely fruitless. 'If I give all my goods to feed the hungry and even hand over my body to be burned, and all without love, it is of no use to me' (1 Corinthians 13:3). So one does not become perfect just by stripping naked, by being poor and despising honours, unless this love of which Paul speaks is there, a love which is found only in the pure of heart. Not being jealous, or puffed up, careless of others, or covetous of what is theirs; not to be glad when others are wronged, nor to plan evil against others – what is all this sort of behaviour but the continuing offering to God of a heart that is perfect and truly pure, a heart free from turmoil of any kind?

John Cassian, *Conferences* 1.6 (compiler's version).

Inward freedom
8.78

There are two wings that raise a man above earthly things – simplicity and purity. Simplicity must inspire his purpose, and purity his affection. Simplicity reaches out after God; purity discovers and enjoys him. No good deed will prove an obstacle to you if you are inwardly free from uncontrolled desires. And if you are free from uncontrolled desires, and seek nothing but the will of God and the good of your neighbour, you will enjoy this inner freedom. If your heart be right, then every created thing will become for you a mirror of life and a book of holy teaching. For there is nothing created so small and mean that it does not reflect the goodness of God.

Were you inwardly good and pure, you would see and understand all things clearly and without difficulty. A pure heart penetrates both heaven and hell. As each man is in himself, so does he judge outward things. If there is any joy to be had in this world, the pure in heart most surely possess it; and if there is trouble and distress anywhere, the evil conscience most readily experiences it. Just as iron, when plunged into fire, loses its rust and becomes bright and glowing, so the man who trusts himself wholly to God loses his sloth and becomes transformed into a new creature.

Thomas à Kempis, *The Imitation of Christ*, tr. Leo Sherley-Price
(Penguin 1952).

Off the treadmill
8.79

Contemporary culture is plagued by the passion to possess. The unreasoned boast abounds that the good life is found in accumulation, that 'more is better'… Furthermore, the pace of the modern world accentuates our sense of being fractured and fragmented. We feel strained, hurried, breathless. The complexity of rushing to achieve and accumulate more and more frequently threatens to overwhelm us; it seems there is no escape from the rat race.

Christian simplicity frees us from this modern mania. It brings sanity to our compulsive extravagance, and peace to our frantic spirit… It allows us to see material things for what they are – goods to enhance life, not to oppress life. People once again become more important than possessions. Simplicity enables us to live lives of integrity in the face of the terrible realities of our global village.

Turn your back on all high-pressure competitive situations that make climbing the ladder the central focus. The fruit of the Spirit is not push, drive, climb, grasp and trample. Don't let the rat-racing world keep you on its treadmill. There is a legitimate place for blood, sweat and tears; but it should have its roots in the call of God; not in the desire to get ahead. Life is more than a climb to the top of the heap.

Richard Foster, *Freedom of Simplicity* (Harper & Row/Triangle 1981).

Wisdom

From infatuation to wisdom
8.80

Seeing the distance is like feeling the immensity of the universe. It is like seeing the giant redwood trees. 'It was very healing to be near them and in the forest,' a friend wrote to me. 'The fatigue of the days dropped from us and we were small creatures again in a big world made by God.' There is a fatigue that comes of living always in our own standpoint without passing over, where the world is small and we are large, where it is up to us to create and sustain and govern the world. It is healing to enter into the greater world that encompasses the smaller, where things are no longer in our hands, God's world like a larger sphere, even an infinite sphere, concentric with the smaller one of the days. Something new begins in us. We are somehow more alive and awake than we have been for a long time. God is starting something, it seems, that we shall see. 'Lead, Kindly Light', if I may use those words myself, is yes to what has begun in me, yes to being alive and awake, yes to what God is starting...

I have loved God more than I thought, I am beginning to realize, loved without realizing I was loving, much as you can be in love, man and woman, without realizing it. My journey, to put it most simply, is to go from infatuation to wisdom – that is my road now, 'the road of the union of love with God'. I have to go from infatuation, from being caught up in everyone and everything I meet, by way of mercy, by passing over to others and coming back to myself, to wisdom, to knowing what is enough for me, to knowing God is enough for me. I come to wisdom, though, as I realize it is God I love, as I realize the love in my life really is 'from God and of God and toward God'. It makes a difference, I can see, to realize you love God. It makes a difference in the love itself. It is like saying you are in love – the love becomes conscious and willing. To love God is indeed to be in love.

John S. Dunne, *The House of Wisdom: A Pilgrimage*
(SCM Press 1985), pp. 21–22.

Wisdom's home with the poor
8.81

What kind of soil can we prepare for Wisdom's growth? The answer is poverty. It was in the poverty of a human life that Wisdom took root; it is in the hearts of the poor that then and ever since the shoots have flourished. It is to the neediness of the lover, as he waits in the streets, that the beloved responds.

The poor Christ, the oppressed, denounced, shunned, tortured and dying Christ, is the place where Wisdom finds a home, now as then. Sometimes those with whom she has moved in do not recognize her until someone points her out. The 'missionary' character of the new church has to be, like Peter's, the discovery and celebration of divine Wisdom very much at home in a place where no one had expected her, and wearing an apron rather than a crown. And surely it is important that it was Peter who was first sent to find this out, Peter who was 'the rock', the leader, in spite of all faults. He has to make that discovery all over again, in our time, and he will find it as hard as he did then to set aside ancient preconceptions and abandon direction and be content to sit down with Wisdom in her new home and learn her language and take a broom in hand.

Rosemary Haughton, *The Passionate God*
(Darton, Longman & Todd 1982), p. 332.

Real talk, real action
8.82

What is *talkativeness*? It is the result of doing away with the vital distinction between talking and keeping silent. Only someone who knows how to remain essentially silent can really talk – and act – essentially. Silence is the essence of inwardness, of the inner life. Mere gossip anticipates real talk, and to express what is still in thought weakens action by forestalling it. But someone who can really talk, because he knows how to remain silent, will not talk about a variety of things but about one thing only, and he will know when to talk and when to remain silent. Where mere scope is concerned, talkativeness wins the day, it jabbers on incessantly about everything and nothing. When people's attention is no longer turned inwards, when they are no longer satisfied with their own inner religious lives, but turn to others and to things outside themselves, where the relation is intellectual, in search of that satisfaction, when nothing important ever happens to gather the threads of life together with the finality of a catastrophe: that is the time for talkativeness. In a passionate age great events (for they correspond to each other) give people something to talk about. Talkativeness, on the contrary, has, in quite another sense, plenty to talk about. And when the event is over, and silence follows, there is still something to remember and to think about while one remains silent. But talkativeness is afraid of the silence which reveals its emptiness.

Søren Kierkegaard, *The Present Age*, tr. Alexander Dru
(Fontana 1962), pp. 78–79.

The treasure of knowledge
8.83

Since you have asked me, John, most dear to me in Christ, how you should go about studying to obtain the treasure of knowledge, I give you this advice. Do not seek to plunge into the sea of knowledge all at once, but go there by way of the many streams that flow into it, since it is wiser to reach the more difficult things by way of the less difficult things. This, then, is my advice and instruction. I charge you to be slow to speak and slow to frequent places where men talk. Embrace cleanness of conscience. Be constant in prayer. Love to dwell in your cell if you would penetrate into the cell of your Beloved. Be courteous to everyone. Do not look too deeply into the deeds of others. Do not be overly familiar with anyone, for too great a familiarity breeds contempt and offers an occasion for being distracted from study. Do not in any way wish to pry into the words and deeds of worldly people. Flee from useless conversations. Do not forget to imitate the ways of the saints and holy people. Do not feel obliged to listen to what everyone says, but commit to memory anything good that you might hear others say. And whatever you read or hear, make an effort to understand it. Make certain of whatever is doubtful and try to remember everything you can, just as if your mind were a jar that needed filling. Do not seek things that are beyond your understanding. By these steps you will bring forth useful branches and fruits in the vineyard of the Lord of Sabaoth while life is in you. If you walk in this way, you may obtain all that you desire.

Thomas Aquinas, letter.

Houses built on sand
8.84

The disease which is most likely to fall upon those who... are trusting implicitly in Christ is the disease of wanting to see signs and wonders, or else they will not believe. In the early stages of my ministry, in the midst of a rural population, I used to meet continually with persons who thought they were Christians because, as they imagined, they had seen signs and wonders; and since then, stories the most ridiculous have been told me by earnest and sincere people, as reasons why they thought they were saved. I have heard a narrative something like this: 'I believe my sins are put away.' 'Why?' 'Well, sir, I was down in the back garden and I saw a great cloud, and I thought, now God can make that cloud go away if he pleases, and it did go away: and I thought the cloud and my sins were gone too, and I have not had a doubt since then.' I thought, Well, you have good reason to doubt, for that is totally absurd. Were I to tell you the whims and fancies that some people get into their heads, you might smile, and that might not be to your profit. Certain it is, that people patch up any idle story, any strange fancy, in order to make them think that they may then trust Christ. Oh, my dear friends, if you have no better reason to believe you are in Christ than a dream or a vision, it is time you began again! I grant you there have been some who have been alarmed, convinced, and perhaps converted, by strange freaks of their imagination; but if you rely on these as being evidences that you are saved, I tell you that you will be resting on a dream, a delusion. You may as well seek to build a castle in the air, or a house upon the sands.

Charles Haddon Spurgeon, 'Marks of Faith', in
Sermons of Rev. C.H. Spurgeon of London (Funk and Wagnalls n.d.).

PART 9

When the Way is Dark

In Times of Temptation

To choose

9.1

I often think the mind is like a videotape that cannot easily be wiped clean. Everything you have ever done, read or experienced is on this tape for good or ill: all the rich and life-giving experiences and all the impoverishing and destructive ones. Much of our life we are able to keep in control, and select from that video what we want. But not always. There are times when the video seems set on random selection, and it turns on to all sorts of things. There are times when I go to church to pray, I kneel before the altar and then instead of prayer, I battle with some of the wickedest thoughts of the week. Because I have stopped busying myself, the mind switches from being fixed in certain tight channels to being free. This experience is by no means rare or new...

We all have minds that are hard to control! But ways have been discovered of helping to keep us reasonably on the right tracks. If the mind records everything we experience, we should be careful what we record on it. We can to some extent choose. There will always be a mixture of good and evil, of life and destruction, but we can influence the mixture by deliberate choice. Quite often, our attitude to what we do will influence our attitude in the future...

This deliberate choice can be called meditation. It happens when we choose certain things and dwell on them. Because we all meditate on things, we should learn to meditate well and discover thought patterns that work well for us. Once again we can turn to the lives of the saints for help – we can learn from those who have tested certain methods and have shown that they work for the good of humankind.

David Adam, *The Cry of the Deer*
(Triangle 1987), pp. 76–78.

The heart's activity
9.2

In my opinion the quality of our thought is to a considerable extent up to us to determine. Whether our thoughts are turned towards things of the spirit or towards things of the flesh depends on ourselves. If we regularly read the scriptures and meditate on them we are leading our minds and memory into a good path. Our regular singing of the psalms aims at producing in us a lively conscience so that, our minds being more concentrated, we lose our taste for earthly things and become absorbed in contemplation of the things of heaven…

This exercise of the mind can appropriately be compared to the action of a mill, driven as it is by the circling pressure of water. The mill has to go on operating as long as the water goes on turning the wheel: it is for the person operating it to decide what sort of grain to grind, wheat, barley or darnel. Only what the person feeds in will be ground.

In the same way, our minds are under constant pressure as long as we live. There is a constant stream of temptations seeking to divert it, and no shortage of disturbing thoughts. But if we are zealous and careful we will decide which of those thoughts can be allowed in and processed. If we steadily meditate on the scriptures, and keep in our minds the things of the spirit, our longing for perfection and our hope of future blessedness, then our thoughts will necessarily be of the spirit and the mind will be held in this path.

John Cassian, *Conferences* 1.17–18 (compiler's version).

Take it easy
9.3

I often hear talk of people committed to social action or in communities who are 'burned-out'. These people have been too generous; they have thrown themselves into activity which has finally destroyed them emotionally. They have not known how to relax and to be refreshed. Those in responsibility must teach such people the discipline of physical rest and relaxation, and the need for spiritual nourishment and for fixing clear priorities. They must also set an example.

Many people get burned out because, perhaps unconsciously, some part of them is rejecting the need to relax and find a harmonious rhythm of life for themselves. In their over-activity they are fleeing from something, sometimes because of deep unconscious guilt feelings. Maybe they do. not really want to put down roots in the community and stay for the long haul. They may be too attached to their function, perhaps even identified with it. They want to control everything, and perhaps also want to appear perfect, or at least a perfect hero! They have not yet learned how to live; they are not yet free inside themselves; they have not yet discovered the wisdom of the present moment, which can frequently mean saying 'no' to people.

These people need a spiritual guide to help them look at themselves and discover why they have not the freedom to stop, and what is the cause of their compulsive need to do things. They need someone who can help them stand back and relax enough to clarify their own motives and become people living with other people, children among other children. God has given each of us an intelligence. It may not be very great, but it is great enough for us to reflect on what we need to order to live what we are called to live – community. These over-active people, it seems, can be fleeing from their own cry for friendship and love, from their own sensitivity and maybe from their inner anguish and agitation. They may be afraid of their emotions, of their own sexuality. They need to reflect on their own deep needs and to refind the child in themselves which is crying because it feels alone. Our bodies need to relax, but so do our hearts, in secure and unthreatening relationships.

Jean Vanier, *Community and Growth*
(Darton, Longman & Todd 1991), p. 177.

Worse than useless

9.4

Let us now see if we can gather up Jesus' arguments against worry.

(i) *Worry is needless, useless and even actively injurious.* Worry cannot affect the past, for the past is past... It is not that a man can or ought to dissociate himself from his past; but he ought to use his past as a spur and a guide for better action in the future, and not as something about which he broods until he has worried himself into a paralysis of action.

Equally, worry about the future is useless... Worry about the future is wasted effort, and the future of reality is seldom as bad as the future of our fears.

But worry is worse than useless: it is often actively injurious. The two typical diseases of modern life are the stomach ulcer and the coronary thrombosis, and in many cases both are the result of worry. It is a medical fact that he who laughs most lives longest. The worry which wears out the mind wears out the body along with it.

Worry affects a man's judgment, lessens his powers of decision, and renders him progressively incapable of dealing with life. Let a man give his best to every situation – he cannot give more – and let him leave the rest to God.

(ii) *Worry is blind*. Worry refuses to learn the lesson of nature. Jesus bids men look at the birds, and see the bounty which is behind nature, and trust the love that lies behind that bounty. Worry refuses to learn the lesson of *history*... The man who feeds his heart on the record of what God has done in the past will never worry about the future. Worry refuses to learn the lesson of *life*. We are still alive and our heads are still above water; and yet if someone had told us that we would have to go through what we have actually gone through, we would have said it was impossible. The lesson of life is that somehow we have been enabled to bear the unbearable and to do the un-doable and to pass the breaking point and not to break. The lesson of life is that worry is unnecessary.

(iii) *Worry is essentially irreligious*. Worry is not caused by external circumstances. In the same circumstances one man can be absolutely serene, and another man can be worried to death. Both worry and serenity come, not from circumstance, but from the heart.

William Barclay, *The Gospel of Matthew*, vol. 1 (Saint Andrew Press 1987), p. 259.

'Resist the beginnings'
9.5

The starting point of all evil temptings lies in inconstancy of mind and small confidence in God. The slack man who abandons his fixed resolve is battered by all kinds of temptation like a ship with no steersman, driven to and fro by the waves.

Iron is proved in the fire, and the upright man in temptation. We often do not know what we are capable of till temptation reveals what kind of persons we are.

All the same, when temptation first appears, we must be especially alert, because it is easier to defeat the enemy if we do not allow him to set foot inside the door of the mind but meet him on the step as he knocks. As an ancient writer once said: 'Resist the beginnings – cure is provided too late' (Ovid, *Remedium Amoris*, 1.91). For first of all, a thought simply crosses the mind, then it grows stronger and takes shape; then comes pleasure, an evil impulse, and consent. So our malignant enemy gradually obtains complete entry if we do not resist him at the start. If a man is slow in stirring himself up to resist, he will grow weaker every day, while the enemy forces grow stronger.

Thomas à Kempis, *The Imitation of Christ,* tr. Betty I. Knott
(William Collins 1979), p. 54.

Anchor yourself
9.6

The devil can bring us into all kinds of trouble. 'Oh,' people say, 'if only I had a spiritual director to talk to! I get the most fearful ideas, and I am in a dreadful state.'

Well, my dear child, I know a lot about the ideas the devil can put in our minds, and my advice is this – what the devil puts in your mind, you put out again; be at peace and turn your heart to God. Pay no attention to such ideas, do not let your thoughts dwell on them; just let them pass out of your mind. You will often suffer such painful experiences; this is the devil's doing, and it comes from inordinate melancholy. He will end by bringing you to despair. 'It is no use,' you will say.

What ought you to do then? Lay the burden of all your cares on God, anchor yourself in him. When sailors are in danger and think they are going to run aground on the rocks, they throw their anchor overboard and it sinks to the bottom of the Rhine, and that saves them. We should do the same; when the devil attacks us with dreadful temptations of mind or body, there is nothing for it but to throw our anchor overboard, the anchor of perfect trust and hope in God. Never mind about the oars and the rudder, the anchor is all you need; and this is what you must do in every distress of soul or body.

Johann Tauler, *Spiritual Conferences*.

Good and bad habits
9.7

We gain nothing by our decision to renounce earthly things if we do not abide by it, but continue to be attracted by such things and allow ourselves to keep thinking about them. By constantly looking back like Lot's wife towards what we have renounced, we make clear our attachment to it. For she looked back and was turned into a pillar of salt, remaining to this day an example to the disobedient. She symbolizes the force of habit, which draws us back again after we have tried to make a definitive act of renunciation.

What does the law mean when it commands anyone entering the temple not to return, after finishing his prayers, by the door through which he entered, but to go straight out through the opposite door without changing direction? It means that we should keep to the path that leads straight to holiness, not allowing any doubts to make us turn back. By habitually thinking about what we have left behind, we undermine our determination to advance and we are pulled in the opposite direction, returning to our old sins. It is a terrible thing when the force of habit holds us fast, not allowing us to rise to the state of virtue which we possessed initially. For habit leads to a set disposition, and this in turn becomes what may be called 'second nature'; and it is hard to shift and alter nature. For though it may yield a little to pressure, it quickly reasserts itself. It may be shaken and forced to give way, but it is not permanently changed, unless through prolonged effort we retrace our steps.

> Neilos the Ascetic, in *Ascetic Discourse*, *The Philokalia*, tr. G.E.H. Palmer,
> Philip Sherrard and Kallistos Ware (Faber & Faber 1979), pp. 236–37.

A sure promise
9.8

The prophet expresses a plain comforting promise of God against all temptation, where he says: 'Whoever dwells in the help of the most high God shall abide in the protection or defence of the God of heaven.' Who is it that dwells in the help of the high God? Surely it is the one who through a good faith abides in the trust and confidence of God's help, and never for lack of that faith and trust in his help despairs of all help, nor departs from the hope of his help to seek help for himself of the flesh, the world or the devil.

... For to such a faithful, well-hoping person the prophet in the same psalm says further: 'With his shoulders shall he overshadow you, and under his feathers shall you trust.' Lo here has every man and woman a sure promise that in the burning heat of temptation or tribulation – for they are so coincident that the devil uses every tribulation for temptation to bring us to impatience and thereby to murmuring and grumbling and blasphemy, and every kind of temptation to a good person that fights against it and will not follow it is a very painful tribulation – in the burning heat I say therefore of every temptation God gives the faithful one that hopes in him the shadow of his holy shoulders, which are broad and large, sufficient to cool and refresh us in that heat, and in every tribulation he puts his shoulders for a defence between. And then what weapon of the devil can give us any deadly wound while that impenetrable shield of the shoulder of God stands always between?

> Sir Thomas More, *A Dialogue of Comfort*, 2.10
> (partly modernized).

Along the way
9.9

Victorious living does not mean freedom from temptation. *Nor does it mean freedom from mistakes.* We are personalities in the making, limited and grappling with things too high for us. Obviously we, at our very best, will make many mistakes. But these mistakes need not be sins. Our actions are the result of our intentions and our intelligence. Our intentions may be very good, but because the intelligence is limited the action may turn out to be a mistake – a mistake, but not necessarily a sin. For sin comes out of a wrong intention.

Therefore the action carries a sense of incompleteness and frustration, but not of guilt. Victorious living does not mean perfect living in the sense of living without a flaw, but it does mean adequate living and that can be consistent with many mistakes. *Nor does it mean maturity.* It does mean a cleansing away of things that keep from growth, but it is not full growth. In addition to many mistakes in our lives, there will be many immaturities. Purity is not maturity. This gospel of ours is called the way. Our feet are on that way, but only on that way; we have not arrived at the goal.

Nor does it mean that we may not occasionally lapse into a wrong act which may be called a sin. At that point we may have lost a skirmish, but it doesn't mean we may not still win the battle. We may even lose a battle and still win the war. One of the differences between a sheep and a swine is that when a sheep falls into a mud hole it bleats to get out, while the swine loves it and wallows in it. In saying that an occasional lapse is consistent with victorious living I am possibly opening the door to provide for such lapses. This is dangerous and weakening. There must be no such provision in the mind. There must be an absoluteness about the whole thing. But nevertheless, victorious living can be consistent with occasional failure.

E. Stanley Jones, *Victorious Living* (Hodder & Stoughton 1941), p. 78.

No gloomy faces!
9.10

Blessed Francis used to say, 'Although I know that the devils envy me the blessings that God has given me, I also know and see that they cannot harm me through myself, so they plan and try to hurt me through my companions. But if they cannot hurt me either through myself or through my companions, they retire in great confusion. Indeed, whenever I am tempted or depressed, if

I see my companions joyful, I immediately turn away from my temptation and oppression, and regain my own inward and outward joy.'

So the father used to censure those who went about with gloomy faces, and once rebuked a friar who appeared with a gloomy face, saying, 'Why are you making an outward display of grief and sorrow for your sin? This sorrow is between God and yourself alone. So pray him in his mercy to pardon you and restore to your soul the joy of his salvation, of which the guilt of your sins has deprived it. Always do your best to be cheerful when you are with me and the other brethren; it is not right for a servant of God to show a sad and gloomy face to his brother or to anyone else.'

'The Mirror of Perfection' 96, tr. Leo Sherley-Price in *S. Francis of Assisi: His Life and Writings as Recorded by His Contemporaries* (A.R. Mowbray 1959), p. 118.

Trials of a seeker after God
9.11

Now during the time that I was at Barnet, a strong temptation to despair came upon me. Then I saw how Christ was tempted, and mighty troubles I was in; sometimes I kept myself retired in my chamber, and often walked solitary in the chace there, to wait upon the Lord. I wondered why these things should come to me; and I looked upon myself and said 'Was I ever so before?' then I thought, because I had forsaken my relations, I had done amiss against them; so I was brought to call to mind all the time that I had spent, and to consider whether I had wronged any. But temptations grew more and more, and I was tempted almost to despair; and when Satan could not effect his design upon me that way, he laid snares for me and baits to draw me to commit some sin, whereby he might take advantage to bring me to despair. I was about twenty years of age when these exercises came upon me; and continued in that condition some years, in great troubles, and fain I would have put it from me. I went to many a priest to look for comfort, but found no comfort from them.

... After this I went to another priest... and reasoned with him about the ground of despair and temptations; but he was ignorant of my condition: he bade me take tobacco and sing psalms. Tobacco was a thing I did not love, and psalms I was not in a state to sing; I could not sing.

... My troubles continued, and I was often under great temptations; I fasted much, and walked abroad in solitary places many days, and often took my Bible, and went and sat in hollow trees and lonesome places till night came on; and frequently, in the night, walked mournfully about by myself: for I was a man of sorrows in the times of the first workings of the Lord in me.

... Though my exercises and troubles were very great, yet were they not so continual but that I had some intermissions, and was sometimes brought into such a heavenly joy, that I thought I had been in Abraham's bosom. As I cannot declare the misery I was in, it was so great and heavy upon me, so neither can I set forth the mercies of God unto me in all my misery. Oh, the everlasting love of God to my soul, when I was in great distress! When my troubles and torments were great, then was his love exceeding great.

George Fox, Journal, ed. Norman Penney (J.M. Dent 1924), pp. 3–6.

The demon of *acedia*
9.12

The demon of *acedia* – also called the noonday demon – is the one that causes the most serious trouble of all. He presses his attack upon the monk about the fourth hour [10 a.m.] and besieges the soul until the eighth hour. First of all he makes it seem that the sun barely moves, if at all, and that the day is fifty hours long. Then he constrains the monk to look constantly out the windows, to walk outside the cell, to gaze carefully at the sun to determine how far it stands from the ninth hour [dinner time], to look now this way and now that to see if perhaps one of the brethren appears from his cell. Then too he instills in the heart of the monk a hatred for the place, hatred for his very life itself, a hatred for manual labour. He leads him to reflect that charity has departed from among the brethren, that there is no one to give encouragement. Should there be someone at this period who happens to offend him in some way or other, this too the demon uses to contribute further to his hatred. The demon drives him along to desire other sites where he can more easily procure life's necessities, more readily find work and make a real success of himself. He goes on to suggest that, after all, it is not the place that is the basis of pleasing the Lord. God is to be adored everywhere. He joins to these reflections the memory of his dear ones and of his former way of life. He depicts life stretching out for a long period of time, and brings before the mind's eye the toil of the ascetic struggle and, as the saying has it, leaves no leaf unturned to induce the monk to forsake his cell and drop out of the fight. No other demon follows close on the heels of this one (when he is defeated) but only a state of deep peace and inexpressible joy arise out of this struggle.

Evagrius Ponticus, in Evagrius Ponticus – The Praktikos and Chapters on Prayer,
tr. John Eudes Bamberger OCSO (Cistercian Publications 1970).

The danger of boredom
9.13

A man in danger of boredom may pass a little of each day in gambling. Try giving him each morning the money he might expect to win during the day so that he need not gamble: you will make him anything but happy. It may be pleaded for him that what he seeks is the pleasure of play, and not the winnings. Well, then, make him play for nothing: he will get no excitement out of that at all and will merely be bored by the game. So it is not the mere pleasure of the game that attracts him: a mild pastime without a strong motive of excitement will merely bore him. He needs to get excited, and to delude himself with the thought that he may have the happiness of winning something (which he would not take if you offered it to him to stop him from gambling), so long as he can satisfy a craving for excitement, and stimulate his desire, his anger, his fear upon an illusory object which he has proposed to himself: just like those children who frighten themselves with a face they have themselves blackened.

How comes it that a man who, a few months ago, lost his only son, and who this very morning was deep in troubles, harassed by lawsuits and disputes, no longer gives these things a thought? Do not be surprised. He is now completely absorbed in watching for the coming of the boar, which his hounds have been following closely for the last six hours. He needs nothing more. A man of sorrows he may be, but if you can induce him to take up some amusement, he will be happy while it lasts. And however happy a man may be, if he is not distracted and completely absorbed in some passion or pursuit which keeps away boredom, he will soon become morose and unhappy. Without amusement there is no joy; with it, there is no sadness. This it is, also, which makes the happiness of persons of position who, having many people about them, are always provided with entertainment, and have the means to continue in that state.

But... when they fall into disgrace they are dismissed and banished to their estates, where they have no lack of material things, nor of servants to minister to every need; yet they are still wretched in the knowledge that they have been dropped, since they no longer have anyone to tear their thoughts away from themselves.

Blaise Pascal, *Pensées*, 116 ('Distractions') in
The Essential Pascal, sel. and ed. R.W. Gleason and tr. G.F. Pullen
(Mentor–Omega Book 1966), pp. 57–58.

In the face of suffering
9.14

How does the Christian conquer the temptation of suffering? Here the end of the Book of Job is a great help to us. In the face of suffering Job has protested his innocence to the last, and has brushed aside the counsels to repentance from his friends who try to trace his misfortune back to a particular, perhaps hidden sin of Job. In addition, Job has spoken high-sounding words about his own righteousness. After the appearance of God Job declares: 'Therefore I abhor myself, and repent in dust and ashes (Job 42:3, 6). But the wrath of God is not now turned against Job, but against his friends: 'for ye have not spoken of me the thing that is right, as my servant Job hath' (Job 42:7). Job gets justice before God and yet confesses his guilt before God. That is the solution of the problem. Job's suffering has its foundation not in his guilt but in his righteousness. Job is tempted because of his piety. So Job is right to protest against suffering coming upon him as if he were guilty. Yet this right comes to an end for Job when he no longer faces human beings but faces God. Face to face with God, even the good, innocent Job knows himself to be guilty.

Dietrich Bonhoeffer, *Temptation* (SCM Press 1955), pp. 36–37.

In Times of Suffering

Delighting to endure

9.15

There is a spirit which I feel that delights to do no evil, nor to revenge any wrong, but delights to endure all things, in hope to enjoy its own in the end. Its hope is to outlive all wrath and contention, and weary out all exaltation and cruelty, or whatever is of a nature contrary to itself. It sees to the end of all temptations. As it bears no evil in itself, so it conceives none in thoughts to any other. If it be betrayed, it bears it, for its ground and spring is the mercies and forgiveness of God. Its crown is meekness, its life is everlasting love unfeigned; it takes its kingdom by entreaty and not with contention, and keeps it by lowliness of mind. In God alone it can rejoice, though none else regard it, or can own its life. It is conceived in sorrow, and brought forth without any to pity it, nor doth it murmur at grief and oppression. It never rejoiceth but through sufferings; for with the world's joy it is murdered. I found it alone, being forsaken. I have fellowship therein with them who lived in dens and desolate places in the earth, who through death obtained this resurrection and eternal holy life.

James Nayler, in *Quaker Spirituality: Selected Writings,* ed. Douglas V. Steere (Paulist Press 1984), p. 96.

Bearing in our bodies the death of Jesus

9.16

The Christian message about the death of Jesus as the beginning of new life gave deeper meaning and clarity to our own indigenous beliefs through the vivid imagery of the scoured, crowned-with-thorns, crucified Jesus of Nazareth. Our ancient icons were now assumed by the suffering Jesus. At the same time, the Christian belief in the communion of saints gave a deeper and more exciting meaning to our ancient belief of the continuity of the ancestors.

Far from dwelling in some far-off mysterious place, they were now enjoying the eternal and unending feast! Our own *mitotes* (Indian word for community-wide feasts) were now seen to be the images and foretaste of the future unending feast in heaven. In this religious *mestizaje*, the elements of our new identity were being forged and shaped.

For a people who have consistently been subjected to injustice, cruelty and early death, the image of the crucified is the supreme symbol of life in spite of the multiple daily threats of death. If there was something good and redemptive in the unjust condemnation and crucifixion of the God-man, then, as senseless and useless as our suffering appears to be, there must be something of ultimate value in it. We don't understand it, but in Jesus, the God-man who suffered for our salvation, we affirm it and in this very affirmation receive the power to endure it without its destroying us. Even if we are killed, we cannot be destroyed. This is the curious irony of our celebrations of the dead: they appear to be dead, but they are not really dead! For they live not only in God but in our hearts and in our memory. Those whom the world thinks are dead, those who have been killed by society, defy death and are alive in us.

Virgil Elizondo, 'Popular Religions as Support of Identity' in
Spirituality of the Third World (Orbis Books 1994), p. 61.

How God feels for us
9.17

If he came down to earth, it was out of compassion for the human race. Yes, he suffered our sufferings even before suffering the cross, even before taking our flesh. Indeed, if he had not suffered, he would not have come down to share our life with us. First he suffered, then he came down. But what is this passion that he felt for us? It was the passion of love. And does not the Father himself, the God of the universe, 'slow to anger and abounding in steadfast love' (Psalm 103:8) also in some way suffer with us? Are you not aware that whilst governing human affairs he has compassion on our sufferings? Look how 'the Lord your God bore you, as a man bears his son' (Deuteronomy 1:31). In the same way as the Son of God 'bore our griefs', God bears with our behaviour. The Father is not impassible either... He has pity, he knows something of the passion of love, he has merciful impulses which it might seem his sovereign majesty would have forbidden him.

Origen, Sixth Homily on Ezekiel 6.6, in Olivier Clément, *The Roots of Christian Mysticism*,
tr. Theodore Berkeley and Jeremy Hummerstone (New City 1993), pp. 45–46.

Nothing is certain
9.18

Eleven months have passed since the cancer in my body was first detected – eleven months of the limited life I am expected to have left, the original sentence being about one year. The medical prognosis is still the same, and the latest scan showed a further increase in the tumour. The future officially is bleak, and I am getting used to people looking at me as a dying man under sentence of death. Nothing is certain. I'm not out of the wood yet. Everything is a matter of faith…

The opposite to faith is fear, and I have found that there is a constant running battle between the two. In one sense, fear is faith in what you do not want to happen. Job once said, 'The thing I fear comes upon me, and what I dread befalls me' (3:25). There is a powerful truth in that statement. When we are afraid of something, we almost pre-condition it to happen. Our fears, however unfounded and irrational they may be, can trigger the fulfilment of those fears.

Fear has been described as the greatest threat to health in our generation, simply because fear is so widespread. Fear is a great deceiver and destroyer. It robs our minds of peace; it breaks our relationships; it ruins our health; it goads us into foolish, impulsive and sometimes violent action; it paralyzes our thinking, trusting and loving…

God never promises to protect us from problems, only to help us in them. If we leave God out of the picture, those difficulties might so strip away our sense of security that we feel vulnerable, anxious and afraid. On the other hand, those same difficulties could drive us back to God and so strengthen our faith. We might feel just as vulnerable, but we *have* to trust God because there is really no alternative; and then we discover that God is with us in the dark as in the light, in pain as in joy. When I was going through a traumatic time in my life, a friend of mine said, 'You cannot trust God too much.'

David Watson, *Fear No Evil: A Personal Struggle with Cancer*
(Hodder & Stoughton 1984), pp. 152–53.

Treasures of darkness
9.19

When I was once passing through a very dark phase, due largely to physical illness – and of course when we are physically ill we all suffer both from a degree of anxiety and from regression to a more infantile level – I did not know whether to accept an onerous and very demanding position or withdraw from it. One day my wife said she thought the darkness could be part of God's training for the job. I came to accept that view. Fear itself can be *used* by God to equip us for our tasks, so long as we take the right attitude to it and do not let it cow us into surrender or into any of the many avenues of escape which the frightened mind suggests to us. I can only write down this simple testimony. Like everybody, I love and prefer the sunny uplands of experience, when health, happiness and success abound, but I have learned far more about God and life and myself in the darkness of fear and failure than I have ever learned in the sunshine. There are such things as the treasures of darkness. The darkness, thank God, passes. *But what one learns in the darkness, one possesses for ever.* 'The trying things,' says Bishop Fénelon, 'which you fancy come between God and you, will prove means of unity with him, if you bear them humbly. Those things that overwhelm us and upset our pride, do more good than all that which excites and inspirits us.'

Leslie D. Weatherhead, *Prescription for Anxiety* (Hodder & Stoughton 1956), p. 32.

Jesus' presence
9.20

If you seek, you will find God in your good will. Though you may feel many conflicts, do not for that reason feel that your will is deprived of desiring God. No indeed, this is the reason why the soul mourns and suffers, because it is afraid of offending God. So it ought to be full of joy and gladness, and not fall into confusion because of its struggles, since God keeps its will good, and makes it hate grave sin.

I remember that I heard this said once to a servant of God, and it was said to her by the sweet first truth, when she was dwelling in very great pain and temptation, and among other things felt the greatest confusion, so much so that the devil said 'What will you do? For your whole life you will remain in this anguish, and then you will have hell.' She answered bravely, without any fear, and with proper self-hatred: 'I do not avoid pains, for I have chosen pain for my refreshment. And if at the end he gives me hell, I will not for that reason abandon the serving of my creator. For I deserve to abide in hell, because I have wronged the sweet first truth; so, if he were to give me hell, he would do me no wrong, since I am his.' Then our Saviour, with sweet and true humility, scattered the shadows and torments of the devil, as happens when the cloud passes and there is the sun: suddenly there came the presence of our Saviour. Then she melted into a flood of tears and glowing with love asked: 'Sweet and good Jesus, where were you when my soul was so afflicted?' And Jesus, spotless lamb, replied: 'I was beside you. For I do not move, and I never leave my creature, unless the creature leaves me through grave sin.' And she carried on her sweet conversation with him and asked: 'If you were with me, how did I not feel you? How could I be by the fire, and feel no heat? I felt nothing but freezing cold, sadness and bitterness, and I seemed to myself to be full of deadly sins.' Then he replied sweetly, saying, 'Do you wish me to show you, my daughter, how in these conflicts of yours you did not fall into grave sin, and how I was beside you? Tell me, what is it that makes sin grave? Is it not your will? For sin and virtue consist in the will's consent; there is neither sin nor virtue, except by act of the will. And the will to sin was not in you; if it had been, you would have been pleased at the devil's suggestions; but since that will was not in you, you were distressed over them, and at the thought of doing wrong. So you see that sin and virtue consist in choice – so I tell you that you should not fall into confusion because of these conflicts. My will is that you should gain the light of self-knowledge from this darkness... knowing that I abide in you secretly. The will is a sign to you that I am there with you; for if you had an evil will, I should not be in you by grace... for I often withdraw feeling to myself, but I do not withdraw grace, since grace is never lost, except by grave sin. And do you know why I do this? Only to make the soul reach true perfection. You know that the soul cannot be perfect unless borne on these two wings, humility and charity. Humility is won through the knowledge of itself, into which it enters in the time of darkness; and charity is won by seeing that I, through love, have kept its will holy and good.'

Catherine of Siena, letter to Sister Bartolomea della Seta, in *Letters of St Catherine of Siena*, ed. and tr. Vida D. Scudder (J.M. Dent/E.P. Dutton 1905), pp. 161–63 .

In passion and in action
9.21

A bishop of the church, a man of long and great achievement, became towards the end of his life totally blind and so much afflicted with a number of different illnesses and disabilities that he was confined to bed and almost deprived of the power of movement. He lay supine on the bed, his arms limp, the palms of his hands upwards, so that his very posture suggested his total exposure to whatever might be done to him, his total dependence and helplessness. As one stood beside him on a particular morning some weeks before his death, one had a sudden and overwhelming impression that something of extraordinary significance was going on before one's eyes – something that even surpassed in its significance all that the bishop had done in his years of activity and achievement and service. This impression did not arise from the manner in which the patient reacted to his condition – from any obvious evidences of his cheerfulness or courage: for he spoke hardly at all, and there could be no other expression of his thoughts or feelings. The impression seemed to come, strangely, from the totality of his helplessness and exposure. He was now simply an object exposed to the world around him, receiving whatever the world might do to him; yet in his passion he seemed by no means diminished in human dignity but rather, if that were possible, enlarged.

In the years of activity and achievement the bishop was rightly known as a godly man, as one in whom the image of God is less marred than in most. Was that image obliterated in him, or effaced, or distorted when he entered his final phase of passion? Did he now less bear the likeness of God than when he worked and achieved? The memory of him and the indelible impression which one received at his bedside makes it impossible to answer these questions in the affirmative, and gives added urgency to our task of discovering how it can be that human beings may bear, in passion no less than in action, the image of that impassible God of whom Christianity has for so long spoken.

W.H. Vanstone, *The Stature of Waiting*
(Darton, Longman & Todd 1982), pp. 67–68.

Give it time
9.22

I cannot leave you without help in the heart-rending state of mind, which you describe in your letter. You are absolutely right to think that this is due to physical reasons. But what is to be done? Merely what one does in the case of every physical malady; give it time to pass away and give it no cause to grow or become chronic.

You will get through it as you got through winter or as you come out of a nightmare on waking up. But as you take all desirable material care of yourself, you must be sure that this physical state has no reality in the soul and in our innermost nature. There is a great comfort in this thought, it is like the relief felt by the audience at a play, when they realize that the play only belongs to the theatre, and that no one in it really comes to harm.

And you are wonderfully in harmony with this thought when you say yourself that your distress is baseless and is only a direct result of your illness. How often I myself, in similar circumstances, have woken up in the night in a state of terror, caused by no justifiable reason or any reason at all. I was terrified without knowing of what I was afraid. There was a physical feeling of fear, but no motive for this terror. It is what some young people with unstable temperaments go through and are said to be 'scared'. When you ask them what they are scared of, they reply 'anything, when the feeling comes on'. We are sometimes deluded by this. We imagine, for no other cause than that of ill health, that the first object we see is the origin of our fear. This is similar to the behaviour of people who are exhausted by fatigue or who suffer from some stomach trouble and who fly into a bad temper with everything and imagine that anything they encounter is the real cause of their 'blues'.

Your experience and judgment are exactly the same as what I know and have personally felt. One must also see God as more tender, loving and sympathetic to the glorious state of dejection which we must at times endure.

You would be sorry for another's troubles: imagine then what admiring pity God has for his children, who endure them so 'splendidly' as St Francis de Sales would say.

Henri de Tourville, *Light and Life: Notes and Letters on the Spiritual Life*, ch. VI, tr. Vincent Girling (Dacre Press 1961), pp. 77–79.

Today's strength is for today's burden
9.23

The battle always has to be fought before the victory is won, though many people think they must have the victory *before* the battle. The conflict with worry and fear is almost always there – each person must overcome or be overcome. But we must fight each battle of our lives in the strength of Jesus' victory. He said, 'As the Father has sent me, even so I am sending you' (John 20:21). We are to be like Jesus – one of whom Satan is afraid!

When we worry, we are carrying tomorrow's load with today's strength; carrying two days in one. We are moving into tomorrow ahead of time. There is just one day in the calendar of action – today. The Holy Spirit does not give a clear blueprint of our whole lives, but only of the moments, one by one.

We all have the same enemies – we are all preyed upon by frustration and worry. In India, Australia, Japan, Germany – we need the same Holy Spirit. We need to remember that we are children of God, living within his constant care. God knows and is interested both in the hardest problems we face and the tiniest details that concern us. He knows how to put everything in place, like a jigsaw puzzle, to make a beautiful picture.

Corrie ten Boom, *He is More than Able*
(Kingsway 1978), p. 31.

Universal struggle
9.24

It would be surprising to find, in a bouquet, flowers which were ill-formed or sickly, since these flowers are picked one by one and artificially grouped together in a bunch. But on a tree which has had to struggle against the inner accidents of its own development and external accidents of climate, the broken branches, the torn leaves, and the dried or sickly or wilted blossoms have their place; they reveal to us the greater or lesser difficulties encountered by the tree itself in its growth.

Similarly in a universe where each creature formed a little enclosed unit, destined simply for its own sake and theoretically transposable at will, we should find some difficulty in justifying in our own minds the presence of individuals whose potentialities and upward-soaring drives had been painfully impeded. Why this gratuitous inequality, these gratuitous frustrations?

If on the other hand the world is in truth a battlefield whereon victory is in the making – and if we are in truth thrown at birth into the thick of the battle – then we can at least vaguely see how, for the success of this universal struggle in which we are both fighters and the issue at stake, there must inevitably be suffering. Seen from the viewpoint of our human experience and drawn to our human scale, the world appears as an immense groping in the dark, an immense searching, an immense onslaught, wherein there can be no advance save at the cost of many setbacks and many wounded. Those who suffer, whatever form their suffering may take, are a living statement of this austere but notable condition: they are simply paying for the advance and the victory of all. They are the men who have fallen on the battlefield.

Pierre Teilhard de Chardin, *Hymn of the Universe*
(William Collins 1981), p. 104.

Singing in times of trouble
9.25

Any fool can sing in the day. When the cup is full, a person draws inspiration from it. When wealth rolls in abundance round about him, anyone can sing to the praise of the God who gives a plenteous harvest, or sends home a loaded argosy. It is easy enough for an Aeolian harp to whisper music when the winds blow; the difficulty is for music to come when no wind is blowing...

No one can make a song in the night by themselves. They may attempt it, but will feel how difficult it is. Let all things go as I please – I will weave songs, weave them wherever I go, with the flowers that grow upon my path. But put me in a desert, where no flowers are, and wherewith shall I weave a chorus of praise to God? How shall I make a crown for him? Let this voice be free, and this body full of health, and I can sing God's praise; but stop this tongue, lay me upon the bed of languishing, and it is not easy to sing from the bed and chant high praises in the fires. Give me the bliss of spiritual liberty, and let me mount up to my God and get near the throne, and I will sing, aye, sing as sweet as seraphs. But confine me, fetter my spirit, clip my wings, make me exceeding sad, so that I become old like the eagle – ah! then it is hard to sing.

It is not natural to sing when in trouble, 'Bless the Lord, O my soul, and all that is within me bless his holy name,' for that is a daylight song. But it was a divine song that Habakkuk sang when in the night he said, 'Though the fig tree shall not blossom… yet will I trust in the Lord, and stay myself in the God of Jacob'… Songs in the night come only from God; they are not in human power.

Charles Haddon Spurgeon, 'Songs in the Night' (1856), in
Spiritual Power, ed. S.E. Wirt (Crossway Books/Lion 1989), pp. 31–32.

Having cancer
9.26

Two years ago I found myself having to speak at the funeral of a sixteen year-old girl who died in our Yorkshire dale. I said stumblingly that God was to be found in the cancer as much as in the sunset. That I firmly believed, but it was an intellectual statement. Now I have had to ask if I can say it of myself, which is a much greater test.

… How does one prepare for death, whether of other people or of oneself? It is something we seldom talk about these days. Obviously there is the elementary duty (urged in the Prayer Book) of making one's will and other dispositions, which is no more of a morbid occupation than taking out life insurance. And there is the deeper level of seeking to round off one's account, of ordering one's priorities and what one wants to do in the time available. And notice such as this concentrates the mind wonderfully and makes one realize how much of one's time one wastes or kills. When I was told that I had six months, or perhaps nine, to live, the first reaction was naturally of shock – though I also felt liberated, because, as in limited-over cricket, at least one knew the target one had to beat. My second reaction was 'Gosh, six months is a long time. One can do a lot in that. How am I going to use it?'

... In fact 'preparing for death' is not the other-worldly, pious exercise stamped upon our minds by Victorian sentimentality, turning away from the things of earth for the things of 'heaven'. Rather, for the Christian it is preparing for 'eternal life', which means real living, more abundant life, which is begun, continued, though not ended, *now*. And this means it is about quality of life not quantity. How long it goes on here is purely secondary. So preparing for eternity means learning really to live, not just concentrating on keeping alive. It means living it *up*, becoming *more* concerned with contributing to and enjoying what matters most – giving the most to life and getting the most from it, while it is on offer.

> John A.T. Robinson, from the sermon, 'Learning from Cancer',
> in Eric James, *The Life of Bishop John A.T. Robinson*
> (Collins 1987), pp. 304, 307–308.

Suffering transfigured
9.27

The transfiguring of suffering is attested in Christian life. Sometimes a person suffers greatly, and the suffering continues and does not disappear; but through nearness to Christ there is seen a courage, an outgoing love and sympathy, a power of prayer, a Christlikeness of a wonderful kind... In the testimony to these experiences in the apostolic writings perhaps the most moving instance is near the end of chapter eight of the letter to the Romans.

> Who shall separate us from the love of Christ? Shall tribulation, or distress, or persecution, or famine, or nakedness, or peril, or sword?... No, in all these things we are more than conquerors through him who loved us. (Romans 8:35, 37)

I love the comment of Karl Barth on the passage:

> Thus our tribulation, without ceasing to be tribulation, is transformed. We suffer as we suffered before, but our suffering is no longer a passive perplexity, but is transformed into a pain which is creative, fruitful, full of power and promise. The road which is impassable has been made known to us in the crucified and risen Lord.

... Such is the transforming of circumstances, not by their abolition but by the lifting of them into the orbit of a crucified and risen Jesus.

> Michael Ramsey, *Be Still and Know*
> (Collins Fount/Faith Press 1982), pp. 66–67.

Drained of energy
9.28

A vague feeling of anguish is prowling around in me like a caged beast, immobilizing my energies and concentration. The feeling has no shape and I don't know what to call it. I am its prisoner. I've got to shake it off. I need all my energy at the moment, at every moment, if I'm to live my life in its fullness. But I won't be free of it until I've let the bad feeling wash over me, then faced it without fear, grabbed it with both hands and offered it to God who can bring new life out of sin.

I can understand the awful pain of those who are suffering from depression. It's a paralyzing of one's whole being, while others whisper: 'He should pull up his socks! Control himself!' But the trouble is *he can't*. It's an ordeal, one of the worst. He needs drugs, perhaps. But he also needs someone always to be there, patient, sensitive, to help him set free the little pieces of life which are stagnating in him, polluting his source. And if he is a believer, he must also be helped to offer it all to God.

Michel Quoist, *With Open Hearts*, tr. Colette Copeland
(Gill & Macmillan 1983), p. 173.

Receiving God's peace
9.29

According to the Bible the peace which God gives is not a freedom from the storms of life, but a mysterious strength and comfort amid the storms; not the removal of pain, but the bestowal of a precious gift. The gift is God himself, the comforter, the one who stands alongside us.

Though in an overriding and abiding sense I believe God has put to death our feeling of abandonment, I feel I must qualify the statement. I do not mean to paint a rosy picture of suffering. Pain hurts! And often pain is very lonely. It is not as though Christians walk tranquilly hand in hand with God through all hardship. During my own times of greatest suffering, feelings of betrayal and abandonment have often gripped me rather than joy and peace. Sometimes I have felt totally alone, as though God were against me and not for me. Then I have felt not trust in him but doubt, not love for him but anger and even hate.

The awareness of God's presence and of his being on my side has come only in retrospect, long after the dark depression has passed. After the ordeal I have been able to say that I know God was with me and for me, but any momentary sense of these truths during the ordeal resulted more from the active, hard work of believing by faith, *despite feelings to the contrary*, rather than through passive acceptance. In times like this, God's peace isn't like a blanket which a father drapes over his child, but like a blanket at the end of the bed which the child must pull up. The father provides the blanket, but the child has to put forth much of the effort. Receiving God's peace may not be automatic; it may require the work of faith.

Charles Ohlich, The Suffering God (Intervarsity Christian Fellowship
1982/Triangle 1983), pp. 102–103.

The butt of anger
9.30

Depressive illnesses are not my subject: they take many forms, and doctors still disagree as to their origin and their treatment. And yet almost always there is in true depression a basis of anger, and it may be that the only 'religious' feeling possible is the attempt to tap and understand some of that repressed resentment and anger and direct it at God. Once again that will only be possible if our understanding of God has progressed from one of fear to one of childlike trust, confidence and love. 'Unless you become like little children...' The God of Jesus Christ offers himself as the butt of people's anger. He knows what it is to be strung up on a cross, spat and railed at and abused. If we are going to come to terms with our inner selves at any but the most superficial level, then being honest with God (which includes being angry with God) may be the starting point. God is not shocked by our rage or resentment. And he alone can absorb it and from it bring something creative.

So, once again, that which has most to say to the sick or suffering person – in this case the depressive – is the cross of Christ. The cross shows us at our most hateful and destructive: equally it shows us God in Christ at his most forgiving and creative. Whatever we do or fail to do, whatever we feel or fail to feel, though the heavens seem barred against us when we try to pray and no answer comes, yet there is no diminution of his love. 'If I go down to hell thou art there also.'

It is hard for a person with severe depression, someone who may be suicidal, to have any sense that God is with them in the darkness. Here, too, you cannot act by yourself. Just as in my own worst time of sickness – even though it was more of a long-drawn-out despondency – I needed to depend on the prayers and sympathetic understanding of others, so someone suffering from a depressive illness depends on that quality of compassionate understanding which does not dismiss their black despair as nonsense, or treat it as something of which one should be ashamed.

Michael Mayne, *A Year Lost and Found* (Darton, Longman & Todd 1987), pp. 62–63.

Allowing pain to be pain
9.31

It is one thing to be empty. It is an even deeper thing to be emptied. Pain does this. It empties us, if we allow it to.

Today in America – and every day in America – seventy-six million Valium will be swallowed. In addition, some thirty million people will glue themselves to soap operas on television. It would seem that our culture is not well adapted to deal with pain. Pain is today's unmentionable reality, much as sex was unmentionable in the Victorian period. And pain is everywhere – deep, ineffable, unfathomable, cosmic pain. And it needs to be named for what it is so that we can pray our pain, that is, enter into it. That is the only way a dentist resolves the pain of a toothache – by entering into its source in an inflamed cavity. Covering our pain up with drugs, alcohol, soap operas or shopping is no release from the pain. It is more acquiescence, of a perverse kind, to the pain. It is letting pain run our lives instead of letting Eros and our love of life run our lives…

Facing the darkness, admitting the pain, allowing the pain to be pain, is never easy. This is why courage – big-heartedness – is the most essential virtue on the spiritual journey. But if we fail to let pain be pain – and our entire patriarchal culture refuses to let this happen – then pain will haunt us in nightmarish ways. We will become pain's victims instead of the healers we might become. The Japanese poet Kenji Miyazawa left us a powerful image of dealing with pain when he said that we must embrace pain and burn it as fuel for our journey. The image that comes to my mind on hearing this advice is the following: we pick up our pain as we would a bundle of sticks for a fireplace; we necessarily embrace these sticks as we move across the room to the fireplace; then we thrust them into the fire, getting rid of them, letting go of them; finally we are warmed and delighted by their sacrificial gift to us in the form of fire and heat and warmth and energy. This is the manner in which we can and indeed must deal with our pain. First comes the embrace, the allowing of pain to be pain; next comes the journey with the pain; then the letting go, but in a deliberate manner, into a fire, into a cauldron where the pain's energy will serve us. And finally comes the benefit we do indeed derive from having burned this fuel.

Matthew Fox, *Original Blessing* (Bear & Co. 1983), pp. 141–43.

Touching our sorrow
9.32

There is a striking parallelism between the natural world and the world of the spirit. A spirituality that refuses to acknowledge the winter of the heart, the great sorrowfulness of human experience, is not only refusing to take seriously the life that people actually lead: it is in danger of encouraging too much leaf and too little fruit.

In that sense, our 'sorrows' are not *only* negative, destructive and painful. Yes, they are those things: it would be as misleading as it would be dangerous to deny that. That is not, however, all they are. They are also the necessary period of die-back, perhaps the continuing process of die-back, which is a precondition of fruitfulness.

It is therefore important to be in touch with our sorrows, to recognize them, to honour them even. So often we imagine there is virtue in pretending they don't exist. We treat them as Victorian *grandes dames* treated the wayward son, labelling him 'black sheep' and dispatching him to the colonies, so that he could be forgotten or ignored until he returned reformed, rich and famous. There is reason for that, of course. Having him around is painful, not least to the family pride.

In the same way, living in the presence of our sorrows is always painful, and one of the bits of us that is hurt most of all is our pride. I hate to acknowledge that I cannot love my mother; that I despise my brother; that I have made a mess of my career or my marriage. How much more comfortable to my self-esteem to push all those feelings away, to pretend to myself and everyone else that everything in the garden is lovely, that summer will last for ever.

Charles Elliott, *Praying through Paradox* (Fount 1987), p. 97.

What if...?
9.33

There is another consideration which, when you know it and think it over, will give you reasonable comfort in external damage, pain and discomfort. A man travels by a certain road, or takes up or quits a certain job. Then he gets hurt, breaks a leg or an arm, loses an eye or gets sick. Then he is likely to think: Ah! – if you had only gone the other way or had done or not done that job, this wouldn't have happened to you; and so he continues to be distressed and is bound to suffer. He would do much better to think: if you had gone by another road, taken up or quit another job, still greater damage or harm might have been your portion. Thus he might reasonably find comfort and be glad at heart.

Or consider this. You have lost a thousand dollars. Stop weeping over the thousand you lost and, instead, thank God that he gave you a thousand to lose and let go, so that you might be exercised in patience and virtue and be worthy of life eternal – as many thousands of people are not. Or take this to your comfort. A man who has been well-off for many years, loses it all. He ought then to reflect wisely and thank God for his misfortune and loss, for only then will he realize how well-off he was before. He ought to thank God for the well-being he enjoyed so many years – and not growl about it.

Meister Eckhart, *The Book of Divine Comfort*, ch. 2, in *Meister Eckhart: A Modern Translation*, tr. Raymond B. Blakney (Harper Torchbooks 1941), pp. 56–57.

In trial and conflict
9.34

Being in agony, [Jesus] prayed 'more earnestly'. As his grief and sorrow increased upon him, he increased in the strength and fervour of his prayer. And yet, as he proceeded to repeat his request, the language of acquiescence became more absolute; at first he says, 'if it be possible let this cup pass', but afterwards he says, 'if this cup may not pass, your will be done' – as if he felt what that will was and meekly placed himself in harmony with it. We have reason to believe, however, that he did obtain, if not the thing he sought, that which was sufficient to supply its place… He was not literally delivered from death; nor from those deadly mental pangs so much worse than the cross itself. But he was saved from sinking under them. He was strengthened by an angel sent to him from the Father and was thus enabled to bear up till the darkness had passed away… In the trials and conflicts of the Christian life, in every season of suffering and sorrow, let us learn to imitate the example of Jesus. However we may value or desire the sympathy of others, let us not depend on it. Let us never forget that in conflict with temptation and in wrestling with God, we must of necessity act alone. Let us pray with fervour, importunity, repetition: if the surges rise and overwhelm the spirit, if, like the Lord, we have agony and anguish, let us learn to pray 'the more earnestly' – to pray, if needs be, with prostration and tears. The grace of Christ will never be denied to the sincere and sorrowful, though its manifestation may be delayed. He lives 'a faithful and merciful High Priest, in that, he himself having suffered being tempted, he knows how to succour them that are tempted.' Imitating his example and confiding in his mercy, succour and light will come at last. No

Christian must ever expect to be without Gethsemanes, but the one that faints not, but continues to pray without ceasing, will always find that there is no Gethsemane without its angel.

Thomas Binney, 'Gethsemane', sermon delivered in
King's Weigh House Chapel, London (1850).

All the way
9.35

One night a man had a dream. He dreamt he was walking along the beach with his Lord. Across the sky flashed scenes from his life. For each scene he noticed two sets of footprints in the sand, one belonging to him, the other to the Lord. When the last scene in his life flashed before him he looked back at the footprints on the sand. He noticed that many times along the path of his life there was only one set of footprints. He also noticed that it happened at the very lowest and saddest times of his life. This really bothered him, and he questioned the Lord about it. 'Lord, you said that, once I decided to follow you, you would walk with me all the way. But I've noticed that during the most difficult times in my life there is only one set of footprints. I don't understand why, in times when I needed you most, you would leave me.' The Lord replied, 'My precious child, I love you and would never leave you during your trials and sufferings; when you see only one set of footprints, it was then that I carried you.'

Margaret Fishback Powers, 'Footprints'.

Part of the fabric of life
9.36

Whether we like it or not, pain is part of the whole fabric of life. To escape suffering completely, we would have to live in some sort of sterilized and cushioned modules, with no risk of infection or accident. If there were no trouble, pain or difficulty in life, there would be no courage, patience, forgiveness or compassion either. We would never learn from our mistakes or grow through struggles and hard challenges. Goodness would just be the automatic response of puppet-people, because the freedom to choose good or evil would not be allowed. The more we try to imagine a painless and flawless world, the more impossible it becomes. Difficulty and suffering are an inescapable part of the mystery of being alive.

This does not make suffering any easier to bear. We still protest and fight against pain when it comes our way. We also complain about how unfair it all seems. If someone who is known to be a Christian faces illness or any other kind of hardship, people often say, 'Why did God let it happen to him if he's a believer?' We sometimes reduce God to a petty wonder worker who will intervene to protect his favourites from trouble. Some religious books come dangerously near to making God into a convenience, a Heavenly Rescue Service to be summoned when it suits us – as long as we have enough faith.

This approach is a far cry from the call of Jesus to give our all, take up our cross and follow him. Discipleship can let us in for more suffering, not less.

Angela Ashwin, *Heaven in Ordinary* (McCrimmon 1991), p. 55.

The pain and unfairness of life
9.37

Most people would like to think there is a God, a creative power behind and within the universe, and that this power is personal and loving. But they find it hard to relate that truth to the pain and unfairness of life. The world doesn't feel or look as if it is made by a God who is love. Yet it is exactly at that point – where what we long for and what we experience do not seem to fit or make sense – that God answers us with his word. His word made flesh. God is not indifferent. God immerses himself in his creation and is born a man, one exactly like ourselves, and at the crib in Bethlehem the image of God as a power to be afraid of, as somehow speaking through the blind forces of nature, that image dies. We see God in human terms: not up there, somewhere far off and over against us, but here, made flesh, for us and with us and in our midst.

Only the passion and death of Jesus can reconcile those two apparently irreconcilable truths: that God is in love with us, and that at some point in our lives we all experience suffering, pain and dereliction. Either God was not in Christ and the cross is the ultimate symbol of all the meaninglessness that can destroy us, the absence of God, the triumph of the secular powers. Or God was in Christ and the cross is the final word of a God who shares the pain and the dirt, the loneliness and the weakness, even the frightening sense of desolation and the death we may be called upon to experience ourselves. That was the audacious claim of the first Christians, that God is now revealed as the one who pours himself out in love, a serving, foot-washing, crucified God, whose love cannot be altered or diminished.

Michael Mayne, *A Year Lost and Found* (Darton, Longman & Todd 1987), pp. 55–56.

God's silence
9.38

The person of hope is the person who waits, and with a pessimistic waiting, for *normally* nothing should happen. The only thing we can reckon on is frustration and derision. How could it be otherwise in God's silence? Job waits, and his friends never tire of proving to him that this is absurd (which it is), that he is wrong (which he is), that God will not come (which is true). They take pains to explain to him *why* God will not come (Job is guilty), and to make fun of him, since his attitude either is one of a godless rebellion or of an absurd expectation. Still Job waits.

Just as Job is the one who attests that a person serves God for nothing, so he is the one in whom the fullness of waiting is actualized. His whole life is filled with waiting. He never lets himself be diverted to the right or to the left by his own attempts to transform the situation. He has penetrated to the bottom of the problem with lucidity. He knows that in the last analysis it is an affair between God and himself, that all the rest, the things that happen, are only the outward aspect of the quarrel with God. He does not work hard and courageously to recover his riches. He does not set out in pursuit of the brigands, or the foreign soldiers, in an attempt to get back his oxen and his camels. He rejects all those human reactions because he knows that the root of the problem is not there. Nothing of serious consequence can be done until satisfaction is had from God. He leaves activity and work to one side, since the one important thing is to wait for God.

Jacques Ellul, *Hope in Time of Abandonment*
(Seabury Press 1973), p. 259.

Thoughts of one near to death
9.39

Don't think of me as one buoyed up on a tide of spiritual consolation; my only consolation is to have none on this side of the grave. As for the instruction I get, our Lord bestows that on me in some hidden way, without ever making his voice heard. I don't get it from books, because I can't follow what I read nowadays; only now and again, after a long interval of stupidity and dryness, a sentence I've read at the end of my prayer will stay with me; this for example: 'You want a guide to dictate your actions to you? Then you must read in the book of life, which contains the whole science of loving.' The science of loving, yes, that phrase wakes a gracious echo in my soul; that;s the only kind of science I want – I'd barter away everything I possess to win it, and then, like the Bride in the Canticles, think nothing of my loss. It's only love that makes us what God wants us to be, and for that reason it's the only possession I covet. But how to come by it? Our Lord has seen fit to show me the only way which leads to it, and that is the unconcern with which a child goes to sleep in its father's arms. 'Simple hearts, draw near me,' says the Holy Spirit in the book of Proverbs (9:4) and elsewhere he tells us that it is the insignificant who are treated with mercy (Wisdom 6:7). In his name the prophet Isaiah has revealed to us that at the Last Day he will 'tend his flock like a shepherd, gather up the lambs and carry them in his bosom' (Isaiah 40:11). And as if all this were not enough, the same prophet, penetrating with his inspired gaze the depths of eternity, cries out to us in God's name: 'I will console you then, like a mother caressing her son: you shall be like children carried at the breast, fondled on a mother's lap' (Isaiah 66:12, 13).

Thérèse of Lisieux, *Story of a Soul*, tr. Ronald Knox in *Autobiography of a Saint*
(Harvill Press 1958), pp. 227–28.

In Times of Loss

A kind of rehearsal
9.40

Our ability to use suffering creatively and grow by it will be influenced by earlier important life events. We are born losers. Birth brings the loss of life within the womb. If one imagines talking to a baby a few days before birth and asking whether he would like to leave his warm, dark, safe home where he is fed without effort, bathes in lovely fluid and is as close as possible to his mother – asking, too, whether he would care to make a painful journey and be squeezed through a narrow channel while his mother cries in pain – the baby would no doubt reply that he would prefer to stay where he is. Yet, if the mothering is good enough, the baby will soon learn the joy of being at the breast, of discovering its independent existence, and of being held and adored and smiled upon, of being able to laugh and gurgle. The world becomes a most interesting and exciting place, and a return to a womblike existence unthinkable. What at the time seemed loss has now become gain. The same sort of process will be repeated with weaning. What baby wants to leave the loving breast? If the weaning is handled sensitively the baby will in fact learn to appreciate a wider variety of food, throwing it on the floor, stirring it about…

I suppose all loss is a kind of rehearsal for the final loss of independence, health and life itself. If my experience of life has been that change usually brings new possibilities and fulfilment, I hope I shall look upon death in the same light.

Anthony Faulkner, *To Travel Hopefully*
(Darton, Longman & Todd 1994), pp. 56–57.

Only truth will do
9.41

My husband's illness and death were for me a confrontation with reality, a fiercely purgative experience that confirmed in me a desire for truthfulness in all my dealings. I determined that I would not 'play games' or allow myself to be manipulated by others. Yet this was not so much a decision I made as the way things were with me.

A widow quickly learns that she and her affairs are regarded as public property. I was horrified at how soon, after my husband died, people wanted to know my future plans. I had none and intended to have none until I was ready. I knew that I had to deal with my husband's death and all that it meant in my own way and I was determined to do so. But it was hard.

I needed space – not space *for* anything, just space. I found coping with the curious and the would-be organizers of my life a great trial at a time when I was spiritually, physically and emotionally exhausted. There are still people I keep at a distance because of their insensitivity during my husband's illness and after his death. They are few but I remain aware of them. 'But what are you going to *do*?' I was asked rather hysterically in a busy shop. My reply, 'Go on living, I suppose' coupled with the information that the pants and socks still needed washing was not what had been expected.

Anger is part of bereavement. And it is all right. If it is not anger experienced directly against God, then it may be experienced as I experienced it – anger against other people, more particularly those Christians who offer cheap consolation from a place of comparative security. The church rightly proclaims resurrection and hope in her liturgy. That is very different from the text-mongering and ill-conceived pieties of those who are not themselves in the desolation of loss. To know that they needed me to be 'all right' so that they might themselves feel reassured did little to lessen my anger. A few people heard a little more truth than they could perhaps take. A few letters were torn up in rage and one or two books were thrown across the room. Sometimes I screamed aloud in an empty house. The exercise gave me a sore throat but it did me good.

Eileen Mable, in *Married to the Church?*, ed. Shelagh Brown
(Triangle 1983), pp. 77–78.

Grief at bereavement
9.42

The earthly beloved, even in this life, incessantly triumphs over your mere idea of her. And you want her to; you want her with all her resistances, all her faults, all her unexpectedness. That is, in her foursquare and independent reality. And this, not any image or memory, is what we are to love still, after she is dead.

But 'this' is not now imaginable. In that respect H. and all the dead are like

God. In that respect loving her has become, in its measure, like loving him. In both cases I must stretch out the arms and hands of love – its eyes cannot here be used – to the reality, through – across – all the changeful phantasmagoria of my thoughts, passions and imaginings. I mustn't sit down content with the phantasmagoria itself and worship that for him, or love that for her.

Not my idea of God, but God. Not my idea of H., but H. Yes, and also not my idea of my neighbour, but my neighbour. For don't we often make this mistake as regards people who are still alive – who are with us in the same room? Talking and acting not to the man himself but to the picture... we've made of him in our own minds? And he has to depart from it pretty widely before we even notice the fact. In real life – that's one way it differs from novels – his words and acts are, if we observe closely, hardly ever quite 'in character', that is, in what we call his character. There's always a card in his hand we didn't know about.

My reason for assuming that I do this to other people is the fact that so often I find them obviously doing it to me. We all think we've got one another taped.

And all this time I may, once more, be building with cards... Am I, for instance, just sidling back to God because I know that if there's any road to H., it runs through him? But then of course I know perfectly well that he can't be used as a road. If you're approaching him not as the goal but as a road, not as the end but as a means, you're not really approaching him at all. That's what was really wrong with all those popular pictures of happy reunions 'on the further shore'; not the simple-minded and very earthly images, but the fact that they make an end of what we can get only as a by-product of the true end.

Lord, are these your real terms? Can I meet H. again only if I learn to love you so much that I don't care whether I meet her or not?...

When I lay these questions before God I get no answer. But a rather special sort of 'No answer'. It is not the locked door. It is more like a silent, certainly not uncompassionate, gaze. As though he shook his head not in refusal but waiving the question. Like, 'Peace, child; you don't understand.'

C.S. Lewis, *A Grief Observed* (Faber & Faber 1961), pp. 52–54.

Sorrow turning to joy
9.43

Neither our natural attachment to life nor our courage in bearing suffering, neither earthly wisdom nor even faith – however great – none of these can preserve us from sorrow for the dead. Death is a twofold phenomenon: there is the death of the departed, and the suffering and deadening in our own soul, occasioned by this painful process of separation. But the path of hopeless sorrow, gloom and despondency is forbidden to the Christian. He must not recoil when faced with suffering nor remain impotently passive before it. He must exert his spiritual powers to the utmost in order to pass through suffering, and to emerge from it stronger, deeper, wiser.

No matter if we are weak in our faith and unstable in our spiritual life – the love we bear towards the departed is not weak; and our sorrow is so deep, precisely because our love is so strong. Through the tension of our love, we too shall cross the fatal threshold which they have crossed. By an effort of our imagination, let us enter into the world which they have entered; let us give more place in our life to that which has now become their life; and slowly, imperceptibly, our sorrow will be turned into joy which no one can take from us.

Alexander Elchaninov, *The Diary of a Russian Priest*
(Faber & Faber 1967), pp. 126–27.

Battling with self-pity
9.44

Even five or six years after Peter's death I found that my journey through the valley was still a running battle with self-pity...

At a dinner party I would find myself the only single person there. Always I knew that my hostess had not meant to be thoughtless. It is hard for anyone who has known only an unbroken family to imagine how this particular situation makes the single person feel. Try as I might to overcome it, I would find that being in the presence of couples threw my aloneness into sharpest perspective.

What then is the solution? It must lie somewhere in the realm of relationship. As solitaries we can wither and die. We long to be needed; we yearn to be included; we thirst to know that we belong to someone. The question is – how can we achieve that sense of belonging?

There is a price to be paid. The first tribute exacted is a modicum of modesty with ourselves. On the one hand, do we want to be rid of loneliness so much that we will allow ourselves no more wallowing in the luxury of pity-parties? On the other hand, how badly do we want to make connection with other people? For let's admit it, there are pluses in having only oneself to think of.

In the light of honest answers to questions like these, I decided I need not be lonely unless I chose to be. The first step was recognizing the necessity for a new dimension and the decision to perform a freshening-up on myself.

Catherine Marshall, *Meeting God at Every Turn*
(Hodder & Stoughton 1980).

To a widow

9.45

For you, I fear that the hard time is on you. It is so pitiful when the last bit of *active* love has been paid to the dead, and there is no more opportunity for tender ministry, and only the grim silence remains, and the cold facts are to be faced, and the loneliness wraps round, and the business of common things has to be taken up, without its inspiration or its purpose, and the past has to be left behind and the new life undertaken. For you, with your deep roots... it is a moment of strange pain.

There is nothing to be done but to set the face forward. Out beyond the edge of life, the hope of the recovery lies. You will look for him again, not by raking in the past, but by moving out towards the home not made with hands. There your treasure all lies. You will find it again. He is faithful that promised. So you will carry with you, as you journey on, all the blessed wealth of the joy that has been yours – for you will take it as a pledge, that it can never be lost, and will be found again. You will bear it in your heart, as an appeal to God to justify what he has begun.

Henry Scott Holland, letter to Mary Drew, 11 April 1910.

The horror of death

9.46

I must... tell, however briefly, of the truly awful catastrophe which occurred in the January of that year... What human family has not known death? Is not death as common as birth? Animals and flowers die around us every day. By the very fact of living we are acclimatized to death. And if 'in Adam all die' are we not all 'made alive' in Christ? Do we not believe it? Is it only a notion; is it impossible to make the belief affective? If any family had ever been brought up to believe, that family was ours. Sentimentally and dogmatically we had been taught to believe from our infancy. Perhaps, to our realistic young minds, our father had often embarrassed us with his poetical and scriptural eloquences. The miracles of the gospel story – of Lazarus, of the centurion's daughter and that other child, of the resurrection itself – and the stories of the son of the Sunamitess and of the boy raised from death by Elijah – these things we knew almost by heart, yet the death of our sister Cicely was, not only to our father and mother but to me also, a more grievous thing than I had ever imagined possible.

... She was alive in Christ, but she was not alive to us. She was not here. The most lovely, the best, the most dear – dead – gone for ever. There was nothing left but a grave in the cemetery and the cold comfort of a text – Talitha kumi. The loveliest text – but what good is even the loveliest text? What poetry can bring the dead to life? I wept, I almost screamed with misery. I dreamed dreams of her return. It was a mercy that the new-found fields, the new flowers and hills of a medieval city imposed themselves upon my attention, though for a time even this delight was spoiled by the thought that we could not share it and explore it together.

Eric Gill, Autobiography (Jonathan Cape 1940), pp. 77–79.

Screaming to God
9.47

'My God, my God, why hast thou forsaken me?' This is not a 'hymn of trust' as some have held, oversimplifying the text in the light of later verses of the psalm. But neither is it a 'cry of despair' as others have thought as a result of disregarding the fact that it *is* an appeal to God. It is a death not simply accepted in patience, but endured screaming to God: God remains the final support in death, a support however which is incomprehensible to the one who is abandoned unsupported to suffering.

Here is the peculiarity of this death. Jesus died *not merely* – and this is toned down in Luke and John – *forsaken by men, but absolutely forsaken by God.* And it is only here that the most profound depth of this death finds expression: that which distinguishes this death from the 'beautiful death' – so often compared with it – of Socrates, who had been charged with atheism and corrupting youth, or of some Stoic sage. Jesus was utterly abandoned to suffering. There is no mention in the gospels of serenity, inward freedom, superiority, grandeur of soul. This was not a humane death, coming gently by hemlock poisoning, after seventy years, in ripeness and repose. It was a death coming all too soon, breaking off everything, totally degrading, in scarcely endurable misery and torment. A death not characterized by lofty resignation, but by absolute and unparalleled abandonment. And yet, for this very reason: is there a death which has shaken but perhaps also exalted humankind in its long history more than death so infinitely human-inhuman in the immensity of its suffering?

Hans Küng, On Being a Christian, tr. Edward Quinn
(Collins 1977), p. 341.

Pictures of Heaven

All creation's praise
10.1

'And I heard every created creature which was in heaven, and upon the earth, and beneath the earth, and on the sea, and all things in them, saying:

> Blessing and honour and glory and dominion for ever and ever to him who sits upon the throne and to the Lamb.'

Now the chorus of praise goes so far that it cannot go farther, for it reaches throughout the whole of the universe and the whole of creation. There is one vast song of praise to the Lamb...

The creatures which are in the heaven add their praise. Who are they? More than one answer has been given and each is lovely in its own way. It has been suggested that the reference is to the birds of the air; the very singing of the birds is a song of praise. It has been suggested that the reference is to the sun, the moon and the stars; the heavenly bodies in their shining are praising God. It has been suggested that the phrase gathers up every possible being in heaven – the living creatures, the elders, the myriads of angels and every other heavenly being.

The creatures which are beneath the earth add their praise. That can only mean the dead who are in Hades, and here is something totally new. In the Old Testament the idea is that the dead are separated altogether from God and humankind and live a shadowy existence. 'In death there is no remembrance of thee; in Sheol who can give thee praise?' (Psalm 6:5)...

Here is a vision which sweeps all this away. Not even the land of the dead is beyond the reign of the risen Christ. Even from beyond death the chorus of praise rises to him.

William Barclay, *The Revelation of John* (Saint Andrew Press [1959] 1976), vol. 1, pp. 180–81.

For those who sleep in Christ
10.2

For them that have slept in Christ, as Christ said of Lazarus, 'Lazarus sleepeth, but I go that I may wake him out of sleep,' he shall say to his Father: 'Let me go that I may wake them who have slept so long in expectation of my coming.' 'And those that sleep in Jesus Christ [saith the Apostle] will God bring with him'; not only fetch them out of the dust when he comes, but bring them with him, that is, declare that they have been in his hands ever since they departed out of this world. They shall awake as Jacob did, and say as Jacob said, 'Surely the Lord is in this place,' and 'This is no other but the house of God, and the gate of heaven.' And into that gate they shall enter, and in that house they shall dwell, where there shall be no cloud nor sun, no darkness nor dazzling, but one equal light, no noise nor silence, but one equal music, no fears nor hopes, but one equal possession, no foes nor friends, but an equal communion and identity, no ends nor beginnings, but one equal eternity. Keep us Lord so awake in the duties of our callings, that we may thus sleep in thy peace, and wake in thy glory, and change that infallibility which thou affordest us here, to an actual and undeterminable possession of that Kingdom which thy Son our Saviour Jesus hath purchased for us, with the inestimable price of his incorruptible blood. Amen.

John Donne, in *Twenty-Six Sermons*, from Sermon XV
(29 February 1627/8).

The soul's purifying
10.3

As for paradise, God has placed no doors there. Whoever wishes to enter, does so. All-merciful God stands there with his arms open, waiting to receive us into his glory. I also see, however, that the divine essence is so pure and light-filled – much more than we can imagine – that the soul that has but the slightest imperfection would rather throw itself into a thousand hells than appear thus before the divine presence. Tongue cannot express nor heart understand the full meaning of purgatory, which the soul willingly accepts as a mercy, the realization that that suffering is of no importance, compared with the removal of the impediment of sin. The greatest suffering of the souls in purgatory, it seems to me, is their awareness that something in them displeases God, that they have deliberately gone against his great goodness. In a state of grace these souls fully grasp the meaning of what blocks them on their way to God. This conviction is so strong, from what I have understood up to this point in life, that by comparison all words, sentiments, images, the very idea of justice or truth, seem completely false. I am more confused than satisfied with the words I have used to express myself, but I have found nothing better for what I have felt. All that I have said is as nothing compared with what I feel within, the witnessed correspondence of love between God and the soul.

Catherine of Genoa, *Purgation and Purgatory*, tr. Serge Hughes,
in *Catherine of Genoa* (Paulist Press 1979), p. 78.

Eternal life and us
10.4

I should like to set down my own belief. In so far as I am willing to be made an instrument of God's peace, in that far have I already entered into eternal life. Heaven to me is here, and whatever else it may be, I can know it now in so far as I am the instrument of that peace. What happens to me after I die, I do not know, nor do I really want to know. I have no evidence on which to deny that there is life after death, but what kind of life it would be, I have no idea. That a man who, in the words of Francis [of Assisi], was in God's will remains in that will, I am prepared to believe, because Francis, when death came, welcomed it; he called death, Sister Death, and said to his doctor, 'She is to me the gate of life.' So should I like to die.

There are some diffident Christians who cannot believe that they are now in eternal life, not only because they continue to think of eternal life as a reward for this one, but because they think it is far too grand a way to describe the prosaic way in which they live. They feel that such descriptions must be reserved for the saints and perhaps the clergy! Yet the gospel is a gospel for *us*, it is good news for *us*. When Jesus said, 'You are the light of the world,' he was not speaking to the saints and the clergy, he was speaking to people like *us*. So let us think and reflect more on the proposition that we are even now in eternal life, and whatever happens after the physical death, we do so continue, for we are in God's will, and God's will continues.

Two last points: the dying of the first death is not always a dramatic encounter; sometimes it takes a long time. The second point is that we do not cease to be sinners because we enter into eternal life; both St Paul and St Francis claimed to be superlative sinners.

Alan Paton, *Instrument of Thy Peace* (Collins Fontana 1970), pp. 117–18.

Ascending and descending
10.5

'He has given his angels charge over you, to keep you in all your ways.' What are the ways of the holy angels? Surely they are those spoken of by the only-begotten when he said 'You will see the angels of God ascending and descending upon the Son of man.' So their ways consist in ascending and descending: they ascend because of him, and they descend, or rather they condescend, because of us. Just as those blessed spirits descend by contemplating God, so they descend out of compassion for you, so that they may 'keep you in all your ways'. They ascend to God's face, and descend at his bidding, for 'he has given his angels charge over you'. And yet in descending they do not lose the vision of his glory, because 'they always behold the face of the Father'...

When the angels ascend to contemplation, they are seeking truth, and in desiring truth they find satisfaction, and in satisfaction they desire. But when they descend to us they show us mercy, that they may keep us in all our ways. These spirits are our ministers, sent to serve us. It is clear that they are our ministers and not our masters. And in this they imitate the example given by the only-begotten, who came not to be served, but to serve, who stood among his disciples as one who serves. The fruit of these ways for the angels themselves is their happiness and loving obedience. The fruit for us is that by them we obtain divine grace and are guarded in all our ways here below. So then, he has given his angels charge over you to keep you in all your ways, in all your needs, in all your desires. He has not charged his angels with turning you from your ways, but with keeping you in them, and directing you by their ways into his ways. How do they do this? An angel acts purely out of love alone; you too, at any rate from your own need, descend and condescend – that is, you try to show mercy to your neighbour, and then, lifting up your desires with the same angel, you strive to ascend with all the eagerness of your soul to sublime and eternal truth... Do not be astonished that those who condescend to keep watch over us condescend to admit us with them into the ways of the Lord, or rather, they direct us into them. They follow in mercy and truth – but he himself is truth itself and mercy itself.

Bernard of Clairvaux, Sermon on the Psalm 'He Who Dwells', adapted from translation in *Sermons on Conversion* (Cistercian Publications 1981), pp. 206–11.

The hope of heaven
10.6

A gay person turning to scripture and the Christian tradition for an image of heaven is in for some pleasant surprises. In heaven there is no marriage (Matthew 22:30; Luke 20:35); gay people will not find themselves on the margins of heaven because they are excluded from the socially validating institution of marriage... The hope of heaven does not rest on fitting in with the way of the world but on the Lion and the Lamb (Revelation 5:5) – on the beauty of a king who strives for justice and the love of a gentle friend who takes to himself our pain and failure.

It is interesting to ask why contemporary Christianity, particularly in its evangelical form, has lost its vision of heaven. The loss of a sense of heaven from modern culture has come about through a series of moves – economic, philosophical and scientific. However, one of the most powerful of these has been the diversion of human desire and social affection from God, the public realm and the world to come. While modern evangelical Christianity struggles to gain a hearing in society and to make an impact on issues that it regards as close to the heart of the gospel, it is largely ignorant of the extent to which it has bought into the modern project. Its recurrent anxiety over 'family issues' is a measure of how deeply it has sold its soul to the destructive idols of Western culture: the reduction of the sense of beauty to 'heterosexual love' and the elimination of bonds of affection in the search of prosperity through the market. Its hostility to gay people is not so much a sign of its loyalty to scripture as a mark of the extent to which it has not heeded St John's advice, 'Little children, keep yourselves from idols' (1 John 5:21).

Recovering a vision of heaven cannot be achieved simply by biblical exegesis, intellectual rigour, artistic passion or cultural nostalgia. It has to emerge as human beings in their diversity encounter the friendship of Jesus within the brokenness and confusion of human life. Restoring the fractured imagination of Western Christianity involves turning away from the idols that destroy and fragment our society. Reconciliation with gay people's experience of Christ is simply part of a more extensive act of healing that needs to take place.

Michael Vasey, *Strangers and Friends: A New Exploration of Homosexuality and the Bible*
(Hodder & Stoughton 1995), pp. 248–49.

A certain kind of life

10.7

Now let us take the idea of *eternal life*. It is far better to speak of *eternal* life than to speak of *everlasting* life. The main idea behind eternal life is not simply that of duration. It is quite clear that a life which went on for ever could just as easily be hell as heaven. The idea behind eternal life is the idea of a certain quality, a certain kind of life. What kind of life? There is only one person who can properly be described by this adjective eternal (*aionios*) and that one person is God. Eternal life is the kind of life that God lives; it is God's life. To enter into eternal life is to enter into possession of that kind of life which is the life of God. It is to be lifted up above merely human, temporary, passing, transient things, into that joy and peace which belong only to God. And clearly, a person can only enter into this close communion and fellowship with

God when they render to God that love, that reverence, that devotion, that obedience which truly bring them into fellowship with God.

William Barclay, *The Gospel of John*, vol. 1 (Saint Andrew Press 1965), p. 118.

Nothing is lost
10.8

The last message from the one whom we loved is: 'Death is nothing at all. It does not count. I have only slipped away into the next room. Nothing has happened. Everything remains exactly as it was. I am I, and you are you, and the old life that we lived so fondly together is untouched, unchanged. Whatever we were to each other, that we are still. Call me by the old familiar name. Speak of me in the easy way which you always used. Put no difference into your tone. Wear no forced air of solemnity or sorrow. Laugh as we always laughed at the little jokes that we enjoyed together. Play, smile, think of me, pray for me. Let my name be ever the household word that it always was. Let it be spoken without an effort, without the ghost of a shadow upon it. Life means all that it ever meant. It is the same as it ever was. There is absolute and unbroken continuity. What is this death but a negligible accident? Why should I be out of mind because I am out of sight? I am but waiting for you, for an interval, somewhere very near, just round the corner. All is well. Nothing is hurt; nothing is lost. One brief moment and all will be as it was before. How we shall laugh at the trouble of parting when we meet again!'

... There is no severance, no gulf fixed. We can send our hearts over the silent frontier into the secret land. We hold converse with them that are gone from us. Not a tie is cut. They know it, we know it. The spirit bands hold... True, we shall not be able to keep that mind. Alas! it will pass from us. The long, horrible silence that follows when we become aware of what we have lost out of our daily intercourse by the withdrawal of the immediate presence will cut its way into our souls. We shall feel it impossible to keep at the high level without a word, without a sign, to reassure us of its truth. The blank veil will hang on unlifted, unstirred. Not a glimpse to be had of the world inside and beyond!...

Yes, but for all that our high mood was real, though it passes. It was a true experience: it gave us authentic intelligence... Though we have returned to the twilight of the valleys, yet we will ever recall the moment when we stood upon the sunlit heights and saw the far horizons. It was a true value that we gave then to life and death.

Henry Scott Holland, 'The King of Terrors', *Facts of the Faith*
(Longmans & Co. 1919), pp. 126–28.

The hope of glory
10.9

The body you now have is sown in *weakness*: it must be watched and tended, continually, to be safe – in weakness, not only during infancy, but always exposed to falls, and bruises, and broken limbs; in weakness, so as to tire with employment, and unless its springs, like those of a clock, be wound up every night by sleep, good for nothing; in weakness, soon reduced, by disease, to lie upon a bed, not able to help itself; and then placed in the tomb, where it soon becomes the prey of worms. This your body, shall be raised in *power*, strong and mighty; never subject to weariness; swift to move, as with eagle's wings; in no more need of dull sleep, the image of death, to recruit its strength; in power, to persevere, without intermission, in the great services to which it shall be appointed; and able to bear 'an exceeding and eternal weight of glory', a very small part of which would sink the body of flesh into a swoon and fear, great as was seen in the beloved disciple, who fell as dead at the feet of Jesus.

Your body was sown a *natural* body – at your birth, to be sustained, like all other animals, by the fruits of the earth, and by the elements; fashioned to relish nothing higher than what can be seen by the eye of flesh, and handled with the hands; so that its joys and griefs, fears and hopes, and all its sensations, are low, and like the brutes. But it shall be raised up a *spiritual body*, that is, one every way accomplished to see, admire, and delight in spiritual objects and exercises; no more a hindrance and clog to the glorified soul; but an aid and help, sinless in all its tendencies – all eye, all ear, all sense, respecting the visible works of God: and an excellent medium of conveying still greater bliss to the soul than it would know without the body. Otherwise it would not be re-united to its former inmate.

The inhabitants of such an incorruptible glorious body, mighty and spiritual, I hope to see my sons and daughters; and, in such infinite dignity, dwell with the Lord our God, who hath formed us for himself, for ever. May this our future eternal existence be ever before our eyes, realized to our minds, and the desire of our hearts! Amen! and Amen!

Henry Venn, letter to his daughter (1786), *Letters of Henry Venn* (1835).

Passing into beauty
10.10

We do not want merely to see beauty, though, God knows, even that is bounty enough. We want something else which can hardly be put into words – to be

412

united with the beauty we see, to pass into it, to receive it into ourselves, to bathe in it, to become part of it. That is why we have peopled air and earth and water with gods and goddesses and nymphs and elves – that, though we cannot, yet these projections can enjoy in themselves that beauty, grace, and power of which nature is the image... For if we take the imagery of scripture seriously, if we believe that God will one day *give* us the morning star and cause us to *put on* the splendour of the sun, then we may surmise that both the ancient myths and the modern poetry, so false as history, may be very near the truth as prophecy. At present we are on the outside of the world, the wrong side of the door. We discern the freshness and purity of morning, but they do not make us fresh and pure. We cannot mingle with the splendours we see. But all the leaves of the New Testament are rustling with the rumour that it will not always be so. Someday, God willing, we shall get *in*. When human souls have become as perfect in voluntary obedience as the inanimate creation is in its lifeless obedience, they will put on its glory, or rather that greater glory of which nature is only the first sketch. We are summoned to pass in through nature, beyond her, into that splendour which she fitfully reflects.

C.S. Lewis, *The Weight of Glory* (Macmillan 1980), p. 16.

Two worlds
10.11

There are two worlds: our universe, the place of God's natural creatures; Christ's heaven, the place of God's glorified creatures. In either world God is everywhere present by his power and his grace; but more fully in that other world where the hearts of the redeemed offer no obstacles to his invisible action, and most fully in the glorious man, Jesus Christ, whom he has made personally one with his divine life. The mind of God speaks from his lips to the citizens of that country; they see the love of God in the kindness of his eyes.

There are two worlds, then; and if we do not call that other world 'heaven', then what are we to call it? Those theologians who say that 'heaven' is an image which means nothing to our age had better be careful what they say. To localize infinite God in heaven, or anywhere else, is a gross metaphysical error in this or in any other age. But if there is not a society of persons in bliss, new-created and centred on a glorified Jesus, then our Christ is nothing but a dead Jew and to talk of Christianity is sentimental folly. But we know a living Christ, and we know he is not unaccompanied; and what shall we call that company, but heaven?

There are two worlds, the old and the new creations of God; but if they are two, then how are they related to one another? Surely the answer of our faith is plain. Our world does not contain Christ's, but Christ's world embraces ours. Since Christ's world is not physical, it is no part of our universe: for our universe is nothing but an interaction of energies, a tissue of dynamic space, and what is not physical has no place in it. No lines of radiation which any telescope can follow will reach it, no curvature of light will show the pull of its influence. But our world is in Christ's heaven: for that is a world where spirit touches spirit. Those heavenly minds can know whatever minds are opened to them by God's will and permission: so we are present to Christ; and so he inflows upon us.

Austin Farrer, *The End of Man*, ed. Charles C. Conti (SPCK 1973), pp. 37–38.

The absolute future
10.12

What kind of kingdom will this be?

It will be a kingdom where, in accordance with Jesus' prayer, God's name is truly hallowed, his will is done on earth, human beings will have everything in abundance, all sin will be forgiven and all evil overcome.

It will be a kingdom where, in accordance with Jesus' promises, the poor, the hungry, those who weep and those who are downtrodden will finally come into their own; where pain, suffering and death will have an end.

It will be a kingdom that cannot be described, but only made known in metaphors: as the new covenant, the seed springing up, the ripe harvest, the great banquet, the royal feast.

It will therefore be a kingdom – wholly as the prophets foretold – of absolute righteousness, of unsurpassable freedom, of dauntless love, of universal reconciliation, of everlasting peace. In this sense therefore it will be the time of salvation, of fulfilment, of consummation, of God's presence: the absolute future.

Hans Küng, *On Being a Christian*, tr. Edward Quinn (William Collins 1977), p. 215.

The promise of glory
10.13

Perfect humility dispenses with modesty. If God is satisfied with the work, the work may be satisfied with itself; 'it is not for her to bandy compliments with her Sovereign.' I can imagine someone saying that he dislikes my idea of heaven as a place where we are patted on the back. But proud misunderstanding is behind that dislike. In the end that face which is the delight or the terror of the universe must be turned upon each of us either with one expression or with the other, either conferring glory inexpressible or inflicting shame that can never be cured or disguised. I read in a periodical the other day that the fundamental thing is how we think of God. By God himself, it is not! How God thinks of us is not only more important, but infinitely more important. Indeed, how we think of him is of no importance except in so far as it is related to how he thinks of us. It is written that we shall 'stand before' him, shall appear, shall be inspected. The promise of glory is the promise, almost incredible and only possible by the work of Christ, that some of us, that any of us who really chooses, shall actually survive that examination, shall find approval, shall please God. To please God... to be a real ingredient in the divine happiness... to be loved by God, not merely pitied, but delighted in as an artist delights in his work or a father in a son – it seems impossible, a weight or burden of glory which our thoughts can hardly sustain. But so it is.

C.S. Lewis, 'The Weight of Glory', in *Transposition and Other Addresses*
(Geoffrey Bles 1949), pp. 28–29.

Seeing in a new way
10.14

But how may we think of heaven?... In his work *The City of God*, St Augustine told of heaven thus: 'We shall rest and we shall see, we shall see and we shall love, we shall love and we shall praise, in the end which is no end.'

Rest: we shall be freed from the busy and fussy activity in which we get in our own light and expose ourselves to our self-centredness. Resting, we shall find that we see in a new way, without the old hindrances. We shall see our neighbours as what they really are, creatures and children of God in whom is the divine image, and that image will become newly visible to us. We shall see ourselves too as God's infinitesimally small creatures: and we shall begin to see God himself in his beauty. Seeing, we shall *love*, for how shall we not love God in his beauty and how shall we not love all our neighbours in whom the image of God is now visible to us? *Praise* will be the last word, for all is of God and none is of our own achievement, and we shall know the depth of gratitude and adoration. St Augustine adds 'in the end which is no end'. It will be the end, for here is perfection and nothing can be more final. It will be no end, for within the resting, seeing, loving and praising there is an inexhaustible adventure of new and ceaseless discovery. Such is the heaven for which we were created.

Michael Ramsey, *Be Still and Know* (William Collins 1982), p. 122.

Heaven and hell
10.15

The full meaning of life is heaven that the world cannot imagine and hell that it hardly knows.

The trouble has been that both heaven and hell have been pictured as places rather than states, and located simply the other side of death. Of course, for the Christian, they are realities that are not *ended* by death. But all he can usefully say about them is from his present experience.

In a real sense the definition of heaven and hell is the same: being with God – for ever. For some that's heaven, for some it's hell: for most of us it's a bit of both.

The Christian believes that life has a grain running through it. The world is made a certain way – for love. To try to live one's life across it is ultimately hell: there is no peace that way.

But the grain is not like something in wood. It's more like something in a person. And to be across a person in whom eternally one lives and moves and has one's being is a most ghastly prospect. It is Sartre's 'hell is other people', only more so.

I do not believe in a God who is content for any finally to live with him and find it hell. But I cannot take the love of God – or for that matter human love – seriously without taking the agony of it equally seriously.

In that sense I believe in hell. It's no kindness to encourage anyone to think that life can be lived at any depth without the shadows. Being in love – and that's what the Christian thinks is our ultimate element – is a searing process.

But God forbid that we should use hell as a stick to keep anyone moral.

John A.T. Robinson, *But That I Can't Believe!* (Collins Fontana 1967), pp. 48–49.

Is heaven perfection?
10.16

'Heaven,' says George Bernard Shaw, 'as conventionally conceived, is a place so inane, so dull, so useless, so miserable, that nobody has ever ventured to describe a whole day in heaven, though plenty of people have described a day at the seaside.'

The trouble with perfection is that it is indescribable, so seldom do we come across it. Shaw's somewhat acerbic comment is too near the mark to make us feel anything other than uncomfortable. The reason for this lies not in 'heaven' itself but in what the great critic and playwright calls its conventional conception. 'Misconception' would be a far more accurate way of describing the heaven characterized by popular imagination: its inanity caused by the endless plucking of myriad harps; its dullness a result of the sheer monotony of the same boring routine; its uselessness due to the absence of anything to do but rest eternally; its misery a direct consequence of the removal of all challenge from the lives of its inhabitants.

Yet this is emphatically not the heaven of scripture, where activity is one of its keynotes, and the worship of God the most significant component of that activity. Somewhere along the line, the Christian understanding of heaven has been derailed or shunted into a particularly curious siding. That state of perfection, which we often describe as 'heavenly', is in fact a mode of existence of which we already experience tantalizing glimpses. Some of those liftings of the curtain are revealed in the beauty of nature and in those awe-inspiring natural phenomena which, though we can now explain them scientifically, still have the power to strike awe into our hearts. The sight of a volcano in full eruption or the sound of a violent thunderstorm immediately overhead, can leave few of us totally unmoved, whatever our understanding of their genesis.

David Shearlock, *When Words Fail: God and the World of Beauty*
(Canterbury Press 1996), p. 150.

Looking beyond death
10.17

Death for the Christian, it is sometimes said, is like the old family servant who opens the door to welcome the children home. Although it would be a mistake to base our beliefs on the experience of those who have clinically died but later have been restored to life, it is worth noting that of those who were Christians nearly all speak of walking peacefully into a garden full of staggeringly beautiful colours and exquisite music (or some similar description), so that it is with great reluctance that they came back to earth again.

It never worries me that we are not able to grasp more clearly the true nature of heaven. We can understand something of which we have no first-hand experience only by describing something with which we are familiar. We are limited by language. But for those who know God and who are trusting in Christ as their Saviour and Lord, there is nothing to fear, and it is sufficient to know that we shall be like him and perfectly with him. Nothing could be more wonderful than that. Never fear the worst. *The best is yet to be.*

When I die, it is my firm conviction that I shall be more alive than ever, experiencing the full reality of all that God has prepared for us in Christ. Sometimes I have foretastes of that reality, when the sense of God's presence is especially vivid. Although such moments are comparatively rare they whet my appetite for much more. The actual moment of dying is still shrouded in mystery, but as I keep my eyes on Jesus I am not afraid. Jesus has already been through death for us, and will be with us when we walk through it ourselves.

David Watson, *Fear No Evil: A Personal Struggle with Cancer*
(Hodder & Stoughton 1984), p. 168.

Behold, your redemption draws near!
10.18

Be not weary, be not faint in your minds: the time of your complete redemption draweth nigh. In heaven the wicked one shall cease from troubling you, and your weary souls shall enjoy an everlasting rest; his fiery darts cannot reach those blissful regions: Satan will never come any more to appear with, disturb or accuse the sons of God, when once the Lord Jesus Christ shuts the door. Your righteous souls are now grieved, day by day, at the ungodly conversation of the wicked; tares now grow up among the wheat; wolves come in sheep's clothing: but the redemption spoken of in the text will free your souls from all anxiety on these accounts; hereafter you shall enjoy a perfect communion of saints; nothing that is unholy or unsanctified shall enter into the holy of holies, which is prepared for you above: this, and all manner of evil whatsoever, you shall be delivered from, when your redemption is hereafter made complete in heaven; not only so, but you shall enter into the full enjoyment of all good. It is true, all saints will not have the same degree of happiness, but all will be as happy as their hearts can desire. Believers, you shall judge the evil, and familiarly converse with good; angels: you shall sit down with Abraham, Isaac, Jacob and all the spirits of just men made perfect; and, to sum up all your happiness in one word, you shall see God the Father, Son, and Holy Ghost; and, by seeing God, be more and more like unto him, and pass from glory to glory, even to all eternity.

But I must stop: the glories of the upper world crowd in so fast upon my soul, that I am lost in the contemplation of them. Brethren, the redemption spoken of is unutterable; we cannot here find it out; eye hath not seen, nor ear heard, nor has it entered into the hearts of the most holy men living to conceive, how great it is. Were I to entertain you whole ages with an account of it, when you come to heaven, you must say, with the queen of Sheba, 'Not half, no, not one thousandth part was told us.' All we can do here, is to go upon Mount Pisgah, and, by the eye of faith, take a distant view of the promised land: we may see it, as Abraham did Christ, afar off, and rejoice in it; but here we only know in part. Blessed be God, there is a time coming, when we shall know God, even as we are known, and God will be all in all. Lord Jesus, accomplish the number of thine elect! Lord Jesus, hasten thy kingdom!

> George Whitefield, 'Wisdom, Righteousness, Sanctification and Redemption'
> (1 Corinthians 1:30), *Select Sermons*, pp. 69–70.

The blessings of the heavenly Jerusalem
10.19

If thou wilt aught wit of the restful place of the high Jerusalem, I shall tell thee, blabbering as I can. It is a place highest, brightest, widest and strongest. There is fellowship best, worthiest, fairest, most fervent in charity, each one to other knit together, with clean love that never shall stint nor cool. There shall we have our Lord that is worthiest, mightiest, wisest, richest, fairest, sweetest, most rightwise, most bounteous and most homely and courteous, and in love and in goodness without measure. There shall be clear sight of the blessed Trinity, stable beholding without blench, charity confirmed, love delightable, praising continual, meekest reverence and wondering highest, deepest ransacking and most plenteous finding, mirth without measure and joy without end... And then shall our Lord with his blessed hand wipe away the tears from our eyes. For after that we shall never hear telling of death, nor of woe, nor of sorrow, for that is passed. And there shall be fulfilled what the prophet said: 'As the mother cherisheth her child, so shall I comfort you, saith our Lord, ye shall be borne in arms and ye shall be cherished on knees.'... And we shall be led into the inner joy, and what without and what within, we shall be so overfilled with joy that we shall be as it were dissolved therein. And if thou wilt wit what joy it is, I cannot tell thee, but as the prophet saith, 'that heart may not think, not ear may hear, nor eye see, what it is Lord that thou hast prepared for the lovers of thee.'

> Walter Hilton, *The Goad of Love*, ed. Clare Kirchberger
> (Faber & Faber 1952), pp. 212–13.

Epilogue

God's banquet
10.20

Let everyone who loves God rejoice in this festival of light!
Let the faithful servant gladly enter into the joy of his Lord!
Let those who have borne the burden of fasting come now to reap
    their reward!
Let those who have worked since the first hour receive now their just wage!
Let those who came after the third hour keep this festival with gratitude!
Let those who arrived only after the sixth hour approach with no fear:
    they will not be defrauded.
If someone has delayed until the ninth hour, let him come without
    hesitation.
And let not the worker of the eleventh hour be ashamed: the Lord
    is generous.
He welcomes the last to come no less than the first.
He welcomes into his peace the worker of the eleventh hour
    as kindly as the one who has worked since dawn.
The first he fills to overflowing: on the last he has compassion.
To the one he grants his favour, to the other pardon.
He does not look only at the work: he sees into the intention of the heart.
Enter then all of you into the joy of your Master.
First and last, receive your reward...
Abstinent and slothful celebrate this feast.
You who have fasted, rejoice today.
The table is laid: come all of you without misgivings.
The fatted calf is served, let all take their fill.
All of you share in the banquet of faith:
    all of you draw on the wealth of his mercy.

John Chrysostom, *Paschal Homily*, tr. Theodore Berkeley
(New City 1993), pp. 53–54.

INDEX OF SOURCES

INDEX OF THEMES

ACKNOWLEDGMENTS

We would like to thank all those who have given us permission to include extracts in this book, as indicated on the list below. Every effort has been made to trace and acknowledge copyright holders of all the extracts included in this anthology. We apologize for any errors or omissions that may remain, and would ask those concerned to contact the publishers, who will ensure that full acknowledgment is made in the future.

Extract from *Prayer,* by Abhishiktananda (Henri Le Saux), pp. 3–5. Published by SPCK 1967.

Extracts from *The Book of the Blessed Angela of Foligno* (*Memorial* and *Instructions*), by Angela of Foligno, ch. 1 and Instruction XXXV in *Angela of Foligno: Complete Works,* tr. Paul Lachance OFM, pp. 130–31 and 308–309. Published by Paulist Press 1993.

Extract from *Proslegion,* by Anselm of Canterbury, ch. 1, tr. M.J. Charlesworth, Oxford: Clarendon Press 1965. Copyright © Oxford University Press, 1965. Reproduced by permission of Oxford University Press.

Extracts from 'Women's Experience of God in Emerging Spirituality' from *With Passion and Compassion: Third World Women Doing Theology,* by Luz Beatriz Arellano, ed. Virginia Fabella and Mercy Amba Oduyoye, copyright © Orbis Books 1988.

Extract from 'Second Discourse on Psalm 32', 8 [V. 3] and from 'First Discourse on Psalm 36', 12 [V. 11] in *St Augustine on the Psalms: Psalms 30–37,* tr. and ed. Dame Scholastica Hegbin and Dame Felicitas Corrigan, pp. 111–12. Published by Newman Press/Longmans, Green & Co. 1961.

Extract from *Daily Study Bible New Testament: The Gospel of Matthew I,* by William Barclay, vol. 1, p. 259. Published by The Saint Andrew Press 1987.

Extracts taken from *School for Prayer,* by Metropolitan Anthony (Anthony Bloom) published and copyright 1971 by Darton, Longman & Todd Ltd and used by permission of the publishers.

Extracts from *Encountering Myself,* by Harry James Cargas, pp. 6 and 108. Published by SPCK 1978.

Extract from *Letters of Catherine of Siena,* by Catherine of Siena, tr. and ed, Vida D. Scudder, pp. 161–63. Published by J.M. Dent.

Three excerpts from *Freedom of Simplicity,* by Richard J. Foster. Copyright © 1981 by Richard J. Foster. Reprinted by permission of HarperCollins Publishers.

Extract from *Original Blessing,* by Matthew Fox, pp. 141–43. Published by Bear & Co. 1983.

Extract from *Christian Uncertainties,* by Monica Furlong, copyright © Monica Furlong 1975. Reproduced by permission of Sheil Land Associates Ltd.

Extracts from *The Shaping of Prophecy,* by Adrian Hastings, pp. 40 and 173–74. Published by Geoffrey Chapman 1995. Reprinted by permission of Cassell plc.

Extracts from *The Passionate God,* by Rosemary Haughton, pp. 18, 218–19 and 332. Published by Darton, Longman & Todd 1982.

Extract from *The Knife Edge of Experience,* by Rosemary Haughton, pp. 31–32. Published by Darton, Longman & Todd 1972.

Extract from *The One Who Listens,* by Michael Hollings and Etta Gullick. Used by permission of the publishers, McCrimmon Publishing Co. Ltd.

Extract from *The Way of the Cross,* by Richard Holloway, reproduced by permission of HarperCollins Publishers Ltd.

Extracts from *The Discipline of Love: The Ten Commandments for Today,* by Martin Israel, pp. 80–81 and 84–85. Published by SPCK 1985.

Extract from *The Four Loves,* by C.S. Lewis, published by HarperCollins Publishers Ltd (UK). Copyright © 1960 by Helen Joy Lewis and renewed 1988 by Arthur Owen Barfield, Harcourt Brace & Company (US).

Extract from *A Grief Observed,* by C.S. Lewis, pp. 52–54. Published by Faber & Faber 1961.

Extracts from 'The Weight of Glory' in *Transposition and Other Addresses,* by C.S. Lewis. Published by Geoffrey Bles 1949.

Extract from *A Year Lost and Found,* by Michael Mayne, pp. 55–56 and 62–63. Published by Darton, Longman & Todd 1987.

Extract from *New Seeds of Contemplation,* by Thomas Merton, p. 1. Published by Burns & Oates Ltd 1962.

Extracts from *Meditations on the Sand,* by Allessandro Pronzato, pp. 9–10 and 57. Published by St Paul Publications 1982.

Extracts from *Every Bush is Burning,* by Joan Puls, pp. 51–52 and 74–75. Published by the World Council of Churches 1985.

Extracts from *The Power of the Cross,* by Sally B. Purvis, pp. 53 and 88. Published by Abingdon Press 1993.

Extracts from *Rich Christians in an Age of Hunger: A Biblical Study,* by Ronald J. Sider, pp. 120, 159–60, 195. Published by Hodder & Stoughton 1977. Reproduced by permission of Hodder and Stoughton Ltd.

Extract from *Jesus in Latin America,* by Jon Sobrino, copyright © Orbis Books 1987.

Extracts from *The Inward Road and the Way Back,* by Dorothy Soelle, tr. David L. Scheidt, pp. 21–22 and 132–33. Published by Darton, Longman & Todd 1979.

Extracts from *Hymne de l'Univers,* by Pierre Teilhard de Chardin, copyright © Editions du Seuil 1961, English Translation © 1965 by William Collins Sons & Co. Ltd, and Harper & Row. Copyright Renewed. Reprinted by permission of HarperCollins Publishers.

Extracts from *Story of a Soul,* by Thérèse of Lisieux, tr. Ronald Knox, *Autobiography of a Saint,* pp. 227–28 and 234–35. Published by Harvill Press 1958.

Extracts from *Stepney Calling: Thoughts for Our Day,* by Jim Thompson, pp. 33–35 and 82–83. Published by Mowbray 1991. Reprinted by permission of Cassell plc.

Extracts from *The Shaking of the Foundations,* by Paul Tillich. Published by SCM Press 1949.

Extracts from *Hope and Suffering,* by Desmond Tutu, pp. 79–80, 81 and 137–39. Published by Collins Fount 1984.

Extract from *Collected Papers of Evelyn Underhill,* by Evelyn Underhill, p. 118. Published by Longmans, Green & Co. 1946.

Extracts taken from *Community and Growth,* by Jean Vanier published and copyright 1979 and 1993 by Darton, Longman & Todd Ltd and used by permission of the publishers (UK); copyright © 1979 by Jean Vanier. Used by permission of Paulist Press (US).

Extracts from *The Divine Pity,* by Gerald Vann. Published by William Collins Sons & Co. 1956.

Extracts from *Strangers and Friends: A New Exploration of Homosexuality and the Bible,* by Michael Vasey, pp. 236 and 248–49. Published by Hodder & Stoughton 1995. Reproduced by permission of Hodder and Stoughton Ltd.

Extracts from *Five for Sorrow, Ten for Joy* by Neville Ward, pp. 75–76 and 117. Published by Epworth Press 1971.

Extracts from *Fear No Evil: A Personal Struggle with Cancer,* by David Watson, pp. 152–53 and 168. Published by Hodder & Stoughton 1984. Reproduced by permission of Hodder and Stoughton Ltd (UK Commonwealth and Canada) and by permission of William Neill-Hall Ltd (rest of world excluding US).

Extracts from *The Joy of God,* by H.A. Williams and C.R. Mitchell, published by Mitchell Beazley.